GOD, HUMANS, AND ANIMALS

GOD, HUMANS, AND ANIMALS

An Invitation to Enlarge Our Moral Universe

Robert N. Wennberg

William B. Eerdmans Publishing Company
Grand Rapids, Michigan / Cambridge, U.K.

Wm. B. Eerdmans Publishing Co.
255 Jefferson Ave. S.E., Grand Rapids, Michigan 49503 /
P.O. Box 163, Cambridge CB3 9PU U.K.
www.eerdmans.com

Printed in the United States of America

07 06 05 04 03   7 6 5 4 3 2 1

Library of Congress Cataloging-in-Publication Data

Wennberg, Robert N.
God, humans, and animals: an invitation to enlarge our moral universe / Robert N. Wennberg.
p. cm.
Includes bibliographical references (p.).
ISBN 0-8028-3975-4 (cloth: alk. paper)
1. Animal welfare — Religious aspects — Christianity.
2. Christian ethics. I. Title.

BT746.W46 2003
241'.693 — dc21

2002029498

CONTENTS

PREFACE

This is a book about animals and the moral life. It is, first, an attempt to educate readers about some of the history of ethical concern for animals and the nature of that concern. Second, it is an invitation to reflect on the ethical issues raised by the existence of animals in our world. It is an invitation to take these issues seriously, while at the same time granting the reader considerable latitude in reaching his or her own conclusions. Third, it is intended, in particular, to articulate a moral concern for animals from a perspective that is sensitive to church history, Christian theology, the Jewish and Christian Scriptures, and the best philosophical thought on these matters.

The British philosopher and historian of ideas Richard Sorabji has argued that in the West, under the profound and far-reaching influence of Augustine, a very healthy debate over the moral status of animals came to an end.[1] Prior to Augustine, there was at least a debate, both in the church and in the larger community. With Augustine the debate ended, and animals were declared to be inappropriate objects of direct moral concern. Animals simply did not count morally. Though there were dissenting voices here and there, the prevailing and standard approach to ethical matters became exclusively human-centered.

In the past thirty years that pre-Augustinian debate has vigorously re-emerged in the larger community, especially among philosophers. Ani-

1. Richard Sorabji, *Animal Minds and Human Morals: The Origins of the Western Debate* (Ithaca, N.Y.: Cornell University Press, 1993).

mal rights and animal welfare organizations have proliferated and their memberships have grown, often with the more radical groups garnering the most publicity. Additionally, an impressive body of literature has been produced, including the founding of journals devoted to just this subject. It would seem that it is time this discussion found its way into the Christian community. Although this is happening in a few places, the Christian church (at both the academic and the pastoral levels) lags well behind the secular community. Indeed, studies indicate that there is a correlation between the degree of one's "religiosity," and one's sensitivity to animal welfare issues and knowledge about the nature of animals themselves. It seems that the greater one's religiosity, the greater one's insensitivity to animals and to animal concerns, and the greater one's ignorance. This ought not to be so.

Having said this, I should also indicate that I am not a crusader on the issue of moral concern for animals. Nor am I just a curious intellectual dabbler. I am someone who is still journeying, someone whose thoughts and sensitivities are still being shaped. Since my moral journey is still in progress and the conclusions that I am at this time prepared to affirm are relatively moderate ones, I think I may be able to speak more effectively to those morally serious people who are "turned off" by those animal activists who strike them (perhaps wrongly) as rabid or fanatical. The fact is, there are important issues here, and they should be the concern of all of us. Perhaps in my own way I can speak an effective word and help some others to begin their journey, as well as speak to those whose journey is in progress. I hope, for these reasons, that those who may be more advanced in these matters, who are more passionate in their advocacy and who are convinced that my conclusions are too conservative, will view my efforts charitably. Despite this moderation, my main conclusion — the necessity for moral recognition of animals — is substantially at odds with the controlling anthropocentric ethic of our society and of the church. Moral recognition of animals means that there are things we are not to do to animals even when it is in our interest to do them. That is what moral recognition means. That is also something most of us are reluctant even to hear about. So, although there may be those animal liberationists who will find my conclusions too restrained, this will not be so in the larger world of thought and practice. In that context these words may even be revolutionary.

But this is more than a book about the ethical treatment of animals. It is an invitation to a richer, more sensitive, and more complex moral life in general, because reflecting on the place of animals in the moral universe necessarily raises for us issues that illumine, challenge, and augment our understanding of the moral life even as it relates to humans. It does this in numerous ways. Consider the fact that women are more sensitive to the suffering and destruction of animals than are men. In general, women are said to have different ethical priorities than men, of which this difference over animals is but one. How, then, do we construct an ethic that is sensitive and respectful of these gender differences? Or consider that in discussions of animal suffering, the charge of emotionalism is often directed at those protesting the cruel treatment of animals. The implication is that a cool rationalism undistorted by emotion is the desirable way to go about our moral business. But can we even conceive of the moral life devoid of emotion, devoid, say, of sympathy or compassion? What, then, is the place of emotion in the moral life? Or consider the attempt to argue for a special moral status for humans, while at the same time acknowledging the appropriateness of a serious moral concern for animals. This involves one in defending the claim that humans are in some crucial ways superior to animals, a superiority that justifies a preferential moral treatment but not a preferential treatment that allows just any human interest to override any and all animal interests. Or consider the claim by the animal advocate that the predation we see in nature, with all its pain, dismembering, suffering, and death, is a tragic state of affairs, even though, as it is argued by some, predation works for the best overall. There is nothing, of course, that we can do to change matters without making things worse. This raises for us the important and more general question of how the morally good person should respond to those tragic elements in our world and in our life, about which we and others can do absolutely nothing. In these and many other ways, reflecting on the moral standing of animals occasions reflections that can only deepen and enrich our moral life in general.

In arguing for the moral recognition of animals with whom we share this planet, I am arguing for something that ought to receive a more receptive hearing among Christians (and religious believers in general) than among secularists — the reverse of what is presently the case. After all, for those religious believers who have a doctrine of creation, animals are not simply here on this planet. Rather, they are here because of the good purposes of God. They themselves have been declared "good" by their Creator. This establishes a presumption that there is in the animal kingdom that which merits respect and appropriate treatment. Therefore, the task of discovering what that appropriate treatment might be and what form that respect is to take is an important and worthy enterprise. It is that task to which this book is devoted.

In enlarging our moral vision so that it embraces animals, we are not simply imposing on ourselves and on others one more unwelcome set of moral burdens. Gaining an enlarged moral vision is not like that. Rather, it is to see old things with a new appreciative eye, to come to hold dear and valuable what was once viewed indifferently, and it is this new "holding dear" that lightens the load and makes new burdens anything but burdensome. After all, in caring for what God cares for there should be joy. So this book is not only an invitation to enlarge our moral universe, it is also an invitation to new joys.

CHAPTER 1

Animal Advocacy and the Christian Tradition: The Lay of the Land

A LITTLE HISTORY: THE EIGHTEENTH AND NINETEENTH CENTURIES

On a Sunday morning, on the eighteenth of October in the year 1772, James Granger, Vicar of the Parish Church of Shiplake, Oxfordshire, England, preached a sermon entitled, "The Abuse of Animals Censured." This was an impassioned plea on behalf of animals and a stern condemnation of the English treatment of them. In that sermon, special attention was directed to the horse, the common mode of transportation at the time, and therefore an animal far more numerous than it is today. Horses were widely owned and apparently used in any way judged acceptable by the owner alone. Too often, according to Granger, the horse was "whipped, spurred, battered and starved to death." No wonder, he pointed out, that England is proverbially referred to as "the Hell of horses."[1] The "barbarous custom of baiting" also came under Granger's severe condemnation. Baiting, an ancient English "sport," involved tethering an animal, usually a bear or a bull, but sometimes even a horse or

1. England may have been referred to as "the hell of horses," but it must be acknowledged, in fairness to England, that all was not heaven elsewhere. For a discussion of the nineteenth-century commercial use of horses in the United Sates, especially New York City, see Gerald Carson, chapter 9, "Horses Are Cheaper Than Oats," in *Men, Beasts, and Gods* (New York: Charles Scribner's Sons, 1972). Referring to the use of horses to pull passenger vehicles, Carson observes, "It was a matter of common observation to one who cared to look that New York was a hell for car horses" (p. 90).

other more vulnerable animal, so that it could not flee, and then setting upon it relays of specially trained dogs, such as mastiffs. Then followed the rending, tearing, slashing, wounding, bleeding, and sometimes the death of both attackers and attacked. Bears, though, were valuable commodities and therefore were not killed in a single go. Indeed they were often not killed at all, but experienced such attacks repeatedly. This was done for the entertainment of those who witnessed what was for Granger a sad and ugly spectacle.[2] At just such practices the Reverend Mr. Granger aimed his text for that Sunday morning, Proverbs 12:10, "A righteous man regardeth the life of his beast: but the tender mercies of the wicked are cruel" (KJV). The results of that sermon were, however, decidedly disappointing. In a postscript of a published version, Granger admitted: "The foregoing discourse gave almost universal disgust to two considerable congregations. The mention of dogs and horses was censured as a prostitution of the dignity of the pulpit, and considered as proof of the Author's growing insanity."[3]

The parish of Shiplake might have considered itself better served had it not had the Reverend James Granger as its parish priest but, instead, the Reverend Thomas Newton, who not only found baiting unobjectionable but personally made the arrangements to have bear baits at his annual parish festival (or Wake). Instead of writing a sermon protesting bear baiting as Granger had done, he wrote a letter to secure the services of one William Smith, a bearward (a keeper of bears for baiting purposes). The letter read in part:

> In about a month's time, that is on the 28th of this month, it is our Wake and if you think it worth your while to come over with a couple of bears I can only say that you shall be welcome to your meat and drink in our house and we will get you a bed somewhere in the town — and I can find a place upon my premises for your bears and I will be looking for some provisions for them. . . . if you come you must bring

2. The historian James Turner provides the following account of a bull bait: "A bull, securely tethered to a stake in the ground by a rope long enough to allow him freedom of movement, was set upon by dogs . . . while the enraged bull defended himself — tossing, shaking, goring unlucky attackers — the dogs tried to slip in and clamp the bull's sensitive lips or nostrils in their vise-like jaws. The skill of the attackers, the tenacity of the bull, his bellows of anguish, dogs hurling through the air with their bellies ripped open, gallons of beer, and the clink of silver all blended in a fever-heat of uproar and excitement" (*Reckoning with the Beast* [Baltimore: Johns Hopkins University Press, 1980], pp. 20-21).

3. Quoted in E. S. Turner, *All Heaven in a Rage* (New York: St. Martin's, 1964), p. 72. For the account of this sermon see Turner, pp. 67-73.

a dog or two with you to run at the bears – and bring also that pointer dog that I saw in the yard when I was at your house.[4]

The attitudes, then, of these two representatives of the gospel could not have been more opposed. For Granger, bear baiting was barbarous, a moral outrage, an expression of cruelty and a violation of scriptural teaching. For Newton, it was appropriate entertainment for a church festival celebrating the parish patron saint. Accordingly, one could write a letter making arrangements for a bear bait with no more compunction than when securing the services of a caterer to provide food and drink or a band to provide music. No need for scruples in the case of food and music, and no need for scruples in the case of an entertaining bear bait either.

With regard to animals, Granger and Newton inhabited different moral universes, and such differences continue to this day, among Christians and among the population at large. Some people have a moral concern and compassion for animals that others apparently lack, and those with that concern, now as then, appear to be in a minority and are often viewed as having eccentric and misdirected sympathies. To be sure, over the years sensitivities have been refined and bear baits at church festivals have become a thing of the past, suggesting that the Grangers of the world, though not always warmly received in their own day, have had a positive influence in changing attitudes and behavior toward animals. Indeed, in the century after Granger preached his sermon, there were radical changes in people's attitudes toward animals. And not only toward animals, for the nineteenth century witnessed an unprecedented expansion of humane sensibilities, as charitable organizations for a wide variety of concerns emerged on the scene: compassionate treatment for the mentally ill, education for the blind and deaf, the founding of hospitals, the passage of child labor laws, improvement of public health, philanthropic housing for the poor, and the crusade to abolish slavery. In this plethora of charitable concerns animals were not forgotten. Indeed, during the second half of the nineteenth century, the Royal Society for the Prevention of the Cruelty to Animals (RSPCA) became the largest and arguably the single most influential voluntary charitable organization in all of England,[5] attracting royalty to its membership along with generous and wealthy supporters. In the United States, in the same century, SPCA's multiplied.

4. Quoted in Turner, *All Heaven in a Rage,* p. 108. The letter was originally quoted in the *Sporting Magazine* of August 1801, for what purpose Turner does not inform us.

5. James Turner, *Reckoning with the Beast,* p. 117 n. 6.

Thus on both sides of the Atlantic, humane concern for animals became a popular concern. Further, legislation to protect animals was passed, including the outlawing of baiting, and the various local SPCA's undertook educational projects to sensitize people to the objectionable character of cruelty to animals.[6]

This new concern with animal welfare was initiated at the end of the eighteenth century with considerable leadership provided by the evangelical community,[7] though it is often alleged that evangelicals, in opposing baiting, for example, were as concerned with the drinking, gambling, and rowdiness that accompanied baiting as they were with the suffering of the animals. Whatever the motives, animals were the beneficiaries of this evangelical concern. Then, throughout the nineteenth century, sermons by pulpiteers of all religious persuasions abounded on the subject of cruelty to animals, with such concern becoming religiously mainstream; no longer was it considered a "prostitution of the dignity of the pulpit." So it would seem that if the eighteenth century belonged to the Reverend Thomas Newton, the nineteenth century belonged to the Reverend James Granger.

Furthermore, in the latter part of the nineteenth century, in both Great Britain and the United States, there emerged a strong anti-vivisection movement. Literally "anti-vivisection" means "against" (anti), "live" (vivi), "cutting" (section) of animals, and signifies opposition to the painful use of animals in research, whether or not the procedures involve invasive techniques, though, of course, they often did. At this point in history experimental physiology had developed into a separate academic discipline, and vivisection was integral to its professional operation; therefore it became a target for attack by many who were concerned with animal welfare. Evangelicals were far from being marginal figures in all this; on the contrary, it was, as Professor Lloyd Stevenson has pointed out, "a striking fact that Evangelicals, and those of similar faith and sympathy, occupied almost all the chief positions in the anti-vivisection soci-

6. There is no need to glorify the animal welfare movements of the nineteenth century. Indeed, they often had mixed motives, too often being concerned with the blood sports of the working class (bull baiting, cock fighting) but indifferent to the blood sports of the middle and upper classes from which RSPCA's membership was drawn. A particularly dramatic instance of this double standard was found in the person of the Baroness Burdett Couts, arguably the most influential single voice in the RSPCA in the latter half of the nineteenth century, who apparently saw nothing wrong with allowing hunting on her estate which involved the impaling of live bait!

7. Turner, *Reckoning with the Beast,* p. 16.

eties."[8] Further, it would not be at all unusual for clergy, including those of evangelical conviction, to be opposed to vivisection. In part, this clerical opposition was fueled by a belief that vivisection was expressive of a materialistic philosophy that underlay science itself. Materialistic science and materialistic medicine, reducing everything to matter, denied, it was thought, the spiritual component in human nature, the very element that gives rise to compassion and kindness, replacing it with cold, calculating, heartless rationality. It was charged that only a materialist, one who was devoid of compassion, could "hog-tie" an animal and then proceed without benefit of anesthesia to surgically explore the animal's inward parts simply for the sake of new knowledge. Thus, in the nineteenth century opposition to vivisection was partly prompted by what was perceived to be the unacceptable philosophy that lay behind it.

It is ironic that today there is often a suspicion that those who *support* animal welfare causes are the ones prompted by an unacceptable philosophy, possibly some form of New Age pantheism. In both cases, then and now, it is uncritically assumed that if a cause finds support from a philosophy considered to be mistaken, then that cause itself is somehow suspect, as if it could not be given adequate support by a more acceptable point of view. But historically, in response to the attacks of the antivivisectionists, those involved in vivisection organized themselves in defense of their activity, and increasingly that defense was found persuasive by the general public. Thus, as we move into the twentieth century it is the defender of vivisection who is mainstream and the critic who is viewed as morally eccentric, standing in the way of what are believed to be the significant benefits that vivisection can bring to the human community. The roles of critic and defender, then, have been reversed.

A LITTLE MORE HISTORY: THE TWENTIETH CENTURY

With the passing of the Victorian era, a new kind of animal concern began to manifest itself, a concern that we have come to call "ecological."[9] That is, we have a shift away from concern with the individual animal to a concern for species survival and the place of species in an environment that must be respected as a well-functioning totality, not to be disturbed by in-

8. Lloyd Stevenson, "Religious Elements in the Background of the British Anti-Vivisection Movement," *Yale Journal of Biology and Medicine* 29 (November 1956): 155.

9. Turner, *Reckoning with the Beast,* p. 125.

sensitive and destructive human intrusions. This new ecological or environmentalist movement, with its concern with species survival, ecosystems, and the whole biosphere, is not simply a new, possibly scientifically more sophisticated version of the older animal welfare movement. It is rather something quite different, indeed possibly something that is ideologically at odds with the animal welfare movement and that has its own competing agenda, as we shall see in the next chapter.

Throughout the twentieth century, this environmental movement grew, and there was articulated an environmentalist ethic that evoked commitment from large numbers of people. Alongside this new movement, the older Victorian tradition with its concern for the welfare and fate of individual animals was continued by various animal welfare groups, such as the American Society for the Prevention of Cruelty to Animals (ASPCA) and the Humane Society of the United States (along with their British counterparts). They are, as most of their forebears were, mainstream organizations rejecting radical stances and generously supported by a faithful membership. These groups accept most current uses of animals and are not at fundamental odds with the society at large. They seek only to reduce the suffering and pain of animals as they are used in traditional ways. Their strategy is to promote public education, the creation of shelters, and the enactment of protective legislation for animals.

In 1975, with the publication of Peter Singer's *Animal Liberation,* the cause of animal advocacy took a dramatic turn, as the book, in conjunction with forces already at work, served to radically change the entire arena of moral concern for animals. Here we have the beginning of the animal rights or animal liberation movement as a pervasive presence on the contemporary scene. Indeed, things have not been the same since. Singer's apologetic sought to justify the deep emotions that drove and shaped those animal advocates who wanted to move well beyond the staid methods and more conservative objectives of the welfarists.[10]

10. Whatever the general public's attitude toward these new animal rights activists – and it is often negative – they are not bereft of intellectually able and rigorous defenders. Singer may have been the first but others have followed, providing alternative modes of philosophical and theological defense that are carefully reasoned. Indeed, a new subdiscipline in the field of philosophical ethics now addresses in a systematic way the issues raised by this new movement. So one is seriously mistaken to think that all of this is lacking in intellectual substance. These defenders are mostly philosophers (Christians among them), who, along with some theologians, have been articulating and with considerable rigor defending a full platform of rights for animals, including a right to life.

It is the growing strength of the animal liberation or animal rights movement in recent years that has attracted the most public attention. As a consequence, new energy has been given to a wide range of animal concerns: the anti-vivisection movement (though Singer himself is not opposed to *all* painful animal experimentation); opposition to the use of animals for substance testing; advocacy of moral vegetarianism (rejecting meat eating on moral grounds); opposition to factory farming (the techniques associated with intensive farming); opposition to the fur trade and the trapping of animals; opposition to the exploitation of animals for entertainment; and so forth. Although this movement is by no means ideologically or programmatically monolithic, many within it would share the conviction that animals have a strong right to live their lives free from human interference. Though this new movement is typically dated from 1975, the ideas associated with it are not new nor are the objectives new. There have always been individuals who have shared the kind of concerns for animals expressed in Singer's book. What is new is the intellectual rigor of their defense and the coalescing of such large numbers in its support.

The 1980s saw a rapid increase in the number of animal rights organizations. It is estimated that by the end of that decade there were some two hundred such organizations with a membership of 500,000 to 1,000,000 in the United States.[11] Perhaps the most influential of these organizations is People for the Ethical Treatment of Animals (PETA), with a membership of approximately 300,000 and a monthly magazine, *Animal Agenda.* It is interesting to note that during this same period the traditional animal welfare organizations, though much criticized by the new animal rights groups for their tepid advocacy, also grew by leaps and bounds. For example, the Humane Society of the United States in the latter part of the 1980s added new members at a rate of 100,000 a year. Altogether the welfare organizations have a membership between ten to fifteen million. Thus, despite the rapid growth of animal rights groups, it is still in the traditional animal welfare organizations that we find the largest contingent of those with animal concerns.

If we use the term "animal advocacy" to include everything from mainstream animal welfarists to animal rights advocates, we might judge that animal advocacy is alive and well. Upon further consideration, however, we might wonder whether this is so, for despite the impressive numbers in these organizations, a substantial portion of our population, in-

11. James M. Jasper and Dorothy Nelkin, *The Animal Rights Crusade* (New York: Free Press, 1992), p. 37.

deed a controlling majority, is indifferent and in some cases hostile to animal advocacy in any form. It is certainly true that the Christian community is at best ambiguously related to all of this; often Christians are bemused by the animal welfarist and hostile toward the animal rights advocate. This unease with animal advocacy is expressive of a feeling that our concern, passion, energy, and resources should be directed to the needs of humans, not animals, and that animal advocacy is an illegitimate diversion of our moral energy and resources.

ANIMAL LOVERS AND PEOPLE LOVERS

At this point, it is worth pausing to reflect on the uneasiness, particularly among Christians, about the legitimacy of spending moral energy on animal advocacy in the face of ever-present human needs. Concern with animals, it may be feared, may so deplete our reservoir of moral concern that there will be too little left for humans. If history is a reliable guide, however, the nineteenth century would suggest that concern for animals does not have to so divert one's moral energies that one becomes less concerned with humans as a result. Indeed, many of those individuals prominent in the animal welfare movement were also passionately committed to the improvement of the human condition.

Thus, William Wilberforce, evangelical Christian and perhaps the single most powerful force for the abolition of the British slave trade, led the fight to outlaw bull baiting and was a founding member of the Royal Society for the Prevention of Cruelty to Animals. Thomas Fowell Buxton, Wilberforce's successor as the anti-slavery leader in the British parliament, was not only a generous philanthropist and a prison reformer but also served with Wilberforce in the RSPCA. Another evangelical, Anthony Ashley Cooper, the Seventh Earl of Shaftesbury, was a tireless worker on behalf of the insane and factory children, assisted Florence Nightingale in army welfare work, *and* served as vice president of the RSPCA. Frances Power Cobbe, called "the grande dame of English anti-vivisection,"[12] invested much of her life in educating slum children. In the United States, Samuel Gridley Howe, Head of the Perkins School for the Blind, was a strong advocate of prison reform, improved treatment and care for the mentally retarded, and promoted the abolition of slavery, as well as serving as a director of the Massachusetts SPCA. Harriet Beecher Stowe,

12. Turner, *Reckoning with the Beast,* p. 36.

famed for kindling anti-slavery sentiment in her writings, performed a similar function in sensitizing people to cruelty to animals. Additionally, as James Turner writes, "The great clans of reforming Quakers – the Gurneys, the Peases – found themselves involved with animal protection as naturally as temperance and anti-slavery."[13] Certainly, it would seem, "animal lovers" can also be "people lovers." And when one reflects on the importance of the current writings of Peter Singer for the animal liberation movement, it is worth noting that he also argues forcefully for radical sacrifice to relieve human suffering, indeed a sacrifice so radical that it leaves most people, including Christians, feeling challenged well beyond their comfort level.

RESENTMENT TOWARD ANIMAL WELFARE

Rosemary Rodd has argued, "Too many people oppose considerate treatment of animals not in order to secure benefits for humans, but simply on the principle that if humans cannot have them then no one shall."[14] Is this true? Or is it too harsh a judgment? Certainly many people object to efforts to help animals, especially organized efforts, and they do so on the expressed ground that the energy thus expended ought to be directed to humans. Thus the philosopher Peter Carruthers passionately declares, "I regard the present popular concern with animal rights in our culture as a reflection of moral decadence. Just as Nero fiddled while Rome burned, many in the West agonize over the fate of seal pups and cormorants while human beings elsewhere starve or are enslaved."[15] Although the ostensible reason for opposing serious concern with animals' welfare is that it reduces our concern with human welfare, one suspects that the real reason is simply resentment toward animal welfare efforts whether they take away from human welfare or not. Rosemary Rodd makes the same point: "This attitude will be familiar to anyone who has been involved in collecting money on behalf of animal welfare charities. Such collectors are frequent recipients of critical comments of the form, 'I wish you took some interest in children's welfare.' Presumably those making this criticism would not make similar remarks to people who were merely engaged in

13. Turner, *Reckoning with the Beast,* p. 36.

14. Rosemary Rodd, *Biology, Ethics, and Animals* (Oxford: Clarendon, 1990), p. 182.

15. Peter Carruthers, *The Animal Issue* (New York: Cambridge University Press, 1992), p. xi.

private entertainment: that is, going to the cinema."[16] So, again, the suspicion is that the resentment is more over helping animals than it is over not helping humans. It is simply not believed that animal needs are real needs, that our meeting those needs is a significant contribution to making the world a better place, nor is it believed that meeting those needs can be a form of Christian service. Now, the suggestion here is not that *all* who oppose organized animal welfare efforts are of the conviction that what makes such efforts unacceptable is simply that they are designed to help animals. On the contrary, there may well be critics who have some appreciation for animal welfare needs, but who do not see how they can be realistically addressed in the face of overwhelming human needs. And they may genuinely be concerned that efforts on behalf of animals will divert much of our moral energy away from humans.

Arguing that such concerns spring from a faulty understanding of love, Mary Midgley relevantly puts to interesting use the tale told by Nathan the prophet in confronting King David with his sin of having Uriah the Hittite killed so that he could marry Bathsheba. Nathan's approach to David is initially subtle and indirect. He begins by telling David the following story:

> There were two men in a certain city, the one rich and the other poor. The rich man had very many flocks and herds; but the poor man had nothing but one little ewe lamb, which he had bought. He brought it up, and it grew up with him and with his children; it used to eat of his morsel, and drink from his cup, and lie in his bosom, and it was like a daughter to him. Now there came a traveler to the rich man, and he was unwilling to take one of his own flock or herd to prepare for the wayfarer who had come to him, but he took the poor man's lamb, and prepared it for the man who had come to him. (2 Samuel 12:1-4)

David, on hearing this, becomes incensed: "As the LORD lives, the man who has done this deserves to die." Having thus drawn David out, Nathan springs his trap: "You are the man!" Midgley focuses on the naturalness with which both Nathan and David accept the relationship between the poor man and his ewe lamb. They fully understand his embracing it with "parental cherishing" as it lay "in his bosom" and was like a daughter to him. Further, the man was not childless, driven by some need for a "child substitute," but had children of his own who shared in the enjoyment of the lamb. And David does not respond to this tale with moral punctili-

16. Rodd, *Biology, Ethics, and Animals,* p. 182.

ousness, suggesting that rather than "sentimental pet keeping" the man would have served the cause of humanity better by adopting a human orphan. Then, Midgley makes the following pertinent observation: "The ewe lamb did not come between the poor man and his children. Instead it formed an extra delight which he could share with them, and so strengthened the family bond. (That, surely, is why Nathan mentions the children). One sort of love does not need to block another, because love, like compassion, is not a rare fluid to be economized, but a capacity which grows by use."[17] It may very well be that the reason we consider moral concern for animals and compassion for them as competing with our moral concern and compassion for humans is that we are misled by a faulty picture or a misleading analogy. We wrongly view moral concern and love as a "rare fluid to be economized" rather than as a "capacity which grows by use."

THE LOGIC OF THE LINE

Yet, the objection persists: "There are so many *human* needs in the world – why be concerned with animals?" Indeed, without question, there are many human needs in the world – so many that it is overwhelming: souls need to be saved and sanctified; bodies need to be fed, clothed, and cured of disease; minds need to be educated and schooled in virtue; society needs to embrace justice and conquer prejudice; the unemployed need jobs; drug addicts need to overcome their addiction; strife-torn families need to be made whole; warring nations need to make peace; crime needs to be controlled; the pollution of the environment needs to be arrested and reversed; and so on and so on.

Of course, what is being suggested in the complaint is not that there are no animal needs, but rather that there are so many human needs that, if we did things in their proper order, humans first and animals second, then there would simply be no time and energy left for helping animals (or writing books about helping animals). The picture that comes to mind here is that of an enormously long line of needy individuals, with humans at the front of the line where they belong and animals at the rear of the line where they belong. And our task as Christians and humanitarians is to start at the front of the line and work systematically back toward

17. Mary Midgley, *Animals and Why They Matter* (Athens, Ga.: University of Georgia Press, 1983), p. 119.

the end of the line. The assumption is that, since that part of the line where humans are located is so long, we will never get to animals, unless we do what we should not do, namely, skip over humans in order to get to animals who are positioned at the back of the line.

A similar logic has prompted some Christians to argue that *all* our efforts as a Christian community ought to be devoted to saving souls, for at the very front of this enormously long line that we are imagining are not only humans but unsaved humans, individuals with the desperate need for spiritual redemption. Since this is the greatest of needs and since there are so many souls in need of salvation, we simply will never get to those humans who have lesser needs – the sick, the starving, the oppressed, the lonely. They must simply wait their turn, a turn, which, it so happens, will never come because spiritual needs always take precedence over all other needs. On this logic there will be no cup of water given in the name of Jesus, only gospel tracts and an invitation to accept the message found in those tracts. For those of us who take that message seriously, it may come as a shock to us when we first discover that Jesus and the biblical tradition of which he is the culmination never adopt "the logic of the line." Rather, needs are met as they are encountered: a call to repentance here, a cup of water there, a physical healing required next, followed by removal of an ox from a ditch on the Sabbath, and so forth. The needs that are met are varied, and Jesus had no rigid set of priorities. Indeed, as in Scripture, so in life, people with needs do not come to us in a long line efficiently ordered by providence; rather, we find ourselves enmeshed in a tangle of human needs and sometimes animal needs too, suggesting a more complicated providence. To sort them out and give exclusive attention to only a small spectrum of those needs is not to follow the biblical model but to adopt a deviant logic of our own devising.

To be sure, some of us may sense a call to specialize in meeting certain needs. For us it may be evangelism or world hunger that becomes our primary focus, or possibly ecology or issues of justice, but we do not specialize in this way because we think that only evangelism or only world hunger or only ecology or only justice is worthy of one's life. Rather, it is because we judge that that is *our* calling because of our particular circumstances, talents, and passions. Other Christians may invest their lives differently but together, we believe, we constitute the Body of Christ, ministering in the world as Christ would minister: doing evangelism, fighting hunger, respecting the environment, and siding with justice. But even when Christians do specialize in this way – and not all do – there still remains in the lives of such specialists a place for the meeting of needs beyond the scope of their specialty — the evangelist is not above offering the cup of cold water for its own sake, the Christian ecologist is not above bearing explicit witness to the death and resurrection of Jesus, the one who is devoted to world hunger may take time to protest racial injustice. So also, a person, whatever his or her calling, should not be beyond taking a dog hit by an automobile to a veterinary clinic, there to be treated and to have its suffering relieved. The dog should not be required to wait at the end of some mythical line, that is, to wait forever. And if animals are, in some set of circumstances, being cruelly abused, then that cruelty should be protested; and we should not be misled by the logic of the line into thinking that silence is appropriate because we must first protest every conceivable abuse of humans before we ever raise our voices on behalf of animals. Indeed, had the Reverend James Granger and all subsequent generations accepted the logic of the line, no voices would ever have been raised against animal baiting and that cruel sport would be with us to this day.

Maybe there is a perfectly good reason why God does not confront us with a providentially ordered line where we are simply to meet individual needs one after another in the order that God has nicely arranged them for us. To be forced to live life that way would, I suggest, produce morally and spiritually constricted people; it would produce people who would not develop the *full range* of compassions, sympathies, and concerns that ought to be characteristic of those being conformed to the image of Christ. For we are to be a people of broad and expansive sympathies — sympathies that extend not only to persons floundering without spiritual direction, and to persons victimized by racial and gender prejudice, and to persons lacking sufficient food to sustain life, and to persons lonely and friendless, but also to that badly injured dog whimpering at the side of the road, having been struck by a passing automobile. This is part of what we are to be as people who aspire to be perfect as our Father in heaven is perfect — a people of just such broad and expansive sympathies.

There is no moral and spiritual wholeness where people narrowly restrict their sympathies. On the contrary, there is something distorted about the person who feels concern only about issues of ecology and has no sensitivity to victims of racial or gender prejudice; there is something deficient in the person who weeps over the spiritually lost but cares not one wit about those crushed by poverty. These and others like them are spiritually distorted; they have departed from the wholeness we are called to develop in Christ. And at this point it may be appropriate to note that all of us are in varying degrees less than whole; all of us are more or less distorted. The task, then, for each of us is to overcome our moral narrowness and increasingly become morally and spiritually whole persons. Indeed, one might characterize the Christian life as the process whereby, time and again, we begin to hear what previously we did not hear, overcoming our spiritual deafness. And because a concern for animals is, I suggest, part of Christian wholeness, it is part of being what we are called to be as followers of Christ; it is simply to share the concern of the Creator, who brought animals into existence, saw them as "good," and "blessed them" (Gen. 1:21, 22), "who gives to the beasts their food, and to the young ravens which cry" (Ps. 147:9), who provides Sabbath rest not only for humans but for beasts as well (Exod. 23:12; Deut. 5:14), and whose saving compassion extends even to animals (Jonah 4:11). To share such concern is simply a part of what it means to be morally and spiritually whole, as God is whole. This, then, is why we are to be concerned with animals when there are so many human needs in the world.

TAKING ANIMAL ADVOCACY SERIOUSLY

I want to suggest that the Christian community rather than being dismissive of animal advocacy should take seriously appeals made on behalf of animals. Not all moral appeals, of course, should be respected. Nor should they all be honored by being granted a *continuous* hearing, as I shall argue animal advocacy deserves. To be sure, to take seriously and to respect a moral position it is not necessary to agree with all that is being advocated. What is required is to recognize at least *the real possibility* of substantial truth in that position and to allow oneself to be shaped and influenced by that recognition, even if one may dissent at certain points.

It is clear that the moral vision of the Christian community should include compassionate sensitivity toward animals and a respectful appreciation of them as God's creatures. How that is nuanced, how that is worked out in practical advocacy, can become problematic and troublesome. But at least basic compassion and respect for animals should be present as we think through our differences and seek to create attitudes and make commitments that are acceptably Christian. Even those within the Christian community who will in the final analysis be critical of animal advocacy ought to be both tempered and sensitive in that criticism if they are to be true to the Christian vision. One's moral vision, after all, shapes not only what one advocates and how one advocates it, but also what one criticizes and how one criticizes it. Not all criticism of animal advocacy will be acceptably Christian.

Consider for a moment the character of a moral vision. It is not simply a listing of all those moral propositions that one accepts, coupled with a listing of those moral propositions that one rejects. This is too limited a conception of a moral vision, too abstract and too removed from its embodiment in an individual life. For moral visions are found in people, not in books; therefore, a moral vision also involves how one holds those propositions – how confidently, how deeply, how tenaciously, how rigidly, how self-critically, how tentatively, how judgmentally, how qualifiedly, and so on. A moral vision, therefore, can be skewed or distorted and in need of correction not merely because the wrong propositions are affirmed but because there is something in the character of the affirmation itself (that is, how the moral belief is held) that is inappropriate and in need of correction. And obviously this applies to beliefs that one rejects as false as well as to beliefs that one accepts as true: one's moral vision shapes and is shaped by the manner of one's acceptance and the manner of one's rejection of those moral beliefs.

Thus, two people who reject the same moral position, one viewing it as, say, silly and foolish, and another viewing it as attractive and plausible but on balance mistaken do not fully share the same moral vision; they have in fact significantly different moral sensitivities and these differences may well function to shape their moral lives in quite different ways. So, if one were to reject animal advocacy it would be important whether one rejects it as silly and foolish, or whether one rejects it as morally plausible but on balance mistaken. I shall argue, minimally, that the church should be in the company of those who have moral sensibilities sufficient to see the moral attractiveness and plausibility of animal advocacy and that to fail to see this constitutes a serious deficiency. It is not merely a failure to grasp certain abstract arguments but a failure to see and to feel in appropriate ways.

ATTITUDES TOWARD ANIMALS

Human attitudes toward animals vary widely; indeed, when it comes to human attitudes toward animals, even a cursory survey of our friends and acquaintances reveals a wide spectrum of attitudes. In a helpful study, Stephen Kellert and Joyce Berry of Yale University surveyed the basic attitudes toward and understanding of animals in American society. In their study they identified ten basic types, which I have listed below along with the percentage of Americans that they conclude are in each category.[18]

Naturalistic	10%	Primary interest and affection for wildlife and the outdoors
Ecologistic	7%	Primary concern for the environment as a system, for interrelationships between wildlife species and natural habitats
Humanistic	35%	Primary interest and strong affection for individual animals, principally pets
Moralistic	20%	Primary concern for the right and wrong treatment of animals, with strong opposition to exploitation or cruelty toward animals
Scientific	1%	Primary interest in the physical attributes and biological functioning of animals
Aesthetic	15%	Primary interest in the artistic and symbolic characteristics of animals
Utilitarian	20%	Primary concern for the practical and material value of animals or the animal's habitat
Dominionistic	3%	Primary interest in the mastery and control of animals, typically in sporting situations
Negativistic	2%	Primary orientation in active avoidance of animals due to dislike or fear
Neutralistic	35%	Primary orientation a passive avoidance of animals due to indifference

The most common attitudes, then, among the American population are the humanistic, moralistic, utilitarian, and neutralistic attitudes. The moralistic[19] and utilitarian[20] attitudes are of special interest because one of our concerns in this book can be expressed as follows: to what extent should our own attitudes toward animals be moralistic ("opposes most exploitative uses of animals, particularly where death or presumed suffering are involved") or utilitarian ("typically supports such activities if sub-

18. Stephen Kellert and Joyce Berry, *Knowledge, Affection and Basic Attitudes toward Animals in American Society,* Phase III (Washington, D.C.: U.S. Government Printing Office, 1980), pp. 42ff.

19. The term "moralistic" may in some contexts have a pejorative overtone, but that is not the case here.

20. "Utilitarian" is not to be strictly identified with the moral theory known as utilitarianism.

stantial human benefits result")? In large measure the current work of animal advocates is an attempt to convert those of utilitarian persuasion into those of moralistic persuasion. Also of interest is the high number of those in the neutralistic camp, those who have an attitude of indifference toward animals. In the language of T. L. S. Sprigge, these are people who are blind to the "ontology of animal reality."[21] These are people for whom animals don't exist as objects of interest or concern and for whom the kinds of questions raised in this book would hold little or no interest. Of course, a neutralist today need not be a neutralist tomorrow, and what at one time in a person's life is a matter of indifference may subsequently become a matter of passionate concern. In some sense this change would represent a new way of seeing, seeing what was there all along to see — a kind of conversion, whereby a substantial part of the created order comes into focus for the first time and brings with it new appreciations, new wonders, and new perplexities.

Almost 60 percent of those surveyed indicated that they were more concerned about the suffering of individual animals than they were about species population levels. In this regard, there is a congruence between American attitudes and the focus of this book, where the emphasis is on the suffering and fate of the individual animal and not on species survival. Over 75 percent of the public objected to the use of steel leg-hold traps to catch animals, and 77 percent of those surveyed *denied* that they admired "a person who hunts hard to obtain a large trophy animal." Additionally, 86 percent of the national sample rejected the claim that love is an emotion appropriately directed only toward humans but never toward animals.[22] That is, they are saying it is legitimate to love animals — to love one's cat or dog, say. This goes counter, as we shall subsequently see, to the thought of those like Thomas Aquinas who judge that love is appropriately directed toward humans only.

A significant part of Kellert and Berry's work was a study of the distribution of the various attitudes (the ten listed above) among a wide range of demographic groupings — age, sex, race, education, income, occupation, urban/rural residence, region, participation in religious activities, and marital status. For the Christian community and religious believers in general, the following two quotations from their study should

21. T. L. S. Sprigge, "Metaphysics, Physicalism and Animal Rights," *Inquiry* 22, nos. 1-2 (1979): 101.

22. Kellert and Berry, *Knowledge, Affection and Basic Attitudes toward Animals in American Society,* p. 48.

be of some considerable interest as well as the cause for some measure of concern.

> 1. [R]espondents who rarely or never attend religious services had among the highest knowledge scores of any demographic group in contrast to those who participated once a week or more who had very low knowledge scores.[23]
>
> 2. Strong differences also existed in concern for the ethical treatment and exploitation of animals and their natural habitats. Specially, those rarely or never participating in formal religious activities scored far higher on the moralistic and lower on the utilitarian scales than respondents who attended services at least once a week or more.[24]

So it seems that the animal's best friend is not to be found in the church but among those of a secular persuasion. Both as to knowledge about animals and concern for them, the secular and not the religious communities appear to be the pacesetters. Sadly, it will not be the first time that the latter needs to learn from the former. Perhaps the case for animal advocacy has not yet been presented to the Christian community within their usual framework for making moral inquiries, that is, one that takes biblical and theological categories seriously.

Finally, the study also shows – significantly – a greater ethical and humanistic concern for animals among females than among males. Females were far more opposed to hunting and rated higher on the moralistic scale, while males scored significantly higher on the utilitarian and dominionistic scales. Males revealed greater knowledge of animals than females, but "it appeared . . . that males possessed a more generalized interest and understanding of animals, but in a somewhat emotionally detached and matter-of-fact manner not found among females."[25] Greater concern for animals among the general female population has translated into a higher percentage of women than men involved in political activism on behalf of animals. Anthropologist Susan Sperling, referring to the renewed animal activism witnessed in recent years, has commented, "Ob-

23. Kellert and Berry, *Knowledge, Affection and Basic Attitudes toward Animals in American Society,* p. 102.

24. Kellert and Berry, *Knowledge, Affection and Basic Attitudes toward Animals in American Society,* p. 107.

25. Kellert and Berry, *Knowledge, Affection and Basic Attitudes toward Animals in American Society,* p. 59.

servation suggests that the new activists are typically white, college educated, from middle-class urban and suburban backgrounds, in their early to middle thirties, and female."[26] Certainly it seems that if one were an animal, it would be better to have one's fate in the hands of a female — and a secular female at that!

CHRISTIANITY AS CULPRIT

The blame for the historical roots of both our ecological crises and our maltreatment of animals is often laid at the doorstep of the Christian church. The charge is that, with its anthropocentric moral vision, the church sees only humans as of value to God and sees nature, including animals, as nothing more than a resource to be used for human advantage. Indeed, these historical roots, it is claimed, reach back to the Old Testament itself, where humankind is given "dominion" over all animals (Gen. 1:26-28) and where it is declared, "the fear of you and the dread of you shall be upon every beast of the earth . . . into your hand they are delivered" (Gen. 9:2). Or as the Psalmist puts it, "Thou hast given him dominion over the works of thy hands; thou hast put all things under his feet, all sheep and oxen, and also the beasts of the field" (Ps. 8:6-7). In this connection Roderick Nash comments,

> The image is that of a conqueror placing his foot on the neck of a defeated enemy, exerting absolute domination. Both Hebraic words [the Hebraic words translated "subdue" and "have dominion over," or "rule"] are also used to identify the process of enslavement. It followed that the Christian tradition could understand Genesis 1:28 as a divine commandment to conquer every part of nature and make it humankind's slave. Certainly such an interpretation proved useful over the centuries as the intellectual lubrication for the exploitation of nature.[27]

In response to such statements, it is not sufficient simply to question the interpretation given the dominion verses or to quote other verses that qualify and supplement them or to introduce biblical notions of

26. Susan Sperling, *Animal Liberation* (Berkeley and Los Angeles: University of California Press, 1988), p. 85.

27. Roderick Nash, *The Rights of Nature: A History of Environmental Ethics* (Madison: University of Wisconsin Press, 1989), p. 90.

stewardship or to argue in a myriad of other ways that the exploitation of nature and animals is antithetical to a theocentric vision of nature. For what is at issue here is not an exegetical or theological claim but a historical one; at issue is not what Christianity *means* or what the Bible *means* but how it has been interpreted and applied, and the historical impact of this interpretation and application. The claim is that the impact has been a negative one, that Christianity as interpreted down through the centuries has not been an influence for good when it comes to the treatment of animals and nature.

It is even argued that the pagan animism that Christianity replaced was actually, in contrast, a beneficial force, inhibiting the exploitation of nature. The pagan animists populated nature with a range of spirits that were associated with flora and fauna, rivers and mountains, earth and animals, all rendering nature sacred and worthy of a kind of respect that was subsequently eliminated with the triumph of Christianity. Thus with Christianity's appearance and the desacralization of nature, to fell a forest or to pollute a stream or to kill a herd of deer was no longer to violate the sacred but to give free expression to our human right to dominion. The pagan animists, though inhibited by their spiritual vision of nature, would still use nature for human ends, but because it was a spiritually risky venture to do so, it would only be done with reservation and a strong sense of restraint. The philosopher John Passmore comments that the

> desacralization of nature certainly left man free to exploit it with none of the qualms which, in many other societies, he would have felt when he cut down a tree or killed an animal. There are societies in which the axeman or the slaughterer before taking up his axe or his knife, would first have begged the tree's or the animal's pardon, explaining the necessity which forced him to destroy it. Indeed, such an attitude to nature lingered on among German foresters as late as the nineteenth century.[28]

But such inhibitions are predicated upon a view of nature as sacred, something inimical to the biblical tradition with its worship of one God, who alone is sacred, a God who is transcendent and who is not to be equated with nature. Indeed, if a reading of the Bible communicates anything at all, it is that God alone is to be worshiped, that God is the creator of nature, and that to worship nature (that is, to put nature into the category

28. John Passmore, *Man's Responsibility for Nature* (New York: Charles Scribner's Sons, 1974), p. 10.

of the sacred) is idolatry. So if the pagan restraints on the use of nature were beneficial (as it is often argued), then Christianity has indeed played a destructive role by removing those restraints and failing to replace them with others.

Ecologically sensitive and biblically informed Christians would argue, however, that there are strong and plausible biblical grounds for exercising stewardly care and restraint in our use of nature, grounds that we have too often neglected or overlooked. And it may be that they were overlooked in part because the Christian community was overreacting to pagan animism, more concerned with rejecting pagan error than with adequately affirming Christian truth. And, of course, this is often – indeed, too often – the case: our own beliefs and attitudes are themselves shaped by the very falsehoods that we rightly seek to repudiate. In the very act of repudiation we twist and distort the truth that prompted the repudiation. Thus it turns out that repudiating error is not the simple matter many of us have supposed it to be.

In this case, we rightly repudiate pagan animism and with it its attendant belief that nature is sacred, and we do so in the name of the God who is the creator of all nature and who alone is sacred and worthy of worship. But in doing so we may be in danger of overstating our own position from fear of falling prey to the error we are rejecting. Indeed, what better way to ensure that we do not succumb to the errors of animism than to treat nature as if it were at the farthest remove from the sacred, as if it had only instrumental value, as if it were a disposable product to be used in any way we choose. Contrariwise, to begin to speak of the respect owed nature because of its intrinsic value, it is feared, is to compromise Christian belief, to teeter on the edge of idolatry and possibly to go over the edge, down the slippery slope to animism. So it may turn out that our attitudes toward nature are shaped as much by animism and our reaction to it as they are by our own positive theological vision. Forgotten is the insight that whereas "nature is not God, it is God's" and therefore should be treated with an appropriate circumspection, caution, and care. Ignored is the fact that God declared creation good even before creating humans. Neglected is the possibility that God can call into existence that which has intrinsic value and expect it to be treated appropriately without being worshiped. So whereas we do not want to fall prey to animism, neither do we want our rejection of animism by itself to shape our attitude toward nature and animals.

Though we may regret what has been an overreaction to pagan animism, we certainly do not want to glorify the merits of animism either, as perhaps some on the current scene have done. For one might well wonder what a world living off the spiritual heritage of pagan animism would be like. Might it not be a world where not the triumph of Christianity but its defeat would be deplored, as we focused on our failure to use nature in legitimate ways to find solutions to many of the ills that afflict humankind: pain, suffering, disease, infant mortality, premature death, and so on? It is, after all, the use of nature that has enabled us to secure important benefits for the human community. To fantasize that the world of the pagan animists would be an idyllic world is to romanticize "what might have been" and not to be fully realistic. Still, this does not overturn the charge that Christianity has historically been interpreted in ways that have not been beneficial to the environment, to nature, and to the world of animals. And the Christian may well regret that the restraints of animism on the use of nature that were removed with the triumph of Christianity were not replaced by other restraints, theologically more appropriate and biblically grounded, restraints that in recent years the Christian community has sought to articulate. Perhaps this delay in providing such restraints should not altogether surprise us, since, after all, it took eighteen hundred years before human slavery, which was often defended theologically and biblically, was finally challenged by a critical mass within the Christian community.

The claim, however, that Christianity's attitude toward the natural order is *the* cause of the modern exploitation of nature can be questioned. A better case, I would judge, can be made for commercial incentives as the real culprit. And it is a dubious proposition that pagan animism could have prevented abuse of nature that is driven by perceived economic advantage. Further, as Keith Thomas notes, "in modern times the Japanese worship of nature has not prevented the industrial pollution of Japan. Ecological problems are not peculiar to the West; for soil erosion, deforestation and the extinction of species have occurred in parts of the world where the Judaeo-Christian tradition has had no influence. The Maya, the Chinese and the people of the Near East were all capable of destroying their environment without the aid of Christianity."[29] One might perhaps be forgiven for being sufficiently cynical as to suggest that if the exploitation of nature is to be stopped it will happen only when we humans perceive it to be in our economic interest to stop it; theological calls to stewardship of the created order will, by themselves, most likely do little to

29. Keith Thomas, *Man and the Natural World* (New York: Pantheon Books, 1983), pp. 23-24.

reverse the recent course of ecological history. One should want, nevertheless, to be on the right side, whether or not one's presence is causally significant in changing things for the better.

WHAT IS AN ANIMAL?

This book is concerned with animals and though we have already spoken extensively of animals, it might be useful to clarify at this point what precisely we mean by an "animal." In common parlance an animal is any of the "lower" members of the animal kingdom, to be distinguished from human beings. Further, as the Oxford English Dictionary notes, "The term is often restricted by the uneducated to quadrupeds; and familiarly applied especially to such as are used by man as a horse, ass, or dog." So only what has four legs, in the thinking of some, is an animal, which means that when the term "animal" is used by some people, they not only do not think of humans but they also exclude from their thinking such life forms as birds, insects, and snakes. But in point of fact all of the following are animals: humans (Homo sapiens), chimpanzees, monkeys, hedgehogs, dolphins, sharks, salmon, wolves, sheep, rats, kangaroos, crows, pigeons, eagles, ostriches, crocodiles, lizards, snakes, frogs, toads, newts, bees, spiders, centipedes, beetles, earthworms, and (according to some) one-celled animals called "protozoa." Just from this meager listing – and there are, keep in mind, over *one million* different species of animals – one can see that to speak of animals is to cover a wide spectrum of life-forms. Thus, talk of animal rights or moral standing for animals or the appropriateness of compassion for animals may stand in need of some qualification. Do we really wish to direct the same moral concern to protozoa as to chimpanzees, to centipedes as to dolphins?

The term "animal" is used in two distinct ways, depending on whether or not humans are included, and there is something more significant here than a piece of arbitrary linguistic usage. As Mary Midgley points out, the exclusive and inclusive uses of the term reflect a deep-seated ambiguity in our own attitudes and feelings toward animals. When we speak of ourselves as part of the animal world (the inclusive use of the term), we see animals as our kin and we transfer to them some of the goodwill and favorable attitude we have toward our own species. Thus, Midgley observes, "If a small child asks us what an animal is, we are likely to choose the first meaning [inclusive], and our answer will probably be wide, untroubled and hospitable, more especially if we are scientifically oriented people. We shall explain that the word can include you and me and the dog and the bird outside, the flies and the worms in the garden and the whale and elephants and polar bears and Blake's tiger."[30] This generosity of spirit toward animals when we include ourselves in their number may in part be why it is that those who wish to make a case for better and more respectful treatment of animals often stress that we humans too are animals and often seek to blur the distinction between humans and nonhuman animals.

But when we use the term "animal" in its exclusive sense, leaving humans out of the picture, then the term often stands for what is "unhuman" or "anti-human." Thus, as Midgley also comments,

> "You have behaved like animals!" says the judge to defendants found guilty of highly complicated human social offenses, such as driving a stolen car while under the influence of drink. What is the judge doing here? He is, it seems, excluding the offenders from the moral community. His meaning . . . is something like this. . . . You have crashed through the barriers of culture. . . . The horror of your act does not lie only in the harm you have done to your victims, but also more deeply, in the degradation into which you have plunged yourselves, a degradation which may infect us all.[31]

In acting like animals, the offenders have, in the judge's view, acted in a manner that is foreign and alien to what is truly human. By characterizing the offenders' behavior as animalish he disowns it as something belonging to a dangerous realm outside of culture, civilization, and morality. There is an implicit recognition that in "behaving like animals" we may have failed to restrain something that is — ominously — *part* of our nature but which is the *entire* nature of nonhuman animals.

This means that people who struggle with the place of animals in the moral community — do they have a place there or not? — will often be tugged back and forth by deep emotions and unconscious attitudes that are at odds with each other, reflected in our dual use of the term "animal." Thus, not all progress in this area is a product simply of surface rationality, whether we are quoting Scripture or offering technical arguments. There are also some deep underlying feelings at play, which are characterized by considerable ambiguity. Throughout this book, however,

30. Mary Midgley, "Are You an Animal?" in *Animal Experimentation,* ed. Gill Langley (New York: Chapman and Hall, 1989), p. 1.

31. Midgley, "Are You an Animal?" pp. 1-2.

reference to "animals" will refer (with few exceptions) only to nonhuman animals. This simply reflects the specific concerns of this book, for we want to ask ourselves whether we have duties to nonhuman animals, whether nonhuman animals have moral standing or rights, what is the appropriate attitude that we should have toward nonhuman animals, what are nonhuman animals like, what is God's purpose for nonhuman animals, why does a good God allow nonhuman animals to suffer, and so forth. We are simply dropping the qualifier "nonhuman" for the sake of brevity, but this is not meant to convey any negative attitude toward animals.

Our fundamental concern, then, is with nonhuman animals, not with humans and not with plants. Animals are regularly distinguished from plants, animals and plants typically being said to constitute the two basic kingdoms of living organisms. Although there is no single criterion that enables us to distinguish animals from plants, there are a number of criteria that, taken together, work reasonably well (though not perfectly, according to experts): (a) method of obtaining food – plants produce their food from inorganic substances, while for animals, food is already organized into organic substances; (b) possession of a nervous system and sense organs – possessed by animals but not plants; (c) locomotion – animals have greater mobility, along with specialized means of locomotion, but plants do not; (d) the nature of tissue cells – in the case of plants they are enclosed in rigid walls of cellulose and in the case of animals in delicate membranes; (e) motor response to stimulation – rapid in the case of animals, not so in the case of plants.

These criteria may help us distinguish animals from plants, but do they provide any reason for considering animals better prospects for moral standing than plants? Most of them appear irrelevant. Why should we consider locomotion or the particular method of obtaining food or the nature of tissue cells in any way relevant to determining one's moral standing? Rather, what makes animals better candidates for moral standing than plants is that we suspect that many animals, but not plants, are conscious and have an inner psychological life that goes better or worse for them, and we judge this to be somehow relevant. Thus, some animals, we believe, are conscious, experience pleasure and pain, and may even be self-conscious, and have desires and an inner mental life of some degree of complexity. Whatever doubts we may have about this, we nevertheless believe it more plausible that this is so in the case of animals than in the case of plants, and therefore we consider animals better candidates for moral standing than plants. Physiologically, a crucial difference is that some animals have brains and a central nervous system, whereas no plants do. Animals, therefore, have the requisite biological basis for "mind," something that plants lack.

A fundamental division in the animal kingdom is that between vertebrates (animals with a backbone consisting of a series of vertebrae) and invertebrates (animals lacking a backbone). In the category of vertebrates are mammals, birds, reptiles, amphibians, and fish, all of which have a spinal cord with a brain enclosed in a cranium. In the category of invertebrates are everything from sponges (debated) to jellyfish, flatworms, and mollusks. One subdivision (a phylum) of invertebrates, arthropods, is worth noting simply because it comprises over 600,000 species, including insects, spiders, and centipedes, and it constitutes 90 percent of the animal population. Invertebrates do have brains but they are less developed, though there is some evidence suggesting that even insects feel pain.

For research purposes, the animal world is organized into phylum, class, order, genus, and species. In the case of humans we are of the *phylum* chordates (this includes vertebrates), the *class* of mammals, the *order* of primates, the *genus* Homo, and the *species* Homo sapiens. Of the genus Homo, only we humans survive; all other members, such as Neanderthals and Homo Erectus, are extinct. Therefore, whatever problems, theological or other, they may pose for us, they do not pose any moral problems. Mammals are the highest class of vertebrates, are warm-blooded, and are the class of animals that we tend to most closely identify with (contrast our differing emotional responses to dolphins and sharks). Our closest relatives are found among the primates, who are mammals with hands that have movable fingers. There are some two hundred living species of primates, ranging from the very primitive insect-eating tree shrew to humans. The term "ape" applies to certain primates, indeed the most intelligent of the primates (excluding humans): gorillas, chimpanzees, orangutans, and gibbons. So the animal world is a vast world, inhabited by creatures of varying capacities, and we suspect that these differences of capacity (especially relating to consciousness and the ability to experience pleasure and pain) will turn out to be morally significant differences.

SUMMARY

In this chapter the issues raised and the points made were wide-ranging and varied. Historically, we observed that the nineteenth century witnessed an unprecedented expansion of humane sensibilities, including concern for animal welfare; this new attitude of concern manifested itself in everything from sermons preached to SPCA's founded, from new laws to protect animals (including the abolition of baiting and other blood sports) to educational efforts to sensitize people to animal suffering. With the coming of the twentieth century ecological concerns emerged, with a focus on species survival and ecosystems supplementing the older nineteenth-century concern with the welfare of individual animals, the latter concern continuing in such organizations as, for example, the Humane Society of the United States. The publishing of Peter Singer's *Animal Liberation* in 1975 signaled the beginning of the contemporary animal rights or animal liberation movement. Whereas the older animal welfarist did not challenge most traditional uses of animals but simply wanted to ameliorate the pain and suffering caused them in the process of that use, this new movement articulates and defends a full platform of animal rights and rejects most traditional uses to which animals have been put. The term "animal advocacy" was introduced to include both traditional animal welfarists and animal rights supporters.

In exploring and ultimately rejecting what we called "the logic of the line" we sought to blunt the charge that moral concern for animals will unacceptably divert moral energy from human beings. It is not the case, we argued, that because there are so many human needs animal needs should be ignored. Rather, as Christians, we are called to be a people of broad and expansive sympathies, concerned not only with the full range of human needs (spiritual, physical, mental, etc.) but also possessed of a compassion that is sensitive to animal suffering as well. All this is part of Christian wholeness, part of being perfect as our Father in heaven is perfect. The journey from moral and spiritual distortion to moral and spiritual wholeness involves, among many other things, a concern for God's animal creation.

It was also argued that the Christian community ought not be dismissive of animal advocacy but that such advocacy should, rather, have a recognized place within the Christian church as it speaks to the church and challenges the church, even if, in varying degrees, that message is not fully embraced. To take animal advocacy seriously is to allow for the real possibility of substantial truth, and to allow oneself to be shaped and influenced by that recognition, even if one may dissent at crucial points.

A survey of American attitudes toward animals was presented. Two interesting findings, especially noteworthy for our purposes, were underscored: (1) regular church attenders are both less knowledgeable about and less ethically concerned with animals than those of a secular persuasion, and (2) females, much more than males, have an ethical and humanistic concern for animals.

The charge that the teachings of Christianity with its anthropocentric moral vision are the major source of our ecological crises and of our maltreatment of animals was examined. It was acknowledged that when Christianity triumphed over pagan animism and desacralized nature, it may have failed to replace animism's restraints on the use of nature with its own restraints. Indeed, it is not enough to reject animism's contention that nature is sacred. It must also be shown why nature and its animal inhabitants, though not sacred and therefore not legitimate objects of worship, are, nevertheless, worthy of an appropriate respect and treatment. That is a task currently being carried out by the Christian community as it draws upon biblical and theological resources to do so – resources that are, I am convinced, sufficient to the task. But even if there has been a delay of centuries in executing this task, it is not necessary to accept the claim that Christian teachings are the cause of the ecological crises. Alternative explanations were suggested.

Finally, we broached the topic "what is an animal?" We saw that the term "animal" covers a wide spectrum of life forms since there are over one million different species of animals. We may well expect, therefore, that the appropriate moral stance toward an animal may depend on the kind of animal it is – centipede or chimpanzee, earthworm or eagle. Relevant features in this regard may be the extent to which the animal is sentient, that is, has an inner conscious life that goes better or worse for it, and the extent to which it has a complex mental life. To speak of moral concern for animals is not to put all animals on a moral par. Clearly, qualifications have to be made. Formal criteria for distinguishing animals from plants were listed, and it was observed that sentience, a feature characteristic of animals (or many animals) but one not possessed by plants, is what makes animals, but not plants, good candidates for moral standing. Finally, the term "animal" can be used in two ways: (1) including humans and (2) excluding humans. The emotional bias that attaches to these two uses was indicated, and it was stipulated that in this text, unless otherwise noted, "animal" will be used in its exclusive sense, referring only to nonhuman members of the animal kingdom.

CHAPTER 2

Animal Advocacy and Environmentalism Contrasted

INTRODUCTION

This is a book on animal advocacy. It is not a book on ecology nor is it an attempt to construct an environmental ethic, for animal advocacy and environmentalism are not the same thing. Indeed, according to some, they are not only not the same thing, but they are seriously at odds with each other, so much so that ultimately one will have to choose between the agenda of the animal advocate and that of the environmentalist.[1] Certainly one senses, even without a great deal of specific knowledge, that the Sierra Club is doing something quite different from the local Humane Society or PETA (People for the Ethical Treatment of Animals). Whether these are merely different activities or ultimately incompatible activities depends on how we construe each and what theoretical justification each is given. In this chapter, we shall explore the relationship between animal advocacy and environmentalism and use it as an opportunity to clarify our own views. We will attempt to put into perspective our duties to humans, to animals, and to the environment, as well as attempt to come to a greater appreciation of the complex moral relationship that holds among them. The issues we shall raise are of fundamental importance for our understanding both of animal advocacy and, more generally, of the character of the Christian's moral universe.

1. Consider the title of the following book: *The Animal Rights/Environmental Ethics Debate,* ed. Eugene C. Hargrove (Albany: State University of New York Press, 1992). This is a collection of articles that traces the history of this dispute and seeks a resolution of it.

No doubt the environmentalist has a higher standing in the community, both inside and outside the church, than does the animal advocate, who is often viewed with a great deal of suspicion. Clearly, environmentalism is more acceptably mainstream than is animal advocacy, even if the message of the environmentalist is too often ignored. Certainly, one can more readily get a hearing in one's church, for example, if one is a Christian environmentalist, coming with a message of ecology and a plea for responsible stewardship of the created order, than if one is an animal advocate talking of human obligations to individual animals and possibly raising such touchy subjects as vegetarianism or animal experimentation or factory farming.

There may be a number of reasons for the embrace that is given to environmentalism in contrast to the "arm's distance" at which animal advocacy is typically held. First, for some people, animal advocacy conjures up visions of illegal activity, such as breaking into medical laboratories, smashing equipment, and "liberating" animals from their cages – the sort of activity that we associate with the Animal Liberation Front, a radical animal rights group. Such occurrences have received a great deal of publicity and are fairly well known among the general public. Although perhaps less well known, environmentalism also has its radical side. For just as animal advocacy has its Animal Liberation Front, so environmentalism has its "Earth First!" And just as members of the former group believe that individual animals have a right to exist for their own sake, apart from any benefit for humans, so "Earth Firsters" believe that the earth and its wilderness have a right to exist for their own sake, apart from any benefit to humans, and both groups have been quite prepared to break laws to achieve their respective goals of gaining recognition for the strong rights they believe are possessed by animals and ecosystems. For example, radical environmentalists have spiked trees (spikes are driven deep into a tree so when hit by the saw of the lumberjack they explode with lethal force – at least one lumberjack has been killed); on Earth Day in 1990 radical environmentalists sabotaged electrical transmission lines, cutting off power to 140,000 people near Santa Cruz, California; in Canada, environmentalists blew up a hydroelectric substation; in Europe they have destroyed bridges, dams, and electrical towers.[2] Thus, in spite of public perception, it is not at all clear that the record for illegal or violent activity is held by radical animal advocates rather than by radical environmentalists.

2. See Daniel J. Kevler and the literature he reviews in "Some Like It Hot," *The New York Review of Books* (March 26, 1992), pp. 31-39.

But people act on perceptions nevertheless, and the perception is that animal advocacy is the more violent. It should not surprise us, however, that when passionate calls for fundamental reform fall on deaf ears, there will always be some who are willing to use violence and illegal activity to get their own way. Furthermore, unacceptable though violence and lawbreaking may be, we need to remember that if, over the centuries, we had turned our backs on all those calls for reform that have been accompanied by such actions, there would have been much good reform that never would have taken place. The fact is, however, that lawbreaking and violence are very much a fringe activity among both animal advocates and environmentalists, and the message of neither group should be discounted simply because of highly publicized cases of lawbreaking.

Second, it may be that environmentalism receives a better reception in the general public than animal advocacy because animal advocacy is viewed as anti-scientific, whereas environmentalism is seen as scientific. While animal advocacy in a number of its forms opposes animal experimentation, which most see as an important medium for the acquisition of scientific knowledge, environmentalism, with its emphasis on ecology, is first and foremost a scientific understanding of how our environment works as an integrated and interdependent whole. It does seem that scientists and scientifically oriented people often take the lead in environmentalism but that many of these same scientists constitute one of the main forces opposing animal advocacy. To be sure, there are some environmentalists who oppose virtually all modern technology, which is the practical application of science, viewing it as environmentally intrusive and destructive, as well as going counter to some supposed ideal of a primitive oneness with nature. Still, one would suspect that the scientific community gives much higher marks to environmentalism than to animal advocacy. And, given the extent to which our society is predisposed to view favorably what is considered scientific, it should not be surprising that in general the environmentalist's cause is accorded more respect than the animal advocate's. We should keep in mind, however, that we are here dealing with an ethical and not a scientific issue, and that scientists are as morally fallible as the rest of us, struggling as we all do for moral clarity and truth.

A third and perhaps more important reason for the general public's suspicion of animal advocacy is that it is viewed as running counter to human interests, whereas environmentalism is seen as *serving* human interests. Certainly when two advocacy groups have something to tell us, one having a message that is in our own interest (protecting and preserving the environment for *our own* benefit) and the other having a message that is in someone else's interest (protecting animals for *their* sake), it is clear which one we will be more inclined to hear. Environmentalists may, of course, wish to impose sacrifices on us, but these can reasonably be interpreted as short-term sacrifices for long-term human gains, the beneficiaries being, if not ourselves, at least our children and our children's children. So if we as a community are strongly anthropocentric, that is, a community that sees as fundamentally good only that which benefits humans, then it will be the message of the environmentalist, should it be an anthropocentric message, and not that of the animal advocate, that will be more readily received.

We must bear in mind, however, that the environmentalist's message is not always an anthropocentric one ("protect the environment for *your* own sake"). There is increasingly in it another component, "protect the environment for *its* own sake." Indeed, at the present time a good number of theoreticians writing in the area of environmental ethics argue that the environment has intrinsic value, worthy of respect for its own sake. This means, among other things, that some human sacrifice may have to be made for the sake of the environment itself. And they are correct, I believe, to so argue, because a satisfactory environmental ethic cannot be built on exclusively anthropocentric grounds. Such a conclusion is supported, as we shall see, both by theological reflection and by deep convictions that most of us have (at least on reflection) about the value of nature. Nevertheless, it is easier, at first glance, to construe environmentalism exclusively in terms of human benefit than it is to make a similar anthropocentric case for animal advocacy. Clearly the sine qua non of animal advocacy is that the life and the welfare of the animal is important for the sake of the animal, not merely for the sake of humans.

TWO PERSPECTIVES ON THE INDIVIDUAL ANIMAL

Environmentalists, of course, have a wider set of concerns than do animal advocates, for they are concerned not only with animals but with flora and fauna, with land, forests, rivers, lakes, oceans, ecosystems, indeed with the whole terrestrial biosphere. So it might seem that animal advocacy is merely one part of the larger environmentalist agenda. Such an interpretation would be mistaken, for the kind of concern that each has with animals is typically quite different. The environmentalist is fundamentally concerned with the preservation of animal *species* and with the role of animals in delicately functioning ecosystems, whereas the fundamental concern of the animal advocate is with the *individual* animal and its welfare.

To underscore this difference — and also to provide some support for the concerns of animal advocacy — reflect on two accounts of the taking of animal life and consider how our concern with what is happening might be quite different, depending on whether we view the matter from the perspective of an environmentalist seeking to preserve species or from the perspective of an animal advocate. The first is an account of the killing of a whale. Tom Regan prepares us for the description that is to follow when he writes, "The fabled days of the hunt, the individual Ahab pitted against the treacherous whale, must remain the work of fiction now. Whaling is applied technology; from the use of the most sophisticated sonar, to on-board refrigeration; from tracking helicopters to explosive harpoons, the latter a technological advance that expedites a whale's death. Time to die: about five minutes, sometimes twenty."[3] Regan then quotes a whaling captain's own description of what is involved in making a catch:

> The gun roars. The harpoon hurls through the air and the whale-line follows. There is a momentary silence, and then the muffled explosion as the fuse functions and fragments the grenade. . . . There is now a fight between the mammal and the crew of the catching vessel — a fight to the death. It is a struggle that can have only one result. . . . Deep in the whale's vast body is the mortal wound, and even if it could shake off the harpoon it would be doomed. . . . A second harpoon buries itself just behind the dorsal fin. . . . There is another dull explosion in the whale's vitals. Then comes a series of convulsions — a last despairing struggle. The whale spouts blood, keels slowly over and floats belly upward. It is dead.[4]

Now, if we are concerned that should this be done too often we will no longer have any great blue whales — which is the kind of whale that was killed in the above account — then we have an environmentalist's concern. And certainly to eliminate the great blue whale from our oceans would be a tragedy, for this massive whale is the largest animal ever to have lived on the planet earth — larger than thirty elephants, larger than three of the largest dinosaurs laid end to end. To hunt them to extinction with their

3. Tom Regan, "Animal Rights, Human Wrongs," in *Ethics and Animals,* ed. Harlan B. Miller and William H. Williams (Clifton, N.J. : Humana, 1983), p. 20.

4. Regan, "Animal Rights, Human Wrongs," p. 20.

unique and irreplaceable genetic pool would be a tragedy, and to be concerned over such a possibility is certainly an appropriate concern. It is not, however, the only concern that one might legitimately have. For we might be concerned not merely (nor even primarily) with the survival of the great blue whale as a species and its role in a web of oceanic life, but rather we might be concerned with that *particular* great blue whale — concerned with its death, its pain, its value, its survival — in which case we have moved to a concern other than that of environmentalism. Indeed, if we seriously question whether we are justified in killing *that particular whale* in order to get candle wax, soap, oil, pet food, margarine, fertilizer, and perfume, *even if* it were not a member of an endangered species, then we have the kind of concern associated with animal advocacy.

The second account describes the killing of a gibbon (a member of the ape family), and once again Regan prepares us for the account that is to follow. "In Thailand, at this moment, another sort of hunt, less technologically advanced, is in progress. The Thai hunter has hiked two miles through thick vegetation and now, with his keen vision, he spots a female gibbon and her infant sleeping high-up in a tree." Then Regan quotes an observer who describes what happens next.

> Down below, the hunter rams the double charge of gun-powder down the barrel with a thin iron rod, then the lead shot. The spark flashes from two flints, and the gun goes off in a cloud of white smoke. . . . Overhead there is an uproar. The female gibbon, mortally wounded, clings to life. She still has enough strength to make two gigantic leaps, her baby still clinging to the long hair of her left thigh. At the third leap she misses the branch she was aiming for, and in a final desperate effort, manages to grasp a lower one; but her strength is ebbing away and she is unable to pull herself up. Slowly her fingers begin to loosen her grip. Death is there, staining her pale fur. The youngster flattens himself in terror against her bloodstained flank. Then comes the giddy plunge of a hundred feet or more, broken by a terrible rebound off a tree trunk.[5]

If we are concerned that if we do this too often, we won't have enough gibbons in the world or that it will upset the balance of nature in the Thai

5. Regan, "Animal Rights, Human Wrongs," p. 20. If we wonder why the Thai hunter is killing gibbons in the fashion described, it is to catch the infant gibbon should it survive the fall, which it often does not, in order to sell it. The infant gibbon ultimately finds its way to a zoo or a laboratory or a store for exotic pets.

jungle, we have an environmentalist concern. But we move in a different direction if we are concerned with that individual gibbon — its baby, its pain, its anguish, its death. And if we feel a touch of sadness over the account of the killing of the great blue whale and possibly even a bit of horror at the killing of the gibbon and its baby, we should not feel compelled to suppress those feelings, according to the animal advocate, as if they were illegitimate or sentimental, for, after all, they are genuine feelings directed at real pain, real anguish, and real death. We do not need to apologize for them as if they are somehow inappropriate.

The different concerns of an animal advocate and many an environmentalist are, in part, captured by noting these different possible reactions to the killing of the great blue whale and the gibbon. Of course, I could have a dual set of concerns: I could be concerned both with the fate of the individual animal and with the survival of the species of which it is a member, lamenting the death of the individual animal (taken by itself) and also disturbed by the additional fact that this death may make the survival of the species less likely. But it is also possible to be an environmental activist concerned with species survival and not care about the fate of individual animals apart from that larger concern. So if there were sufficient great blue whales in the ocean and sufficient gibbons in the Thai jungle, then, under those circumstances, the fate of these two individual animals would be of no moral consequence. And it is also possible to be an animal advocate concerned with the suffering of individual animals and concerned with environmental issues only in so far as they impinge on the former concern, as, of course, they often would, since the preservation of habitats and ecosystems will be crucial for the survival of individual animals.

Significantly, environmentalists have a much greater willingness to preserve species at the expense of individual animals, that is, to preserve members of an endangered species at the expense of members of a plentiful species. But if the locus of rights or value is the *individual* animal, not the species, as the animal advocate insists, then it is not morally permissible to sacrifice members of a plentiful species in order to preserve members of a scarce species, as the environmentalist is willing to do. For the animal advocate, the fact that an animal is a member of an endangered species does not give it greater intrinsic value or a greater claim to life than a member of a flourishing species. To conclude otherwise is somewhat analogous, it might be argued, to imputing a greater value and a more stringent claim to life to members of an endangered race, preserving their lives at the expense of members of a race blessed with large numbers.

The analogy is not quite right, of course, because members of different racial groups are nevertheless members of the same species (Homo sapiens). Nevertheless, from the perspective of the animal advocate, to grant one animal a greater claim to life over another animal of equal cognitive capacity because of the endangered status of its species, makes no more moral sense than giving a similar preference to members of an endangered racial group. The logic here is, as Bryan Norton states, "When one justifies differential treatment of individuals because of the status of their species, one treats individuals as means to the preservation of species and denies that they are ends-in-themselves."[6] But the individualism of animal advocacy affirms that the individual is the bearer of intrinsic value and therefore cannot be reduced to a means by which the preservation of endangered species is to be achieved. Thus, to extend preferential treatment to a member of an endangered species at the expense of another individual of another species, who is identical in all other relevant aspects, is simply to engage in unjust discrimination.

This difference between the animal advocate and the environmentalist in their views of species preservation is of more than theoretical interest because conserving endangered species will, in practice, often have to be done at the expense of members of more plentiful species. This does mean that environmentalism and animal advocacy will have different implications for environmental protection. Thus, laws protecting the endangered great blue whale in turn put pressure on the sperm whale and other plentiful whale species, making the survival of some of their members less likely. The environmentalist or species preservationist will enthusiastically endorse such regulation; the animal advocate will judge it to be a failure to accord equal treatment to individuals with equivalent levels of consciousness.

ENVIRONMENTALISM: THREE VERSIONS

The significant practical differences that may exist between animal advocacy and environmentalism are a product of the different theoretical justifications that each can be given. For this reason these justifications are worth looking at. Certainly, concern with ecology has been motivated and justified, first, anthropocentrically — that is, justified in terms of benefits

6. Bryan Norton, *Why Preserve Natural Variety?* (Princeton, N.J.: Princeton University Press, 1987), p. 165.

that will be brought to humans by being environmentally responsible. Within this framework, concern with species or animal habitats or ecosystems or with the whole biosphere is justified in terms of benefits that accrue to humans. To destroy the environment is to destroy *our* environment and threaten not only *our* well-being but our very existence. It is wrong because it threatens us. Further, to destroy a species, including an animal species, is to remove from our world a group of living organisms that *we* can study, enjoy, and simply have the satisfaction of knowing are there. Something like this, I believe, is how the general public tends to view environmentalism – protecting the environment for our human sake. Certainly, such an anthropocentric view of environmentalism is animated by a different spirit than is animal advocacy with its concern with animals for their own sake. If an environmentalist judges that only humans have intrinsic value and only human needs are legitimate objects of moral concern, then there is no basis for animal advocacy. There is only human advocacy, and concern with the environment is merely an extension (though no doubt an important extension) of human concern.

Here I would at least suggest that an anthropocentric environmentalism will not prove satisfactory. That is, preserving the environment solely for reasons of human survival and well-being will not justify the preservation of all that most of us feel ought to be preserved. As the philosopher Martin Schönfeld has argued, we "could survive quite well in a completely cultivated environment with low level pollution; one that contains tree farms instead of forests, fields instead of wetlands, lawns instead of meadows, and cattle or pets instead of wildlife. Human interest in the continued existence of mankind sets a standard for the integrity of the biosphere that is too minimal to serve as a basis for the ethical undesirability of environmental degradation."[7] Indeed, in Schönfeld's scenario, something of value has been lost. Gone are the forests, the wetlands, the meadows, and all the wildlife, and in their place are these human constructs that serve humans just as well (we may suppose) as nature's originals. So although human ends are equally well served, something of value has been lost and has not been fully replaced. And are not these intuitions supported by a theological vision that sees the earth as God's *doubly* good handiwork, good in its own right and good as a human habitat?

In principle, of course, there is no reason why one could not em-

7. Martin Schönfeld, "Who or What Has Moral Standing?" *American Philosophical Quarterly* 29 (October 1992): 355.

brace environmentalism both because it is good for humans and because it is good for animals. This, of course, is just what many in the animal rights movement would do. Thus we have a second approach to justifying environmentalism. This position is known as sentientism: whatever is sentient, but only what is sentient, has moral standing. That is, only that which can suffer, or, more broadly, only that which has an inner conscious life that can go better or worse for it, has moral standing and is of intrinsic value. This means that only humans and certain animals have moral standing, since only they are sentient, while such objects of environmental concern as species (as such), ecosystems, and the biosphere are not. Concern for the environment on such a view is to be justified by reference to its significance for sentient creatures, human and animal. No doubt this will go some way to amending the deficiencies that one finds in a purely anthropocentric environmentalism. It will surely permit less degradation of the environment, and the preservation and protection of far more of it, since we need to secure not only human but also animal habitats. But even this view seems to fall short of accounting for our deepest intuitions and our theological convictions. For on such a view an ecosystem consisting only of plants and nonsentient organisms would have no intrinsic value. It could be treated with total indifference and would count for nothing on the grounds that it contributes nothing to human or animal life. But that seems to be mistaken.

But there is a third way to justify environmental concern. Indeed, more often than not, environmentalism is given neither an anthropocentric nor a sentientist justification, at least by theoreticians writing in this field. On the contrary, it is argued that species, ecosystems, and the whole biosphere have an intrinsic significance apart from any value they may have in furthering and serving either human or animal interests. This is frequently called "deep" ecology and is to be contrasted with "shallow" ecology, which views ecological concern as merely an extension of human and animal interest. Deep ecology, on the other hand, acknowledges fundamental obligations to nature that transcend human and animal interests. According to deep ecology, to destroy an ecosystem is wrong not because such destruction will hurt individual animals and plants or even individual humans, but because the ecological whole, as a harmonious interdependent system, has intrinsic value. Indeed, in certain prominent forms of environmental ethics, the constituent parts that compose the biosphere, including humans, take on their value *solely* from the contribution they make to the whole. Here, I suggest, things become morally and theologically problematic.

One of the most radical yet influential deep ecologists was Aldo Leopold, whose book *A Sand County Almanac* (1949), especially the twenty-five page manifesto at the end of the book, has become "the intellectual touchstone for the most far-reaching environmental movement in American history."[8] Indeed, Aldo Leopold has been lionized by the likes of former Secretary of the Interior Stewart Udall, has been the subject of a PBS television documentary, and has been referred to as an "American Isaiah" and an "American Moses." But despite the influence and prominence of Aldo Leopold, his ideas, taken at face value, are not only well outside the pale of received ethical opinion, but they also provide the environmental movement with a theoretical justification that places it in serious conflict with animal advocacy. According to Leopold, the individual animal has no value whatsoever, apart from its proper functioning as part of the larger ecological whole to which it is connected.

Consider the oft-quoted words of Leopold: "A thing is right when it tends to preserve the integrity, stability, and beauty of the biotic community. It is wrong when it tends otherwise."[9] As interpreted by the philosopher J. Baird Callicott, a follower of Leopold, this means "that the good of the biotic *community* is the ultimate measure of the moral value, the rightness or wrongness, of actions."[10] This is an instance of "ethical holism," where the individual parts derive their value from their contribution to the functioning of the whole. Thus what we do to the individual parts (kill an animal, fell a tree, uproot a plant, drain a swamp) *becomes* right or wrong solely by reference to the impact it has on the larger biotic community — its "integrity," "stability," and "beauty." So, can we kill that deer, we wonder? Should we chop down that tree, we ask? It all depends on the impact it would have on the biotic community. If the killing of that deer would helpfully reduce the overpopulation of deer, which are overgrazing and threatening the ecosystem of which they are a part, then it would be justified. If, on the contrary, the killing of the deer would disturb the delicate balance of nature, threatening the ecosystem in some way, it would be wrong. It is not, according to Leopold, that by killing that deer (or a number of deer) we stabilize the ecosystem and thereby save a great many other deer from extinction and painful death by starvation (ethical indi-

8. Roderick Frazier Nash, *The Rights of Nature: A History of Environmental Ethics* (Madison: University of Wisconsin Press, 1989), p. 63.

9. Aldo Leopold, *A Sand County Almanac* (New York: Oxford University Press, 1949), pp. 224-25.

10. J. Baird Callicott, "Animal Liberation: A Triangular Affair," *Environmental Ethics* 2 (Winter 1980): 320.

vidualism) but that we save the ecosystem itself (ethical holism). So it is not that deer are slain for the sake of other deer but rather deer are slain for the sake of the ecosystem. Thus, the biosphere or the biotic community as a whole (again, its "integrity," "stability," and "beauty") is the source from which all value derives.

Furthermore, because not only animals and plants, but also bodies of water and land, are essential parts of this functioning whole, they too have value and possess a similar derivative moral standing. Indeed, the land or the water may be even more essential to the functioning of the whole, and thus may have more value than animals or plants. It is in this way that moral standing is extended not only to what is animate but to what is inanimate and inorganic. Thus, there is no category of being on this planet which has special moral status, not even that which is sentient or conscious or self-conscious or rational or spiritual or whatever. What *is* relevant – and the only thing that is relevant – is one's contribution to the biotic community as a smooth, functioning totality. In contrast, most traditional moralists have wanted to say that human life has special value just because it is conscious and self-aware, and animal advocates have wanted to say that animal life also has some special value because it is at least conscious (and maybe even in some cases self-conscious). This is precisely what is denied by the deep ecologist. For the deep ecologist, a respect for animals is appropriate only out of a primary respect for the ecological whole of which animals are a functioning part.

The deep ecologist's respect for animals as integral and important parts of a well-functioning biotic community does not, however, extend to domesticated animals. The deep ecologist views the domestication of animals with considerable suspicion and even hostility. This is so for two reasons. First, in domesticating animals we have removed from these animals their beautiful wildness, their fierce autonomy, and have turned them into docile and dependent pets. This is viewed as a kind of desecration. One senses something of the deep ecologist's concern when one witnesses a performing bear moving across a stage, precariously balanced on top of a rolling ball. To see what we judge should be a free and independent creature, in a carnival atmosphere, moving at human command at the flick of a whip, more clown than beast, is for many a sad spectacle. To the deep ecologist what we do to a single performing bear is what we do to whole species when we domesticate them. Second, and crucially, domesticated animals are seen as destructive intrusions into the surrounding ecosystems that have evolved without a niche for domesticated animals. Thus, sheep and cattle have, in great numbers, pushed out into the environment, taking over land formerly used by other animals, upsetting the balance of nature, which has no place for massive numbers of these human creations. Because animals, like all elements that constitute the biotic community, take on their value (positive or negative) from their contribution to the biotic community, and because domesticated animals are a destructive force on the environmental scene, it follows that they are a disvalue and are to be treated accordingly. So, on such a view, while a call to save the whale or the coyote may be justified, it is not similarly justified in the case of sheep or cattle, and for sound ecological reasons.

For animal advocates, in contrast, the same concern is directed to domesticated animals as to wild animals. For the animal advocate, whether animals are wild or domesticated, just as whether they are endangered or not, is irrelevant to their moral status. What *is* relevant is whether they are conscious, experience pain and pleasure, and have interests that can be respected, something that cannot be said of a tree, a mountain, or a lake. Indeed, it could even be argued, contrary to deep ecologists, that we have a greater obligation to domesticated animals since they have become dependent on us in ways that wild animals have not. Thus, in taking a dog or a cat into our household we may well conclude that we have assumed some special obligations that we would not otherwise have.

Though we are primarily concerned in this book with nonhuman animals, we might explore briefly the implications of an unqualified deep ecology for our attitude toward humans. If all value derives from the biotic community, then the value or disvalue of humans, like that of the value or disvalue of deer, is derived from the biotic community. Can we, then, cull humans just as we cull deer? It would certainly seem so. The logic of the theory appears to demand it. Callicott, for one, dances dangerously close to giving a "yes" to this question when he comments, "The biospheric perspective does not exempt Homo sapiens from moral evaluation in relation to the well-being of the community of nature taken as a whole. The preciousness of individual deer, as of any other specimen, is inversely proportional to the population of the species. Environmentalists however reluctantly and painfully do not omit to apply the same logic to their own kind."[11] Such a view is truly breathtaking. That is, the more members of a species we have, the less valuable individuals among them become. By this account individual humans are less valuable today, with the increased population, than they were two hundred years ago when our human numbers were significantly fewer. It would thus appear that kill-

11. Callicott, "Animal Liberation: A Triangular Affair," p. 326.

ing humans or letting them starve is less serious an offense today (if an offense at all) than it was two hundred years ago. Why? Because when we get too many of them, they threaten the ecologically sound functioning of the whole.

Certainly the Christian community will have grave doubts about any view in which the meaning and purpose of individual human life is accounted for exclusively in terms of its contribution to the biotic community. The Christian church can seriously entertain the possibility that the biotic community, as a divinely created, harmoniously functioning whole, has a value that ought to be respected in its own right as God's good creation. But what Christian reflection would not allow is accounting for the value of individual human life solely or even principally in terms of its contribution to the biotic community. From a Christian perspective human life has a purpose, the value and significance of which transcends any such function. For the Christian, individual human life is the divinely conferred occasion to pursue life purposes and to shape an ultimate spiritual destiny. More specifically, it is the opportunity to come to know God and to participate in a process of moral and spiritual transformation. One can helpfully add that a part of that transformation is coming to appreciate and respect the whole created order, and to assume one's proper role as a caretaker of it. Although reference to a caretaker role captures some of what the more radical deep ecologist wants, the Christian cannot grant all that the deep ecologist wants, namely, exhaustively accounting for the value of human life in terms of its contribution to the biotic community. That would be to deify the biotic community, making it the source of all value, all significance, and all purpose. In short, it would be idolatrous.

So, for the Christian, individual *human* life has value by virtue of the divine purpose for it, and that purpose is not simply to contribute to ecosystem functioning. We must then reject the implications of Leopold's ethical holism for human life, but what about its implications for animals? Do individual animals have some intrinsic value? Or are animals, in contrast to humans, valuable only to the extent that they contribute to the larger biotic whole, beyond which they have no value at all? That is, are deep ecologists wrong about humans but right about animals? Animal advocates argue that deep ecologists are wrong about both, that neither humans nor animals take on their value solely from their contribution to the biotic community; rather, *both* have a significant value independent of any such contribution. What should the Christian community conclude about this? Should we agree with the deep ecologist or with the animal advocate on the status of animals?

DEEP ECOLOGY CONTRASTED WITH TRADITIONAL MORALITY

As we continue to reflect about these matters let us note that there is a certain tough-minded realism attaching to the kind of "deep ecology" that we have been examining. As we look at the structure of nature, as we look at the functioning of the biotic community, we do see the essential role played by pain, killing, and death. It is this reality we are asked by advocates of deep ecology to come to terms with. We are asked to accept it as good, and not to be alienated from it, and therefore from nature, of which it is an integral part. As Callicott comments, "To live is to be anxious about life, to feel pain and pleasure in a fitting mixture, and sooner or later to die. That is the way the system works. If nature as a whole is good, then pain and death are also good."[12] Here we see the logic of ethical holism once more at work: because the integrity, stability, and beauty of the biotic community is the supreme value from which all other value derives, then it follows that because pain, death, and killing all contribute to its integrity, stability, and beauty, they too are good. Pain is good because it informs us of bodily injury and prevents us from persisting in a range of self-destructive behaviors. A world without pain, therefore, would be "biologically preposterous." Death is good because it prevents overpopulation; killing and eating what is killed is good because it sustains life, all part of nature's food chain. Indeed, "this is how the system works," and if the system as a whole is good, then these particular workings of the system are also good.

This reality is just what animal advocates fail to see, according to deep ecologists. They fail to accept the order of nature, which involves pain and the imposition of pain, death and the imposition of death, the eating of meat and the legitimate role of predators. Instead of accepting all this, including our own role in this, as natural and good, animal advocates have sought to exempt animals from the order of nature. They believe that animals have rights, that animal pain is an evil, and that we ought to feel compassion for animals who are hunted down by predators. All of this, it is claimed by the deep ecologist (and by others), bespeaks an alienation from nature and a refusal to accept natural activities and processes as good — good because they contribute to the good of the whole.

But it is not only animal advocates, according to deep ecologists, who are alienated from nature. In mistakenly seeking to remove animals (along with humans) from the fabric of nature in which they are embed-

12. Callicott, "Animal Liberation: A Triangular Affair," p. 333.

ded, animal advocates are simply the worst offenders. The rest of society is implicated as well, for they have been guilty, at least according to this radical version of deep ecology, of removing *humans* from the fabric of nature. Both animal advocates and society at large have forgotten that all of us, animals and humans, are a part of nature, part of the biotic community, and that we are to be seen, valued, and understood in these terms. Notice what Callicott has to say in this regard, in an interesting and provocative passage:

> Rather than imposing our alienation from nature and natural processes and cycles of life on other animals, we human beings should reaffirm our participation in nature by accepting life as it is given without a sugar coating. Instead of imposing artificial legalities, rights, and so on on nature, we might take the opposite course and accept and affirm natural biological laws, principles, and limitations in the human, personal and social spheres. Such appears to have been the posture toward life of tribal peoples in the past. The chase was relished with its dangers, rigors, and hardships as well as its rewards: animal flesh was respectfully consumed; a tolerance for pain was cultivated; virtue and magnanimity were prized; lithic, floral, and faunal spirits were worshipped; population was routinely optimized by sexual contingency, abortion, infanticide, and stylized warfare; and other life forms, although certainly appropriated, were respected as fellow players in a magnificent and awesome, if not altogether idyllic, drama of life.[13]

All this suggests the following three very different moral visions: the individualism of traditional morality, the individualism of animal advocacy, and the holism of "radical" deep ecology.

(1) *The two-world moral universe of certain forms of traditional morality:* ethical individualism applies to humans and ethical holism applies to animals. That is, individual human life has intrinsic value and therefore traditional moral concerns apply to humans, whereas individual animals have value only to the extent that they contribute to the biotic whole.

(2) *The one-world moral universe of animal advocacy:* ethical individualism applies to both humans and animals since both have intrinsic value; therefore, traditional moral concerns are to be extended (in ways appropriate) from the human world into the animal world.

(3) *The one-world moral universe of radical deep ecology:* ethical holism

13. Callicott, "Animal Liberation: A Triangular Affair," p. 334.

applies both to humans and to animals since neither has intrinsic value but only a value derived from its contribution to the biotic community.[14]

Many people adhere to something like the first position, which assumes a middle ground between the other two. (Here, perhaps we need to be reminded of what is sometimes called "the fallacy of the golden mean," which is committed whenever we assume that a middle position, midway between two alternatives, often labelled "extremes," is automatically true or correct.) According to such a view, when we deal with humans we appropriately invoke and are guided by traditional morality, but none of this applies to our dealings with animals. Thus, should I go hunting, I shed my traditional morality since it does not apply to my conduct in the world of nature. Here I become a predator, something I must not become vis-à-vis other humans, but which is acceptable, on the present view, when the hunted is an animal. It is as if I step out of one moral world into another; it is as if I leave behind human society with its rules and regulations and become myself a part of nature, part of the cycle of pain, killing, and death that we accept because it is natural. What I do is no more wrong and no more questionable than what a lion does who hunts and kills a zebra. We both are predators, we both are part of the drama of nature, and in neither case is there a cause for moral concern. Indeed, when hunting I may even be motivated by a concern for the overpopulation of deer, which may be due to a lack of predators (say, wolves), and I may seek to restore a proper balance in nature by culling the deer population. Here I view the deer as part of nature, and I apply to my hunting a justification that derives from a respect for natural processes, that includes a recognition of the ecologically important niche filled by various predators, a role that I now assume as hunter.

This, of course, would not be how we respond to human overpopulation on the first view. In traditional morality, we don't even think of culling the human herd. Yet human overpopulation represents a far more seri-

14. We need not interpret Aldo Leopold himself as saying that the welfare of the biotic community is the *only* good and that we humans can do anything whatsoever to each other so long as we do not compromise the beauty, stability, and integrity of the biotic community. Rather, we can interpret Leopold as saying, in the words of Lawrence Johnson, that "*when it comes to dealing with the land community,* here is the way to tell right from wrong" (*A Morally Deep World* [New York: Cambridge University Press, 1991], p. 240). Traditional morality continues to apply to other humans but the biocentric ethic applies to our behavior toward the environment. Leopold, then, would be a deep ecologist but not a "radical" deep ecologist, since he does not believe that the land ethic that he proposes is also the sole arbiter of right and wrong between humans.

ous threat than deer overpopulation. What is going on here? In part it is this: we view deer as a part of nature in a way that we do not view humans, and so the logic of nature applies to our dealings with them but not with humans. Thus, there are two worlds: the world of humans and the world of nature. Each has its own moral logic, and each is more or less sealed off from the other, though we humans can step from one world into the other, changing moralities as we do so. It is this moral vision that is under siege by two groups who wish to create a single moral world. On the one hand, animal advocates propose to extend the moral concern that traditionally has been reserved for humans to animals; on the other hand, certain "radical" deep ecologists propose just the reverse, to extend the ethic of nature from animals to humans. So the question remains, wherein lies the truth? I believe the truth lies with the animal advocate and not with the environmentalist. To begin to see why this is so let us look at the embeddedness of animals in the often violent and disinterested workings of nature.

NATURE, ANIMALS, PREDATION, AND EVIL

Nature as a whole is good, deep ecologists have told us; therefore, they conclude, its constituent parts and their ecologically healthy functioning are also good. Because nature is good, so are pain and death, which are essential aspects of nature's harmonious functioning. One often hears this line of thought repeated by people who know nothing of deep ecology but who are perhaps trying to make peace with pain and death in their own thinking. "Death must come to all of us because that is the way nature works and it is all for the best." Indeed, one sometimes hears *Christians* speak in this way. I believe that upon reflection, however, we will see that such talk is better set aside. Whereas Christians will agree that creation or nature is good, we do not assert that it is *perfectly* good. Christians recognize that a good creation is in certain respects marred by the presence of evil — or what is called natural evil[15] — and have officially recognized the relation of natural evil to the doctrine of the fall, a doctrine that embraces both humans and nature and declares that neither corresponds fully to the original divine intent. Neither humans nor nature, as it is now found

15. Natural evil refers to the pain and suffering traceable to nature's functioning and not (at least on the surface) traceable back to a misuse of human freedom, which would be moral evil. To be struck by a lightning bolt is a natural evil; to get hit on the head with a baseball bat swung by an angry neighbor is a moral evil.

in this world, is as God fully wants it to be. Certainly, the ancient dispute over the problem of evil testifies to the reality of natural evil: critics of Christianity (and of theism in general) have argued that the presence of natural evil in the world is incompatible with a rational belief in a good and all-powerful Creator, and Christians have responded in a variety of ways, denying this incompatibility. But on one thing critics and defenders alike agree: nature is not perfect; it is not what one would expect as coming from the hand of a good and all-powerful God. So we in the Christian tradition cannot automatically conclude, as do deep ecologists, that because something is a part of the natural order, it is therefore good. However we account for it, creation is distorted by evil. And to say that there is evil in the natural order is to acknowledge that there is in nature that which, all else being equal, it would be better not to have there; therefore, there is in nature that which one might remove or alter and, if successful, thereby improve the world in which we live. This we call natural evil.

But what, more specifically, is natural evil? Traditionally we have tended, anthropocentrically, to identify as evil only that in nature which adversely impacts humans, that which brings them pain, suffering, disability, and death, but we tend to ignore the workings of nature which adversely impact animals. When it comes to animals we seem to accept the holism of deep ecology and with it the assumption that nature is perfectly good, reasoning that what befalls a particular animal (say, a painful and unpleasant death) is good because it is the way the system works and this particular working is on the whole for the best. Thus, in matters related to humans, we reject this line of thinking and actively use all our ingenuity and strength to fight the pain, suffering, disability, and death that nature would bring our way. This resistance is justified, we judge, because nature is not perfect. It is fallen, and when nature prevents individual human flourishing, we judge it to be evil. When our human resistance is unsuccessful, as it often is, we accept the outcome not as good, but as tragic. In doing this, we recognize a tragic dimension to human existence — evil that we cannot escape and must finally accept. Should a human be mauled and killed by a lion, we would view such an event as tragic, not as somehow acceptable because part of the workings of nature. It is at least worth asking whether this approach might not also be appropriate in dealing with animal pain. Is not the pain and death that befalls the young zebra when it is killed by the lion also tragic?

For it is important that what actually is tragic in life be viewed by us as tragic. What we are as moral and spiritual beings is to a considerable extent a product of how we view the drama of life as it unfolds around us.

That is, what we view as sad or regrettable or deplorable or tragic, or, for that matter, wonderful or admirable or praiseworthy, goes some considerable way to defining our moral character, determining who we are as moral and spiritual beings. Christians (and all humans) are called not merely "to do" and "to act" but also – and perhaps more importantly – "to be," and an important part of "being" is how one feels toward a range of things, including those things one cannot alter or in any way influence. Thus, to take but one simple example, suppose we read in the newspaper of parents, lovingly and caringly providing for their young daughter dying of leukemia. These are not people we know or can contact or in any way support and influence for good (prayer aside); it is for us only a written account that we have before us in the newspaper. But our response should be – should it not? – one of admiration, respect, and praise for the parents, compassion for the child, and a sense of sadness for the tragedy of the situation. There is, in other words, a morally and spiritually appropriate response to the content of that article that will characterize the good person. That response is not a celebration of leukemia as a means of reducing human population. Rather, it is to recognize that here there is genuine tragedy.

The animal advocate calls us to a recognition that there is tragedy in the animal world as well as in the human world, tragedy that should call forth from the good person recognition and compassion for those who suffer it. Does not the evil that mars the natural world impinge upon its nonhuman as well as its human inhabitants? Consider the fact of predation in nature – animals killing and eating other animals. As has often been observed, predators have their important ecological niche, that of helping keep animal population within appropriate limits. Thus the carnivores prey upon the herbivores and by reducing their number keep them from overgrazing the land and thereby destroying the habitat that both need for their survival. Without predators, then, the system would break down and the existence of the very species that is preyed upon would be threatened. And, of course, the carnivores must kill and eat meat in order to survive. So, as unpleasant as the sight of a lion killing and devouring a Thomson's gazelle may be for many of us, the lion must engage in such activity if it is to survive. To deny the lion its prey is to deny the lion its life, and the life of the lion is as valuable as the life of the Thomson's gazelle. Predation, then, is part of the working of a system that works for the good of the whole. This is what the environmentalist stresses. The animal advocate, on the other hand, invites us to consider the fact that the good of the Thomson's gazelle is sacrificed for the sake of the larger good and that this is tragic. And it is here that the Christian, I believe, has more reason to side with the animal advocate than with the deep ecologist. That we should regret that it has to be that way is simply to say that we can envision a better world, a world where the good of the Thomson's gazelle does not have to be sacrificed either for the good of the lion or the good of the system as whole — even if this is a world that we ourselves could never bring about.

The Christian believes that there is just such a vision of a better world, a vision of a future age when the Messiah will establish his Kingdom on earth and there will be fully realized God's original intent for creation. At that time, we are told,

> The wolf shall dwell with the lamb,
> and the leopard shall lie down with the kid,
> and the calf and the lion and the fatling together,
> and a little child shall lead them.
> The cow and the bear shall feed;
> their young shall lie down together;
> and the lion shall eat straw like the ox. . . .
> They shall not hurt or destroy
> in all my holy mountain. (Isa. 11:6-9)

In this vision of a better and a more harmonious world animals will not "hurt or destroy" each other because "they shall not hurt or destroy in all my holy mountain." This is a better world because the lion does not prey upon the Thomson's gazelle but yet the lion survives and flourishes. This is not a world, certainly, that we humans can bring about, but it is a better world nonetheless. And if we so much as acknowledge that it is a better world, then we must also acknowledge the appropriateness of regret over the present ecological arrangement that requires predation — regret, that is, over the fallenness of our world that has introduced a tragic element into the natural order of things. It would truly be better if there were no predation but sadly that cannot be. Therein lies the tragedy. And part of our being the kind of people we ought to be is to recognize that tragedy.

Though we, as Christians, might recognize with the deep ecologist that predation may serve a larger good, we do not conclude that predation is an *unqualified* good. As with so many things in life that serve good ends (as, for example, when a leg must be amputated to save a human life from cancer), it would nonetheless be better if the good did not have to be achieved at such a cost. Similarly, the recognition of the ecological necessity of predation does not transform the killing of the gazelle by the lion into an unqualified good, nor does it render regret and the recognition of its tragic dimension inappropriate. Rather, it provides the very basis for that recognition.

Significantly, whether we view predation as tragic or merely as a part of nature and therefore good without qualification will determine what we believe we ourselves can legitimately do with animals. If the pain, suffering, disability, and death that nature visits upon animals is viewed as tragic, then we ourselves should be reluctant to replicate that tragedy in our own treatment of animals, and we will not offer as a justification for our behavior the observation that what we are doing to them is no worse than the fate that befalls them in nature, as if what befalls them in nature is not itself problematic. Indeed, if what happens to them in nature, even if ecologically necessary, is not fully good but tragic, then only with strong justifying reasons should we voluntarily become extensions of nature's harsh workings. We may well debate what constitutes an adequate justification for our replicating nature's harsher side, but we should not sally forth to such activity without a strong sense that what we do needs a justification and a strong one at that. Thus, to recognize that there is a tragic dimension in nature that affects both humans and animals is to take a major step toward extending moral concern to animals — to reject, in other words, the single moral world of the radical deep ecologist and the dual moral world of the traditional moralist. It is to recognize that there is in nature that which (a) affects animals adversely and which (b) all else being equal it would be better it were not so. This is to begin to speak in terms of "ought" and "ought not." Minimally, we ought not to enlarge on nature's tragedy, gratuitously inflicting pain, sickness, disability, and death. Indeed, there may even be particular circumstances where we ought to actively prevent or remove these evils. To embrace the messianic vision of Isaiah 11 is not only to recognize that animals are involuntary participants in the tragic drama of life but also that they too can become objects of our moral concern as we seek to make the world more what it ought to be and more what one day it will be.

The observation that animal suffering and predation are evils sometimes evokes the response, "are we not, then, foolishly committed to policing the animal creation to prevent this very evil, helping the Thomson's gazelle escape from the lion, the rabbit from the fox, etc.?" Not at all. For as Steve Sapontzis, himself a strong animal liberationist, has rightly noted, what we are morally obliged to prevent is "predation whenever we can do so without occasioning as much or more unjustified suffering than the predation would create. . . ."[16] And seeking to police the animal world would certainly cause as much or more suffering as the predation itself would cause. This is but to underscore the tragedy of the situation: there is very little, perhaps nothing, that we can do to improve on nature's working.

ENTERING A MORE COMPLEX MORAL WORLD

We have made a number of suggestions in the course of this chapter, suggestions that, admittedly, make one's moral universe more complex than it might otherwise be, suggestions that render moral decision-making a more complicated and a less certain affair. But it is better, I judge, to have a more complicated and perhaps even unwieldly morality than to have one that purchases certainty and precision at the cost of oversimplification, denying moral realities that ought to be recognized and factored into our moral assessments, moral realities that are part of the universe in which we have been placed by God. Based on our thinking so far, we have identified three such complicating factors: first, individual humans have intrinsic value; second, individual animals have intrinsic value; third, the biosphere and its various ecosystems have intrinsic value. In saying that something has intrinsic value I mean only to assert that it has significance in and of itself, that it has significance to God apart from any contributions it makes to other parts of God's creation. So something has intrinsic value when its continued existence, its flourishing and its integrity, is ethically desirable for its own sake. Something that has intrinsic value can, of course, also have instrumental value. Thus, for example, suppose the terrestrial biosphere does have intrinsic value, it being something that God is pleased with in its own right. It may also have instrumental value by virtue of providing, as it does, a supporting environment in which individual human and animal life can flourish and fulfill God's purpose for them. Thus, we can work to save the environment for our own human sake, for the sake of animals, and for the environment's own sake as God's intrinsically good creation.

To acknowledge that something has intrinsic value is to recognize that it ought to be treated with appropriate respect and care — appropriate, that is, to the intrinsic value that it has. After all, some things may have

16. Steve Sapontzis, *Morals, Reasons, and Animals* (Philadelphia: Temple University Press, 1987), p. 247.

more intrinsic value than others and therefore merit greater respect and care. To say, then, that the biosphere, humans, and animals all have intrinsic value is not to say that they all have the same intrinsic value. It is to say, however, that they all merit some moral consideration, and that their mere existence places limits on our moral freedom. It is to say that we cannot just do anything we please to animals, to the biosphere, or to fellow humans and act rightly. Because they have intrinsic value, our own interests do not automatically justify just any treatment of them, though our interests may in some cases override theirs. Consider John Kleinig's prosaic example of the termite: "There is something coarse about a person who kicks open a termite hill, destroying its complex structure of tunnels, exposing its occupants to the destructive rays of the sun. True, such affirmative value as termites have may be outweighed by other values. Those that set up their colonies in the timbers of our houses may find their affirmative value of little help to them."[17] Rightly so, but where the activities of the termite are not in a position to threaten other greater values, there we should let them be, honoring the value that they have. So because something has less intrinsic value than humans does not mean that any and every human interest, even a whim, takes precedence over the needs of the other.

If the biosphere has intrinsic value, then we humans should make some sacrifices for it, apart from consideration of any possible benefit to ourselves (though such benefit may often result). But because we humans also have intrinsic value there are limits to the extent of sacrifices that we should make for the environment's own sake. Further, if animals have less intrinsic value or a lower moral standing than humans (something that some animal rights advocates would refuse to concede), then there may be sacrifices for the sake of the biosphere that we can impose on animals that we would not be justified in imposing on humans. Orchestrating all these considerations in making actual decisions will not be easy, and no doubt morally sensitive and informed people will not always agree on how this is to be done and exactly what moral weight is to be assigned to the various relevant factors. But what needs to be stressed is that all these are relevant factors that should be taken into account. Furthermore, in acknowledging the ambiguity and complexities of the situation, we should also acknowledge that some things seem clear. For example, this position involves a fourfold rejection: first, a rejection of those variants of deep ecology that claim that only the terrestrial biosphere has intrinsic value and that all other value is derivative from this; second, a rejection of an

17. John Kleinig, *Valuing Life* (Princeton, N.J.: Princeton University Press, 1991), p. 105.

anthropocentric ethic that sees only human life as having intrinsic value; third, a rejection of that variant of animal advocacy which grants to animal life the same intrinsic value as to human life (a point that will be discussed at greater length in chapter 8); fourth, a rejection of those views that attribute intrinsic value only to that which possesses consciousness (sentientism), thereby denying intrinsic worth to ecosystems and to the terrestrial biosphere.

As we noted earlier, to say that something has intrinsic value is to say that it is valuable and worthy of respect apart from any contribution it makes to other parts of God's creation, though it may very well make such a contribution, thereby even increasing its worth. Thus, God, in creating, has made many good things, each good in his eyes, and each to be appreciated and treated with an appropriate respect. But what does it mean to respect creation?

One way to understand respect for creation is in terms of respect for the telic development of living organisms, a notion employed by John Kleinig as part of his own attempt to understand the value attaching to all living things, though he himself does not place this notion in a theistic context. "Each living organism," he comments, "has its own *telos* or pattern of development – whether limited, as in the case of plants, or relatively open-ended, as in the case of humans. . . ."[18] Thus the "livingness" of such organisms "is not constituted by *stasis* but by the dynamic outworking of an end, a maturation or summation, and this, it might be argued, represents a good, albeit – again – not an overriding one."[19] So, as we look at individual life, we see it to be dynamic and developing, moving toward an end, the fulfillment of its inherent potential. To respect creation is, then, first, to see this goal-directedness as intended by God and, second, to honor that divine intention by not unnecessarily impeding or frustrating an organism's telic fulfillment and, perhaps in some cases, by positively assisting it. What this means in particular cases, in a world of competing claims and values, will need to be thoughtfully worked out (indeed it may pose for us a never-ending agenda), but what is being emphasized here is simply a basic attitude toward living things that ought to characterize those who seek to respect a good creation. Albert Schweitzer seemed to capture the spirit of this when he observed that what is troublesome is not "the farmer who has mowed down a thousand flowers in his meadow as fodder for his cows" but rather the same farmer who on his

18. Kleinig, *Valuing Life,* p. 50.
19. Kleinig, *Valuing Life,* p. 172.

way home "strikes off in wanton pastime the head of a single flower by the roadside."[20] In a world of competing needs, the flowers, even by the thousands, may have to be used to sustain the farmer's cows, but to wantonly destroy one such flower is a failure to appreciate the goodness of creation, a failure to recognize the claim to our moral consideration of that one, solitary flower by the side of the road.

And respect for the telic development of individual life-forms generates, it is reasonable to believe, respect for those complex wholes called ecosystems, which are not themselves organisms in the strict sense. (This, of course, would be contested by proponents of the Gaia hypothesis. Named after the Greek goddess of the earth, this theory argues that the biosphere, with all its interrelated parts that function much like the cells, tissues, and organs of the human body, is itself a super organism.[21]) That is, when one begins by considering the telic development of, say, the bee, one cannot do so in isolation from its role in the more complex social life of the hive, nor in isolation from the larger world of flowers and pollination, and so on. Quickly one is drawn into a much larger web of life, indeed a web of forces and powers and entities, both organic and inorganic, that interrelate in such a way as to make possible each other's existence and development, along with the creation of that finely tuned, larger whole, the ecosystem. And that complex whole is, I suggest, to be respected as something desirable in its own right, and therefore as something worthy of being sustained for its own sake.

AVOIDING SOME DANGERS

In talking of humans, animals, plants, ecosystems, and the like all having intrinsic value, there are at least two dangers that need to be avoided. First, there is the danger that this will be interpreted to mean that they all have the same intrinsic value. This is the "doctrine of species organismic equality," a doctrine that has been held by few in the Western world.[22] It would awkwardly follow from such a doctrine that all possess-

20. Quoted in Kleinig, *Valuing Life,* p. 172.

21. See James Lovelock, *Gaia: A New Look at Life on Earth* (London: Oxford University Press, 1974); James E. Lovelock, "Gaia: The World as Living Organism," *New Scientist* 112 (1986): 25-28. In assuming, on the contrary, that the biosphere is not a living organism, I do not here gain any advantage for my own arguments — quite the contrary.

22. One of those few is Paul W. Taylor, *Respect for Nature: A Theory of Environmental Ethics* (Princeton, N.J.: Princeton University Press, 1986).

ors of intrinsic value, be they humans or plants, have an equal claim to our moral consideration and concern. In contrast to this, I am affirming a doctrine of gradations in intrinsic value, some possessors of intrinsic value having less, others having more such value. And the greater one's intrinsic value, the greater one's claim to moral consideration. It needs to be emphasized that there is nothing in the notion of intrinsic value, as I am using the term (i.e., having value and being worthy of respect apart from any contribution to other parts of the created order) that requires that all possessors of intrinsic value possess it equally. One is free to construe this notion of intrinsic value as one judges most reasonable, graded or equal, and I am suggesting that our moral universe is to be understood as inhabited by many diverse and wonderful things, all worthy of the kind of respect and moral concern appropriate to their particular degree of intrinsic value.

The second danger is that once we have introduced the notion of gradations of intrinsic value it will be understood as licensing the imposition of any and all sacrifices on that which has less intrinsic value for the sake of furthering the interests of that which has more intrinsic value, no matter how trivial those interests might be. Thus humans, who have more intrinsic value than the rest of creation (as I shall assume at this point but defend later on), could use creation in any way they see fit, for whatever advantages they can thereby bring to themselves. But such a position would be indistinguishable from an anthropocentricism that affirms that only humans have intrinsic value, with everything else on the planet having merely instrumental value. Indeed, this would undercut the very point of recognizing that animals, plants, and ecosystems have intrinsic value, the point being to place moral limits on what we humans, despite our greater value, can do with and to them for our own benefit. Therefore, we must reject the view that says that whenever there is a clash of interests, the interests of that which has greater intrinsic value always prevail over the interests of that which has less intrinsic value. On such a view, whenever there is a clash between human interests and the flourishing of animals, plants, or ecosystems, human interests would automatically prevail. Accordingly we could fell a thousand-year-old tree to provide Sequoia coals over which to cook our meals (John Kleinig's example). But this is the very thing that the recognition of nonhuman intrinsic value is designed to exclude: giving priority to every human interest whenever there is a conflict with the flourishing and the telic development of nonhuman life and ecological wholes.

In essence we are seeking to avoid two extremes: (1) only humans have intrinsic value and there are no moral limits to the use to which the world of animals and nature may be put for human advantage, and (2) humans, animals, plants, and ecosystems all have equal intrinsic value and therefore much of the legitimate use to which we put nature in the pursuit of important human interests is forbidden, possibly imperiling human existence itself. So the avoidance of these extreme positions seems morally necessary, but the acceptance of the middle position is fraught with ambiguity and moral uncertainty. This is, however, often just the case in the moral life: extreme positions provide clear direction but that direction is at the same time strongly counterintuitive, whereas the mediating position does not have counterintuitive implications but neither does it provide clear direction. In the case at hand, we have argued that humans, animals, plants, and ecosystems have some intrinsic value as God's good creation, but they do not all have the same intrinsic value. And whatever has intrinsic value makes claims upon us because its continued existence and flourishing is a good. This, in turn, means that the forfeiting of some of our own interests or at least assuming some inconveniences for the sake of other centers of intrinsic value may be required of us — more in the case of that which has more intrinsic value and less in the case of that which has less intrinsic value. But how much sacrifice or how much inconvenience is required in a given instance is what is uncertain and controversial. And there are no formulas to tell us how much inconvenience and forfeiture of our interests for the sake of animals, plants, and ecosystems is required. We may at least be certain that it is more than our anthropocentric culture has historically been willing to assume. And it is discovering what this "more" involves, and acting on it, that is one of our tasks as a Christian and human community.

We should note, finally, that burdens do not have to be burdensome. Although sacrifice and inconvenience may be required of us, surely there must be a sense of joy as we exercise faithful stewardship over a creation that contains so many wonders and beauties, a sense of privilege as we care for what God cares for. Indeed, when we come to recognize and fully appreciate the goodness of God's creation, then the efforts we expend on its behalf and whatever sacrifices we make for it will not be offered grudgingly but willingly and gladly. What is called for is a renewal of spirit, one in which we share God's openness to the good things he has made. In the words of Princeton Theological Seminary professor Daniel Migliore, "When we confess God as the creator, we are saying something about the character of God. We are confessing that God is good, that God gives life to others, that God lets others exist alongside and in fellowship with God, that God makes room for others."[23] As with God, so with those of us who are God's stewards, we are to exist alongside and in fellowship with what God has made. As we worship, serve, and love this God who makes room for others, we shall become a people who also make room for others. This *does* mean that God must be worshiped *as* the one who makes room for others, indeed as the one who makes room not only for humans but for animals and plants, for forests, wetlands, and meadows, for ecosystems and the biosphere. The call to moral and spiritual renewal is in these matters, as always for the Christian, a call to a renewed understanding of the God we worship and seek to serve. It is service, including sacrifice and inconvenience, that arises out of true worship that is accompanied by joy and peace.

SUMMARY AND CONCLUSIONS

In this chapter we have been exploring the relationship between animal advocacy and environmentalism, which has served to raise central questions for us as we have reflected on our obligations to humans, animals, and nature. In the course of our discussion we have rejected an exclusively anthropocentric justification of our moral concern for animals and we have rejected an exclusively anthropocentric justification of our moral concern for the natural environment. Indeed, we went further and rejected the view known as sentientism, the view that the natural environment (i.e., ecosystems and the whole biosphere) is valuable and to be protected only to the extent that it furthers and serves the interests of sentient creatures (human and animal). This was rejected in favor of a view that sees, in more complicated fashion, forests, wetlands, meadows, wildlife, ecosystems, and the whole biosphere as good in its own right, as well as good as a habitat for sentient creatures. That is to say, the natural (nonsentient) environment is God's doubly good creation, good intrinsically (worthy of respect in its own right) and good instrumentally (furthering human and animal interests).

Finally, we rejected the holism of radical deep ecology, which sees humans and animals as being valuable only to the extent that they contribute positively to the maintenance and integrity of the biosphere, which then becomes the source of all value. We rejected such a view, first

23. Daniel Migliore, *Faith Seeking Understanding: An Introduction to Christian Theology* (Grand Rapids: Eerdmans, 1991), p. 85.

and foremost, because it sees humans as being nothing more than servants of the biosphere. We affirmed that from a Christian point of view human life has a value quite apart from its place within an ecosystem. Theologically understood, human life is the divinely conferred occasion to pursue life purposes and to shape an ultimate spiritual destiny. So, although the biosphere or the biotic community, as a harmoniously functioning whole, has an intrinsic value that ought to be respected in its own right as God's good creation, nevertheless, this is not the whole story. The other part of the story is that the biosphere takes on much of its value (though not all) from the individual human lives it sustains and makes possible – lives that are embraced within a special divine purpose.

This means that the Christian's moral universe is populated by humans, animals, and plant life, along with complex wholes such as ecosystems, all of which have intrinsic value. In other words, they all are valuable and worthy of respect apart from any contribution they make to other parts of God's creation. This is not to say that they all have the same intrinsic value, but it is to say that they all have some intrinsic value and that this has serious implications for human conduct. And if there are gradations in intrinsic value (which seems reasonable), then in cases of serious conflict that which has less intrinsic value can be sacrificed for that which has more intrinsic value. To conclude that animals and plants, along with ecosystems, can be sacrificed for the furtherance of certain human interests does not mean that the furtherance of just any human interest will justify such sacrifices, else talk of nonhuman reality having intrinsic value is simply empty moral chatter. On the contrary, the recognition of nonhuman intrinsic value means that there are sacrifices and inconveniences that we humans must bear for the sake of nonhuman entities.

In the course of our discussion, we also addressed the issue of predation, and we examined the claim that, because the functioning of nature as a harmonious whole is good, therefore so are the pain and death that are essential to that harmonious functioning. In contrast to this view we argued that nature, though good, is not perfectly good, but rather is marred by the presence of evil, a recognition of which is captured by the doctrine of the fall. Thus there is that in nature which affects animals negatively – pain, sickness, disability, and death – which is an evil, but one which it is not in our power to eliminate without creating even more evil. There is, then, in nature a tragic dimension that we can only experience with some sadness as we contrast it with that messianic age when "They shall not hurt or destroy in all my holy mountain."

CHAPTER 3

Animal Advocacy, Women, and Feminist Theory

INTRODUCTION

In talking with people about issues of animal welfare it does not take long before one senses that there is a greater sympathy for animal suffering among women than among men, and that women, more often than men, give animal advocacy a receptive hearing. If it is true that animal advocacy receives its most sympathetic hearing among women (a claim supported by systematic empirical research), and if it is also true that our society is one whose controlling attitudes are those of the dominant sex, namely male, then it seems to follow that the cause of animal advocacy and the cause of women's liberation are intimately connected. For in liberating the female experience, that is, in giving that experience an equal role in shaping our society and culture, we will be empowering attitudes and sensitivities that can only benefit animals. Indeed, feminist theorists have noticed this connection, and one finds in their writings strong identification with animal advocacy, along with sharp criticism of the patriarchal culture that, in their view, has spawned abusive attitudes toward animals and toward nature in general. The issues raised by animal advocacy intersect, then, with issues of feminism. Together they have the makings of an explosive mix, one that can evoke strong emotional responses from all directions.

We shall, first, look at empirical studies supportive of the claim that women are more sensitive to animal suffering than men, and that they, more than men, respond to moral claims made on behalf of animals.

Then we shall briefly take note of the work of Carol Gilligan and her claim than women typically approach moral or ethical problems differently than men, operating from what she calls "the care perspective" in contrast to the male "justice perspective." These empirical studies have inspired feminist thinkers to engage in the task of constructing a female ethic, that is, in constructing an ethic that reflects those particular moral tendencies that are said, according to those very studies, to characterize women in general. We shall examine those special features that are said to characterize a female ethic and shall reflect on their implications for the treatment of animals. We shall see not only that women are likely to be friends of animals but that a female ethic is squarely on the side of animal advocacy. After that, we shall examine eco-feminism, the systematic attempt by feminist thinkers to critique patriarchal attitudes toward animals (and nature in general) and to offer a feminist correction. Finally, we shall seek to sort out what all this means for the moral legitimacy of animal advocacy.

GENDER DIFFERENCES, AGAIN

Personal experience does seem to indicate that men and women differ in their attitudes towards animals, and that they respond differently toward cases of perceived animal suffering and abuse. This is supported by systematic studies by professional researchers. As has already been noted, in reporting the work of Kellert and Berry, there is strong empirical evidence supporting the claim that there are *significant* differences between men and women in their attitudes toward animals. In a later study, focusing exclusively on gender differences, they characterize this difference as "dramatic"[1] and offer a range of observations that make it abundantly clear that differences in attitude toward animals is a product of gender more than of virtually anything else. One of the important conclusions that Kellert and Berry reach is that "without question women are far more bothered than men about the possible infliction of pain and suffering on individual animals."[2] This conclusion was supported by the very different responses made by women and men when confronted by the following statements:

1. Stephen R. Kellert and Joyce K. Berry, "Attitudes, Knowledge, and Behavior toward Wild Life as Affected by Gender," *Wild Life Society Bulletin* 11.5 (1987): 363-71.

2. Kellert and Berry, "Attitudes, Knowledge, and Behavior," p. 367.

(a) "Laboratory experiments which cause great pain to animals should be stopped even if these experiments are important to scientific or medical research." Women tended to agree with this statement more than men and in the "strongly agree" category there were twice as many women as men.

(b) "I think rodeos are cruel to animals." Once again women tended to agree with this statement more than men and in the "strongly agree" category there were almost twice as many women as men.

(c) "I see nothing wrong with using leg-hold traps to capture wild animals." Men were more likely to agree with this statement than women; although men tended as a group to disagree with this statement, women did so in greater numbers.

(d) "I think it's all right to kill an animal to make a fur coat as long as the species is not endangered." Despite the fact that women, more than men, are associated with the wearing of fur coats, they more than men questioned the acceptability of this practice.

(e) "I approve of hunting for recreation and meat." Here the "strongly agree" category had twice as many men as women.

The responses made to these statements do not show that all or even a majority of women oppose laboratory experimentation or oppose rodeos but they do show that more women than men oppose them and that in general women are more reluctant to kill or cause pain to animals than are men. Moreover, a larger proportion of women are involved in efforts to stop such practices as harvesting harp seals or using leg-hold traps to catch animals. Significantly, 80 percent of the membership of animal-welfare organizations is made up of women.[3] In contrast, 85 percent of the total number of animal hunters is male, with 29 percent of all men reported having hunted during the previous two years, while this is true of only 4 percent of the female population. In general, Kellert and Berry inform us, "Females especially valued wild animals as objects of affection and expressed considerable concern regarding the consumptive exploitation of wildlife. Males were far more knowledgeable and less fearful of wildlife and more inclined to value animals for practical and recreational reasons."[4]

It is not that men are ecologically or environmentally insensitive, quite the contrary: 62 percent of the membership of environmental pro-

3. The predominance of women in animal welfare organizations is not a recent phenomenon, but has been true since the founding of SPCA's in the early nineteenth century. See James Turner, *Reckoning with the Beast* (Baltimore: Johns Hopkins University Press, 1980), pp. 58, 76.

4. Kellert and Berry, "Attitudes, Knowledge, and Behavior," p. 371.

tection organizations are males, reflecting the fact that men are more concerned with *species* survival and habitat preservation while women are more concerned with cruel treatment and exploitation of *individual* animals. That is, women are more likely to be receptive to animal welfare appeals (in contrast to simply environmental appeals) and men less so.

Finally, when men and women were asked to rank various animals on a like-dislike scale the results were interesting but not altogether surprising. Women gave their higher ratings to familiar domestic animals (e.g., cats, dogs) and to animals that we generally view as attractive and nonthreatening (e.g., swans, ladybugs, butterflies, robins). Men, in contrast, were far more likely to favor predatory animals (e.g., wolves, snakes), game animals (e.g., trout, moose), and invertebrates (e.g., beetles, spiders).[5] Though not pretending to understand all that this reveals to us about the male and female psyches, nevertheless one might suppose that our world would in some ways be better off with more people who identify with swans, ladybugs, butterflies, and robins rather than with wolves, snakes, and other predators. This, of course, may have less to do with what these animals are in and of themselves and more to do with what our identification with them signifies in light of our construal of them.

There are, then, significant differences between men and women in their attitudes toward animals. Research indicates that women are more sensitive to animal suffering and tend to focus more on the individual animal, while men are less sensitive and tend to be more concerned with species survival. But how do we account for these differences? Are they perhaps expressive of differences at a more fundamental level? One possibility is that they are reflective of differences in moral orientation: women and men react differently to animal welfare because they bring to the moral life differing ethical perspectives.

CAROL GILLIGAN AND THE FEMALE MORAL VISION

The work of Harvard's Carol Gilligan, *In a Different Voice,*[6] has achieved almost mythic status, as well as being Harvard University Press's all-time best-selling paperback. In this important and groundbreaking work, Gilligan studied the cognitive and moral differences between men and

5. Kellert and Berry, "Attitudes, Knowledge, and Behavior," p. 367.

6. Carol Gilligan, *In a Different Voice* (Cambridge, Mass.: Harvard University Press, 1982).

women. She concluded that because men and women are socialized differently, they bring to the moral arena different ethical perspectives; they speak, as she puts it, with different voices. Because the dominant public "voice" has traditionally been male, the different "voice" with which the female speaks has been little heard. It is the male voice and its perspective that has become the official approach to morality, standardized in the ethics textbooks and articulated in the public arena. But it is the female voice that Gilligan wishes to identify and contrast with its male counterpart.

The metaphor of voice is a particularly powerful one, as Lawrence Hinman has pointed out.[7] Whereas the "language of theories" leads quickly to a "competitive and combative" stance, one theory over against another, "voices may be different without excluding one another."[8] Further, some voices may, I might add, be so loud that they overwhelm other voices. Consequently, some voices may never be heard and never have the opportunity to be fully developed. And what we do know is that the beauty of a voice, or the wisdom and moral insight given expression by a voice, is not measured in decibels. To speak, as Gilligan does, of a different voice, one widely present but yet little heard, is a call to listen; it is perhaps a call for some to be temporarily silent while others speak. Something else is interesting about the metaphor of voice. That is, voices can vary among women (from soprano to contralto) and among men (from counter-tenor to bass); yet, nevertheless, there are certain identifiable tendencies — women tend to have higher voices and men to have lower voices. So in seeking to identify the different moral voice with which women speak, we need not assume that there are no significant differences among them. Nor need we assume that because of the differences among women's voices there is not *a* female voice to be found but only female voices. After all, a female chorus sounds different from a male chorus, differences within the choruses notwithstanding.

In part, Gilligan's research was a reaction to earlier work in the area of moral psychology. This work assumed that the moral development of males was normative and whatever was found to deviate from male developmental norms, as females seemed to, was to be considered deficient. Or as Jean Grimshaw put it, "Women have been measured against male norms and found wanting."[9] Freud gave expression to this assumption of

7. Lawrence Hinman, *Ethics: A Pluralistic Approach to Moral Theory* (Fort Worth, Tex.: Harcourt Brace Jovanovich, 1994), pp. 327-29.

8. Hinman, *Ethics: A Pluralistic Approach,* p. 329.

9. Jean Grimshaw, *Philosophy and Feminist Thinking* (Minneapolis: University of Minnesota Press, 1986), p. 187.

male normativeness when, within the context of psychoanalytic theory, he wrote,

> I cannot evade the notion (though I hesitate to give it expression) that for women the level of what is ethically normal is different from what it is in men. Their superego is never so inexorable, so impersonal, so independent of its emotional origins as we require it to be in men. Characteristics which critics of every epoch have brought up against women — that they show less sense of justice than men, that they are less ready to submit to the great exigencies of life, that they are more often influenced in their judgments by feelings of affection or hostility — all these would be amply accounted for by modification in the formation of the superego which we have inferred above.[10]

Freud claims that there is a difference in what is "ethically normal" for men and women. From the above quotation we see what he takes those differences to be. First, for women, feelings and emotions have a more important place in the moral life. Thus, to provide an example, compassion directed toward immediate suffering will be more central in moral decision-making. Second, women have a weaker sense of justice. Thus women, *less* often than men, for example, will be heard to say in response to a plea for mercy, "No, I can't do that, it wouldn't be fair to others." Third, for women, the conscience is not so impersonal in its judgment-making. Thus, for women, the concrete specifics of a situation will loom larger in moral decision-making. That this is my mother or my son or my friend will not so readily defer to impersonal or abstract considerations.

The literature in the psychology of moral development after Freud continued to view male moral development as normative, and either to ignore female moral development or to view it as somehow deficient or defective. This is true of the work of Jean Piaget,[11] Erik Erikson,[12] and more recently Lawrence Kohlberg.[13] The latter's longitudinal study of over seventy males over a twenty-year period purported to discover a fixed sequence of developmental stages that individuals pass through on the way

10. Freud, "Some Physical Consequences of the Anatomical Distinction between the Sexes," in *On Sexuality,* vol. 7, ed. A. Richards (Harmondsworth: Penguin, 1977), p. 342.

11. Jean Piaget, *The Moral Judgment of the Child* (New York: Free Press, 1965).

12. Erik H. Erikson, *Identity: Youth and Crises* (New York: W. W. Norton, 1968).

13. Lawrence Kohlberg, *The Philosophy of Moral Development* (New York: Harper and Row, 1981).

to moral maturity. Not all people reach the higher stages; indeed, the sixth and final stage is seldom reached. Initially, research seemed to indicate that females suffered from arrested moral development, finding themselves, more often than males, stuck at the following stage:

> ***Stage 3:*** "The right is playing a good (nice) role, being concerned about other people and their feelings, keeping loyalty and trust with partners, and being motivated to follow rules and expectations."

In contrast, it was more often the male that continued to develop (and more quickly), achieving the higher stages. These higher stages are as follows:

> ***Stage 4:*** "The right is doing one's duty in society, upholding the social order, and maintaining the welfare of society or the group."
>
> ***Stage 5:*** "The right is upholding the basic rights, values, and legal contracts of a society, even if they conflict with the concrete rules and laws of the group."
>
> ***Stage 6:*** "This stage assumes guidance by universal ethical principles that all humanity should follow."[14]

In all of this, Kohlberg assumes that morality has to do with what males tend to excel in, namely, abstract, legalistic moral reasoning. The good person, therefore, is an individual adept at using these rules and principles, deducing from them the appropriate moral conclusion and then acting upon it.

Gilligan was understandably suspicious of the claim that males are morally more advanced than females. For why assume that when females do not score as well relative to norms established by studying males that the problem is with females rather than with the norms?[15] Gilligan set

14. Kohlberg, *The Philosophy of Moral Development,* pp. 410-12.

15. Indeed, initially it was believed, as mentioned previously, that females lagged behind males in moral development based on Kohlberg's six-stage analysis. Cf. Lawrence Kohlberg and R. Kramer, "Continuities and Discontinuities in Child and Adult Moral Development," *Human Development* 12 (1969): 93-120. But more recently those conclusions have been reversed. In fact, a systematic, statistical analysis of eighty studies that submitted ten

about the task of studying female moral development. She constructed her own developmental scheme based on what she maintained was the distinctive female moral orientation. Working with both female and male subjects (women and girls, men and boys), she concluded that males tend to have what she called "the justice perspective." Accordingly, men (tend to) stress individual rights, especially the right to be left alone and not to be interfered with by other people. These are not primarily welfare rights or rights of recipience, but rights of autonomy, that is, the right to proceed in one's life free from interference by others. Moreover, for the male, moral dilemmas and moral disputes are interpreted as conflicts among rights that are to be resolved by determining which right has priority, which right, in other words, is "stronger." And males, in contrast to females, who place a greater emphasis on reconciling people and meeting everyone's needs, tend to view one side of a moral dispute as having the stronger right and therefore being in the right, while the other has a weaker claim and is viewed as the moral loser — someone to whom, therefore, nothing is due. Further, the justice perspective places greater stress on abstract rules, tending to discount the particulars of the situation, with its pain, suffering, and peculiar circumstances, in favor of the dictates of abstract universal principles or truths.

In contrast to this, women tend to have what Gilligan calls "the care perspective." Here the emphasis is on caring, compassion, and meeting the needs of others. In other words, it is an ethic of nurture. The aim of morality is to avoid hurting others and to maintain relationships. Moral dilemmas and moral conflicts are interpreted as conflicts between needs and competing ways of caring that are to be resolved through communication and maintaining sensitivity to all interests involved — but not by imposing rules. Thus women, as they enter the moral arena, are more likely to view themselves in the role of caretaker and nurturer, and not as a referee "counting out" the losers and declaring the winners in the battle of rights. The analysis that Gilligan offers may account for the tendency of men to support the Republican party (the perceived "justice party") and women to support the Democratic party (the perceived "care party").

Of course, these are only broad tendencies. Large numbers of women vote Republican and large numbers of men vote Democratic. In a

---

thousand subjects to Kohlberg's basic testing procedure and scoring system revealed no significant differences between male and female. That is, it seems that females can play as well as males the moral game as Kohlberg conceives it. Cf. Lawrence J. Walker, "Sex Differences in the Development of Moral Reasoning," *Child Development* 57 (1986): 522-26.

similar way, the care perspective is simply more commonly characteristic of women; that is, women are more likely to have less confidence in rules, to give special attention to the particularities of the concrete moral case before them, to work harder to reconcile and meet the needs of all people involved in a moral dispute, to work harder to maintain relationships throughout (despite differences), to not view moral matters as a contest of competing rights, and so forth. Inspired by these empirical studies, feminist thinkers have sought to construct a female ethic that takes seriously these very tendencies, just as in the past traditional ethicists have tended to work out, in their formal treatises, tendencies and perspectives that were in fact more reflective of the male experience. Such an undertaking is worthwhile in its own right, but it may also have some important implications for animal advocacy.

A FEMALE ETHIC

Jean Grimshaw has identified certain main themes to be found in a female ethic. She identifies these themes not on the basis of empirical studies like Gilligan's that seek to determine how girls and women go about the task of making moral decisions but on the basis of her acquaintance with the work of those feminist thinkers who consciously seek to articulate a female ethic. These ethicists take themselves to be working out, with greater theoretical care, tendencies that are rooted in the female experience. They understand themselves, therefore, to be constructing an ethic reflecting those moral tendencies that generally characterize females more than males. The three main emphases of a female ethic, according to Grimshaw, are the following:

(1) A critique of abstraction (said to be a male tendency) and a belief that female moral thinking is more contextualized, less bound by abstract rules, and more attentive to concrete circumstances.
(2) A stress on empathy, nurturance, or caring, which women more commonly display than men.
(3) An emphasis on the moral demands of the situation, which are discovered by a process of attention to the particularities of the case confronting one.[16]

16. Grimshaw, *Philosophy and Feminist Thinking,* p. 203.

Let us briefly comment on each of these emphases and make some application to issues of animal advocacy. (These features of a female ethic do appear to overlap, and so an exposition of one of them will invariably involve us in commenting on the others.) The first major theme is the critique of abstraction. This critique, Grimshaw notes, can be understood in two ways. First, it can be understood as critique of the tendency when engaging in moral evaluation to "discount or think away" the unique or special features of a person or situation, giving attention solely to those features that are widely or universally shared and that enable us to employ general concepts, categories, or rules. With a female ethic, in contrast, we have what is called an "ethic of particularity," that is, an ethic that focuses on individual persons with their *particular* needs to be met, goals to be furthered, traits of personality to be enjoyed, features of character to be admired, interests to be respected, and abilities to be fostered. It is the individual in whom all these features (and others) coalesce who is to be celebrated in all her uniqueness and specialness and to whom moral concern is to be directed. As Marilyn Friedman, a feminist philosopher, has pointed out, there is a curious irony in attempts by philosophers (and theologians, one might add) to ground the absolute and irreplaceable value of each individual in some feature that she shares with all other individuals: rationality, soul, image of God, etc. Rather than rendering individuals irreplaceable, this would seem to render them indistinguishable and, in the final analysis, interchangeable and quite replaceable. To be sure, as Friedman herself puts it, "We still deserve equal respect in virtue of our common humanity. But we are also more than abstractly and equivalently human. It is this 'more' to which we commit ourselves when we care for others in their particularity!"[17] And it is this emphasis on particularity — the uniqueness and specialness of the individual — that makes such an ethic a natural ally of animal advocacy with its concern for the life and well-being of the *individual* animal, not just concern for the species or the complex ecological whole. For here we have concern, to make matters specific, not simply with the species "coyote" but with that particular coyote, vainly and in great pain trying to escape from a leg-hold trap.

This tendency to moral abstraction operates not only with regard to persons but also with regard to those situations in which persons find themselves. What is taken to be important and completely determinative

17. Marilyn Friedman, "Beyond Caring," in *An Ethic of Care*, ed. Mary Jeanne Larrabee (New York: Routledge, 1993), p. 270.

for moral purposes according to the "traditional" ethic are those *common* features attaching to a situation that render an act one of lying or stealing or cheating or whatever. What is much less important or possibly not important at all, on such an approach, are those features that make a particular act of lying or stealing different from other acts of lying or stealing. In contrast, a female ethic is said to be more sensitive to features that distinguish acts of lying from each other (or acts of stealing from each other), more sensitive to the particularities of the case before us that calls for moral evaluation. This is to say, there is less confidence in the serviceability of moral rules. A female ethic will, then, be more skeptical about the adequacy of moral rules to provide infallible guidance and thus less confident about judgments based on widely generalizeable features of a situation. The concern here does seem to be reasonable, for it seems possible that too high a confidence and a reliance on moral rules may pose a number of potential problems. There may be a slowness to react to radically new situations that call for a moral response. Because one lacks the guidance of a relevant moral rule, one may be stymied, not knowing what to do. Or perhaps one may judge that it doesn't matter what one does, that it is a matter of indifference, since the new situation is not covered by any of one's present stock of moral rules. One can imagine animals suffering as a result of such a strongly rule-based mentality, since it may not seem that they fall under any of the moral rules one has at one's current disposal. This is presumably because our present rules were formulated in a time when concern for animals was less likely to be a matter of ethical reflection.

There is a second sense of abstraction, Grimshaw notes. This has to do with making moral judgments without considering "the human consequences," without considering "the specific and detailed effects which that course of action might have on human beings." Often involved in this is a "distancing" of ourselves from "the actual or potential reality which would be the outcome of a particular course of action."[18] Such "distancing" from the human consequences of our actions occurs in a wide variety of contexts. For example, when waging war we typically dehumanize our enemy, speaking of them as if they were diseased pests that needed to be exterminated or as objects/things that can be treated as such. Thus, we sought to kill the "Huns" or "Nips" in World War II and the "Gooks" in the Vietnam War. This way of speaking removes from us the reality of the pain, suffering, death, and mutilation that we are caus-

18. Grimshaw, *Philosophy and Feminist Thinking,* p. 205.

ing to living, breathing, family-connected, hopeful-for-the-future human beings like ourselves. Similarly, in the case of our dealings with animals, there are also a range of distancing devices that we employ. Thus we eat "pork" and "beef" and "poultry" – not a particular pig or cow or bird and certainly not "animal flesh." Moreover, as Mary Midgley comments, "In scientific articles, experimental animals never moan, scream, cry, growl, whimper, howl, snarl or whine; they just discreetly vocalize. Similarly, they seldom do anything so vulgar as getting killed. On the contrary, they are politely 'sacrificed'. . . ."[19]

None of these observations are meant to prejudge the morality of particular wars nor even the moral legitimacy of using animals for food and painful scientific experimentation. They are intended to alert us to these distancing devices. They are also to say that to fail to fully reckon with the pain and suffering caused by a given course of action, vividly and honestly confronting it, is not to be in a position to render a trustworthy moral judgment. For by distancing ourselves, we remove ourselves from the full character of what we are doing. And we may indeed be especially prone to do this in our dealings with animals, where we seem to suffer from a peculiar blindness to their psychological and subjective reality. That animals have an inner life that goes better or worse for them, that they experience pain and pleasure, suffering and contentment, is often something we block from our consciousness at critical moments. In contrast to such abstraction, the female correction is "concreteness," which "requires that one experience or vividly imagine such consequences . . . and judge on the basis of that awareness."[20] A female ethic, then, with an emphasis on vividly confronting the full reality of the pain and suffering that we may inflict or that we can relieve can only help the cause of animal advocacy, as well as help make us more honest moral beings.

The second feature associated with a female ethic, according to Grimshaw, is its emphasis on caring and empathy. Drawing on Nel Noddings's work,[21] caring is said to involve "engrossment" (Noddings's term), which is to put aside self and enter into the experience of another as far as possible. Such engrossment, it is said, does not imply deep personal feelings for the other nor need it be part of a long-term relationship. It is, however, the means whereby we "apprehend the reality" of the other,

19. Mary Midgley, "Are You an Animal?" in *Animal Experimentation,* ed. Gill Langley (New York: Chapman and Hall, 1989), p. 15.

20. Grimshaw, *Philosophy and Feminist Thinking,* p. 205.

21. Nel Noddings, *Caring: A Feminine Approach to Ethics and Moral Education* (Berkeley and Los Angeles: University of California Press, 1984).

"trying to grasp what the other is experiencing and how she sees things, and behaving towards her in a way that recognizes and is appropriate to that apprehension."[22] When we do this, we are caring, and when we understand caring in this way we also understand the dangers posed by abstraction.

The third feature of a female ethic, according to Grimshaw, is a stress on the moral demands of a given situation discovered by a process of "attention." In the course of her exposition Grimshaw approvingly quotes the philosopher and novelist Iris Murdoch: "I have used the word 'attention' . . . to express the idea of a just and loving gaze directed upon an individual reality. I believe this to be the characteristic and proper mark of the moral agent."[23] Much of Murdoch's work, Grimshaw notes, is a defense and exposition of this notion. Attention involves, importantly, humility, which is not, as Grimshaw observes, a peculiar style of self-effacement, like speaking with a weak voice or standing in the background. "Rather, it is a capacity for 'self-less' perception of the world; self-less in the sense that attention to and perception of a person or situation are, as far as possible, undistorted by fantasy or by the desires of self."[24] So, crucial to making the appropriate moral response to a situation is attending carefully to the particulars of the situation.

There is much here that is interesting, provocative, enriching, and, of course, in need of further development and much qualification. I would only make one brief observation and then make a short application to animal advocacy. The observation is this. It is easy to be overly concerned with the feminist downplaying of the importance of moral rules, fearing that perhaps what we have with a female ethic is a new antinomianism. It is by no means the case that feminist ethicists simply want to jettison moral rules. Some feminists may move too far in this direction, but they also find themselves criticized by other feminists.[25] Nevertheless, what is generally characteristic of a female ethic is a warning against an

22. Grimshaw, *Philosophy and Feminist Thinking*, p. 231.

23. Iris Murdoch, *The Sovereignty of Good* (London: Routledge and Kegan Paul, 1970), p. 34.

24. Grimshaw, *Philosophy and Feminist Thinking*, p. 235.

25. Referring to Nel Noddings, who seeks to articulate a female ethic in her book, *Caring: A Feminine Approach to Ethics and Moral Education*, Virginia Held has commented, "But I think that the attack on principles has sometimes been carried too far by critics of traditional moral theory. . . . We should not forget that an absence of principles can be an invitation to capriciousness" (Held, *Feminist Morality* [Chicago: University of Chicago Press, 1993], p. 75).

over-reliance on moral rules. And, clearly, one can put moral rules in their place without ceasing to have a healthy moral respect for them. Feminist thinking simply calls our attention to something that we all sense at certain moments: the importance of moral rules can be overrated. Certainly an awareness of this is reflected in the charge of legalism that one hears from time to time in the course of moral discussions, a charge that is directed at a rigid, wooden, insensitive use of moral rules. Implicit in such a charge is a recognition that there is more to being a good person than being a scrupulous observer of moral rules. Being a good person means that one has the wisdom to use rules with sensitivity and discretion. Moreover, moral rules cover only a small portion of the moral life. The vast bulk of moral living is lived out in spheres where we simply have no formulas or rules to guide us. Our dealings with people in the course of a normal day are filled with moral and spiritual occasions for which there are no applicable rules. Here cultivation of "the just and loving gaze" is what will, more likely, prove helpful. As Virginia Held has observed, "Caring, empathy, feeling for others, being sensitive to each other's feelings – all may be better guides to what morality requires in actual contexts than may abstract rules or rational calculation."[26]

As for animal advocacy, the application is this. With an ethic that stresses care and empathy, that emphasizes the importance of the "just and loving gaze," and that operates with less confidence in the adequacy of moral rules to do all the moral work for us, one will be better positioned, I believe, to respond to the needs of animals. One will be less likely to delay one's response because of puzzling over the existence of animal rights, less likely to be morally paralyzed because one lacks a relevant moral rule that covers animals. For what makes one worthy of moral consideration in a female ethic is being needy, not possessing certain rights. To be sure, talk of rights can perhaps be extended to cover animals (as I believe it can), but it may be a demanding and time-consuming task to argue one's way over all the intellectual hurdles put in the way of the claim that there are such things as animal rights. In contrast, compassion and caring do not require the same complicated intellectual feats. If one has compassion toward suffering animals born of care, one simply exercises it, one simply assumes the role of caretaker and nurturer. It would seem, then, that not only do animals have a friend in women but animal advocacy has a friend in a female ethic as well.

26. Held, *Feminist Morality,* p. 52.

ECO-FEMINISM AND THE INSIGHTS OF FEMALE EXPERIENCE

The emergence in the past twenty years of sophisticated feminist theory is one of the most interesting and important intellectual developments of the latter part of the twentieth century. To be sure, much that feminist theoreticians have to say is controversial. And it is often said that we are currently witnessing a widespread disenchantment with the feminist movement as a sociopolitical phenomenon. Nevertheless, whatever the state of feminism as a social movement, the world of feminist theory is alive and well. Books and articles that seek to develop and apply feminist thought to the full range of human experience and activity are being produced at a record pace. As with any burgeoning academic area, one can hardly keep up with the flood of newly published material.

Despite such enormous intellectual activity, feminist theory is little understood among the general public. This is regrettable, because this literature is not only provocative, it is also the bearer of important moral insights. The general public does have some awareness of the feminist movement as it is portrayed in the popular press and some idea of the arguments on behalf of equal rights for women, but they have little sense of feminist theory or what might be called "transformational feminism." This is, like any ideology, a method for analyzing the ills of society and a prescription for putting things right. One of the areas that has been the object of feminist analysis is human treatment of nature and, in particular, of animals. Indeed, feminist theory has been sufficiently concerned with these issues that there exists within feminist theory a subfield called "eco-feminism" that addresses just these concerns.

Eco-feminism is the application of feminist thought and theory to issues of ecology, and it can for reasons of exposition be helpfully contrasted with deep ecology. In the case of deep ecology, as we have seen, the source of the ecological crisis that confronts our world is found in an anthropocentric ethic and worldview, one that sees human good as the only good and sanctions any use of nature so long as it serves human ends. What is needed to correct the situation, deep ecologists tell us, is to jettison our anthropocentric ethic and replace it with an ethic that respects nature as something valuable in its own right, not as something valuable only because it can be used to serve human ends. In contrast, eco-feminism sees the problem as a product of an *androcentric* or "masculinist" worldview. That is, while deep ecology sees the problem as *human,* eco-feminists see the problem as *male.* Or to put it in more familiar feminist terms: the current ecological crisis and the kind of exploitation of animals that concerns animal advocates is a product of a patriarchal culture – a culture that is characterized by the male values of subduing, conquering, mastering, controlling, and dominating. It is these values and it is the men imbued with them that have led to the abuse of nature and of animals. In essence, we abuse because we wish to dominate and master. Referring to patriarchy, Andree Callard, one such eco-feminist, has scathingly commented,

> The treatment of nature and animals is the vilest manifestation of that disease. . . . In patriarchy, nature, animals and women are objectified, hunted, invaded, colonized, owned, consumed and forced to yield and to produce (or not). This violation of the integrity of wild, spontaneous Being is rape. . . . As with women as a class, nature and animals have been kept in a state of inferiority and powerlessness in order to enable men as a class to believe and act upon their "cultural" superiority/dominance.[27]

These are intense and angry words, perhaps too intense and angry to find a sympathetic hearing in some quarters. Nevertheless, it would be a mistake to dismiss these words as nothing more than intemperate rantings. When one looks at the violence in the world, it is, admittedly, overwhelmingly male violence. As one reflects on war (declaring it and waging it), murder, terrorism, rape, spousal abuse, sexual abuse of children, child pornography, violent pornography, bodily assault, gang violence, drunk driving, vehicular manslaughter, trafficking in drugs, and lawbreaking in general, one recognizes that these are predominantly male activities. Indeed, one might expect that the elimination of all *male* violence from the world would virtually eliminate *all* violence from the world. If, in addition to such recognized male social violence, there is the violent exploitation of nature and of animals, one might expect it to be primarily a male activity as well. In fact, one might be surprised if it were anything else but that. So the eco-feminist thesis that what we have here is essentially a *male* problem is not an unreasonable suggestion.

A distinction needs to be made here. It is not that there is a biological problem. Rather, there is a problem, they argue, with males as they are shaped and socialized in a culture dominated by patriarchal values. This, then, is the source of the problem, males imbued with the drive to dominate and master. Women too, it must be acknowledged, can be distorted by patriarchal values, and they too can participate in the world's violence. It happens less often in their case, it would be argued, because women are

27. Andree Callard, *Rape of the Wild* (Bloomington: Indiana University Press, 1989), p. 1.

socialized differently than men and are marginal players on the patriarchal scene, being therefore less influenced by it.

The ills that patriarchy has spawned are a product, it is charged, of an unchecked drive for dominance and mastery, the quintessential features of patriarchy. We see this, it is alleged, in such pernicious patriarchal manifestations as racism (the domination of one race by another), imperialism (the domination of one nation or culture by another), and sexism (the domination of one sex by another). So, too, when it comes to the environmental ills that imperil our world and the abuse to which animals have been subjected. This also, according to the eco-feminists, is a product of the same drive for dominance and mastery.

OBJECTIFYING ANIMALS

In patriarchy, the eco-feminist critique continues, animals and nature are "objectified," that is, viewed as objects with whom one senses no kinship and for whom fellow feelings are absent. To objectify something in this sense is to block from consideration any imaginative awareness of the feelings and sensitivities of the other and to deny them their subjectivity as bearers of an inner life that in some respects corresponds to our own. Thus, scientists in the laboratory, it is claimed, typically view animal research subjects as if they were mere things. Consequently, they describe the functioning of the animal and any deleterious effects of the experimenting on the animal as if they were describing a machine and its malfunctioning. Here there is no sense of connecting with a kindred being, only with an "it." Andree Callard puts it this way:

> From this perspective, the researcher strips the animal of its natural attributes and manipulates it to suit his design. The animal no longer exudes grace, strength and health. Restricted in body and mind, and drastically altered, it is afflicted with physical and mental diseases. The researcher does not identify with, feel connected to, this animal. Rather he coolly observes and measures its reactions to the substances and conditions to which he subjects it. As the animal is forcibly alienated from its essence and isolated from its kin, so it is separated from the researcher and, by virtue of the violence the researcher does to animal integrity, he alienates himself from his own nature and from the rest of humanity.[28]

28. Callard, *Rape of the Wild,* p. 58.

This "scientific objectivity" constitutes a distortion of the reality before us, treating the animal as if it were an abstraction and not a concrete living, breathing, feeling organism. This also reflects, it is claimed, the excessive male emphasis on abstract rationalism and the tendency to separate thought from feeling, both ills that feminists associate with patriarchy.

But why is the objectifying of animals an expression of patriarchy? In part, one might suppose, because what one dominates, harms, and kills is not something one can at the same time experience kinship with. If one is going to *treat* something as an object, one will need to *view* it as an object. Compare this with how soldiers view their enemies: they tend to turn them into things, into what is "subhuman," so that they can proceed in their military missions without crippling inhibitions. Moreover, the patriarchal male, the feminist analysis proceeds, thinks in terms of hierarchies: what is below is inferior to and separate from what is above, and therefore can be dominated by it. The importance of hierarchies, respect for hierarchies, and the controlling place of hierarchies is a central feature, it is said, of patriarchy. And in the case of animals, because they rank below humans and are separate from humans, they can be justifiably dominated by humans and consequently are objectified by them. Women, in contrast, according to feminist theorists, are much less prone to objectifying animals and nature, much less likely to fall prey to patriarchal distortions, including thinking and organizing experience in terms of hierarchies. Women, because of their socialization and life experiences, are presumed to have a greater sense of connectedness to nature and to view the suffering found there more compassionately than does the male. As Callard suggests, "woman's reproductive system . . . enables her to share the experience of bringing forth and nourishing life with the rest of the living world."[29] Women also are assumed to have a greater sense of what it is like to feel helpless just because of their own social experience of vulnerability, and therefore they have a greater capacity for empathy for the vulnerable and helpless in nature.

FEMINISM AND SCIENTIFIC ATTITUDES

For some feminists the real villain in the present mistreatment of animals is the dominance of a scientific method, and, in particular, the dominance of a scientific method that has itself been infected by patriarchal

29. Callard, *Rape of the Wild,* p. 106.

values. Biologist and feminist Zuleyma Tang Halpin argues that the concept of scientific objectivity, as it finds expression in patriarchal science (i.e., science as it has developed in male-dominated societies) involves (1) "the rejection of feelings in favor of the intellect" and (2) "the separation of the subject from the object (what is thought about)."[30] These features of "male" objectivity are, of course, from the feminist standpoint viewed negatively. The current approach to scientific research assumes that if we operate with a cool, detached intellect when doing science, "unencumbered" by feelings or emotions, we will reduce the likelihood of our investigations being unacceptably skewed by personal bias or prejudice. Thus, the closer the mind of the scientist approximates the functioning of an emotionless computer, the better. Or, as Halpin more caustically puts it, "I am a scientist, therefore I cannot feel." But, according to certain feminists, such emotional detachment is not essential for good science. In fact, feminists would argue just the reverse. It is the result of the fact that science has been done primarily by men and has taken on their patriarchal values; that is, this value on detachment is historically contingent to good science.

In making their case, feminists often appeal to Barbara McClintock, MacArthur award winner, Nobel laureate, genius, and biological revolutionary, as an example of female science. In her approach to research she operates with what has been called "a feeling for the organism." This characterization comes from Evelyn Fox Keller, whose biography of McClintock is titled, *A Feeling for the Organism: The Life and Work of Barbara McClintock.* As McClintock herself comments:

> [An organism] isn't just a piece of plastic. It is something that is constantly being affected by the environment, constantly showing attributes or disabilities in its growth. . . . No two plants are exactly alike. . . . I start with the seedling, and I don't want to leave it. I don't feel I really know the story if I don't watch the plant all the way along. So I know every plant in the field. I know them intimately, and I find it a great pleasure to know them.[31]

This style of doing science has often been denigrated by leaders in the fields of molecular biology and genetics, according to Stephen Jay Gould,

30. Zuleyma Tang Halpin, "Scientific Objectivity and the Concept of 'the Other,'" *Women's Studies International Forum* 12, no. 3 (1989): 285.

31. Quoted in Stephen Jay Gould, "Triumph of a Naturalist," *New York Review of Books* (March 29, 1984), p. 6.

biologist and Harvard professor.[32] The contrasting style, favored by critics of McClintock, is characterized by Gould as follows:

> The experimental sciences (like molecular biology) generally work in the reductionist mode, trying to establish a simple linear claim of cause and effect. They prefer explanations rising from the lowest level of molecules and their physico-chemical properties. To reach the "basic" level, they work with the simplest organisms and try consciously to avoid the individuality of any particular creature. They concentrate instead on the repeatable properties of large groups so that a clone of bacteria becomes the analogue of a population of atoms with no individuality by definition.[33]

So, to extend the feminist analysis, we might say that the reductionist style favored by molecular biologists and geneticists is a male style while McClintock's is female. Though, as Gould comments, McClintock's style is actually common in his own subfield of biology, evolutionary and taxonomic biology, so that this particular style may be as much a matter of subfield as it is of gender. Nevertheless, feminists are advocating an approach that, à la Barbara McClintock, involves a "feeling for the organism" both in its totality and in its particularity. This may or may not be a more fruitful way to do biology (that is something for the experts to decide), but it would seem that when the organism studied is an animal, one is more likely with such an approach to appreciate and empathetically engage with the hurts, harms, pains, and frustrations suffered by the animal. In contrast, with a reductionist approach where one focuses at a micro-level (say at the level of molecules, physico-chemical properties, or even C-fibers firing) one is simply not intellectually, appreciatively, and emotionally engaged at a level where those hurts, harms, pains, and frustrations can appropriately register. What we may have then with McClintock's style of doing science is not so much a requirement for doing good biology as a requirement for being a morally perceptive person. It is in essence a way of looking at the world so that one sees what needs to be seen in order to respond with appropriate moral concern. Otherwise one may suffer from a kind of blindness to the way the world is, and thereby we may fail to perceive situations warranting beneficent action or kindly restraint.

According to the second part of Halpin's characterization of scien-

32. Gould, "Triumph of a Naturalist," p. 6.
33. Gould, "Triumph of a Naturalist," p. 6

tific objectivity, the thinking self (of the scientist) is *separated* from the object of study. That is, the scientist views what is studied as an object or thing, "rendering it incapable of eliciting any meaningful emotions from the scientist."[34] Or, to translate this into terminology widely used in feminist circles and by Halpin herself, the object of study is viewed as "the other," a term introduced by Simone de Beauvoir in her classic feminist text, *The Second Sex*. In patriarchal culture, it would be argued, women are "set up as the negative, the unessential, the abnormal to the male."[35] Or, in other words, they are viewed as "the other." This concept has been extended to cover the patriarchal attitude toward animals and nature as well. Halpin is introducing it here to explicate what she understands to be an essential feature of patriarchal scientific objectivity where the object of study becomes "the other" — the male scientist himself being the standard of value and significance and the object of study being relegated to the status of the substandard. On this model, the self is conceived as normal and superior, and the other is conceived as alien, abnormal, and of lesser value. And, indeed, what the scientist studies, the scientist controls and masters. Here there may be no sense of kinship with what is studied but only a godlike sense of superiority.

It is into this scientific culture with its value on emotional detachment and the construal of the object of study as "the other" that animals are brought for the purposes of study and experimentation. In this environment they become or can easily become indistinguishable from other mechanical tools of the scientist's trade. Animals are simply there to be used in whatever way the scientist, unimpeded by emotional sentimentality and licensed by the sense of one's superiority, judges best. If this analysis is anywhere near on target, then the way to a better treatment of animals is not to be found primarily in waging isolated animal rights campaigns, but in transforming the whole patriarchal scientific culture. Specifically, the patriarchal view of objectivity needs to be challenged and transformed, that notion that good science can be done and appropriate results obtained only as scientists emotionally distance themselves from what they study and only as they construe what they study as "the other," with whom they have little or no significant kinship.

This analysis and critique of androcentric objectivity raises issues of considerable interest and controversy. Certainly we would wish to retain

34. Halpin, "Scientific Objectivity and the Concept of 'the Other,'" p. 286.

35. Maggie Humm, *The Dictionary of Feminist Theory* (Columbus: Ohio State University Press, 1990), p. 156.

and endorse scientific objectivity in some important sense of that term. This objectivity would at least call for the elimination of those personal biases and prejudices that can distort the outcome of our research. But surely this can be done without divesting ourselves of feelings, emotions, and a sense of connectedness with the object of our study. What kind of feelings and what sense of connectedness will be appropriate will have to be contextually determined, depending on whether what we are studying is, for example, a mouse or a molecule. Getting clear on this appears, however, to be as much a moral issue as a scientific one. Unquestionably, having "a feeling for the organism" in both its wholeness and its particularity can only help to sensitize us in ways that will prove salutary for the welfare and well-being of those animals that we study and use in experimental research.

SOME REFLECTIONS ON THE FEMINIST CRITIQUE

There are, admittedly, feminist theorists who claim that the female experience of the world and those intellectual, moral, and spiritual categories that flow from it are uniformly superior to the male experience and all that it generates. In some cases the impression one is left with, conveyed through a lively and intense rhetoric, is that all the world's ills are traceable back to the patriarchal male, while all virtue finds its origin in the female experience and understanding – as if, in effect, Adam fell but not Eve. This approach most often serves to alienate rather than to illuminate. For Christians in particular, the biblical doctrine that sin is a universal human condition ought to make the Christian community suspicious of any theory that views all moral evil as generated by one sex and all redemptive possibilities by the other. Basic Christian doctrine affirms that all humans, men and women, are, in various ways, morally flawed and spiritually defective. To suggest otherwise, laying full responsibility for all evil at the foot of the male and suggesting that males only are in need of moral attention, is contrary to the biblical vision of a fallen humanity. Sadly, the main result of such a one-sided view is often a premature dismissal of the feminist's critique in general, as if it were nothing more than so much vituperative male-bashing.

In assessing the feminist critique, it is only fair to stress that it is not a criticism of the male sex (a biological reality) but of the male gender (a social construct); that is, it is a criticism of those male attitudes and behaviors that are encouraged in a patriarchal society. Furthermore, the feminist critique is largely systemic in nature; that is, it is a critique directed not at personal moral failings but at socially embodied patriarchal values and attitudes that are deeply entrenched in the customs, conventions, and practices that govern our social life and that are uncritically accepted as normative by most of us. Most importantly, however, we need not view the feminist critique in stark terms: female vs. male, good vs. evil, and so on. Rather, we can understand the female experience as generating certain sensitivities that males are less likely to possess. These female sensitivities can play a significant role in reshaping our society in beneficial ways and enriching our personal lives. Thus the feminist philosopher Jean Grimshaw speaks of a female ethic that does not "suppose that women as individuals are inherently morally superior to or purer in heart than men. They suppose, rather, that female life and experience creates the possibility for women more easily than for men of perceiving the dangerous and ruinous and inhuman nature of ideologies and actions that have led to so much destruction."[36] There are, then, certain sensitivities, more prevalent among women than among men (but not exclusively female), that need, for all our sakes, to play an enlarged role in shaping who we are as human beings and in shaping our life together in society. If, in fact, women and men are socialized in different ways so that they bring different vulnerabilities, different virtues, and different insights to the world around them, then it makes sense that we would all be better off if the world were more evenly shaped both by the "masculine" and "feminine" perspectives. It is not strange to think that since men have been the most active historically in shaping our social institutions, these institutions would tend to bear more obviously the marks of male fallenness (and male virtues) than the marks of female fallenness (and female virtues).

CONCLUSIONS

In this chapter we have looked at the claim that women are more sensitive to animal suffering and more active in support of animal welfare and animal rights causes than are men. This claim seems to be amply supported by empirical research, by the higher percentage of women involved in animal advocacy organizations, and by personal observation. But where does all this lead us? It might be observed that, from the fact that women tend to be more sensitive to animal suffering than men nothing follows about

36. Grimshaw, *Philosophy and Feminist Thinking*, p. 194.

how sensitive we *ought* to be. That males tend to be *less* sensitive toward animal suffering has as much a claim, on the face of it, to normative status as female tendencies. Indeed, that women tend to be more sensitive to animal suffering than men only serves to raise for us the crucial question: should we cultivate the female or the male tendency? It does not, however, answer the question and tell us which tendency is morally preferable. Perhaps women are too sensitive and not tough-minded enough. But then perhaps men are too insensitive, callous in a way that stands in need of correction. Possibly both of these claims are partially true and the morally preferable attitude toward animal suffering is to be found somewhere between these two broad tendencies, a kind of golden mean, requiring men and women to learn from each other in order to achieve the appropriate balance.

Nevertheless, in raising these questions an important function may, one hopes, be served by rousing us from our "dogmatic slumbers" about animals. Raising the questions may constitute a first step in the process of critically re-evaluating our attitudes toward them. For the official voice, indeed the dominant and controlling voice in our society, has been the male voice, with its particular intellectual and moral tendencies. This is the voice of male preachers, professors, politicians, social commentators, and other shapers of public opinion who determine for us what is morally mainstream or what is considered morally eccentric, including moral concern for animals. Because ours is a male-dominated society, certain tendencies, male ones, have enjoyed an uncritical acceptance. To these dominant tendencies there may always be minor challenges but not the kind of serious challenge that comes when it is backed by a critical mass of opinion and that is therefore more difficult to simply dismiss as morally eccentric. To be sure, that critical mass of opinion may have existed all along in the female of our species, but because female opinion has existed only within a framework of male authority, it has been effectively marginalized and rendered ineffectual in shaping public moral discourse. In this chapter, we have suggested that this dominance of the male voice in our public life may have left us more morally insensitive about animal welfare than we might otherwise have been.

In addition to examining the empirical claim that there is a greater sympathy for animal suffering among women and that they, as a group, tend to be more receptive to animal advocacy, we also looked at some of the feminist theorizing relevant to animals and our treatment of them. One can, of course, in great measure appreciate the significance of this difference between women's and men's attitudes toward animals without entering into or even understanding the feminist critique of patriarchal culture. One can simply view this difference as a challenge to think through "Who has it right?" And one can also accept this challenge and do so with the quite reasonable assumption that the official and culturally dominant attitude toward animals, which largely arises out of the male experience, needs to be qualified by those female sensitivities which hitherto have been marginalized but which bring with them an equal claim to validity. But the feminist critique, of course, often moves well beyond a call to negotiate these gender differences. For it is a call to recognize that the male attitude toward animals is morally substandard and that it is the female attitude which more nearly approximates the attitude that ought to prevail and be manifest in our social policies and practices. And we can be open to the serious possibility that this is indeed so without adopting the view that the female experience is always valid, always superior, and always the last court of appeal.

None of this feminist thinking need be found threatening either to men or to the Christian community. Rather, it should be welcomed. We are in the fortunate position of being able to draw on the wisdom, perceptions, and sensitivities of that portion of the human community that has been, over the centuries, the true silent majority. For all of our benefit, they are no longer silent. And it is not simply that they add to our numbers, but they bring *new* insights, *different* emphases, and *special* perspectives. No doubt there will be new error and folly as well, for such is the human condition, but the excitement centers on new categories and perspectives, along with new challenges to thought and action that have already proved insightful and enriching. To the extent that we view God as the ultimate source of truth and wisdom, and to the extent that we have been unwilling to listen to those who manifest God's image in a different way and therefore speak in a different voice, we have, unknowingly perhaps, prevented ourselves from hearing God's voice in its fullness.

CHAPTER 4

What Are Animals Like?

INTRODUCTION

"What is it like to be an animal? What do monkeys, dolphins, crows, sun fishes, and ants think about? Or do nonhuman animals experience any subjective feelings at all?"[1] With these words, Donald Griffin, a distinguished biologist, raises a question that most of us have asked at one time or another. Who has not looked into the eyes of a dog or a cat or a horse and wondered, "What is going on in there?" As we looked and as we pondered (if only momentarily), it seemed to be a deep mystery, though few of us doubted that the dogs, cats, and horses into whose eyes we peered were in fact conscious, that there was an inner subjective life, and that *something* was, in fact, going on. In the case of ants, houseflies, and their various kindred, we are far more skeptical, tending to view them as automata, little efficient machines, devoid of any inner subjective life. Thus, when we accidently step on the dog's paw and it squeals, we do not doubt that it feels pain, but when, while spading our garden, we cut an earthworm in two and see it writhe (as *if* in pain, we suppose), we do not take seriously the possibility that it might be suffering. Despite these convictions, there is much, we feel, that remains mysterious about both dogs and worms.

The kind of questions that we raise amateurishly and informally, and the kind of questions that Griffin is raising professionally and sys-

1. Donald Griffin, *Animal Thinking* (Cambridge, Mass.: Harvard University Press, 1984), p. 1.

tematically, are not only interesting and intriguing questions in their own right; they are also questions the answers to which have crucial implications for the kind of moral standing we may be obliged to assign to animals. If animals are not conscious at all, then animals can be relegated to the same moral category as plants. But if, on the contrary, it turns out that animals are conscious beings who experience pleasure and pain, then that fact, we might well suppose, should be taken into account in our treatment of them. And if some animals are conscious and others are not, then differential treatment may be appropriate. Of course, if consciousness and the experience of pain extends to houseflies as well as to house pets (as some have argued), then our responsibilities may also extend to houseflies, in which case our moral burdens may be heavier than we had thought. If on the other hand, no animals are conscious and none experience pain (as has also been argued), then our moral responsibilities will be lightened considerably.

ARE ANIMALS CONSCIOUS AND DO THEY EXPERIENCE PHYSICAL PAIN?

Most of us believe that rocks and plants are not conscious and do not experience physical pain and believe that humans are conscious and typically experience physical pain when exposed to the appropriate stimuli. But what do we believe about animals? Again, most people believe, without any hesitation, that many species of animals are conscious, that is, that they have an inner psychic life that goes better or worse for them. Thus, when a dog is hit with a baseball bat, it is believed that the dog experiences pain and that its inner subjective life is made worse. In talking with people about such an incident, there may be disagreement about the *moral implications* of the fact that the dog experiences pain and suffers, but rarely would the fact of suffering itself be questioned. Indeed, one can talk with individuals who deny that we have any direct obligations to animals but who, for all that, are not tempted to deny that animals are conscious and experience pain. Apparently, it is easier to be a skeptic about our obligations to animals than it is to be a skeptic about the reality of their pain and suffering.

It may come as a surprise to many to discover that in the narrower professional circles inhabited by psychologists, ethologists, and philosophers, there has been and continues to be doubts about the existence of animal consciousness. This is all the more surprising when we realize that

Darwinian evolution, with its strong emphasis on the continuities between human beings and animals, has been the working model within which so much reflection about animal life has been carried on in the twentieth century. And, of course, if only humans are conscious and experience physical pain, this would constitute a sharp discontinuity between humans and animals that would cry out for justification on evolutionary grounds. Nevertheless, Daisie and Michael Radner, in summing up the professional state of affairs, observe, "Today, despite the intervening century of research in experimental psychology and evolutionary biology, arguably there is more ambivalence about animal consciousness than there was in Darwin's time."[2] It is not so much that there are direct statements by scientists and others in support of the theory that animals are merely automata, so much "as a reluctance to admit any doctrines alternative to the beast-machine."[3]

But why is there this skepticism about animal consciousness or at least reluctance to affirm such consciousness? In part, this is expressive of a more general unease about consciousness (human or animal) that has characterized much of the scientific and philosophic communities in the twentieth century. This unease has found its most striking expression in behaviorism, which became the dominant approach to the study of human and animal behavior among academic psychologists. Behaviorists rejected the old mentalism or folk psychology (still used by all of us on an everyday basis) that sought to explain human behavior by reference to conscious mental states that cause particular behaviors. A typical example of folk psychology would be the following: "He went jogging because he wanted to lose weight and because he believed that jogging would contribute to weight loss." Here the behavior, jogging, is explained by reference to conscious mental states, a *desire* to lose weight and the *belief* that jogging would be a means to that end. In contrast, behaviorism eliminated any reference to conscious mental states and sought to understand human behavior as a psychological reaction to environmental stimuli and reward. This was an attempt to put the discipline of psychology on a firm scientific footing. It required ridding itself of any concern with consciousness because consciousness was viewed (at best) as an elusive phenomenon that can be directly known only in one's own case (only I know what I'm thinking, feeling, etc.) and disclosed to others only by vague and con-

2. Daisie Radner and Michael Radner, *Animal Consciousness* (Buffalo: Prometheus Books, 1989), p. 122.

3. Radner and Radner, *Animal Consciousness,* p. 122.

fusing introspective reports that in the final analysis are uncheckable. In short, because science deals with what is public, and because consciousness is, by its very nature, private, then psychology, if it wants to be scientific, cannot concern itself with consciousness. By substituting a stimulus-response model of explanation for the conscious mental-state model, all relevant variables (i.e., the physical organism, the stimulus, the response) became publicly observable and therefore amenable to investigation by means of the scientific method. This enabled psychology to move its activity into the laboratory, run experiments that could be verified, identify observable behavior patterns, and, in short, to join the community of scientists. In the process, conscious mental states were eliminated as an explanatory variable, and increasingly their very existence came to be questioned.

A further impetus to skepticism about animal consciousness was scientific naturalism, a philosophical vision that saw all of nature (including humans and animals) as part of a material order wholly governed by the same physical laws. Thus, whether we are seeking to explain Smith's jogging or the earth orbiting the sun or a flower growing, the same body of laws will provide a fully sufficient explanation. This kind of scientific naturalism has a difficulty, however, with consciousness. For if we understand consciousness as a purely mental phenomenon — an immaterial, nonphysical reality that can cause things to happen in the material realm — then it would not be the case that everything that happens in the world is governed and explained by physical law. Instead there would be constant intrusions into the physical realm by minds, that is, by consciousness. One could quite understand how a scientific naturalist would be a bit uneasy, for example, over the notion of God, an infinite mind or center of consciousness, intervening in the physical world (say, parting the Red Sea). This would involve a miracle, in the sense of a suspension of the laws of nature, and something therefore inexplicable by those laws. This would be a case of consciousness, albeit *infinite* consciousness, intruding into a world otherwise completely governed by physical law. Our scientific naturalist might, nevertheless, be able to make peace with this notion, since God is, after all, a reality that lies outside of and is separate from the world of nature into which God occasionally intervenes. Thus, even with God's existence, the universe itself could still remain what the scientific naturalist had always believed it to be: a unified whole governed by a single set of physical laws that can, apart from occasional divine intervention, account for all occurrences in the world.

Far more problematic for the scientific naturalist, however, would be a world in which there are *finite* centers of consciousness, many little gods, as it were, attached to human and animal bodies, who do just what God does when God miraculously intervenes in the world — that is, perform feats that are not explicable by the laws of nature. Indeed, if I raise my hand as a result of a conscious mental act or decision, then my hand's going up appears to be as miraculous as God levitating a table by God's mental act or decision. So, if there are finite centers of consciousness causally affecting the world (i.e., making their bodies do all sorts of things and through their bodies making other things happen), then it would appear not to be the case that all the world is completely governed and explained by the same set of physical laws. This the scientific naturalist could *not* countenance and remain a scientific naturalist.

What then is the scientific naturalist to do? For many it seemed that one must either deny that there is such a thing as consciousness or grant that there is consciousness but deny that it in any way causally impacts the physical world, a world that would therefore remain completely governed by physical laws and be determined totally by antecedent physical causes. In this latter case consciousness would be only an epiphenomenon or a collateral phenomenon (B. F. Skinner's term[4]) — produced by the brain but itself causally inefficacious. In either case, consciousness is relegated by the scientific naturalist to a kind of limbo; it is either nonexistent or, if it exists, it is causally ineffectual, and thus of no interest to any one concerned with explaining any occurrence in the world, including human and animal behavior.

A third factor in reducing the significance of consciousness has been the more recent rise of cognitive science, a discipline drawing upon work in both cognitive psychology and artificial intelligence. This is an effort to understand thinking (or cognition) in humans and animals after the model provided by a digital computer. In this view, the brain, which does the thinking, processes information like a computer. Computers process information by means of symbol manipulation and — crucially — there is no need to introduce talk of conscious mental states in understanding how a computer functions. On the computer model of the brain, then, there is no need to introduce conscious mental states in seeking to understand how thinking occurs in humans or animals. (Of course, sometimes

4. "I do not believe that there is a world of mentation or subjective experience that is being, or must be ignored. One feels various states and processes within one's body, but these are collateral products of one's genetic and personal history. No creative or initiating function is to be assigned them" (B. F. Skinner, *Reflections on Behaviorism and Society* [Englewood Cliffs, N.J.: Prentice Hall, 1978], p. 125).

the discussion has swung to the opposite extreme and it has been proposed that *computers* are conscious.)

All this is to observe that there have been intellectual forces at work that serve to minimize the importance of conscious mental states and even to call into question the very existence of consciousness itself. But how, one might wonder, does this pose a special problem for animals over against humans? For it would seem that behaviorism, scientific naturalism, and cognitive science have implications for humans as much as for animals. If these developments threaten to downgrade animals to automata, would they not have exactly the same implications for humans? And indeed they do, but there are factors, it has been suggested, that have resulted in animals faring less well than humans in an intellectual environment skeptical about the potency and reality of conscious mental states.

In the case of humans, we are at least aware of our own conscious mental states; that is, we feel pain and suffer in a variety of ways, have thoughts and desires, and so on. Further, in the case of humans there is the possibility of linguistic verification: we can talk about our pain, for example, describing where it hurts, when it hurts, and how much it hurts. We can also describe a wide range of other feelings and thoughts. Moreover, our lives are embedded in a social fabric that involves, in addition to everyday informal interactions, participation in moral, legal, and ecclesiastical systems that force us to recognize thoughts and feelings in others.[5] In the church, in the law courts, in the moral arena, in our daily idle chatter, we invoke conscious mental states to describe and understand what is going on in the human community, but in all this animals are quite peripheral. In these arenas, "folk psychology," with its common-sense emphasis on inner subjective states, reigns supreme and thus does not allow us to so easily dispense with consciousness as we might in a laboratory while running rats through a maze. Possibly for these sorts of reasons, the intellectual forces that minimize the role of consciousness and at times question its very existence have had a more pervasive (and some would add "perverse") impact on attitudes toward animals, generating more skepticism about *their* consciousness than about human consciousness.

The fact remains — however exactly we explain it — that in certain professional quarters there is substantial skepticism about animal consciousness. For this reason, those that argue on behalf of moral concern for animals have often felt the necessity to argue on behalf of the claim that animals are conscious and do experience physical pain. In certain set-

5. Bernard Rollin, *The Unheeded Cry* (New York: Oxford University Press, 1989), p. 71.

tings, then, animal consciousness cannot be taken for granted and the claim that animals are conscious must be supported by arguments. Yet this will itself strike many as a very odd undertaking for much the same reason that it struck David Hume as odd, who commented: "Next to the ridicule of denying an evident truth, is that of taking much pains to defend it; and no truth appears to me more evident, than that beasts are endow'd with thought and reason as well as men. The arguments are in this case so obvious that they never escape the most stupid and ignorant."[6] Yet not only have arguments been advanced in favor of animal consciousness but others have responded with counterarguments, indicating that for some, contrary to Hume, the arguments are not obvious.

ANIMALS AS AUTOMATA

Before examining the arguments for and against animal consciousness, it will be helpful to look at some phenomena that may serve to raise skeptical questions about the existence of consciousness in animals. This may prove helpful simply because most of us do not share this skepticism and do not have serious doubts that a broad range of animals are conscious — that dogs feel pain, cats see mice, horses experience hunger, and so on. The phenomena to which I refer may also help us understand what is being claimed by those who suggest that animals are automata, that although animals at times engage in rather complicated behavior, they are nevertheless not aware of what they are doing or what is occurring. The phenomena that I have in mind are certain human behaviors that are divorced from conscious control, have been identified by psychologists, and have been made the objects of scientific investigation. What, in part, makes these phenomena interesting is that they are human behaviors that are typically accompanied by awareness and conscious control but in certain instances are not. It is this very kind of behavior, devoid of awareness, that is being attributed to animals when it is argued that they are automata.

Consider subliminal perception, where an individual's behavior is affected by stimuli below the threshold of awareness. One here thinks of the concern expressed over the possible uses of subliminal messages to control human behavior for purposes that are morally questionable — for example, flashing the words "candy" or "popcorn" on the movie screen so

6. David Hume, *A Treatise of Human Nature,* ed. L. A. Selby-Bigge (New York: Oxford University Press, 1960), p. 176.

rapidly that the viewer is not conscious of what is happening, yet the receiver of the message is prompted to get up and go to the candy counter to purchase candy or popcorn. Here the individual perceives but is not aware that she perceives. In one sense, the individual *sees* the word "candy" or "popcorn," in the sense that the individual processes the visual information and acts on it, but she does so without any subjective awareness of seeing the word. At that point one is partially an automaton. A message is being communicated, received, and acted upon, but the recipient is unaware of what is occurring.

Of related interest are cases of what is called "blindsight," a phenomenon discussed in the professional literature but unfamiliar to most of us. In the case of blindsight, an individual who has suffered a certain kind of brain damage – extensive destruction of the visual cortex – will have a blind field, that is, an area in her former visual field where she no longer has the subjective experience of seeing. In short, she *is blind* or partially blind. Yet, at the same time, when induced by experimenters to participate in certain games calling upon her to make a range of visual discriminations (the location of light, the sizes and shapes of objects, etc.) she can do so with surprising accuracy (in the case of some discriminations with 95 percent accuracy); it would seem she has residual *sight* of which she is *not aware.* The person with blindsight takes herself to be guessing when asked to make various visual discriminations and is astonished to discover the accuracy with which she has succeeded.[7] Thus, an individual with blindsight might walk around a chair that she does not experientially see, that she "guesses" is there, which suggests that visual information is being processed and is guiding her behavior without her being aware of it. We have, then, a kind of "unconscious seeing."

Classic cases of automatism may also be of interest. These are cases in which the individual performs simple or complex actions without full awareness or possibly any awareness at all of what is transpiring. Sleepwalking or what is called somnambulism is an instance of this; here an individual may get up and walk, tending to avoid obstacles, may even talk, then return to bed and have no memory of the incident. Or consider what is called "post-epileptic automatism," where the individual who has had an epileptic seizure will continue an action in process before the onset of the seizure or will engage in new behavior (in some rare cases violent behavior) but do so unaware of what she is doing.

7. L. Weisenkrantz, "Varieties of Residual Experience," *Quarterly Journal of Experimental Psychology* 32 (1980): 365-86.

All these cases are interesting because of what they suggest, *not* because they prove anything one way or the other about animal consciousness. They suggest the theoretical possibility that behavior, which in humans is typically controlled and accompanied by conscious awareness but sometimes is not (as in cases of subliminal perception, blindsight, somnambulism, and post-epileptic automatism), may in the case of animals *never* be accompanied by conscious awareness. So, when we look into the eyes of the cat, dog, or horse and wonder "what is going on in there?" we could conceivably answer, "Much the same thing as is going on in the sleepwalker or the person with blindsight or the individual receiving a subliminal message or the person undergoing post-epileptic automatism." That is to say, information is being processed, and behavior is being controlled in accord with that information, but there is little awareness or possibly no awareness of what is transpiring. To suggest that animals are automata — the beast-machine thesis, as it is called — is to suggest that animals are always in a state of automatism. If so, then they do not have an inner life that goes better or worse for them and it does not matter to them how they are treated. Therefore, it should not matter to us. In essence, there is nothing to be morally concerned about — or at least very little. But should we believe that animals are automata?

ANIMAL CONSCIOUSNESS: POINT-COUNTERPOINT

Those who deny that animals are mere automata and claim, on the contrary, that animals are centers of consciousness with an inner subjective life have a range of arguments they offer in support of their claim. This argumentative enterprise may strike many today, as it did Hume in the eighteenth century, as faintly ludicrous, involving as it does employing considerable mental energy in support of what is taken by many to be an obvious truth. Yet, there are skeptics, and the need has been felt to argue the case on behalf of animal consciousness.

Interestingly, for some, there may actually be more uncertainty about animal consciousness *after* looking at the arguments than before. This is not an altogether isolated phenomenon. Consider a comparable experience that some people have with arguments for the existence of God: they may actually be less certain about their beliefs after their exposure to these arguments than before. Or, better yet, reflect on such basic beliefs as (a) there is a real past or (b) there are other centers of *human* consciousness besides my own or (c) there are material objects that exist independently of our experience of them. These are strong, persistent beliefs that all of us have and they are, I would add, fully rational beliefs. But if one were ever to experience doubt about any of them, it most likely would occur when futilely trying to prove them. We soon discover that our convictions outstrip the cogency of our argumentation. Though, in point of fact, the arguments are largely irrelevant, for these are not beliefs we have come to by argument in the first place, nor are they beliefs that we retain because of arguments. Rather, they are (or appear to be) evident truths that we simply "read off" from the world we live in. These are, after all, fundamental beliefs, and there are few beliefs, if any, that are more fundamental and to which we can make appeal in order to establish them. To be sure, we may not be able to prove that we are reading things properly, but in the course of daily living we experience no need for such proof.

Similarly, I suggest, with our belief that animals are conscious: we do not really argue to this belief so much as we simply "see" the world that way in the course of encountering animals and experiencing their behavior. Rosemary Rodd, after sympathetically surveying various arguments on behalf of animal consciousness, concludes, "It seems, however, that we are still obliged to say that the central reason why we believe other people and animals have experience is that *we* are conscious and we have an innate tendency to ascribe consciousness to entities which act in ways which we recognize as signs of sensation."[8] Indeed, when I step on the dog's paw and it squeals, I automatically interpret this as a sign of pain, and thus I see the dog as sharing with me a sentient kinship. Nevertheless, despite the obviousness of this, there are arguments on behalf of animal consciousness and they are worth looking at. These arguments assume, to begin with, that humans are conscious and then ask, "Are animals conscious too?"

Consider, first, the *appeal to common sense.* That is, people as they come in contact with animals, whether household pets, domesticated animals, or wild animals, naturally and without any reservation attribute to them a range of conscious mental states, including the experience of pain. We do not speak of animals in the same way we speak of plants or computers, neither of which we take to be conscious. Animals are different, we believe, and our common sense mode of discourse reveals this: "The dog is in *pain*"; "The horse is *suffering* terribly so we had better put it out of its misery"; "The chimpanzee enjoys being groomed"; and so forth. Indeed,

8. Rosemary Rodd, *Biology, Ethics, and Animals* (New York: Oxford University Press, 1990), p. 63.

the predator, as it chases its prey, does so, not because it is programmed like a heat-seeking missile, but because, like us, it *sees* the prey – in other words, because it is subjectively aware of its presence, and because it is hungry, experiencing the discomfort that comes from lack of food. Thus, we do not take animals to be organic robots, devoid of consciousness. This is what people in all walks of life, from diverse cultures, from varying religious traditions, raised on farms or in cities, living in different ages, literate and illiterate, uniformly believe about animals: they are experiencing centers of consciousness. This, then, is the appeal to *common* sense or the appeal to what people commonly believe.

Of course, common sense is not an infallible guide to truth. At one time, it was common sense that the earth was the center of the universe and that the sun orbited the earth and the earth was stationary. At one time it was common sense that heavier objects fall faster than lighter objects, that the rock falls faster than the pebble. In each of these instances common sense turned out to be wrong. And in the twentieth century; physics has exploded one common-sense belief after another. Bernard Rollin's graphic comment seems on target: "there is no question that common sense has lost its virginal status after its rape by physics."[9] Here consider the fact that not so long ago we lived in the common-sense Newtonian world of absolute space and time. We believed that space and time were universal constants that provided the uniform and unalterable backdrop against which all events occur. But, apparently not so. For Einstein and twentieth-century physics have, contrary to common sense, told us that time is relative: it is a property that varies according to the motion of an object in relation to the speed of light. For example (to use the standard example), if one traveled for a few months in a spaceship at near the speed of light (were that possible), the space traveler would return to earth to discover that years had passed. Here we would have the very strange notion: the simultaneous existence of different temporal realities. And this, of course, takes the wind out of the sails of common sense, which would say, with Newton, that either only a few months have passed or that years have passed – but not both. But it *is* both, insists the contemporary physicist. Furthermore, and equally startling, space is relative, spatial properties also varying according to the motion of an object in relation to the speed of light. Thus our spaceship traveling at near the speed of light will, from the vantage point of a stationary observer, shrink in size as it accelerates but will remain constant for those in the ship. Once

9. Rollin, *The Unheeded Cry,* p. 4.

again we have, the physicist asserts, the simultaneous existence of alternative realities, not merely a single reality viewed or experienced in different ways as common sense would have it. So, it would seem, common sense is not quite the trusted guide to truth that many of us have supposed. And if we can come to believe in multiple, simultaneous temporal and spatial realities, then we might also be able to accept the suggestion that animals are automata, the chimpanzee as well as the housefly.

In response to this attempt to undermine confidence in common sense, it can be conceded that common sense is not an *infallible* guide (what, after all, is?). There have indeed been occasions where we have been provided with good reasons to reject the deliverances of common sense. But it does not follow that this is one of them. Just because common sense can be wrong, it doesn't follow that it is wrong or untrustworthy here. In the case of animals, common sense has not been overruled by cogent reasons and in view of the absence of such reasons, it is reasonable to favor the deliverances of common sense, which are after all nothing less than the convictions that have emerged in people everywhere and in all generations as they have observed, intimately associated with, and lived with animals. Such a universal conviction is not to be lightly set aside and certainly not in the face of the mere suggestion that animals *might* be automata or that common sense can be wrong.

A second argument – not unrelated to the first – is that for almost all of us it is virtually impossible not to believe that animals are experiencing centers of consciousness. We have no doubts that a dog suffers considerably when hit by a car. Indeed we cannot bring ourselves to believe otherwise. It is not merely, as the common sense argument would have it, that we all in fact believe that animals are conscious, experience pain, and so on, but rather that we cannot help but believe this. It would be as difficult to believe that my dog does not experience pain as to believe that my wife or daughter does not experience pain, and that, I suggest, can be coupled with the following principle: If there is a belief that (a) we cannot help but believe and (b) against which there are no decisive objections, then we are rational to accept that belief, draw out its implications, and act on those implications. In this principle, it should be noted, is both a subjective and an objective condition. The subjective component is that there must be a strong, persistent belief that maintains itself in the face of varying experiences and critical reflection – it remains strong and simply will not go away. Certainly our belief in animal consciousness appears to be in this category – it persists and will not go away. The objective component is that there must be no overriding objections to that belief, meaning that a substantial case against it must not have been made. If that case should be made, then our persistent conviction must be viewed as an illusion and we in turn must resist it, refuse to affirm its truth, and refrain from acting on it. But that case has not been made, and therefore, we can, in good conscience, believe that animals are conscious, experience pain, and can be cruelly treated.

A third line of support on behalf of animal consciousness appeals to the physiological and anatomical similarities between humans and many animals. If we accept that human subjective experiences arise as a result of certain processes in our brains and central nervous systems, then where there are certain critical physiological and anatomical similarities between humans and animals, there we may reasonably conclude there are also similar subjective experiences. To use Stephen Walker's example: Suppose we are wondering whether someone born deaf and dumb who is enthusiastically eating his soup is in fact enjoying it much the same as we are, having, that is, similar enjoyable taste experiences. "If we could know that (a) that soup is the same, (b) his taste-buds, olfactory apparatus and so on are the same and (c) all his brain-states except those involved in speech are the same, we ought to be confident that his conscious appreciation of the soup has a good deal in common with our own."[10] Here, of course, we are dealing with a member of our own species, but where we are dealing with members of other species who have relevantly similar physiological and anatomical structures we may reasonably suppose that they have similar mental experiences. It would also follow that the greater the differences between humans and other species, the greater the difference between our inner subjective life and theirs. Thus, it is more reasonable to believe that apes have conscious experiences similar to ours than that insects do, insects being further removed from us physiologically and anatomically.

In pointing to such anatomical and physiological similarities between ourselves and other animals we strengthen the case for drawing conclusions about the inner mental life of animals. Consider the case of the chicken, an animal that in many ways is quite different from us physiologically. Yet suppose we are concerned with whether the chicken experiences pain when it is debeaked in the course of intensive farm practices. We, of course, do not have beaks, have never had them sliced off, and thus would not be able, on that basis, to impute to the chicken a certain set of painful experiences. Yet there are relevant similarities.

10. Stephen Walker, *Animal Thought* (London: Routledge and Kegan Paul, 1983), p. 106.

> Biological evidence that chickens' beaks consist of an outer layer of horny material covering soft tissue which extends along the length of the beak and is well supplied with blood and nerve fibers, that some of these fibers are of the type generally concerned with the perception of pain in humans, and that these pain receptors are highly active after debeaking adds weight to the common sense concern already aroused by what we observe during the process (that the cut beaks bleed, and that the chickens struggle and squawk).[11]

Rosemary Rodd helpfully contrasts the debeaking of a chicken with the shoeing of a horse.[12] Although the horse may at first be frightened by the noise and smell of the shoeing, it shortly calms down and stands quietly while the shoeing process continues. But in addition to the lack of behavioral indications of pain, the hoof itself, unlike the beak, is made of a tough, solid material devoid of nerve fibers. So the horse, we reasonably conclude, experiences no pain when shoed, unlike the chicken when it is debeaked.

Many, including critics of animal consciousness, judge that the most powerful consideration on behalf of animal consciousness is the argument from evolutionary theory. If we grant that both humans and existing animals developed by a process of gradual change from previously existing forms, and, consequently, if we reject a special creation of each individual species as an immutable life-form, then we have reason to believe that there is no radical discontinuity between humans and all other animals.[13] And certainly if only humans were experiencing centers of consciousness, all other animals lacking an inner subjective life of any kind, then just such a radical discontinuity would exist. If evolution has occurred, then it seems likely that human characteristics have evolved from more rudimentary characteristics found in our nonhuman ancestors and thus found elsewhere in nature. Because it is likely, based on evolutionary theory, that human consciousness has evolved from animal consciousness, it is also likely that animal species closely related to Homo sapiens would have conscious experiences similar to, if not identical with, consciousness.

11. Rodd, *Biology, Ethics, and Animals,* p. 62.

12. Rodd, *Biology, Ethics, and Animals,* pp. 49-50.

13. If one accepts a special creation of each individual species, then it is at least possible that only humans have been endued with consciousness. Of course, a proponent of special creation need not deny that animals have minds and are conscious, and may very well judge that there are good reasons for believing just that, but obviously an appeal to evolutionary theory will not be one of them.

Bernard Rollin states the evolutionary argument as follows:

> In so far as humans represent a step in the evolution of life, they share with other creatures enzymes, proteins, functions, and structures. It would be evolutionarily odd if consciousness had emerged solely in humans, especially in light of the presence in other creatures of brains, nervous systems, sense organs, learning, pain behavior, problem-solving, and so on. Continuity and small variation constitute the rule of living things. If someone wishes to violate the principle of continuity and assert quantum jumps between animals while remaining a proponent of evolution the burden of proof is on him.[14]

That is, one would have to give an evolutionary reason why consciousness has evolved only in humans.

A final argument on behalf of animal consciousness is the argument from explanatory adequacy. Indeed, one reason why we attribute conscious mental states to animals is that it helps us make sense of their behavior; it is a strategy for understanding their behavior and it is a strategy that appears to work. As Bernard Rollin convincingly puts matters:

> By assuming that animals feel and have other subjective experience we can explain and predict their behavior (and control it as well). Why beat a dog if it doesn't hurt him? Why does a lion hunt if it isn't hungry? Why does a dog drool and beg for scraps from the table if they don't taste good? Why does a cat in heat rub up against the furniture if it doesn't feel good? Why do animals scratch if they don't itch?[15]

It is true that skeptical scientists (e.g., strict behaviorists) often stress that the mental experiences of animals and humans cannot be directly experienced and stress that because we cannot directly verify the inner mental life of animals we do better to simply abandon such talk. But, again, Bernard Rollin has commented, "There is no principle between postulating quarks, genes, quanta, and black holes, and postulating mental states. None of these are directly observable . . . why should we make such commitments? Because they provide the best explanation; they allow us to understand, predict, and explain features of the world which we couldn't otherwise deal with."[16]

14. Rollin, *The Unheeded Cry*, p. 32.
15. Rollin, *The Unheeded Cry*, p. 163.
16. Rollin, *The Unheeded Cry*, pp. 196-97.

THE APE-LANGUAGE PROJECTS

A second area, besides consciousness, that has been explored in an effort to determine the nature of animals relative to humans is language. Many have thought that an important difference between humans and animals is the linguistic ability possessed by humans. It is this divide, it is claimed, that accounts for all the significant differences that exist between humans and animals. But the claim that language is the unique possession of humans has itself been challenged. For after all, have not apes been taught to use language?

The 1970s was *the* decade of ape-language projects. These were attempts to teach language, in some form or other, to apes, in particular to chimpanzees, which are widely regarded as the most intelligent of the apes. Washoe and Koko became household names (and to a lesser degree Sara and Lana as well): being the object of considerable media attention, they were written about, appeared on the cover of magazines, and were the subjects of television documentaries.[17] But this excitement and interest was not restricted to the general public. Anthropologist Jane Hill spoke for many (though not all) in the scientific community when she said, "It is unlikely that any of us will in our lifetime see again a scientific breakthrough as profound in its implications as the moment when Washoe . . . raised her hand and signed 'come-gimme' to a comprehending human."[18]

If the attempt to teach language to apes is judged to be successful, then there has been realized what the eighteenth-century French materialist philosopher and physician, La Mettrie (1709-1751), had said was possible when he declared, "I have little doubt that if this animal were properly trained he might at last be taught to pronounce, and consequently to know, a language. Then he would no longer be a wild man, nor a defective man, but he would be a perfect little gentleman. . . ."[19] The challenge, as La Mettrie saw it, was one of getting the ape to pronounce; he believed that

17. I refer, as others have, to the 1970s as the decade of the ape-language projects because it was primarily during this period that results, in some cases from projects started earlier (pride of place goes to the Gardners who began their work in 1967), were disclosed. Projects of this kind proliferated, and enthusiasm was high, both among professionals and the general public. With time, criticism has mounted and interest waned, though ape-language projects continue.

18. Jane Hill, "Apes and Language," in *Speaking of Apes,* ed. Thomas A. Sebeok and Jean Umiker-Sebeok (New York: Plenum, 1980), p. 351.

19. La Mettrie, *Man a Machine* (Chicago: Open Court, 1927), p. 22.

this could be done and had no doubt that the "machine" that constituted the brain of an ape would be up to the task of using language once the ability to utter the appropriate range of sounds was acquired. But that, of course, turned out to be the rub: the ape lacked the appropriate speech organ and therefore one could only speculate as to what would be the case if the ape could articulate sounds as human beings do.[20]

What La Mettrie had said was possible for apes contradicted the thought of influential men like René Descartes (1596-1650), the father of the modern rationalist tradition with its strong emphasis on the uniqueness of the human species — a uniqueness grounded in a rational capacity supposedly possessed by humans alone. Descartes, for one, would not have been impressed by La Mettrie's contention that if we could only get the ape to pronounce, we would then be able to get the ape to speak. Descartes had argued that "men who, being born deaf and dumb, are in the same degree, or even more than brutes, destitute of the organs which serve the others for talking, are in the habit of themselves inventing certain signs by which they make themselves understood."[21] Thus, one need not be able to voice sounds in order to acquire language. One can use hand signs as a linguistic medium, something that deaf and dumb humans have done but that nonhuman animals, including apes, have not. In essence, Descartes argued that if apes, who are destitute of speech organs, actually had the capacity to acquire a language they would have manifested this in the form of sign language.

Possibly, however, the apes needed some human assistance — just what Allen and Beatrice Gardner of the University of Nevada at Reno (and later Roger Fouts of the University of Oklahoma, a student of the Gardners) sought to provide when they introduced Washoe, a young chimpanzee, to American Sign Language (ASL). ASL is a genuine language, with

20. There have been some serious attempts to assist apes to vocalize spoken English. After considerable effort, Keith Hayes and Catherine Nissen taught the chimpanzee Viki to utter a few English words, e.g., "mamma," "papa," "cup." See K. Hayes and C. Nissen, "Higher Mental Functions of a Home-Raised Chimpanzee," in *Behavior of Nonhuman Primates,* vol. 4, ed. A. M. Schriver and F. Stollnitz (New York: Academic Press, 1971). Viki frequently would use her fingers to hold her lips in the right position to vocalize in the required manner, indicating that she was not being limited by intelligence — apparently she knew what was wanted of her — but by the lack of physical control necessary to make the appropriate sounds. Keith Laidler had a bit more success with an orangutan in a similar project but the vocal limitations again proved an impediment to seriously testing La Mettrie's claim. See Laidler, *The Talking Ape* (Glasgow: Collins, 1980).

21. Descartes, "Discourse on Method," in *The Philosophical Works of Descartes,* trans. E. S. Haldane and G. R. T. Ross, vol. 1 (New York: Dover, 1955), p. 117.

rules of grammar and syntax, translatable into other languages, widely used by the deaf (it is the fourth most used language in the United States), and an effective vehicle for the expression of complex thought.[22] And the Gardners were not the only researchers to make such attempts. David Premack of the University of Pennsylvania taught Sara, another female chimpanzee, to use plastic tokens of various shapes and colors that represented words (e.g., a triangular piece of blue plastic would stand for apple) and that could be manipulated for language use.[23] Duane Rumbaugh and Sue Savage-Rumbaugh of the Yerkes Primate Center at Emory University invented "Yerkish," a computer language in which console keys bore patterns that stood for words; they then sought to teach this language to Lana, still another female chimpanzee.[24] At Stanford University, Francine Patterson, a psychologist and doctoral student, worked with a female gorilla, Koko, whose accomplishments, in addition to ASL use, included using a typewriter speech synthesizer designed by Stanford philosopher and logician Patrick Suppes.[25]

In essence, these researchers, and others involved in ape-language projects, were attempting to demonstrate that what La Mettrie had said was possible was indeed possible. And just as La Mettrie had Descartes who argued that it was *not* possible for apes to learn a language, so these twentieth-century researchers had their Descartes in the person of Noam Chomsky. This distinguished and influential professor of linguistics at M.I.T. echoed Descartes's claim, arguing that human grammatical compe-

22. R. A. Gardner and B. T. Gardner, "Teaching Sign Language to a Chimpanzee," *Science* 165 (1969): 664-72; B. T. Gardner and R. A. Gardner, "Two-Way Communication with an Infant Chimpanzee," in *Behavior of Nonhuman Primates,* ed. Schriver and Stollnitz, pp. 117-84; R. S. Fouts, "Language: Origins, Definitions, and Chimpanzees," *Journal of Human Evolution* 3 (1974): 475-82.

23. D. Premack, *Intelligence in Ape and Man* (Hillsdale, N.J.: Erlbaum, 1976); D. Premack and A. J. Premack, *The Mind of An Ape* (New York: Norton, 1983); D. Premack, "On the Assessment of Language Competence in the Chimpanzee," in *Behavior of Nonhuman Primates,* ed. Schriver and Stollnitz, pp. 185-228.

24. D. M. Rumbaugh, *Language Learning by a Chimpanzee: The Lana Project* (New York: Academic Press, 1977); D. M. Rumbaugh and T. V. Gill, "Language and the Acquisition of Language-Type Skills by a Chimpanzee (Pan)," *Annals of the New York Academy of Sciences* 270 (1976): 90-123; D. M. Rumbaugh and T. V. Gill, "Mastery of Language-Type Skills by the Chimpanzee (Pan)," *Annals of the New York Academy of Sciences* 280 (1976): 562-78; D. M. Rumbaugh, T. V. Gill, and E. C. von Glaserfeld, "Reading and Sentence Completion by a Chimpanzee (Pan)," *Science* 182 (1973): 731-33.

25. F. Patterson, "Conversations with a Gorilla," *National Geographic* 154 (1978): 438-65; F. Patterson, "Ape Language," *Science* 211 (1981): 86-87; F. Patterson and E. Linden, *The Education of Koko* (New York: Holt, Rinehart and Winston, 1981).

tence was both innate and unique to the human species. In so arguing, Chomsky and other linguists of a similar persuasion were reacting to their empiricist colleagues who claimed that children were born with no special capacity for language but only with a general ability to learn, an ability that made possible the acquisition of a range of skills, including the use of language. If one viewed matters in this latter way, then granting what was apparent, that is the ability of chimpanzees and other apes to learn at a fairly sophisticated level, one might well expect that chimpanzees could acquire a language, or at least acquire language proportional to their intelligence. Chomsky disagreed: general intelligence and a general ability to learn were not sufficient to account for the acquisition of language. Rather, humans had a specific innate capacity for language, an inherited linguistic blueprint that was rooted in the structure of the human brain. Intelligence by itself was not a substitute for this.[26]

A range of considerations have been found persuasive by those who side with Chomsky. For example, consider the following line of argument set forth by linguist Ronald W. Langacker:

> We know a great deal about language, but despite centuries of serious investigation, we would be at a complete loss to describe exhaustively the structure of any language, even the most intensively studied. But this is essentially what the child does . . . masters the entire set of lexical items and structural principles that constitutes a linguistic system . . . does this on the basis of indirect and fragmentary evidence, and at an age when . . . not yet capable of logical, analytical thought. This remarkable phenomenon can be explained in terms of the rationalist view, but hardly in terms of the empiricist position. . . . With no inborn structural principles to guide him, the child could hardly be expected to discover the nature of the linguistic system that partially underlies the verbal activity of the people around him. He would have no basis even for suspecting the existence of this system. Furthermore, its abstractness and complexity puts it well beyond the possibility of being discovered by trial and error.[27]

26. For a brief summary of Chomsky's theory of language by Chomsky himself see the dictionary article "Language: Chomsky's Theory," in *The Oxford Companion to the Mind,* ed. Richard L. Gregory (New York: Oxford University Press, 1987), pp. 419-21; a statement of Chomsky's Cartesian vision of linguistics with an interesting historical discussion can be found in Noam Chomsky, *Cartesian Linguistics* (New York: Harper and Row, 1966).

27. Ronald W. Langacker, *Language and Its Structure,* second ed. (New York: Harcourt Brace Jovanovich, 1973), pp. 245-46.

Certainly, one cannot but be impressed with the spontaneous ease with which children acquire their initial language: they may lack specific instruction — no attentive parents constantly working with them on language drills — but they learn to talk as they are exposed to others who talk. And as they learn to talk they learn to do what groups of humans everywhere do — *without exception* — communicate by means of language, for all human communities are language communities. Indeed, by about the age of six, children will have mastered the basics of their native language and they will be "in possession of a linguistic system that specifies an unbounded class of sentences that [they] can draw upon in speaking and understanding." They have "the ability to comprehend, effortlessly and spontaneously, sentences that are completely novel to [their] experience."[28] To account for all this, Chomsky and others posit the existence of innate structures for learning language, not a structure for a particular language, say English or French, but for any language, and not a general ability to learn, but a particular capacity to learn language. The reason, then, that nonhuman animals do not possess language is not that they are "stupid," severely lacking in intelligence, but simply that they lack this innate structure.

The rationalistic or Neo-Cartesian linguistics exemplified by Noam Chomsky provided a part of the intellectual environment that existed at the time the ape-language projects were initiated. Chomsky's claim that language was possible only where there was an innate capacity for language and that this was an exclusively human capacity could be refuted very simply: by teaching a nonhuman to use language. To succeed at demonstrating the grammatical competence of apes would constitute a straightforward victory of the empiricists over the rationalists in the debate about language acquisition. But did these researchers in fact succeed? Looking back on these projects, Herbert Terrace, a Columbia University psychologist and a major critic, has commented, "There is considerable agreement that apes . . . are unable to master the basic features of language."[29] Daisie and Michael Radner, sympathetic though they are for claims on behalf of animal intelligence and consciousness, conclude, "With primate language research the more the data are examined the less impressive they are. It seems that you can lead an ape to words but you can't get it to 'speak as we do.'"[30] Though there have always been critics of

28. Langacker, *Language and Its Structure,* p. 239.

29. H. S. Terrace, "Animal Cognition: Thinking Without Language," in *Animal Intelligence,* ed. Laurence Weiskuentz (Oxford: Clarendon, 1985), p. 113.

30. Radner and Radner, *Animal Consciousness,* p. 160.

the ape-language projects, disenchantment has grown rather than lessened with the passage of time. More professionals have joined the number that say, if not that Chomsky's theory of language is correct, at least that he has not been shown to be wrong by the various ape-language projects.

At issue is not whether animals can communicate (there is a large and growing literature on animal communication) but whether they can communicate by means of language. Thus, I might smile and communicate to someone that they are welcome. Though I will have successfully communicated, I have not used language. Similarly an animal might warn others of his kin of the presence of predators by the making of an appropriate warning noise, but the noise, like my smile, doesn't constitute the use of language, if by language we mean (1) the use of words or signs understood by the user to be symbols and (2) the combination of these words or signs in novel ways to constitute phrases, clauses, and sentences in accord with rules of grammar (whether consciously understood or not). It is the claim by certain researchers to have taught apes language in this sense that is controversial, and although defenders of this claim have not been banished from the field, their position is increasingly under siege.

It must be admitted, however, that the kinds of reports that emerged from the ape-language projects were, taken at face value, impressive and even startling. Washoe learned 132 hand signs and was able to improvise by combining them in new ways. When she was shown a Brazil nut she is said to have signed "rock berry" and when she saw a swan gliding in the water signed "water bird."[31] Washoe would also request various kinds of food by signing. Lana also, apparently, had the ability to improvise; lacking a word for either a cucumber or an orange, she came up, respectively, with "green banana" and "the apple which is orange." Sara could answer questions such as "what is the color of . . . ?" and "what is the name of . . . ?" Roger Fouts in working with the chimpanzee Lucy had the following exchange, according to Eugene Linden:

31. The water-bird example has a certain fame because apparently it was often cited by the Gardners as an instance where Washoe joined two previously learned but unconnected signs into a new meaningful combination, thus demonstrating an understanding of these words and the ability to use them linguistically. Critics have suggested that what might have happened is as follows: Washoe saw the water and signed "water" as she had been trained, and then saw the bird and signed "bird" also as she had been trained, and therefore was not joining words into a novel combination. H. S. Terrace, L. A. Petitto, R. J. Sanders, and T. G. Beves, "Can an Ape Create a Sentence?" *Science* 206 (November 23, 1979): 895.

Roger signs "Roger" in saying, "Lucy tickle Roger."
Lucy signs "Roger . . . tickle . . . Lucy."
Roger signs "No" and repeats "Lucy . . . tickle . . . Roger."
Suddenly comprehending, Lucy leaps to tickle Roger.[32]

But it was the work of Francine Patterson and her reported results with the gorilla Koko that were the most startling of all.[33] Koko, who has a vocabulary of 375 words, was said to show "touching sympathy" toward other animals and upon seeing a horse with a bit in its mouth signed "Horse . . . sad." When she was asked why the horse was sad she replied by signing "Teeth." When she was shown a photograph of another gorilla struggling against taking a bath, Koko, who also hates baths, is reported by Patterson to have signed "Me Cry there" while pointing to the picture. Further, Patterson said of Koko, "I've come to cherish her lies, relish her arguments, and look forward to her insults." What kind of insults? Koko's invectives consisted of "You . . . dirty . . . bad . . . toilet." What kind of lies? On one occasion Koko broke a sink by sitting on it and when asked if it was she who had broken the sink, she replied, seeking (it is claimed) to falsely accuse Francine Patterson's assistant, "Kate . . . there . . . bad."

But all of this has come under severe criticism and that criticism (which has always been present in professional circles)[34] became accessible to the general public with the publication of psychologist Herbert Terrace's book *Nim*.[35] Terrace's work represents a watershed in attitudes toward the ape-language projects. In the words of linguist Derek Bickerton, "subsequent to Herbert Terrace's study of the chimpanzee Nim, it has been accepted by most researchers that apes cannot produce genuine sentences."[36] Terrace, at Columbia University, began a project of teaching

32. Eugene Linden, *Apes, Men and Language* (Harmondsworth: Penguin Books, 1976), pp. 100-102. Linden, for one, had no doubt about the success of the ape-language project: "Anyone can now talk to a chimp" (p. 199).

33. All the examples of Patterson's work with Koko are taken from her article "Conversations with a Gorilla," pp. 438ff.

34. Examples of such early critical evaluation include E. H. Lennberg, "Of Language, Knowledge, Apes and Brains," *Journal of Psychological Research* 1 (1971): 1-29; T. A. Sebeok, *Perspectives in Zoosemiotics* (The Hague: Moulton, 1972); G. Mounin, "Language, Communication, Chimpanzees," *Current Anthropology* 17 (1976): 1-7; and J. Lember, "Language in Child and Chimp?" *American Psychology* 32 (1977): 280-95.

35. H. S. Terrace, *Nim* (New York: Knopf, 1979).

36. Derek Bickerton, *Language and Species* (Chicago: University of Chicago Press, 1990), p. 198.

ASL to a male chimpanzee (named Nim Chimsky in parody of Noam Chomsky) and did so with the expectation that he would have much the same success as he thought his predecessors had had in their ape-language projects. Terrace anticipated that Nim would succeed in refuting Noam. At first, Terrace thought he had succeeded. But, after reviewing extensive videotapes of his work, he concluded that not only had he not been successful but neither had his predecessors. In summarizing his own work, which was the first to make a permanent video record of an ape-language project, Terrace says (after analyzing 20,000 individual instances of Nim using two or more signs in combination),

> Superficially, many of Nim's combinations appeared to be generated by simple finite-state grammatical rules (for example, more + X; transitive verb + me or Nim, etc.). However, a frame-by-frame analysis of video tapes of Nim's signing with his teachers revealed that Nim responded mainly to the urging of his teacher to sign and that much of what he signed was a full or partial utterance of his teacher's prior utterance. Thus, unlike a child at stage one of language acquisition . . . Nim's signing was mostly non-spontaneous and imitative.

Furthermore, Terrace goes on to observe, "Analysis of the available films of other signing apes revealed a similar pattern of non-spontaneous and imitative discourse. . . ."[37] The significance that Terrace attaches to cuing is not merely that the chimpanzee is copying the instructor but that the instructor assists in providing the grammatical order. Thus when Nim signs "Me . . . hug . . . cat" an analysis of the videotape shows the teacher signing "you" while Nim signs "me" and "who?" while Nim signs "cat." Here Nim is not cued to sign "cat" rather than "dog," for Nim selects that sign on his own, but he does gain assistance in ordering of the signs.[38] Even so, Nim did *not* have an impressive track record; for example, Nim signed "banana . . . eat . . . Nim" as often as "banana . . . Nim . . . eat."[39]

In sum, Terrace concluded that apes lack any understanding of grammatical word ordering. Rather, use of signs was more akin to the training of pigeons to peck colors in the appropriate order (say, red, green, yellow, and blue) to obtain food and do so even when the positions of the

37. Terrace, "Animal Cognition," in *Animal Intelligence,* ed. Weiskuentz, p. 115.

38. Terrace et al., "Can an Ape Create a Sentence?" p. 897.

39. Terrace et al., "Can an Ape Create a Sentence?" p. 893.

colors were rearranged.[40] Such rote learning and rote performance is not the acquisition of a linguistic skill nor is it the creation of a sentence. Indeed, Terrace comments rather scathingly, "It would be as erroneous to interpret a rote sequence of pecks to the colors, red, green, yellow, blue (in that order) as a sentence meaning Please Machine Give Grain as it would be to interpret the sequence that a person produces while operating a cash machine as a sentence Please Machine Give Cash."[41] Or, as John Heil has argued: a dog that formerly simply whined for food when hungry but is trained to ring five bells in a certain order for a particular kind of food and then in a different order for yet another kind of food, certainly has had its "repertoire of responses" increased considerably, but it is perplexing how this in any way elevates the behavior above its normal whining.[42] Instead of bells rung by a dog, we may have hand-signs made by chimpanzees, but we should not be misled into thinking that "because a certain activity is part of a linguistic repertoire of a language-user, any creative engaging in that activity is thereby using language."[43]

In contrast to apes, young children of three or four years of age are clearly guided by the *meaning* of various grammatical rules; they are not merely mimicking what they hear nor making a trained rote response. This can be seen by the fact that, as pointed out by Stephen Walker, a psychologist at the University of London, children "deduce rules, and are thus led into errors such as 'mans' and 'mouses' and 'falled' and 'comed.'"[44] These errors (and others) are significant because they show that the child is neither mimicking nor making a trained rote response because "mans," "mouses," "falled," and "comed" would not be something the child would ever hear and therefore mimic nor something the child would be trained to repeat by rote. Clearly, the child understands grammatical rules and is following them, and although the understanding may be faulty or incomplete, nevertheless there is the understanding of a rule. That is to say, the child is not merely acting (or speaking) *in accord with* a rule but is actually *following a rule,* and this is a significant difference. Thus a computer may be programmed to function in accord with a rule but it does not thereby follow a rule in the sense that humans fol-

40. R. O. Straub and H. S. Terrace, "Generalization of Serial Learning in the Pigeon," *Animal Learning and Behavior* 9 (1981): 454-68.

41. Terrace, "Animal Cognition," in *Animal Intelligence,* ed. Weiskuentz, p. 116.

42. John Heil, "Speechless Brutes," *Philosophy and Phenomenological Research* XLII, no. 3 (March 1982): 402-3.

43. Heil, "Speechless Brutes," p. 400.

44. Walker, *Animal Thought,* p. 376.

low rules. To follow a rule one's understanding of the rule must play a causal role in what one does or says: I order or frame words the way I do *because* I understand certain rules the way I do. In contrast I could be trained to make certain rote responses in Arabic, a language I do not know, and my responses may well be *in accord* with certain grammatical rules of Arabic, but I would not, because of that fact, be said to be following rules in the sense that my understanding of the meaning of the rule determined the ordered character of my Arabic response. Thus, what is being contested by critics is not only the minimal claim that apes make gestural signs in accord with grammatical rules (which itself may be questionable) but that they *follow* grammatical rules, something that a language user does do.

Despite these difficulties and criticisms, work with ape-language projects continues. But if the sizable number of skeptics is to be convinced that the semantic and syntactic hurdles have been cleared by the undeniably intelligent ape, more impressive evidence will have to be forthcoming. It is reasonable to conclude, then, that it has yet to be *demonstrated* that animals possess linguistic competence: the ape-language projects have not proved sufficiently impressive (to date) to convince a critical mass of professional opinion among psychologists, ethologists, linguists, anthropologists, and philosophers. And even had the ape-language projects been successful, or should they prove successful in the future, that would still leave the vast bulk of the animal world outside the circle of actual language users, and therefore to attach too much importance to the possession of language would certainly have undesirable implications for those who wish to elevate the moral standing of animals. Indeed as Tom Regan puts it, "As for cats and dogs, chickens and hogs, llamas and tigers, for example, since they give no evidence of being able to master the use of a relevant language, they would remain . . . in the category of 'thoughtless brutes.'"[45] And if to be a "thoughtless brute" is to be morally inconsequential, then this would hardly have implications that an animal rights activist and theoretician such as Regan would find congenial. Moreover, matters might even be worse than Regan himself suggests, for if it is the *actual possession* of language that crucially moves one out of the category of "thoughtless brute" and not merely the *potential* for language, then even the vast bulk of apes, those that have not been recipients of the kind of attentive and prolonged instruction given to the likes of Washoe, Koko,

45. Tom Regan, *The Case for Animal Rights* (Berkeley: University of California Press, 1983), p. 15.

Sara, and Lana, whatever their potential, must also be viewed as "thoughtless brutes."[46]

But the advocates of full moral standing for animals, at least the central players on the academic scene, have not pressed the case for the ape-language projects or sought to score moral points by an appeal to those projects. Some, indeed, are quite skeptical. Tom Regan expresses appreciation for the work of Herbert Terrace, the main critic of these projects, and warns against prematurely attributing significant linguistic abilities to nonhumans.[47] James Rachels, who denies that humans are special, nevertheless agrees with the criticisms that have been leveled at the ape-language projects; indeed, Rachels calls them "impressive."[48] Steve Sapontzis in carefully articulating his case for liberating animals does not even refer to the ape-language projects[49] nor does Andrew Linzey in his attempt to make a theological case for animal rights.[50] Other serious advocates of full moral concern for animals have been more positive in their assessment of the ape-language projects, though, in part, this may be due to the earlier publication of their work during a time when enthusiasm for these projects ran high. Thus Peter Singer speaks of their "striking success,"[51] while Bernard Rollin refers to this "remarkable research" and judges that it "supports the claim that no hard and fast line can be drawn between human reason, thought, and sign apparatuses and that of animals."[52] Mary Midgley seems to view the ape-language projects as having succeeded in their goals,[53] but has wisely observed, "what follows if

46. Rosemary Rodd has suggested that one way to view the ape-language projects, should we view them as successful (though she herself is skeptical of their actual success), is that "the signing apes have to some extent been transformed into a semi-human mental condition" (*Biology, Ethics, and Animals,* p. 88). But, of course, the potential for transformation is not itself transformation, and therefore those apes who have not received language instruction will not have been transformed into this semi-human mental condition.

47. Regan, *The Case for Animal Rights,* p. 14.

48. James Rachels, *Created from Animals: The Moral Implications of Darwinism* (New York: Oxford University Press, 1990), p. 139.

49. Steve Sapontzis, *Morals, Reason and Animals* (Philadelphia: Temple University Press, 1987).

50. Andrew Linzey, *Christianity and the Rights of Animals* (New York: Crossroad, 1987).

51. Peter Singer, *Practical Ethics* (Cambridge: Cambridge University Press, 1979), p. 94.

52. Bernard Rollin, *Animals Rights and Human Morality* (Buffalo: Prometheus Books, 1981), p. 27.

53. Mary Midgley, *Animals and Why They Matter* (Athens, Ga.: University of Georgia Press, 1983), p. 61. Midgley also recommends to her readers for an overview of the ape lan-

chimps can, in some sense, talk? Why does it matter so much? There is something most fishy about the idea that big questions could hang on the results of these experiments alone. The experiments matter only if they bring to our notice an important and pervasive fact about the world. If they do, there must be other evidence for it."[54] Midgley, in fact, believes there is other evidence for it and that we have good reason for attributing to animals a complex mental life. To a person, the other animal advocates agree with her. And certainly we should be cautious about concluding that *lack* of language reflects badly on the general intelligence level of animals, since, if Chomksy is correct, it is not the lack of general intelligence that accounts for the inability of animals to acquire a language but the lack of a species-specific capacity for language rooted in the structure of the animal's brain.

Whether or not they judge the ape-language projects to have been successful, animal advocates universally reject a language test for moral standing, arguing that creatures can be rational, have beliefs and desires, control their behavior in accord with those beliefs and desires, be both conscious and self-conscious, have interests, and generally fully satisfy all requirements for full moral consideration (which may include a right to life), and do so despite their lack of language. This does mean that they are in conflict with some very powerful voices in the philosophical world who have argued that, in fact, a great deal hinges on whether or not a creature is in possession of a language, that many of the crucial features that animal advocates wish to attribute to animals cannot sensibly be attributed to languageless creatures. It also means that they are at odds with many in the scientific community, both psychologists and ethologists, who are skeptical about the conscious experience of animals. Despite the fact that there are highly respected philosophers and scientists who are supportive of the claim that animals have complex conscious mental lives without the presence of language, there are clearly problems connected with this claim.

---

guage controversy a rather enthusiastically uncritical book by Eugene Linden, *Apes, Men and Language*.

54. Mary Midgley, *Beast and Man: The Roots of Human Nature* (Ithaca, N.Y.: Cornell University Press, 1978).

LANGUAGE AND THE MENTAL LIFE OF ANIMALS

One of the difficulties in attributing to animals a wide range of mental states is the uncertainty over how exactly to characterize those mental states. Lacking a language, they cannot characterize them for us, and we are then left to conjecture about their exact character. If we attribute beliefs, for example, to animals, how should we characterize those beliefs? Thus, a dog chases a cat up a tree and then barks at the cat while anxiously circling the tree. Quite naturally, many of us will say, "The dog believes the cat is up the tree." But does the dog have a rich enough conceptual reservoir to have this belief? Can the dog conceptually distinguish, for example, a tree from a telephone pole? Does it understand that trees are living and that they grow? That they are, more simply, tallish, solid entities? And what does the dog believe about cats? Does it believe that they are four-legged, furry, and fast? It does seem unclear how we should answer these questions. Thus, we are inclined to attribute beliefs to animals but uncertain how to characterize those beliefs.

The influential American philosopher Donald Davidson is confident enough to conclude that animals lack a rich enough conceptual network essential for something to count as a belief about trees and cats. He argues: "There is no fixed list of things someone with the concept of tree must believe, but without many (such) beliefs, there would be no reason to identify a belief as a belief about a tree, much less an oak tree. Similar considerations apply to the dog's supposed thinking about the cat."[55] But perhaps Davidson is overconfident in concluding that the dog's conceptual network is so impoverished that it cannot possibly possess beliefs about cats and trees. For we can argue, as George Graham does, that the same belief can be held in "varying ways or different degrees."[56] Thus, to use Graham's example, I might believe that Horowitz was a better pianist than Rubenstein, a belief I share with the musicologists in my music department. Their belief is embedded in a far richer and more sophisticated conceptual network than mine, which is decidedly more primitive by comparison. Similarly the dog's beliefs about cats and trees may be much more primitive than mine, yet it could still be the case that the dog and I share the belief that the cat is up the tree. And though we may be uncer-

55. Donald Davidson, "Rational Animals," in *Action and Events: Perspectives on the Philosophy of Donald Davidson,* ed. E. LePore and B. McLaughlin (Oxford: Basil Blackwell, 1985), p. xxx.

56. George Graham, *Philosophy of Mind: An Introduction* (Oxford: Blackwell, 1993), p. 69.

tain as to the precise nature of the dog's belief, our justification in attributing some such belief is found in the dog's behavior as it continues to circle that particular tree (all the while barking) rather than some other nearby tree. Why that particular tree? Because, the answer goes, the dog believes the cat is in that tree and not in a nearby one. The explanatory power of attributing this belief to the dog is what warrants its attribution.

Sometimes it is argued that animals lack beliefs because, lacking linguistic competence, they cannot form sentences. And why are sentences necessary for beliefs? Because to have a belief, it is argued, is to believe that a certain sentence is true, namely, in the case at hand, to believe that the sentence "The cat is up that tree" is true. It is sentences, then, that are true or false, and to have a belief that something is true (or is the case) is to believe that a certain sentence is true. So, if in order to have beliefs one must be able to form sentences, and if in order to form sentences one must possess a language, then, granting a lack of language on the part of an animal, it follows that animals lack beliefs.[57]

But such an argument is not free of serious objections. First, it does not seem to be true in our own case that when we believe something to be so that we are forming a sentence to ourselves and affirming the truth of that sentence. I may believe I'm now in pain, that the sunset I am witnessing is beautiful, that I am now reading (or writing), without, in any of these instances, consciously formulating any corresponding sentence to myself: "I'm in pain" or "The sunset is beautiful" or "I am now reading." Indeed, it rather seems that we sometimes use language to express such beliefs, not that language creates or constitutes the belief. Indeed, we have all had the experience of searching for words to give adequate expression to our beliefs. We have even had the experience of forgetting a very ordinary and often-used word that has temporarily escaped us. Here we may vainly struggle to give expression to what we are thinking or to what we want to say. All this suggests that beliefs can be present though sentences have not yet been formed.

Second, as Lawrence Johnson has noted, if beliefs require linguistic competence, then in the evolution of language, there would have been no beliefs prior to the acquisition of language, but that seems most peculiar. "That there was a sudden leap into language is quite absurd. For that to have happened some cave person (or whatever) must have first started using noises or gestures linguistically. This would have been an amazing ac-

57. See R. G. Frey, *Interests and Rights: The Case Against Animals* (Oxford: Clarendon, 1980), p. 87.

complishment, particularly for a being without beliefs or desires."[58] Indeed without beliefs or ideas to communicate, how would language as a medium to communicate ideas ever emerge? Or, in the case of beginning to teach children to speak and understand a language, we point to certain objects and name them. Thus we point to a certain bouncy, round object and say "ball." Central to this is the child's believing that we are referring to the bouncy, round object when we say "ball." That is, the child must have a pre-linguistic belief (about what is being referred to) in order to acquire the meaning of words. That is, to acquire language one must have beliefs.[59] But if humans must have beliefs prior to possessing language competency then it is possible for animals to have them too. So, to acknowledge, rightly, that animals are not language-users does not force the conclusion that animals lack a range of mental states, including beliefs. We may still wonder, though, how extensive those mental states are.

ANIMAL MINDS

That animals have an inner life that can go better or worse for them, that animals are conscious and can experience pleasure and pain, seems to be among the more confident claims that we can make about the mental lives of animals. Maybe, in the final analysis, that is sufficient for our purposes. For this gives us a reason for not being cruel or abusive to animals (i.e., because it causes animals unnecessary pain) and a reason for respecting the lives of animals (i.e., because to kill may be to cut short an existence that is on the whole pleasurable and satisfying to the animal). Though this may be all we need to generate a satisfactory moral concern for animals, certainly a more varied and interesting mental life than this has been attributed to animals. No doubt most of us are inclined to believe that such a richer mental life is characteristic of dolphins, whales, and chimpanzees. It has been argued (by Darwin, no less) that animals can experience anxiety, grief, dejection, despair, joy, love, tender feelings, devotion, ill-temper, sulkiness, determination, hatred, anger, disdain, contempt, disgust, guilt, pride, helplessness, patience, surprise, astonishment, fear, horror, shame, shyness, and modesty — though even James Rachels, who lists these claims and is sympathetic to them, admits that

58. Lawrence Johnson, *A Morally Deep World: An Essay on Moral Significance and Environmental Ethics* (Cambridge: Cambridge University Press, 1991), p. 8.

59. This argument is found in Regan, *The Case for Animal Rights,* p. 45.

Darwin attributed to animals rather complex mental states on what amounted to rather slender grounds.[60] And, indeed, it is right here that matters become more controversial and less certain.

Donald Griffin, formerly Director for the Institute for Research in Animal Behavior and Harvard professor of biology, has argued for extensive conscious thinking on the part of animals. He bases this conclusion on a confluence of the following considerations:

(1) Versatile adaptability of behavior to novel challenges;
(2) Physiological signals from the brain that may be corrected with conscious thinking;
(3) Most promising of all, data concerning communicative behavior by which animals sometimes appear to convey to others at least some of their thoughts.[61]

Examples from Griffin of adaptive behavior include the account of a green-backed heron in a city park in Japan that finds a twig, breaks it into small pieces, and carries one of them to a nearby pond where she drops it into the water. She watches the drifting piece of twig intently and brings it back after it has drifted a certain distance. She repeats this until small minnows swim up to the floating twig, then she uses her long sharp bill to devour her prey. It is tempting to interpret this in terms of the heron experiencing hunger, wanting to eat, and believing that dropping twigs in the water will attract what she likes to eat.[62] Or, equally impressive, chimpanzees break off a slender twig from a tree, carry it some distance to a termite mound where they insert the twig into the mound, withdrawing it with termites clinging to it. The termites are then eaten.[63] Or think of the many cases of predators cooperating in their hunt for prey. Thus, the lioness will drive prey toward a pride member waiting in a concealed position.[64] Are these behaviors the product of conscious thought? Yes, suggests Griffin. These are not automatic behaviors, the product of inflexible instinct, hard-wired like a computer. Rather, they indicate conscious thought, much like the

60. Rachels, *Created from Animals,* p. 175. The list of mental states that Darwin attributes to animals is extracted from Darwin's *The Expression of the Emotions in Man and Animals* (Chicago: University of Chicago Press, 1965).

61. Donald Griffin, *Animal Minds* (Chicago: University of Chicago Press, 1992).

62. Griffin, *Animal Minds,* p. 2.

63. Griffin, *Animal Minds,* p. 2.

64. Griffin, *Animal Minds,* p. 2.

thought that humans would engage in when solving comparable problems or cooperating in a similar way.

In arguing that communication is evidence of thinking, Griffin gives the example (among others) of the communication skills of vervet monkeys. The vervet monkey has distinct warning calls for eagles, pythons, and leopards. When the warning of an approaching eagle is given the vervets react one way, another way when the python warning is sounded, and yet another way in response to the leopard alarm. Each particular response maximizes the survival chances of the vervet in face of that particular predator. Now, one may wonder, is semantic information really being conveyed by these vocalized alarms? Possibly, upon hearing a particular alarm, the other vervets look at the alarm giver and are able to judge from it the direction from which the predator is coming, then they see for themselves the nature of the threat and react accordingly. But the use of recorded vervet alarm calls, where there would be no companion vervet to cue them, eliminated this possibility. The vervets continue to respond to the different alarms in the manner appropriate to each kind of predator.[65]

It is to just such intelligent and versatile behavior that appeal is made in support of the claim that animals possess a complex mental life. Questions do emerge about these claims, however, for the appeal to such behaviors may "prove" too much or at least "prove" more than seems sensible to many of us. It might establish, for example, that honeybees have a complicated conscious mental life. For, in Griffin's words, "The most significant example of versatile communication known in any animals other than our own species is the so-called 'dance-language' of honeybees."[66] Thus, the direction and location of sources of food is communicated from one honeybee to another by means of agitated dances. But if such behavior is evidence for a conscious mental life in which subjective thought is communicated from one animal to another, then there is evidence that even honeybees have conscious mental lives. Griffin is quite open to this, indeed argues for it.[67] No doubt for many, on the contrary, the conviction that insects are more akin to reflex automata is so strong that there will be an almost irresistibly strong tendency to view these dances by the honeybee as mere tropisms, that is, automatic responses that are not the product of conscious thought at all. (A tropism is a reflex

65. Griffin, *Animal Minds,* pp. 156-60.
66. Griffin, *Animal Minds,* p. 178.
67. Griffin, *Animal Minds,* p. 194.

action that, unlike a knee-jerk reflex, affects the whole body.) But if the communication of the location of food from one honeybee to another is not evidence for conscious, subjective thought, then why should the alarms of the vervet monkey be so understood?

All this suggests three interpretive possibilities. First, all behaviors described by Griffin are to be understood as blind mechanical behaviors on the part of the animal. Second, all these behaviors (whether those of vervet monkeys or honeybees) are expressions of subjective, conscious thought. Third, some of the behaviors described are expressions of subjective, conscious thought but others are not, being mere tropisms. In regard to the latter possibility, it would be argued that where there is a display of highly adaptive behavior in novel situations there we have the best case for there being something more than the hard-wired response associated with bare mechanical instinct. In contrast, where the behavior is repetitive and does not adapt to new changes and changing circumstance, the behavior is perhaps best understood in terms of mechanical reflex.

SELF-CONSCIOUSNESS

It is often claimed that what distinguishes humans from animals is the fact that humans are self-conscious and animals are not. That is, whereas animals might be consciously aware of the world around them and even think about objects and events not present to the senses, they are not aware that these are their own thoughts. Thus, the dog may believe the cat is up the tree, but it does not also believe that it believes the cat is up the tree. This means, if true, that animals do not engage in reflexive thinking about their own thoughts. Animals would not have, then, second-order thoughts, beliefs, and desires. They would not be able to think about their own thoughts, desires, or beliefs. This is certainly not an unconsequential ability. It is central to engaging in an important kind of moral and spiritual self-criticism and growth. But its importance should not be overestimated either, for as Daisie and Michael Radner have commented, "Relatively little of one's own mental activity consists of reflecting upon one's own thoughts or upon the fact that it is oneself who is having them."[68]

It has, however, been argued that self-consciousness is necessary for consciousness. On such an assumption, to deny that animals are self-conscious would be to deny that they are conscious. David Rosenthal con-

68. Radner and Radner, *Animal Consciousness,* p. 30.

tends that mental states become conscious mental states only by becoming the object of a second-order thought.[69] It is thus denied that all mental states are conscious, and it is asserted that mental states become conscious only when one also has the thought that one is in that mental state. So those thoughts that are not the object of thought are not themselves conscious.

None of this, however, strikes me as a serious problem for the claim that animals are conscious. For one could grant Rosenthal's claim that consciousness requires self-consciousness but conclude that because it is reasonable to believe that animals are conscious, it is also reasonable to believe that animals are self-conscious. This is the conclusion that Rosenthal himself reaches.[70] But one might also espouse an alternative view of consciousness, arguing that thoughts are intrinsically self-referential, that is, their conscious character is not dependent upon some second-order mental state. This would mean that thoughts about thoughts are not required for conscious thought. As I reflect on my own thought life, such an analysis appears to be the case.

Of course, it is an empirical question whether or not animals are self-conscious. This is not something that can be decided from a philosopher's armchair. And there is data that suggests self-awareness in animals, even if it does not amount to proof. Thus, animals' self-concealment suggests self-awareness, as they seek to hide themselves from predators or prey. For example, the lion with low-slung stealth will move through the grass toward its zebra prey, "freezing" when the zebra's gaze seems to be directed its way. Also of interest is the reported tactic of grizzly bears who stake out locations from which they can observe human intruders without themselves being observed.[71] Then, as Bernard Rollin points out, "Why not simply take the fact that animals perceive or are able to recognize dangers and threats to themselves as evidence of self-awareness?"[72]

SUMMARY

In this chapter we explored and defended the claim that many species of animals are conscious, that they have an inner subjective life that can go

69. David M. Rosenthal, "Two Concepts of Consciousness," *Philosophical Studies* 49 (1986): 329-59.

70. Rosenthal, "Two Concepts of Consciousness," p. 350.

71. Griffin, *Animal Minds*, p. 249.

72. Rollin, *The Unheeded Cry*, p. 263.

better or worse for them. We examined historical reasons why consciousness in general is suspect in academic circles, for both humans and animals. We indicated why this suspicion has had a negative impact on our treatment of animals. We conceded that our widely shared conviction, for example, that dogs feel pain, cats see mice, and horses experience hunger is not primarily the product of theoretical argument but of a natural and virtually irresistible conviction that emerges in us as we encounter animals acting in ways that we take to be signs of consciousness. Nevertheless, we presented four arguments in support of the claim that animals are conscious.

Next, we looked at the ape-language projects, concerted attempts to teach language, in some form, to apes. We saw that there was some reason to be suspicious of the claim that these projects were successful. We also saw that animal advocates have not uniformly defended the success of these projects but have uniformly rejected a language test for moral standing, arguing that even without language animals can be rational, highly intelligent, have beliefs and desires, and control their behavior in accord with those beliefs and desires.

The most confident claim we can make about the mental life of animals is that they are conscious and experience pleasure and pain. But a more varied and interesting mental life may be attributed to animals based on intelligent and versatile behavior. This would include beliefs, desires, and means-end reasoning. Self-consciousness was given special attention in this chapter, and considerations that support animal self-awareness were mentioned. Finally, it was argued that discussions centering around the nature and relationship between consciousness and self-consciousness do not seriously threaten the claim that animals are conscious and have a rich and varied mental life.

CHAPTER 5

Animals and the World of Moral Theory

INTRODUCTION

A discussion of the morally appropriate treatment of animals cannot even get off the ground until we decide whether or not animals (or at least some animals) are members of the moral community. That is, do animals have moral standing? Should we conclude that they do and that therefore it is wrong to inflict pain on an animal or to kill an animal without a justifying reason, only then can we get on with the business of determining what those justifying reasons are. We may not all agree, but because we believe that animals count morally, we would at least judge that there is something genuinely at stake here, something worth exploring. Should we conclude, on the contrary, that only humans are members of the moral community, then this discussion need proceed no further and our energies can be more fruitfully directed elsewhere.

To say that an individual has "moral standing" is to say that the individual is an appropriate and a required object of "moral concern" for its own sake. Conversely, if an individual lacks moral standing, then it would *not* be an appropriate object of moral concern for its own sake. Rocks, for example, are not proper objects of moral concern for their own sakes. Crucially, what constitutes moral concern depends on the moral theory that one happens to hold. Thus, for those who believe that rights are morally basic, moral concern will take the form of respecting the individual's rights. If one is a rule-theorist, on the other hand, moral concern will take the form of applying the relevant moral rule to the individual. If one is a virtue-theorist, then moral concern will take the form of embracing the individual with one or more of the virtues (e.g., love, compassion, kindness). If one is a moral pluralist – seeing rights, rules, and virtues as *all* relevant expressions of moral concern, depending on the context – then there are multiple forms that moral concern might take. To say, on the contrary, that certain individuals *lack* moral standing would be to say that they are not legitimate objects of moral concern in *any* of these ways. It is not merely to say that they lack rights, but it is also to say that no moral rules apply to them for their own sake, and that they are not to be objects of compassion or kindness for their own sake.

I think that there is, in fact, a widespread conviction that it is possible for humans to be guilty of mistreating animals, that we can act in such a way toward an animal that what we do to it is morally wrong. It is not believed, in other words, that we can do just anything we please with an animal and act morally. It would be wrong, for example, to douse a living, fully conscious dog with kerosene and then ignite the animal, turning it into a flaming torch. Despite widespread belief that this would be wrong, there is not widespread agreement as to why it would be wrong. Indeed, some would argue that it is wrong even though animals themselves don't have moral standing.

The concerns of this chapter and the next are important for several reasons. First, getting clear on *why* it is wrong to inflict pain and suffering on animals in circumstances where we all agree it is wrong (e.g., brutalizing an animal for fun) may give us some help in clarifying our thinking about those more controversial circumstances where we do not yet agree. Second, it is a challenge to see if we can provide a theoretical moral framework for a direct moral concern for animals, something more than just trusting our intuition that such moral concern is required. Finally, it is of interest simply to explore the world of moral theory and to see how various moral theories connect with animals. In some circles, for a moral theory to be unable to give moral standing to animals is a deficiency of sufficient gravity that the theory will either have to be qualified to accommodate animals or the theory itself will have to be rejected. This may be quite right.

DUTIES TO ANIMALS ARE ONLY DUTIES TO HUMANS: AQUINAS AND KANT

Albert Schweitzer has said, "Just as the housewife who has scrubbed the room is careful to see that the door is shut lest the dog should come in and ruin the finished job with its footprints, so European thinkers are on their guard lest animals should intrude into ethics."[1] Two such thinkers are Thomas Aquinas, widely regarded as the greatest Roman Catholic theologian, and Immanuel Kant, one of the giant figures in the history of philosophy. Both wish to keep the door shut to animals because each holds a moral theory that has no place for animals; yet being decent individuals, they do not want to be so insensitive as to be morally indifferent to the cruel and abusive treatment of animals. The trick for them is to morally condemn cruelty to animals without admitting direct moral obligations to animals. It can be done, they judge, by arguing that those who mistreat animals are likely to mistreat humans and that for that reason — and that reason alone — such mistreatment is wrong. Mistreating animals is not wrong taken by itself, but it is wrong derivatively or indirectly, wrong because of what it might prompt us to do to human beings.[2] Only humans have moral standing and mistreating animals, who lack such standing, is not wrong in and of itself but becomes wrong only at that point where it negatively affects those who do have moral standing. Since Aquinas and Kant hold that we do not have *any* direct moral obligations to animals but only to human beings (and, of course, to God), we are therefore forced to ground the wrongness of mistreating animals in some obligation that we do recognize. In this case, it is the obligation *not* to make ourselves the kind of persons who are prone to mistreat other humans, and the assumption is that abusers of animals are likely to become abusers of humans. As Kant puts it, if one "is not to stifle human feelings, he must practice kindness toward animals, for he who is cruel to animals becomes hard also in his treatment of men."[3]

For Aquinas and Kant, then, there are obligations that *concern* animals but no obligations *to* animals, only to humans. Consider a parallel case. My obligation not to burn down my neighbor's house concerns my neighbor's house but it is an obligation to my neighbor not to destroy her

1. Quoted in Karl Barth, *Church Dogmatics,* vol. 3, *The Doctrine of Creation,* part 4 (Edinburgh: T&T Clark, 1961), p. 349.

2. Immanuel Kant, *Lectures on Ethics: Duties Toward Animals and Other Spirits,* trans. Louis Infield (New York: Harper and Row, 1963), pp. 239-41. The interpretation that I am giving to Kant is the prevailing interpretation and the one that is of interest for our purposes. What we wish to do is explore a line of argument that denies to animals moral standing — in other words, denies obligations to animals for their own sake. The prevailing interpretation of Kant provides us with that line of argument. For a somewhat different slant on Kant see Tim Hayward, "Kant and Moral Considerability of Non-Rational Beings," in *Philosophy and the Natural Environment,* ed. Robin Attfield and Andrew Belsey, Royal Institute of Philosophy Supplement 36 (Cambridge: Cambridge University Press, 1994), pp. 129-42.

3. Kant, *Lectures on Ethics,* p. 240.

property. It is not an obligation to the house at all. As with houses, so with animals: I have an obligation that *concerns* animals (not to abuse them), but that is an obligation that I have *to* humans (not to become the sort of individual prone to mistreat humans or to be indifferent to their suffering). So Aquinas and Kant would both concur that brutalizing animals is wrong and thus they would be part of the consensus that would condemn such acts. But for them, it is wrong only because of what it might prompt us to do to other human beings – to brutalize *them* or to become insensitive to *their* suffering.

What Aquinas and Kant ask us to believe, we should note at the very outset, is hard to believe. This is not to say that people don't believe it, because there are people who apparently do. Nevertheless, it should take very little reflection to bring us to the point where we see the serious difficulties attaching to such a view. We are asked to believe that the torture of an animal is wrong only because it might prompt us to mistreat or neglect humans; the animal's pain and suffering counts for nothing and by itself provides no reason whatsoever why we should refrain from our torture. According to such a view, beating a dog with a baseball bat is no more objectionable, taken by itself, than beating a rug. What makes beating dogs wrong is that it may lead to the abuse of humans, whereas beating rugs (apparently) does not and hence is not wrong. Of course, if the world were a different kind of place and beating rugs gave rise to beating wives or husbands or children or neighbors, then beating rugs would be wrong in all the ways that beating dogs is now supposedly wrong. In this sort of world, we would need to admonish people not to beat rugs and to pass laws prohibiting such behavior. But, in our world, it is the beating of dogs and not the beating of rugs that holds out the potential for human abuse, and therefore the beating of the one and not the other is wrong.

Despite it being wrong to beat dogs with baseball bats, it nevertheless remains the case on such a view that dogs and other sentient animals are in their own right no more worthy of consideration than rugs, since neither rugs nor dogs have moral standing. To be sure, when we beat the dog we cause it excruciating suffering, but, by itself, we are told, that provides no more reason for refraining from our act of beating than the fact that beating a rug causes the emission of dust. Neither the dust nor the pain are viewed by themselves as morally relevant considerations. This constitutes, it would seem, a moral absurdity, so that any theory that entails such a conclusion is on the face of it defective. Indeed, I would argue that we can be more confident that the infliction of gratuitous and excruciating suffering on an animal is wrong (taken by itself and apart from any bad consequences for humans) than we can be confident that some complex moral theory that tells us that animal pain counts for nothing is true.

Further, we may well ask: why is it that we tend to view the beating of dogs but not the beating of rugs as likely to spill over into the mistreatment of humans? Why is it that we sense a possible danger in the one instance but not in the other? Is it not because we perceive that beating dogs, unlike the beating of rugs, is itself cruel and wicked, and we fear that cruelty and wickedness in one area of life is likely to extend into other areas? Surely it is not that we view the beating of dogs to be morally innocuous (pain and all) and then surprisingly discover that it may give rise to what actually is wicked and cruel, namely, the beating of humans; rather, we sense that beating dogs is itself wicked and cruel, and understandably we fear that this cruelty might manifest itself in our relationships with human beings. Indeed, the person who is willing to inflict the evil of gratuitous pain on a dog may become all too willing to inflict a similar evil on humans. In recognizing this we seem to be recognizing that both what is done to the dog and what is done to the human are evils. Thus, I suggest, our very fear that beating dogs will give rise to mistreating humans is a recognition that beating dogs is itself an evil.

But will the abuse of animals in fact make us more likely to abuse humans, as Kant and Aquinas assume? This, of course, is a factual question, and I am not aware that we have any hard data that will enable us to conclusively settle the issue. It is possible (contrary to what Kant and Aquinas assume) that abusing animals will actually *reduce* the abuse of humans by serving as a release or outlet for aggression and hostility that otherwise would be directed toward humans (though I must confess to doubts). In this regard the philosopher John Passmore has commented,

> tyrants from Nero to Himmler have been notoriously devoted to animals. It is a matter of common observation, indeed, that kindness to animals is often substituted for kindness to human beings. Whether the inverse also holds, whether those who are cruel to animals are also cruel to human beings, it is more difficult to say. There is certainly no difficulty, at least, in conceiving a situation in which cruelty to man and cruelty to animals are completely dissociated. Kant would have us believe that under these circumstances there would be nothing wrong in cruelty to animals.[4]

4. John Passmore, "The Treatment of Animals," *Journal of the History of Ideas* 36 (1975): 203.

THE CLAIM THAT HUMANS DO NOT HAVE DUTIES TO ANIMALS

Aquinas's and Kant's conclusion that the abuse of animals is not *inherently* objectionable is based on arguments that purport to show that we do not have moral obligations or duties to animals to begin with. From this it follows that we do nothing wrong, we breach no duty, when, considered in isolation, we torture an animal. Aquinas and Kant have their reasons for denying that we have duties to animals and, whether we find those reasons convincing or not, many people initially will be sympathetic to this denial. They will be sympathetic, I surmise, because they find it odd to acknowledge obligations to rabbits, raccoons, squirrels, owls, and other animals. The very idea that humans can be morally beholden to subhuman animals seems to place animals on a level with humans, and many will feel unease over this. So, although there will be widespread concern over the conclusion that Aquinas and Kant reach – that torturing animals is not, by itself, morally objectionable – there will also be a measure of sympathy for the premise from which they derive their conclusion, namely, that humans have no obligations or duties to animals. So, "yes," many would assert, "it is wrong to torture animals because of the suffering it causes the animal," but "no," many of the same number would also be tempted to assert, "we have no duties to animals."

The philosopher Mary Midgley warns us against the temptation to reject talk of "duties" to animals. She observes, "In common speech to say that we have no duty to animals (or anyone else) means that it does not matter how we treat them. It absolves us. It would be awkward and pedantic to say 'this is just a verbal point – you are still bound to behave as you would if there was a duty.'"[5] Indeed, if the act of torturing an animal is inherently objectionable (contrary to Aquinas and Kant), then why be reluctant to speak of a duty to animals, a duty that can be violated should we seriously mistreat them? For what is the point of denying that we have any duties to animals if that denial does not mean what it is typically taken to mean, that we are morally free to behave in any way we please? The risk involved in such a denial is that we will place animals outside the arena of moral concern, viewing any kindness that we extend to them as flowing solely from our largesse, always optional rather than mandatory, never something we are duty-bound to do.

5. Mary Midgley, *Animals and Why They Matter* (Athens, Ga.: University of Georgia Press, 1983), p. 53.

DUTY: AN ANALYTICAL INTERLUDE

Despite a recognition of the danger inherent in denying duties to animals, talk of duties to animals may continue to strike some as awkward or odd. This may be so even for those who are sympathetic to the call for moral concern for animals. In some cases, the reason for this may be that we are operating with a restricted notion of duty, one that understands duties to be those requirements generated by institutional roles and positions. And certainly this is one way that the term "duty" can be understood. Consider in this regard the following dictionary definition of "duty": "obligatory tasks, conduct, service, or functions that arise from one's position."[6] Thus a professor, a judge, a physician, a captain of a ship, a lawyer, and so on all have a range of duties to those individuals they serve or for whom they have some special responsibility. A professor, for example, has the following duties (among others): to conduct class, hold office hours, give examinations, turn grades in to the registrar at the end of the term, and serve on college committees. Additionally, there are those duties generated by one's role as wife or husband, parent or child, citizen, etc. Thus parents have a duty to adequately provide for their children, citizens the duty to vote, and the list goes on. But all such positions and roles are part of human institutions that are concerned with behavior and relationships among members of the human community. It is not clear how animals could be a part of any of this.[7]

There are, in addition to such role-duties, those duties that are created by past acts on our part, whereby we assume or take upon ourselves a particular obligation. Thus we promise to do something, and that promise generates our duty to do what was promised. Sidney Zink has commented with regard to such duties, "We speak of a 'fulfillment' or 'violation' of obligation, meaning a kind of completion or failure to complete that which began with the past commitment or assumption of obligation."[8] So, a further reason why it might be felt strange to speak of obligations or duties to animals (duties being, according to Zink, obligations of a more serious kind) is that there are no social practices whereby we pledge ourselves to animals or make commitments to them, as we do with humans. There may be a partial exception to this in the case of pet-adop-

6. *Webster's New Collegiate Dictionary* (Springfield, Mass.: G. & G. Merriam Company, 1974).

7. Possibly zoo keepers and veterinarians by virtue of their roles do have duties to care for animals in certain ways, though these seem to be duties not so much to the animals themselves as to those individuals who have committed the animals to their care.

8. Sidney Zink, *The Concept of Ethics* (London: Macmillan, 1962), p. 126.

tion, when we do seem to take upon ourselves an obligation to care for the adopted animal; but in general we do not make commitments to animals via pledges, promises, or contracts.

No doubt, viewing the concept of duty in the restricted sense of a moral requirement generated either by one's position or by a specific commitment made renders odd most talk of duties to animals. However, much of what we *ought* to do or refrain from doing even with regard to humans cannot be captured by this restricted notion of duty, for there is much that we morally ought to do and ought to be apart from any appeal to duty in this narrow sense. And no one (even those who wish to narrowly restrict the use of the term) is suggesting that we are morally required to do only what it is our duty to do in this limited sense. So, for example, if my neighbor has locked himself out of his house and needs access to my telephone, I have no *duty* to make my telephone available to him but nevertheless I *ought* to do so. Similarly, I ought to be friendly to my colleagues, to give to charitable causes, to be a tolerant person, and so forth, but none of these are duties narrowly conceived. Therefore, not all "moral oughts" are generated by duties in this restricted sense. This means that to conclude that we do not have duties narrowly conceived to animals is not unduly problematic, since it would not follow that it doesn't morally matter what we do to animals, any more than it would follow that if we didn't have duties narrowly conceived to humans it wouldn't morally matter what we do with them. Indeed, enormous stretches of the moral life would still remain intact, for there are many "oughts" or moral requirements that are unconnected with duties in this circumscribed twofold sense.

There is, however, another, broader notion of duty. Indeed, contrary to Zink (who argues that duties are simply our more stringent obligations) other philosophers have argued that obligations and duties are different from one another, not merely in stringency but in kind. What is claimed is that obligations are those moral requirements that one *undertakes* to do, while duties are moral requirements which apply *apart from* one's having undertaken them. Thus, my promise creates an obligation, not a duty, whereas the principle of truth-telling creates a duty, not an obligation. And so I have an obligation to help my neighbor work on his roof because I promised to do so, but I have a duty to tell the truth whether or not I have pledged myself to tell the truth.[9] On this enlarged understanding, then, it would make sense to say I have a duty not to steal, not to kill (murder), not to torture, as well as a duty to fight for social justice, con-

9. Cf. A. W. Sparks, *Talking Philosophy* (New York: Routledge, 1991), p. 250.

tribute to charitable causes, etc. Who, then, has it right here? Those who propose a narrow interpretation of duty (i.e., role-duties and commitment-duties) or those who favor a broader interpretation (i.e., duties as given)? Professor A. W. Sparks speaks to the point when he comments, referring to the distinction between obligation (as undertaken) and duty (as given), "The distinction is a genuine one and that can be a useful way of making it, provided one announces loudly and clearly that that is how one intends to use the words 'duty' and 'obligation.' It is sometimes worse than bad manners to pretend that these are the only correct meaning of the words."[10] So, rather than be guilty of bad manners, I shall acknowledge that there are a variety of *legitimate* ways we can use the word "duty." The danger is that we shall confuse these uses, as would be the case when we think that because *some* talk of duties to animals is not clearly sensible (duties narrowly conceived) that *all* talk of duties to animals is not sensible (duties broadly conceived).

AQUINAS: THE LESS PERFECT IS AVAILABLE FOR USE BY THE MORE PERFECT

Both Aquinas and Kant offer reasons for denying the existence of duties to animals, reasons that are worth reflecting upon. Aquinas offers us the following argument (here Aquinas primarily has in mind the killing of animals but his argument has application beyond killing to the concerns of this chapter, the infliction of gratuitous suffering):

> There is no sin in using a thing for the purpose for which it is. Now the order of things is such that the imperfect are for the perfect, even as in the process of generation nature proceeds from imperfection to perfection. Hence it is that as in the generation of a man there is first a living thing, then an animal, and lastly a man, so too things, like the plants, which merely have life, are all alike for animals, and all animals are for man. Wherefore it is not unlawful if man uses plants for the good of animals, and animals for the good of man. . . .[11]

Aquinas is telling us that God, through nature, has so ordered matters that plants are available for the good of animals and humans, while plants

10. Sparks, *Talking Philosophy,* p. 250.

11. Aquinas, *Summa Theologica* (New York: Benziger Brothers, 1947), Part 2, Question 64, Article 1.

and animals are available for the good of humans, the less perfect and less valuable being available for the use of the more perfect and more valuable. So in pursuing one's own good, it is legitimate for the more perfect to use the less perfect because the good of the more perfect has a greater claim to be realized than the good of the less perfect.

If Aquinas is arguing that the more perfect have *no* duties to the less perfect, then his argument is seriously problematic. For if a significant aspect of being "more perfect" is being "more intelligent," then it would certainly follow that normal human beings have no duties to chimpanzees, for example, who are less intelligent and therefore less perfect. It would also follow that normal humans have no duties to massively retarded human beings, who are even less intelligent and consequently less perfect than chimpanzees. But the suggestion that we have no duties to the massively retarded is a morally awkward conclusion. Better to jettison, it would seem, the principle that the more perfect have no duties to the less perfect than to find oneself committed to such a conclusion. Further, even if we want to say that animals, because less perfect than humans, are available for human use, we still do not want to say that animals can be used in any way we please without any consideration of the animal; we do not want to say that the well-being of an animal can be sacrificed on a whim, that the interests of the animal, no matter how weighty, can be sacrificed for the interests of human beings, no matter how trivial. This is a conviction that we have already given concrete expression to when we said that it is wrong to torture animals for fun. Finally, we need also to observe that animals (and plants) are not merely given to us for our *use* but they are also entrusted to our *care,* as we respond to the biblical mandate to be caretakers of the natural order. It is the very fact that we humans are more perfect that makes possible our caring for those who are less perfect. There are, in fact, moral limits to the use to which we may put animals, limits that most of us recognize at least in extreme cases of animal abuse. Thus, we cannot automatically assume that the use to which we put an animal is justified simply because we are humans and it is an animal, or, in Thomistic language, because we are more perfect and it is less perfect.

Once we recognize *moral limits* to our use of animals, then many questions legitimately arise: If we cannot torture animals for fun, can we kill them for fun? Granted that we can kill and eat animals for survival, can we kill and eat animals simply because we like the taste of them (which may simply be a close relative of "fun")? Can we inflict, in the course of scientific investigation, considerable pain and suffering on animals for the sake of knowledge that holds out little or no prospect of any practical benefit for humanity? As soon, then, as we qualify Aquinas's account (as it surely must be qualified), all these questions and a host of others become legitimate questions. They are not foolish questions but are appropriate for us to raise and ponder.

AQUINAS AGAIN: ANIMALS ARE NOT TO BE "LOVED OUT OF CHARITY"

Aquinas offers us a second reason for denying moral standing to animals. He denies, as he puts it, that animals are to be "loved out of charity," for only God and human beings, he insists, are to be so loved.[12] Thus, animals are not appropriate objects of love. It follows that people are not to love their cats and dogs, their horses and rabbits, etc. (Aquinas acknowledges that there is, however, a secondary sense in which animals can be loved, as when we seek an animal's welfare and preservation in order to honor God and provide what is useful to humans, though this is ultimately an expression of love of God and love of humans, not love for the animals whose welfare and preservation is sought.)

Aquinas's reason for denying that animals are to be "loved out of charity" is that to be loved out of charity presupposes, as he says, a kind of "friendship" which in turn involves "fellowship," indeed a "fellowship of everlasting happiness." Because friendship and fellowship presumably cannot be had with an irrational creature, therefore animals cannot be "loved out of charity." What precisely Aquinas is saying can best be left to the Thomistic scholar, but this much seems clear. In suggesting that love presupposes the capacity for fellowship and friendship, Aquinas may be suggesting that love at its profoundest level is connected with one's deepest hopes, wishes, and values, and that only rational creatures who are moral and spiritual agents capable of sharing in a fellowship with the divine can be embraced by those hopes, wishes, and values and thus loved in a manner that encompasses them. Aquinas may be correct in this; *in that sense* perhaps we cannot love animals. Further, many Christians may understandably be sympathetic to the claim that there is a circle of love reserved exclusively for what is personal and to which animals cannot gain admittance.

Nevertheless, there is no reason — and Aquinas certainly provides us with no such reason — why we cannot legitimately feel affection for animals, have compassion for them, and make them the object of our con-

12. Aquinas, *Summa Theologica,* Part 2, Question 65, Article 3.

cern when they suffer. Whether one wishes to call this love or not can remain an open question. That the one who suffers is an irrational creature is irrelevant to the propriety of compassion, concern, and care. Indeed, a massively retarded human being can be the legitimate object of our compassionate concern, not because she is a rational creature (which she is not) but because she can suffer. Why, then, should we not be compassionately concerned with animals for their own sake? Aquinas has given us no convincing reason why we should answer this question in the negative.

KANT: WE HAVE DUTIES ONLY TO RATIONAL MORAL AGENTS

Kant, too, has his reasons for denying that we have duties to animals. His, perhaps, are the more famous. He argues[13] that we do not have duties to animals because animals are not rational moral agents. That is, they are not beings capable of choosing between right and wrong, committing themselves to moral ideals, to life goals and projects, to religious outlooks, and so on. For Kant, only moral agents are to be respected as ends in themselves — that is, to be respected in such a way that their choices are not coercively overridden but honored and allowed to stand, to be allowed to choose the ends for which they are to live their lives, and to be fitting objects of duty. Thus, we are not to make persons serve our ends by imposing our will on them by force or by tricking them into doing our will by deceit or fraud, for when we impose our will on others in this way (in contrast to rational persuasion) we treat them as "means." We treat them as if they were mere things to be used for the securing of our goals. Now, whereas human beings are not to use other human beings as means, they *can* use both inanimate objects and animals as means because neither are rational moral agents.

For Kant, then, the moral community (the body of individuals to whom we have moral obligations) consists exclusively of moral agents, those individuals capable of moral choice and therefore capable of shouldering moral obligations and duties. To use the current professional lingo, this is to say that only moral agents are "moral patients," the latter term referring to those individuals to whom we have obligations. But, within the human community, aren't there moral patients who are not moral agents? Examples would be human infants (and fetuses), the massively retarded, the severely senile, and the insane. How extensive our obli-

13. Kant, *Lectures on Ethics,* pp. 239-41.

gations are to these individuals may be a matter of debate, but it would certainly include the obligation not to inflict gratuitous pain and suffering. Such an infliction would constitute a wrong done to those individuals themselves. In contrast, for Kant there are no moral patients who are not moral agents, for only moral agents have moral standing in their own right and only they are members of the moral community.

Kant may not, of course, intend to exclude infants (and others) from direct moral concern and therefore to exclude them from membership in the moral community, but it is not evident how he could consistently exclude animals on the grounds that they are not moral agents but then proceed to include infants, who are not moral agents either. Of course, normal infants will in due course become moral agents and Kant might wish to argue that normal infants are in the same category as sleeping or temporarily unconscious moral agents who are still moral agents worthy of respect. But even if it could successfully be argued that infants are moral agents (their potential for agency counting as agency), it would still remain the case that terminally ill infants (whose moral agency will never be actualized), anencephalic infants (infants born without any higher brain portions), the massively retarded, and the severely senile are *not* moral agents (actually or potentially), and therefore on strict Kantian grounds they would lack moral standing and their suffering by itself would be of no moral concern. They would not be moral patients. Such a conclusion is difficult to accept, as it is difficult to accept the conclusion that suffering gratuitously inflicted on animals is in its own right of no moral concern.

SOCIAL CONTRACT THEORY: ONLY RATIONAL AGENTS HAVE MORAL STANDING

Social contract theory or contractualism has its roots in the writings of Locke, Rousseau, and Kant and has found powerful contemporary expression in John Rawls's important work *A Theory of Justice.* This theory is an attempt to justify principles of justice by showing that they would be the principles freely chosen by rational agents in a carefully specified set of imaginary circumstances. Specifically, in the case of John Rawls, we are asked to imagine that all rational agents who will ever live (or their representatives) are gathered together before the outset of history for the purpose of determining what principles of justice they will adopt. In what is called the "original position" these rational agents are to reach agreement

— to "contract," as it were — on a set of principles that once agreed to cannot be altered, underscoring the necessity to choose carefully and wisely. These rational agents, though knowledgeable about the world that they will one day inhabit, are nevertheless ignorant about certain features of their own particular future situation, operating as they are behind what Rawls calls "a veil of ignorance." They do not know, for example, what their own sex will be, or their race, or their religion. Therefore, they are not able to formulate principles that will favor themselves over others. This insures an appropriate impartiality. Indeed, in formulating principles of justice they will make quite certain that those principles that they choose do not favor one sex or one particular race or religion, lest they unknowingly put themselves at a serious disadvantage. It is in such imagined circumstances as these, though more finely tuned by Rawls, that rational agents are to formulate and agree to principles of justice. Justice, then, consists of those principles that would be agreed to in these very circumstances.

Here I am only hinting at a theory that is worked out with great detail and philosophical mastery by Rawls. It is perhaps the supreme expression of a contractualist theory, and it represents an approach to issues of justice and morality that has gained considerable support in recent years. But it is a theory, crucially for our purposes, that allows for the moral standing only of rational agents. In the original position, behind the veil of ignorance, only rational creatures are admitted and only their interests count. By stipulating that justice consists of those principles that all self-interested rational agents would agree to, one has from the outset effectively placed animals outside the domain of justice. This is characteristic of all social contract theories: animals are excluded as objects of direct moral concern. Only the interests of rational agents count in constructing and agreeing to principles of justice.

SOCIAL CONTRACT THEORY AND CRUELTY

Rawls's own work focuses exclusively on issues of justice and on our role as members of a political community. He is not primarily concerned with morality more broadly construed. Others, however, have taken social contract theory and have sought to construct, in addition to a theory of justice, a theory of morality. Indeed, the philosopher Peter Carruthers not only defends a social contract theory of morality but uses it in a sustained attempt to refute all claims on behalf of moral standing for animals, while at the same time arguing that social contract morality does not permit the kind of outrageous treatment of animals which would be sufficient to cast serious doubt on the moral plausibility of the theory itself.

According to Carruthers, social contract theory or contractualism is the most plausible moral theory on the contemporary scene, superior both to theistic ethics and to utilitarianism (its most credible secular competitor). Therefore, what it has to say on the issue of moral concern for animals is definitive. And what does it have to say? What would rational creatures like ourselves agree to for our own sakes with regard to animals? "Contracting rational agents," we are told, "should agree to try to develop a ready sympathy for one another's suffering and sympathy for animal suffering is . . . merely a side-effect of this general attitude."[14] There are two things to note about Carruthers's comment. First, rational agents should commit themselves not only to certain rules (i.e., not to kill, not to assault, not to lie), but they also should agree "to develop certain positive attachments and dispositions of feeling"[15] that are necessary for creating the kind of community that self-interested rational agents would want to inhabit. Second, these dispositions – say, sympathy and a lack of cruelty – are such that certain behaviors toward animals (e.g., torture) may be expressive of a type of cruelty that is *not* likely to be limited in its expression to animals; and when behavior that hurts animals (or is thought to hurt animals) is expressive of such cruelty, it is to be condemned but condemned solely because of its possible negative consequences for rational agents.

It is claimed, then, that contracting rational agents would see the advantage for themselves of living in a community whose members are characterized by the virtue of sympathy and the absence of cruelty, and to the extent that abusive behavior toward animals is also expressive of a lack of sympathy for or cruelty toward humans, it is to be condemned. Thus, *sadistic* behavior toward animals, torturing them for fun, for example, would be expressive of a character defect likely to infect one's relations with other humans and therefore should be condemned. Certainly one would not hire persons to baby-sit one's children who were known to torture dogs for fun in their spare time. Also to be condemned is the *brutish* behavior manifest in the case of "the hit-and-run driver to whom it never

14. Peter Carruthers, *The Animal Issue* (New York: Cambridge University Press, 1992), p. 154.

15. Carruthers, *The Animal Issue,* p. 153.

occurs to stop, in order to help the dog left howling in pain at the side of the road, as well as the one who drives on because late for an appointment at the hair dresser. . . ."[16] This also seems plausible, for again one would think twice about submitting the care of one's children to people capable of such disregard for suffering. Thus, contractualism would condemn causing animals to suffer for no reason (sadistic cruelty) or for trivial reasons (brutish cruelty) because both would be expressive of a basic character defect that rational agents concerned with their own welfare would not want present in their communities. Contractualism, despite there being no direct moral concern for animals, does not have utterly outrageous implications for our treatment of them.

But many, I think, will judge it outrageous that we are asked by Carruthers to believe that the pain of a dog suffering from massive first degree burns caused by malicious teenagers counts by itself for nothing in our moral calculations — that what alone counts is some deeper cruelty that may be present and that may possibly manifest itself in our dealings with rational agents. It would seem that if one is concerned, as Carruthers is, with having a theory that does not have implications that outrage common moral sense, one should be concerned not only that sadistic and brutish behavior be condemned as common sense dictates, but that it be condemned for the right reason, namely, because of what is done to the animal. This is something that common sense also dictates.

SOCIAL CONTRACT THEORY: SOME AWKWARD IMPLICATIONS

One of the awkward implications of Carruthers's denial of moral standing to animals can be seen in Carruthers's own discussion of the moral relativity of our treatment of animals. He observes, no doubt rightly, that the same conduct toward animals that in one society may be expressive of a cruelty that is likely to negatively impact humans, and therefore is to be condemned, in another society may be free of such cruelty and therefore appropriately be a matter of moral indifference. Carruthers provides a somewhat startling example of such relativism, an example which underscores the moral awkwardness that accompanies any theory, including his own, that views moral concern for animals as only an extension of moral concern for rational agents and nothing else. Thus, he tells us, in a society unlike ours (where animals are not given the status of honorary humans,

16. Carruthers, *The Animal Issue,* p. 154.

where sentimentality toward animals does not abound) "a dog may be slowly strangled to death because it is believed to make the meat taste better, while it never occurs to the people involved that there is any connection between what they are doing and their attitudes to human beings – indeed, there may in fact be no such connection; while such an action performed by someone in our society would manifest cruelty, when done by them it may not."[17] And, indeed, it may not be an expression of cruelty in that society. This seems to show, contrary to Carruthers's interpretation, that painfully strangling a dog slowly to death must be wrong for some other reason, wrong because of what is done to the dog.

Throughout Carruthers's discussion we are exposed to a contractualist's understanding of cruelty, an attitude toward suffering that is likely to manifest itself in damaging behavior toward *humans.* That means that wherever there is a psychological separation between our treatment of animals and our attitude toward human suffering, one can slowly strangle dogs for the sake of better-tasting meat or even torture them for fun without manifesting cruelty. So also, according to Carruthers, one can work in a laboratory using "animals for the testing of detergents, causing them much suffering in the process" or one can be a farmhand "working in conditions that cause considerable suffering to the animals under [one's] care," but because there is no reason to believe that this makes one "any less sympathetic and generous" a person in one's dealings with humans, there is nothing here that is morally problematic.[18] Thus there is no moral reason to seek alternatives to the painful testing of detergents on animals or improvement in the conditions that cause considerable suffering to farm animals. Carruthers admits that these are "controversial consequences," but believes they must be accepted in light of the general plausibility of contractualism.

Carruthers is also understandably concerned about the implications of contractualist theory for nonrational humans – young babies, the massively retarded, and those suffering from senile dementia. Because, according to contract theory, morality has to do with what rational creatures would contract or agree to for the benefit of themselves, what are we to say about nonrational humans? Here matters could become even more problematic than the difficulties that emerge in connection with animals. Are such individuals to be reduced to the status of animals because of their lack of the requisite rational capacity? Indeed, what are the implica-

17. Carruthers, *The Animal Issue,* p. 162.
18. Carruthers, *The Animal Issue,* p. 159.

tions of contractualism for our conduct toward nonrational humans? Carruthers, for one, is going to grant them full moral standing. But on what basis? He argues that because they share human form and many patterns of human behavior with rational agents, to mistreat them will be expressive of a cruelty and an insensitivity that is almost certain, much more certain than in the case of the mistreatment of animals, to manifest itself in mistreatment of those who undeniably are rational creatures. So, in the light of this, rational contractors would agree out of self-interest to extend full moral rights to nonrational humans.

This is done, notice, out of concern for the suffering of rational humans who may be threatened should we fail to extend this protection to those humans who lack rationality, but surely there is something wrong here. We can perpetuate a moral outrage not only by failing to recognize as possessors of rights any group that should be so recognized but also by failing to extend that recognition for *the morally right reasons.* For example, to acknowledge that Jews (or Swedes) ought to be extended all the rights that we extend to non-Jews (or non-Swedes) is simply not good enough, *if* one's sole reason for doing so is that our failing to do so may threaten the welfare of the rest of us, as if only what happens to "the rest of us" genuinely matters. No amount of moral theorizing and sophisticated talk of social contractors or different levels of moral discourse will be sufficient to remove such an outrage. Nor will it succeed in doing so when what we are saying is that torturing and abusing babies and other nonrational humans is objectionable only because it may threaten the welfare of rational humans.

Carruthers's social contract theory has a problem quite the reverse of a standard problem associated with utilitarianism. Utilitarianism begins with a predistributive equality ("everyone counts for one and no one counts for more than one"), but ends up with a radical inequality (i.e., imposing great sacrifices on the few for the benefit of the many). In contrast, Carruthers's social contract theory begins with a predistributive *inequality* (in the original position only rational humans count) but ends up with an egalitarian outcome (i.e., nonrational humans are to be treated equally with rational humans). This predistributive inequality is unacceptable because at the most fundamental level, preparatory to deciding what moral rules, rights, and virtues ought to be endorsed, it is declared that the pain and suffering of nonrational humans counts for nothing. Full rights for nonrational humans are subsequently judged necessary only in order to protect the rights of those who really do count, namely, rational humans. This extension is contingent solely upon our living in a world where we humans are so psychologically constituted that we cannot neglect and abuse nonrational humans without creating a high probability of our neglecting and abusing rational humans.

One has not saved a moral theory from grave objection by observing, even if rightly, that it does not permit the torture of animals, when the suffering of the animal itself is not the reason for that prohibition. For after all, it is our common moral sense that we are seeking to placate by showing that our favored theory does not permit such torture, but it is that same common moral sense that tells us the torture is wrong *because* of the suffering caused the animal. Indeed, our conviction that torturing animals is wrong is simply the conviction that torturing animals is wrong because of the pointless suffering it causes the animal. We are offended and outraged because of what is done to the animal, not because we suspect the existence of some subterranean psychological connection between abusing animals and abusing humans. To say that torturing animals is not wrong because of the suffering that is caused the animal is to offend common moral sense every bit as much as saying that torturing animals is not wrong at all.

UTILITARIANISM: EVERYONE'S HAPPINESS COUNTS

Among ethical theorists, utilitarians have been leaders in advocating concern for animals. Jeremy Bentham and John Stuart Mill in the nineteenth century articulated a moral vision that embraced animals as well as humans;[19] they also laid the foundation for utilitarian ethical theory, their names becoming synonymous with classical utilitarianism. In our own era the work of another utilitarian, Peter Singer, especially his *Animal Liberation* (1975),[20] has given birth to the current animal liberation movement by both stimulating practical advocacy and providing a philosophical foundation for such advocacy. It is understandable why utilitarians have been sensitive to issues of animal welfare and why they have been ready to recognize direct duties to animals. Classical utilitarian moral theory has had an exclusive concern with the production of favorable states of consciousness (e.g., pleasure) and the avoidance of unfavorable states of con-

19. Jeremy Bentham, *The Principle of Morals and Legislation,* chapter 17, section 1; John Stuart Mill, "Three Essays on Religion," in *John Stuart Mill: Essays on Ethics, Religion and Society,* ed. J. M. Robson (London: Routledge and Kegan Paul, 1969), pp. 184-87.

20. Peter Singer, *Animal Liberation* (Berkeley and Los Angeles: University of California Press, 1975).

sciousness (e.g., pain). Thus, as soon as one recognizes that animals are conscious beings capable of pleasure and pain, one will then have to embrace animals as objects of moral concern. Utilitarianism is, then, a moral theory that readily lends itself to moral concern for animals, which is not to say that utilitarians have always seen the implications of their own theory.

Utilitarians are consequentialists, maintaining that the consequences of acts or practices are what render them right or wrong; acts or practices are not, they tell us, inherently or intrinsically right or wrong but only become right or wrong depending on the nature of their consequences. Utilitarians differ as to what consequences are relevant or desirable. For Mill, the desired consequences are happiness (i.e., a favorable balance of pleasure over pain); for Singer it is the satisfaction of preferences; while other utilitarians provide yet other visions of the good consequences that we are obligated to produce. But since the point of moral action is to bring about the best consequence, once one identifies what those desired consequences are, one can then proceed to evaluate actions and practices by ascertaining whether they maximize happiness or the satisfaction of preferences or whatever the desired consequence may be.

Utilitarians have little sympathy for talk of rights and typically engage in such talk only as a concession to popular rhetoric. Brutalizing animals (or humans) is wrong, according to the utilitarian, not because it violates any right that the animal (or a human) has but because it violates the one fundamental principle that generates all obligations, our obligation to maximize the happiness of the greatest number. Thus, in typical utilitarian fashion Jeremy Bentham in a memorable phrase declared, "Natural rights is simple nonsense: natural and unprescriptable rights, rhetorical nonsense – nonsense upon stilts."[21] Why such hostility toward rights? In part, at least, because utilitarians correctly perceive that rights are a moral weapon that can be wielded to thwart the implementation of the principle of utility and thereby frustrate the goal of maximizing overall happiness. Rights can be invoked by the individual to protect his or her own welfare and to insure that it is not sacrificed to further the happiness of the larger community. Thus, according to rights-theorists (i.e., those who believe rights are morally fundamental) there are to be moral restraints on our attempts to achieve the good of the greater number or the

21. Jeremy Bentham, "Anarchical Fallacies," in *The Works of Jeremy Bentham*, ed. John Bowring (Edinburgh: W. Tait, 1843-1859), vol. 3, p. 221.

happiness of the majority or the well-being of the community, and these restraints are expressed in terms of rights that the individual has over against the larger community, rights that can be invoked and that when honored (as they ought to be) may actually frustrate attempts at achieving a gain in total happiness. There are simply certain things you can't do to me even if it would work out for the good of the community as a whole. I, after all, have my rights. Obviously, utilitarians cannot countenance the recognition of moral considerations that limit what is for them the only moral end – maximizing overall good consequences. Peter Singer, for example, who is a central figure in the "animal rights" movement, because he is a utilitarian does not believe in rights for animals or for humans. Singer confessedly engages in such talk solely to be effective at the popular level, where, of course, the main battle for animal welfare has to be conducted.

UTILITARIANISM: EVERYONE'S HAPPINESS COUNTS EQUALLY

Significantly for a discussion of animal concerns, utilitarians have argued that equal interests, needs, desires, and preferences are of equal importance, and that they are to be counted equally in assessing consequences, and therefore counted equally in determining how we ought to behave. Thus the interests, needs, desires, and preferences of each individual count equally, whether the individual is oneself or another, a male or female, white or black, rich or poor – and (crucially for present purposes) human or animal. More specifically, it would be argued, if someone is in pain, that would be equally undesirable, equally an evil, equally worthy of removal no matter whose pain it is. Whereas none of us would say that pain is less of an evil when it is suffered by a female rather than a male, by an African-American rather than a European-American, by a poor person rather than a rich person, by a Christian rather than a non-Christian, we may be tempted to say that pain suffered by an animal is less of an evil than the same pain suffered by a human being. But this is a temptation we ought to resist, it would be argued by the utilitarian. Here, then, we are confronted by the bolder claim that animal pain is an evil equal to human pain, so that we do as much to make the world a better place by relieving animal pain as we do by relieving human pain. Therefore, if one is a consequentialist committed always to securing the best possible state of affairs and if one recognizes that removing animal pain does as much to secure this best possible state of affairs as does removing human pain, then we are as much obligated to remove and to not cause animal pain as we are obligated to remove and to not cause human pain.

In summary, then, the utilitarian provides us with a moral vision that permits animal pain to be treated as an evil in its own right; in this, it accords with our common-sense convictions. In that it counts all pain equally, however, animal and human, it seems to run counter to our common-sense convictions. And yet why should I think that my pain is a greater evil than an equal pain suffered by my dog? Here the utilitarian raises a crucially important issue. To be sure I can quote John 3:16 and my dog cannot. But why should we think that a relevant factor? I can read Heidegger and sometimes understand what he has to say, and my dog cannot. But so what? One doesn't have to be a utilitarian to feel the force of this challenge and rightly wonder how we can justify a preferential concern for human suffering.

If we wish to argue for the moral appropriateness of a preferential treatment for humans over animals, we can argue in one of two ways. First, we can deny that human pain and animal pain are *equal* evils, arguing that human pain is a greater evil than animal pain and more worthy of relief. Thus, we might claim that a little pain suffered by a human is a greater evil than much pain suffered by an animal or even by large numbers of animals. For example, it might be claimed that even though I am suffering from pain that is less intense and less protracted than that suffered by a chimpanzee, who is suffering twice as much for twice as long, nevertheless my pain is a greater evil than the chimpanzee's pain. Indeed, it might even be claimed that my pain is a greater evil than the aggregate pain suffered by a hundred chimpanzees, each of whom is suffering twice as much as I am. It would follow that in trying to make the world a better place with more good and less evil, we should concentrate our efforts on eliminating human pain because it is to count for more on our calculations.

But why should we think human pain to be a greater evil than chimpanzee pain? Because the human has a superior cognitive ability? But, again, why should we think that that by itself is a relevant factor, if the pain is the same? Further, most of us are not prepared to conclude that the pain of a massively retarded human counts for less because of his or her inferior cognitive ability. Most of us would not endorse such a conclusion, although that is just the conclusion we must endorse if the degree of evil attaching to a given pain is determined by the cognitive ability of the individual experiencing it. Should we perhaps argue instead that pain becomes a greater evil simply by being experienced by a member of the human species, regardless of cognitive ability? On such a view my pain or the pain of a severely retarded human being is a greater evil than a comparable pain suffered by a chimpanzee simply because we are human beings. It is not that I or the severely retarded suffer more from our pain than does a chimpanzee. It is not that the chimpanzee is cognitively deficient, for it is cognitively superior to the massively retarded human whose pain we suppose counts for more. It is simply that the chimpanzee is unfortunately a member of the wrong species and therefore its pain doesn't count as much as ours does. But, again, why should one think that the degree of evil attaching to one's pain is a product of one's species, so that the same identical quantum of pain is a greater evil when it is experienced by a member of one species rather than another species?

So, then, let us grant that taken by themselves equal pains are equal evils. Nevertheless, it might reasonably be argued that the same amount of pain in a typical human is more likely to have negative repercussions than it would have in the life of an animal. Thus John Kleinig argues, "In the case of humans the experience of pain can interfere with so much else of normative significance – e.g., the ability to exercise one's distinctively human capacities."[22] This is to assume, as I am quite prepared to do, that there are special values attaching to these distinctively human capacities, values that do not attach to animal life. It is not that having those capacities makes the pain a greater intrinsic evil but that the pain becomes a greater evil instrumentally by frustrating the expression of those singular human capacities. But it needs pointing out that this line of argument does serve to minimize the pain of those individuals (e.g., the massively retarded) whose human capacities are severely truncated and therefore would not be interfered with by the presence of severe pain.[23]

The second way to resist the conclusion that animal pain and human pain generate equal duties is *not* to deny that "equal pains are equal evils, be they human or animal pains" but rather to deny that "equal evils equally oblige us to act for their prevention or removal." I believe this to be true. At this point, however, we depart from a strict utilitarian or consequentialist vision. Thus, it would be granted that, all else being equal, comparable pain in an animal and a human are evils of equal magnitude. That is, it would be granted that my pain and a chimpanzee's pain would be equally evil, assuming that we suffer equally. But it would not be granted that

22. John Kleinig, *Valuing Life* (Princeton, N.J.: Princeton University Press, 1991), p. 179.

23. This issue will be taken up again and at greater length in chapter 8.

comparable pains in an animal and a human, equal evils though they be, place equal obligations on us for their prevention and removal. From the fact that two evils are of equal magnitude, it would not follow that we are equally obliged to prevent or remove them. On the contrary, for a range of reasons, we may actually have a greater obligation to remove one evil rather than another. Indeed, we may have a greater obligation to remove the lesser evil, leaving more evil in the world than would be the case had we acted to remove the greater evil. This is to reject a consequentialist moral vision with its imperative to always maximize the greatest amount of overall good. There are, I believe, a range of considerations that would justify this denial, and they are considerations that do not require an abandonment of concern for the chimpanzee.

For example, the pain suffered by my daughter may be no greater, possibly even less, than the pain suffered by a neighbor's daughter, but all the same my first duty is to care for my daughter. In acting first to help her I do not deny that comparable pain and suffering of some other human being is equally an evil, but what I do deny is that determining my obligation or duty is solely a matter of weighing evils and then seeking to remove the greater one. Thus, I am not simply and solely obligated to create the greatest possible preponderance of good over evil; indeed, if that were true I would then have to neglect my daughter's suffering whenever I could relieve the suffering of another who suffers more. The mere fact that someone is my daughter (or a member of my immediate family) is by itself a morally relevant consideration and is an important factor in determining the direction of my particular efforts to reduce pain and suffering or to increase human happiness. That does not mean that other people don't count or are not to be the objects of my moral concern, indeed even objects of my *sacrificial* moral concern. But whereas each individual's pain is as worthy of relief or removal as any other individual's, my special concern is to be directed to my family. Indeed, if we did not give preferential treatment to family members but directed our time, energies, resources, and affections indiscriminately, the special community that is the family would simply dissolve. The existence of any community, including the family, involves giving privileged status to its members, and demonstrating partiality toward them.

What has just been said about family membership might also be said about our species membership: it too creates special obligations, justifies a range of preferential treatments, and gives moral direction to our efforts at relieving pain and suffering. In other words, the mere fact that someone is a member of the human species does count for something in determining our obligations and priorities. Again, it does not follow that those outside our species are not to be objects of moral concern any more than it follows that those outside our family are not to be objects of moral concern. None of this justifies eliminating moral concern for animals or disregarding their welfare; it would, however, seem to justify some preferential treatment for humans.

Whereas the special obligation to family members is more evident, we might pause to consider the nature of this "species membership" that places its own moral claims upon us. It might be observed, first, that we relate to other human beings in the context of a wide range of cooperative associations; we do this not only as members of families but also as members of neighborhoods and local communities, as citizens of nations, and as members of continental, hemispheric, and worldwide organizations. We engage in cooperative enterprises in which we provide and receive economic and material assistance from one another. We also create art together, trade together, socialize and play together, explore our common history together, do science together, build economic, political, legal, and religious institutions together, and in a myriad of ways work together for common goals. By these efforts and many others we sustain each other in existence and make possible personal fulfillment, as well as carry on the task of building and preserving civilization. Sustaining that cooperative activity requires mutual commitment and concern, a special commitment to and concern for those who are members of the human community. It is a direct and special concern for other humans that creates goodwill and thereby binds us together, creating the very foundation of community. We also, as beneficiaries of this cooperative activity, owe something in return, owe something to those who, like ourselves, are sustained and enriched by being members of this community. For this reason we understandably and rightly give preference and priority to our own species and the needs of its members. And the Christian would also add that we have a calling to build, enrich, and redeem the human community, a community that can only exist and flourish, as the family can only exist and flourish, as we exercise certain preferences toward its members. One such preference is a special moral concern for the pain and suffering of its members and an acknowledgment that human pain and suffering confronts us (in general) with a greater urgency to seek its removal and relief than does animal pain and suffering. Further, we humans are more dependent on other humans for our survival, health, and happiness than are animals. To be sure we humans can have (and have had) a disastrous impact on the welfare of animals, but granting a half-way decent habitat, animals need us much less than we need each other. Therefore, considerations of need and interdependence dictate a priority of concern for other humans.

This line of reasoning is not an instance of "speciesism" giving preferential moral consideration to members of our own species and doing so for no other reason than that they are members of our species. That is not what is going on here; we are not to give preferential treatment to humans simply because they are humans as if that by itself is the last word. Rather, we are to give preferential treatment to humans because we humans are part of an interacting, interdependent community that exists, in part, because of that preferential treatment, just as the family as a special community exists in part because of such preferential treatment. For some, this reason may not seem strong enough nor perhaps even theological enough, but keep in mind we are not here dealing with the questions of why human *life* is to be preferred to animal life (reasons which are forthcoming in a later chapter) but reasons for simply giving priority to human *suffering* over animal suffering.

There is a need to make two further observations. First, the account that we have given in support of preferential treatment of humans might also be embraced by the utilitarian, who could argue that in the long run a certain preferential concern for one's own species, like a preferential concern for one's own family, will maximize overall happiness, will more effectively bring about the best results as we give focus to our energies in accord with the very natural emotional attachments we have for family and fellow humans. Second, nothing that has been said about the legitimacy of preferential treatment for humans justifies the use to which we typically put animals, and none of it is a defense of the status quo in our treatment of them. After all, we did acknowledge that equal pains are equal evils whether experienced by humans or animals and this acknowledgement will by itself complicate attempts at justifying the painful use to which we often put animals. In this connection, the analogy between preferential treatment of family members and preferential treatment of humans can be instructive, for giving preferential treatment to one's family does not justify dismissing the needs of those outside of one's family nor does it permit inflicting suffering on them for the advantage of one's family. Likewise, if the analogy holds, our preferential concern for our own species does not justify dismissing the needs of animals or using them in just any way we please for our advantage.

A PROBLEM FOR UTILITARIANISM

A common criticism of utilitarianism is that it sanctions abusing or mistreating a few individuals in circumstances where such abuse would actually produce a greater amount of overall happiness than any alternative course of action open to us. Thus, on utilitarian grounds, a small number of persons could be made to suffer, unjustly and wrongly, critics would insist, for the considerable benefit of a larger number of individuals. Since it is the total amount of happiness (or preference satisfaction) that the utilitarian is committed to producing, it may be that in some circumstances the path to that goal involves the infliction of considerable pain on the innocent few for the advantage of the many.

This criticism of utilitarianism has also found its way into the discussion of animal welfare. For example, Rosalind Hursthouse finds utilitarianism theoretically deficient as an ethical protector of animals, arguing, "Since bullfighting gives pleasures to thousands at the relatively small cost of a few hours of horror and pain for the bull, a utilitarian should, in theory, be in favor of it for the Spaniards – pending their coming to find some other form of sport which causes less suffering, more enjoyable."[24] It is for just this kind of reason that some who are concerned with animal welfare find utilitarianism deficient and have sought alternative moral grounds for protecting animals. One way to do this (but not the only way), is to appeal to animal rights and to argue that the bull in Rosalind Hursthouse's example has a right not to be victimized, a right that is not overridden or defeated by the fact that it gives pleasure to thousands of spectators. Rights would be invoked here for the same reason that rights theorists invoke rights for human beings, because it is the possession of rights that morally prevents the abuse of the few for the welfare and happiness of the many.

A PRINCIPLE OF BENEFICENCE

Even if one judges utilitarianism to be deficient as a complete moral theory, nevertheless the utilitarian's concern for the welfare of others must be embraced in some form or other by any satisfactory moral theory. Though the pursuit of that welfare must, I judge (contrary to the utilitarian), be directed and even limited by a range of moral considerations that

24. Rosalind Hursthouse, *Beginning Lives* (New York: Basil Blackwell, 1989), p. 154.

are independent of the principle of utility (by individual rights, by considerations of justice, by obligations to family, etc.), it must also, nevertheless, be endorsed. Indeed, the consequences of one's actions for the happiness and welfare of others may not be the whole of morality, generating by itself *all* obligations, as the utilitarian insists. Nevertheless, it is an enormously important part of morality. Therefore, any moral theory that pretends to completeness must include, even though not be totally reducible to, a principle that obligates us to minimize pain and suffering and to further the happiness and interests of others. When such a principle is part of a larger moral vision, but not the whole of that vision, then that principle is usually referred to as a principle of beneficence. A complete moral vision will include such a principle. Additionally, I would suggest, there will be rights, considerations of justice, and a range of special obligations (to family members, for example) that will circumscribe and give direction to how one goes about the task of contributing to the happiness and welfare of others. But the moral point is this: one must make one's life count for others in significant ways.

If the principle of beneficence is a part of any complete moral vision, one that calls each of us to make our contribution to reducing the world's pain and suffering and improving the lives of those that live in this world, then it is this very principle that will obligate us in a range of circumstances to act on behalf of animals and to desist from a range of behaviors that are harmful to them. That is, the principle of beneficence will include within its scope all sentient creatures of whatever species, even if we legitimately give a certain priority to our own species, just as we give a certain priority to our own family. To embrace animals within the scope of the principle of beneficence is to acknowledge that their interests, needs, and desires carry moral weight and give rise to obligations, just as do the interests, needs, and desires of humans. The principle of beneficence by itself does not tell us how we are to orchestrate all our efforts on behalf of a suffering and needy world, but it does say that animals count too and that they are to be given moral consideration. I am, then, to view my life as a potential force for bettering the lives of others, a potential force that is to be activated as pain and suffering is encountered in other lives. And included in this concern is to be the pain and suffering of animals.

A PRINCIPLE OF NON-MALEFICENCE

It may be felt, however, that more relevant than a principle of beneficence, which is after all a positive duty to further the well-being of others, would be a principle of non-maleficence, that is, a principle prohibiting harm to others – not to cause them pain, not to disable them, not to deny them pleasure, not to deny them freedom, and not to kill them, without an overriding justification. This kind of moral concern that we direct to humans will now be extended to cover animals (though what will count as an overriding justification may differ in the case of animals – that is, what might justify harming animals might not be sufficient to justify harming humans). So, no sentient creature is to be subjected to gratuitous pain (that is, pain inflicted without an overriding justification). This, then, is a duty that we have to all animals, and, therefore, they are, at least to that extent, members in good standing of the moral community. Our moral attitude toward animals would not be, as it so often has been, that we can, if it pleases us, cause pain, disable, deny pleasure, deny freedom, and kill unless we can be provided with a reason why we should not. Rather – just the reverse – we are not to do these things unless a clear moral justification can be given for doing so. We might view much of animal advocacy as an attempt to reverse the burden of proof from "You must show me why I should not harm this animal" to "I must offer a good reason why I can harm this animal." The words of William James capture the spirit of this: "Take any demand, however slight, which any creature, however weak, may make. Ought it not, for its own sake, to be satisfied? If not prove why not."[25]

In fact, the principle of non-maleficence may be just the principle we need in order to address most (if not quite all) of the concerns and demands of animal advocacy. Fundamentally, animal advocacy directs its attention to stopping a wide variety of harms done to animals by humans: harming animals by raising them in factory farms, by painfully experimenting on them, by trapping them with leg-hold traps, by confining them in cages, by killing them for sport or food, and so on. In other words, the message on behalf of animals is largely, "Leave them alone; let them be; don't harm them." The principle of non-maleficence not only captures much of the concern of animal advocacy, it also serves to raise the issues that we need to think through in order to come to terms with

25. Quoted in William K. Frankena, *Ethics* (Englewood Cliffs, N.J.: Prentice Hall, 1963), p. 38.

animal advocacy. For the principle of non-maleficence prompts us to consider *how extensive* should our concern with animal harm be? Should it extend to all of the following: causing pain, disabling, denying pleasure, denying freedom, and, finally, killing? Further, it raises for us the important question, how strong do our reasons have to be in order to justify our harming animals? Even in the case of humans we judge that we can cause harm when there is an overriding justification. Thus we might kill or disable humans in waging a just war, or deny freedom to felons as part of our criminal justice system, judging in each case that we have a sufficient justification for doing so. But how strong do our reasons have to be in order to justify harm in the case of animals? The principle of non-maleficence, then, raises for us two central issues: how *extensive* are our obligations not to harm animals and how *strong* are those obligations?

SUMMARY

In this chapter we first examined the claim that animals are not members of the moral community and that we do not have direct moral obligations to them. This conclusion was rejected in large measure because it is strongly counterintuitive: it is simply hard to believe that torturing an animal is not in the least wrong because of the pain and suffering it causes the *animal* but solely because it might prompt us to harm humans, to whom alone (it is claimed) we have obligations. To say that we do have duties to animals, or, more specifically, to say we have the duty to refrain from torturing animals, is just to claim that what we do to the animal, torturing it, is what renders our actions wrong. Contrariwise, to deny that we have any duties to animals is to be forced to conclude that nothing we have ever done or ever could do to an animal, would, by itself, render our actions wrong. So the admission that the gratuitous infliction of pain on an animal *by itself* makes our actions wrong is in essence an admission that we have duties to animals, at least the duty not to torture.

We also looked at arguments by Aquinas and Kant that attempt to block this conclusion, restricting, as they do, the moral community to human beings only. We judged those arguments to be unsuccessful and concluded, on the contrary, that the moral community consists in part of "moral patients" who are not moral agents, that is, individuals to whom we moral agents have obligations but who are incapable of exercising moral responsibility themselves and thus do not have obligations to us (e.g., the unborn, infants, the massively retarded, those suffering from advanced senility). Animals, we argued, are moral patients and therefore in that sense part of the moral community. This still leaves open the question of how strong those duties are relative to other members of the moral community and how extensive those obligations are. But the door has been opened for a consideration of just these issues.

Our examination of social contract theory provided a continuing opportunity to look at a theory that, following Aquinas and Kant, contends that, whatever obligations we have to animals, they are only indirect obligations. In the case of Peter Carruthers, mistreatment of animals is to be of moral concern only when it is expressive of a cruelty likely to negatively influence our treatment of rational agents. This means that cruel treatment of animals is a culturally relative notion, since what is done in one society may not be expressive of a cruelty likely to distort one's treatment of humans, but may in another society be expressive of just such cruelty, likely to infect our dealings with other human beings. Problematically, however, in neither society does the suffering of the animal count on its own merits. Despite Carruthers's desire not to outrage common moral sense with a theory that permits sadistic and brutish treatment of animals, he nevertheless ends up outraging common moral sense by condemning such behavior *for the wrong reason.* For common moral sense not only condemns causing a dog massive first degree burns by soaking it with kerosene and then igniting it, but condemns it because of the gratuitous pain and suffering it causes the dog. For a moral theory to fail to condemn such brutish and sadistic behavior would be a failure of major proportions (as Carruthers recognizes), but it is also a failure to condemn it solely for reasons extraneous to the suffering of the dog (as Carruthers does not seem to recognize).

Having concluded at an intuitive level that we have duties to animals, we next began the search for a moral theory that will help us understand those duties and possibly put us in a position to determine their strength and number. This task, started in this chapter, will continue into the next. We began by examining utilitarianism, a theory that has fully embraced animals as part of the moral community and has provided a model of moral concern for animals. Because animals have an inner life that goes better or worse for them — that is, they experience pleasure and pain — they thereby become fitting candidates, on utilitarian grounds, for moral standing. This seems to be correct, in contrast to Kant's claim that moral concern is to be restricted to rational moral agents. The mere fact that an individual can suffer does seem sufficient, apart from any consideration of rational capacities (which may be morally relevant in other ways) to render it a legitimate object of moral concern. In other words, that an individual is in great pain or is suffering horribly is by itself a morally relevant consideration, and this is so apart from any knowledge of this individual's cognitive capacities. This insight, we argued, can be endorsed and appropriated without accepting the whole moral program of utilitarianism.

In our discussion of utilitarianism the plausible yet provocative claim that equal pains are equal evils and therefore equally worthy of removal was examined. We concurred with this claim, acknowledging that the removal of animal pain will do as much, all else being equal, to make the world a better place as would the removal of an equal quantum of human pain. We denied, however, that animal pain and human pain generate equally strong duties and did so not by denying that equal pains are equal evils but by denying that equal evils equally oblige us to act for their prevention or removal. We gave reasons for giving a preferential treatment to our own species and concluded that normally we have a stronger obligation to remove and prevent human pain and suffering than we have to remove and prevent animal pain and suffering. We argued that this was not speciesism, an arbitrary preference for one's own species, at the same time warning that this does not in any way justify the use and abuse to which we have traditionally subjected animals.

Though we did not in this chapter subject utilitarianism, which comes in many forms and can be nuanced in a great many ways, to careful scrutiny, it is nevertheless a moral theory that I suspect most members of the Christian community would not find fully acceptable (for reasons that have not been fully articulated here). We did, however, critically suggest that in the area of animal welfare, utilitarianism may face the same criticism that it faces in trying to maximize human welfare — an unacceptable willingness to sacrifice the few for the sake of the many, or, as our example had it, sacrificing the welfare of a bull in a bullfight, with its brief and perhaps intense suffering, for the sake of the cumulative pleasures of large numbers of spectators.

Though we rejected utilitarianism as a satisfactory moral theory, we did acknowledge the legitimacy of moral concern for the welfare and well-being of those affected by our actions and the need for any satisfactory moral vision to include a principle of beneficence. That is, we are obligated to make our active contribution toward reducing the world's pain and suffering, contributing to the happiness and welfare of others, enabling them to flourish in ways appropriate to their own kind. But perhaps more to the point in the context of exploring the wrongness of torturing animals would be a principle of non-maleficence, a principle of prohibiting harm to others. We are not to cause others pain, not to disable them, not to deny them pleasure, not to deny them freedom, and not to kill them without an overriding justification – which may, we suggested, be different in the case of humans and animals.

CHAPTER 6

More on Animals and the World of Moral Theory

INTRODUCTION

Here we continue our examination of a variety of moral perspectives from which brutal treatment of animals might be condemned. We shall examine theories that appeal to animal rights (both secular and theological versions), to virtue theory, with its claim that such treatment is expressive of a serious character defect, and, finally, to the biblical notion of stewardship, with its contention that animals are part of a domain that has been entrusted to the human community for appropriate care and preservation.

ANIMAL RIGHTS

One way to understand the immorality of gratuitously inflicting suffering on animals is in terms of rights. Torturing animals is on this view wrong because it is a violation of the rights of the tortured animal. We should note, first, that though most people take for granted the existence of human rights but may be dubious about animal rights, there are many professional ethicists who are dubious about both. It is not that they are moral skeptics, uncertain about any and all moral claims, but rather that they have particular problems with the claim that there are such things as rights. It is not that they judge it to be morally unobjectionable to torture people, or animals for that matter, but rather it is objectionable for reasons other than the violation of rights. In the case of utilitarians, for example, torture is wrong (or is usually wrong) because it violates the principle of utility (or usually does), contributing to a reduction of overall happiness. In the case of the principle of non-maleficence (i.e., the obligation not to cause pain, disable, deny pleasure, deny freedom, or kill, without an overriding justification), to torture a person is wrong because it violates this very principle. Thus there is no need to appeal to rights in order to condemn torture. The principle of non-maleficence, it would be argued, provides us with all the moral ammunition that we need. It is not that it is wrong to cause pain without an overriding justification because people have a right not to be caused pain without an overriding justification. Rather, it simply is wrong to cause people pain without an overriding justification. Though one may wish to justify the principle of non-maleficence, it will not be a justification framed in terms of rights. The appeal to rights is, on such a view, a moral redundancy. Nevertheless, there are those who continue to argue the case for human (and animal) rights, and the appeal to rights is certainly widespread in our society. Moreover, talk about rights does seem to capture something important that might not be fully captured by an appeal to moral principles and their violation.

The rhetoric of animal liberation is in fact filled with appeals to rights. This is consistent with other liberation movements that we have witnessed in recent decades. They have all framed their demands in terms of rights – minority rights, women's rights, gay rights, Third World rights, etc. These groups view themselves as oppressed, and they invoke rights in order to dramatically state their case and, they hope, put an end to their oppression. The animal liberationist also appeals to rights, in this case rights possessed by nonhuman animals. Unquestionably, by stating their case in terms of rights, animal liberationists wish to stress that they are not merely asking for favors and suggesting kind treatment for animals but that they are making moral demands. It is very tempting to view kind and respectful treatment of animals as something optional or discretionary, something that can be chosen as an ideal but not something required or mandatory. In invoking rights, on the contrary, it is being emphasized that maltreatment of animals is a fundamental moral violation, seriously wrong and not to be taken lightly.

Moreover, appeal to rights, more than any other appeal in our moral vocabulary, justifies the use of legal force. So when it is said that rights are being violated, there is an implicit appeal to our legal structure to become cognizant of these overlooked and violated moral rights and to take the steps necessary to secure them as *legal* rights, fully protected by the powers of the state. Thus, all liberation movements have not only made an appeal to the individual conscience but have also sought legal change to preserve and protect the interests of the oppressed. This is also true of animal liberationists. In the case of wanton cruelty to animals (e.g., torture for fun), the claim that an animal's rights are being violated would not only be a demand addressed to the perpetrators of the cruelty (that they stop), but also an appeal to the law (that it make them stop).

Further, the appeal to rights individualizes the offense or maltreatment that is being protested. "You are violating my rights" or "You are violating that person's rights," we might exclaim in the appropriate circumstances. In protesting in this way we sharply focus attention on the person being harmed; we point to the individual (or possibly a group of individuals) whose legitimate claim is being ignored or trampled upon. In contrast, to protest the same offense by appealing to the relevant moral principle that is being violated shifts attention, we may well feel, away from the person being mistreated to a moral abstraction that is not being honored. It is not merely that a universal moral truth is being violated, but that an individual is being violated, an individual who possesses rights and whose legitimate claims are being ignored. The appeal to rights, then, provides a salutary moral focus that might otherwise be lost by mere appeal to universal principles and their violation.

Finally, it is the appeal to rights which, if recognized, ensures that the individual's welfare will not be sacrificed for the good of the larger community. It is rights that place limits on what can be done to the individual in the pursuit of group interests. If we are not to torture one human being for the entertainment value it might bring to millions, it is, according to a rights theorist, the fact that the individual has a right not to be tortured that trumps the pleasure it brings to the millions. Similarly, we may wish to argue that the animal used in a bullfighting exhibition ought not to be brutalized for the pleasure it may bring to a vast crowd, even if the pleasure of the many humans is greater in aggregate than the pain of the one bull. If so, one way to capture this is to speak in terms of rights possessed by animals, in this case a right not to be tortured.

Those in the animal liberation movement appeal to animal "rights" almost as a matter of moral reflex, seeing themselves as historical successors to a series of already legitimized liberation movements. As a matter of strategy, however, one may perhaps wonder whether the appeal to animal rights is the most effective appeal we can make in a community and culture like ours where such talk strikes many as peculiar. In the past, those who have rejected the appeals of various liberation groups have not (typically) denied that members of the group in question have rights or felt that such talk was peculiar. Rather, they have denied that those rights were actually being violated. In the case of animal liberation the appeal to rights itself is highly suspect, and such talk may make many people balk at the whole subject of better treatment for animals. Possibly the appeal "to stop cruelty to animals" would be more effective in reaching people. Nevertheless, we should still want to know, tactical issues aside, do animals in fact have rights? Does such a claim make moral and conceptual sense? Is torturing an animal wrong because it violates a right that the animal possesses or is it wrong for some other reason?

THE QUICK ROUTE TO ANIMAL RIGHTS

There is one way to argue on behalf of animal rights that attempts to avoid much of the tangled discussion that typically accompanies any serious attempt to (a) establish the existence of moral rights (denied by utilitarians and others), (b) establish exactly what those rights are (some theorists arguing for a long list of rights, others for a more abbreviated list), and (c) establish what category of being possesses those rights. These are complicated and difficult issues. To avoid such complications, one could simply *assume* from the outset that human beings have rights and that they have those basic rights that are asserted in such documents as the United Nations Declaration of Human Rights. Most people would grant that much. The challenge that animal rights advocates then put to us is the following: if human beings have rights, it is incumbent upon those who deny rights to animals to point to some relevant property that one must possess in order to have rights, a property possessed by human beings but not possessed by animals. The burden of proof, then, rests on the shoulders of those who would deny rights to animals to show that animals lack the relevant property. Indeed, it could be claimed that just as in the law individuals are presumed to be innocent until proved guilty, so animals should be presumed to possess basic rights until it is proven that they lack that crucial property or properties that one must possess in order to possess rights.

It would be granted that in the case of many rights possessed by humans it is easy to show that they are not possessed by animals, for clearly there are rights that it would make no sense to attribute to an animal. For example, the right to freedom of worship is not a right that is sensibly attributable to an animal. An animal is disqualified from having this right because it lacks an identifiable property essential to its possession, namely, the capacity to worship. But contrast the right to worship with the right not to be tortured, a right that the United Nations Declaration of Human Rights also asserts is possessed by every human being. Whereas animals cannot worship, they can feel pain, they can suffer, they can be tortured; therefore, we cannot disqualify them as holders of a right not to be tortured in the same way that we can disqualify them as holders of a right to worship.

We may be tempted to think that animals do not have rights of any kind because they cannot invoke rights, protest the abuse of their rights, forego the exercise of their rights should they choose, or, in general, do the sorts of things that people do with their rights. Thus it might be argued that in order to have a right one must be able to wield that right, something that humans can do but something animals cannot do. It would follow, however, from such a line of thought that not only animals but also the (human) unborn, infants, the massively retarded, those with advanced senile dementia, the insane, etc., have no rights – not even the right not to be tortured – because they, like the animal, lack the capacity to wield rights. This would be an unpalatable conclusion to have to reach. It would seem more plausible to believe that if there were a proxy who could invoke rights on behalf of a given individual (whether or not that proxy actually does so), then that would be sufficient – as, for instance, other members of society might invoke rights on behalf of the unborn, infants, the massively retarded, the senile, and the insane. Thus, in order to have a right it is not essential that individuals be able to invoke rights on their own behalf but simply that there be those who can invoke those rights for them. And just as people may invoke rights on behalf of infants, so others may invoke rights on behalf of animals.

In order to have rights, it is often argued, it is a necessary condition (and possibly even a sufficient condition) that one have interests; this is the so-called "interest condition" for rights. Thus, those who lack interests cannot have rights. And why must one have interests in order to have rights? Because rights, the argument runs, are protective moral coverings for interests. They are moral entitlements to have certain of one's interests respected. But one cannot have a moral entitlement to have one's interests respected if one has no interests or is not the kind of being that can have interests. Thus, rocks cannot sensibly be said to have rights because rocks lack interests; therefore, lacking as they do that which rights morally protect, they can have no rights either.

The question is, do animals have interests and therefore do they satisfy the interest requirement for possessing rights? Or are they merely like rocks – without interests and therefore without rights? It would certainly seem that they have interests. Indeed, it seems contrary to my dog's interest to be beaten and deprived of adequate quantities of food and water; and it is in his interests to be fed and exercised regularly. Perhaps on a generous understanding of interests even plants could be said to have interests. For example, it might be observed that it is in a plant's interest to be watered regularly because the plant needs water and lack of water will harm the plant, threatening its existence as a self-maintaining organism. However, for those who argue that interests are not merely a necessary prerequisite for having rights but are by themselves a sufficient condition for having rights (i.e., all who have interests also have rights simply by virtue of those interests), this broad understanding of interests may prove to be too broad, since it would turn out that plants, having interests, also have rights.

If one wants to avoid this implication, one might construe "interest" more narrowly. Thus we might speak of "affective interests." Indeed, both humans and animals, but not plants, have interests that concern how they feel, that relate to their conscious sense of well-being. Because humans and animals have an inner psychological life that they can experience as more or less pleasant, more or less satisfying to them, they therefore have affective interests, interests that relate to that inner psychological life. Thus, it is both in humans' interest and in animals' interest not to have their lives made miserable by suffering; this is not, however, something that can be said of plants, which have no inner psychological life, and cannot be made miserable. Therefore, animals, as well as humans, but not plants, have affective interests. So if by the interest condition we mean that having affective interests is a necessary condition for having rights, then sentient animals cannot be disqualified as holders of rights in the same way that rocks or plants can.

TOM REGAN AND ANIMAL RIGHTS

When discussing animal rights, one cannot overlook Tom Regan's book, *The Case for Animal Rights.*[1] This wide-ranging and carefully argued work is

1. Tom Regan, *The Case for Animal Rights* (Berkeley and Los Angeles: University of California Press, 1983).

still the single most important discussion on this topic. In the academic arena, Regan is, along with Peter Singer, one of the two most influential and respected defenders of the moral requirement of concern and care for animals. In terms of practical advocacy, there may be little to separate Regan and Singer. At the theoretical level, nevertheless, they are worlds apart, for they place their moral concern for animals and their respective claims that we humans have duties to animals in radically different moral frameworks. One can best appreciate the character of Regan's argument from rights theory by setting him over against Singer's utilitarianism.

What is at issue between Regan and Singer, then, is not the belief that animals have moral standing and that humans have important duties to animals, for these are shared beliefs. Nor do they significantly differ as to the implications of these beliefs — both call for a radical reorientation of traditional attitudes toward animals, along with sweeping changes in our treatment of them. Where they differ is in the theoretical basis for their conviction and in their understanding of the adequacy of various moral frameworks. Thus, it is Singer's utilitarianism and Regan's rights theory, not the appropriateness of moral concern for animals, that is at issue. Both are attempting to make the case that animals have significant moral standing, but they are also seeking to make a case for their respective moral visions into which moral concern for animals is to be placed. Regan and Singer both believe that their particular moral theory does the best job of providing a theoretical basis for an appropriate moral concern for animals. At issue, then, is not merely the welfare of animals but the welfare of one's own moral theory.

Although Regan's talk of animal rights may strike many in the Christian community (and in the larger community as well) as suspect, he is in fact bringing to the moral debate about animals an ethical perspective that many Christians will find quite congenial. Suppose we were talking not about animals but about human beings; in that case there would be considerable agreement with what Regan has to say. Regan would argue that human beings have rights and that those rights cannot be set aside simply because the larger community's interests could be furthered by doing so. Thus, 1 percent of the population cannot be enslaved for the benefit of the other 99 percent, even if there will be a net gain in overall happiness; in other words, the right of the 1 percent not to be enslaved morally defeats the appeal made by the 99 percent to this desirable increase in their net happiness. Further, many in the Christian community would concur with Regan's assessment of utilitarianism: utilitarians wrongly view human beings as mere "receptacles of value," as Regan puts it.[2] By this Regan means to charge that utilitarians teach, in effect, that what is of value in individuals is the content found in the receptacle – pleasure or happiness (according to classical utilitarianism) or the satisfaction of one's preferences (according to Singer) – not the receptacle itself. So, according to utilitarianism – or at least according to certain versions of it (i.e., according to what is called "total utilitarianism") – our moral goal is to produce as much of this valuable content as we possibly can. Such a moral vision seems analogous (in certain respects) to a farmer whose herd of cows has value only to the extent that the cows produce milk – the more the better. The cows have no value in themselves but only as containers or producers of what is of recognized value. So, just as the point of a dairy farm is to produce as much milk as one possibly can, it being legitimate to treat cows in any fashion that will maximize the output of milk, so the point of morality is to maximize the production of the total amount of happiness (or satisfied preferences). It is then legitimate to treat persons in any way that will maximize the desired total output of happiness. On such a view, each of us becomes a sort of hedonic cow, our value depending on our production of pleasure or happiness.

In contrast to a view such as utilitarianism that construes individuals as mere "receptacles of value," Regan declares that the receptacles themselves are of value. As such, they merit respect. Their value does not ebb and flow according to their content, which is to say that they have inherent value or worth. Unlike the farmer's cows, who have value to the extent that they produce milk, humans are not valuable only to the extent that they produce happiness in themselves or in others. Indeed, this is what Regan calls "the postulate of inherent value," and it is a *denial* that one's value depends either on one's own experiences (the content of the receptacle) or on the contribution one makes to the experiences of others (improving the content of other receptacles). That is, my inherent worth is not dependent on either my being happy or my making others happy. Indeed, as Regan comments, "the lonely, forsaken, unwanted, and unloved are no more nor less inherently valuable than those who enjoy a more hospitable relationship with others."[3]

This postulate of inherent value, according to Regan, generates a further principle, "the Respect Principle," which declares that individuals who have inherent value are to be treated in ways that fully respect that inherent value. This is but to say that individuals with inherent value have rights.

2. Regan, *The Case for Animal Rights,* p. 236.

3. Regan, *The Case for Animal Rights,* p. 237.

That is, they are morally entitled by virtue of their inherent worth to be treated and respected in certain ways appropriate to that worth. Further, inherent value is not something one has in degrees, as if some individuals have greater inherent value and therefore are worthy of more respect than other individuals. Rather, inherent value is something you either have completely and totally or not at all. The consequence of this is that each individual who is a bearer of inherent value is worthy of the same moral respect as any other individual. Thus, each individual with inherent value has, for example, the same right to be free from torture. Unhappy individuals don't have less inherent value and weaker rights than happy individuals, nor do individuals who contribute little to the happiness of others have less inherent value and weaker rights than those who contribute more. All have the same inherent value and the same strong right not to be harmed.

To the extent that all of this is taken to apply to human beings, it might be relatively uncontroversial, but Regan, of course, is not just talking about human beings. He is also talking about animals — they too have inherent value, they too are to be respected, and they too possess rights. Here, of course, matters become controversial, especially as we reflect that, according to Regan, all who have inherent value, be they animals or human beings, have inherent value to the *same* degree, humans and animals commanding thereby the same respect (though that respect may take different forms). Regan's crucial move is to argue that all who are "subjects-of-a-life" have inherent value, have the same inherent value, and therefore are to be equally respected as possessors of rights. And all "normal mammalian animals aged one or more" are, he tells us, "subjects-of-a-life" and thus possessors of inherent value. To be the subject-of-a-life, one must be more than just alive, indeed one must be more than merely conscious; one must have the following features:

(1) beliefs and desires
(2) perception
(3) memory
(4) a sense of one's own future
(5) an emotional life
(6) the ability to experience pleasure and pain
(7) preference and welfare interests
(8) the ability to initiate action in pursuit of desires and goals
(9) a psycho-physical identity over time.[4]

4. Regan, *The Case for Animal Rights,* p. 243.

This is an impressive list of features and one might be tempted to agree that those who have these features have, as Regan argues, "a distinctive kind of value — inherent value — and are not to be viewed or treated as mere receptacles."[5] If it were agreed that all possessors of these characteristics have inherent worth, then all one needs to do in order to show that all normal mammals aged one year or more possess inherent value — with all the rights, privileges, and respect attaching thereto — would be to show that they possess these features. But do all normal mammals one year of age or older possess these characteristics? Regan argues that they do.

Consider, as an example, a one-year-old dog, Fido. Regan contends that Fido is not merely living or alive but crucially is the subject-of-a-life, possessing all the features enumerated above, and hence is one of those who has inherent value. Fido, it so happens, has buried a bone in the backyard and, at a later point in time, returns to the backyard, unearths the bone, and eats it. According to Regan's analysis, all the following are involved: beliefs and desires (the dog *believes* the bone is buried in the backyard and *desires* that bone); perception (the dog *sees* and *recognizes* the bone); memory (the dog *recalls* where the bone is buried); the initiation of action in pursuit of desires and goals (the dog goes to the backyard and digs *in order to* unearth the bone); a sense of one's own future (the bone was buried for one's own use at a later time and, also, when the dog begins to unearth the bone it does so in anticipation of having it in the very near future). Further, Fido has an emotional life (experiencing fear over certain threats, joy when petted and played with); experiences pleasure and pain (eating is pleasurable, being beaten causes pain, etc.); has both preference and welfare interests (to be beaten is contrary to its welfare and contrary to what it wants or prefers for itself); and has a psycho-physical identity (the Fido who feels sore today is the same Fido who was beaten yesterday). Thus Fido fulfills all the conditions essential to being a subject-of-a-life and therefore has inherent value.

Regan acknowledges that a critic of all this might offer a stimulus-response analysis of what Fido did in burying and later retrieving his bone, not an analysis that attributes to the dog beliefs, desires, memories, acting to achieve goals, and so forth. But one can also offer a stimulus-response analysis of human behavior devoid of references to beliefs, desires, etc. Indeed, Regan argues that the dog's behavior no more requires a stimulus-response analysis than does human behavior. To put matters differently, Fido's burying the bone is as legitimately analyzed in terms of

5. Regan, *The Case for Animal Rights,* p. 243.

beliefs and desires as is a pirate burying and retrieving his treasure. So a stimulus-response analysis of behavior no more threatens the claim that Fido is the subject-of-a-life that goes more or less well for him than it threatens the claim that a treasure-burying pirate is the subject-of-a-life that goes more or less well for him.

All this brings us to the central question of the present chapter: why is it wrong to inflict gratuitous pain and suffering on an animal in circumstances where all of us would agree it to be wrong? According to Regan's account, it is wrong because it violates a right that the animal has not to be harmed without an overriding justification. This right is generated in the following way: *the postulate of inherent value* (i.e., individuals with a subjective life at least comparable to that of a one-year-old mammal have value in their own right) gives rise to *the postulate of respect* (i.e., individuals with inherent value are to be treated in a manner respectful of that value) which next gives rise to *the harm principle* (i.e., individuals with inherent value are not to be harmed in the absence of an overriding justification).

One may feel that all of this is unnecessarily complicated, if all one is interested in showing is why it is wrong to inflict gratuitous pain on animals. For why must one successfully argue that the animal has inherent worth in order to show that it is wrong to torture it? Isn't it enough that there is suffering and it is gratuitous? If a creature can suffer, it is clearly in that creature's interest not to be made to suffer gratuitously and it would seem as easy to generate a right not to be tortured from these considerations alone as it would by adding complex discussions of inherent worth. But we must keep in mind that Regan has even bigger fish to fry, for he also wants to argue that one-year-old mammals also have a right to life and for this kind of claim talk of inherent value may be essential.

ANDREW LINZEY: A THEOLOGICAL CASE FOR ANIMAL RIGHTS

If one wants a distinctly theological case for animal rights one must begin by looking at the writings of Andrew Linzey, who has been described by Tom Regan as "the foremost theologian working in the field of animal/human relations."[6] In keeping with his desire to make a theological rather than a purely philosophical case, Linzey seeks to ground animal rights in

6. On the back cover of Linzey's book, *Christianity and the Rights of Animals* (New York: Crossroad, 1987).

God, who alone, he contends, is the possessor of absolute rights and thus the distributor of all rights, and not, as Regan does, in the inherent worth that animals possess simply by virtue of their own natural capacities. Accordingly, Linzey does not even speak of "animal rights," as Regan does, but rather of the "theos-rights" of animals (or, in other words, the "God-rights" of animals), thereby stressing that the rights animals possess they possess because God has the right to have what he has created and what he values appropriately respected – and animals have been created by God and are valued by God. Therefore animals are appropriate objects of respect and concern.

Linzey sums up his theory of animal rights with the following three propositions:

(1) that God as Creator has rights in his creation;
(2) that Spirit-filled, breathing creatures, composed of flesh and blood, are subjects of inherent value to God; and
(3) that these animals can make an objective moral claim which is nothing less than God's claim upon us.[7]

In the first of his three propositions, Linzey asserts that the basis for all rights is the right of God as Creator to have what he has made and what he values appropriately honored and respected. For this reason, all rights, human and animal, are not merely rights but are theos-rights and thus constitute, as Linzey stresses in his third proposition, nothing less than God's claim to have his creation respected in the ways he wants it to be respected. To violate theos-rights, therefore, is ultimately to wrong God and ignore his claims as Creator.

In his crucial second proposition, Linzey identifies those who are bearers of theos-rights: all animals who are (a) Spirit-filled, (b) breathing, and (c) made of flesh and blood. "The Spirit-filled," the crucial notion for Linzey, are those individuals into whom the Creator-Spirit has breathed a certain minimal capacity for psychic life. Thus, fish, insects, and microbes, though subjects of value simply because they are alive, are nevertheless not bearers of theos-rights because they lack the minimal requisite psychic capacity or, as Linzey puts it, they lack (or are not known to possess) "spiritually analogous lives to those of humans."[8] Basically, bearers of theos-rights are mammals. In this regard Linzey observes that his

7. Linzey, *Christianity and the Rights of Animals,* p. 69.
8. Linzey, *Christianity and the Rights of Animals,* p. 84.

"Spirit-filled" criterion for theos-rights has "some correspondence" with Tom Regan's "subject-of-a-life" criterion that includes all mentally normal mammals of a year or more. For Regan and Linzey, then, there is fundamental agreement as to which animals possess rights, but they differ over the theoretical basis for those rights: for Regan, these particular animals have rights because their psychic life is of inherent value, whereas for Linzey those same animals have rights because God especially values their level of psychic life (i.e., they "are subjects of inherent value to God").

Linzey's rejection of Regan's claim that it is solely because of their natural capacities that mammals have value and his own claim that it is solely because God values them that mammals have value are not problem free. Clearly, Linzey fears that Regan's view leaves no role for God, animals having value by virtue of what they are, independently of any bestowal of value on them by God. God seems morally dispensable, and this, Linzey judges, is theologically unacceptable. To rectify this, he argues that it is not natural capacities per se but the fact that God values those natural capacities that gives them their value and ultimately gives animals their theos-rights. As Linzey puts it, "the theos-perspective does not locate the value of beings in any faculty or capacity, but in the will of God, which may be deduced from the givenness of Spirit-filled individuals."[9] It is God the valuer, then, that is morally foundational, not what is valued, in this case, Spirit-filled, breathing creatures, composed of flesh and blood. But here the old theological conundrum cannot be avoided: does God value animals because *they* are valuable (a theistic variant of Regan's position) or are they valuable because God chooses to place value on them (Linzey's apparent position)?

To appreciate the difference between these two positions briefly consider a comparable theological dispute that centers not over animals but over humans and what it means to say that humans are valuable because they are in the image of God. Though many disputes swirl around the concept of the image of God, one of them is a disagreement between those who understand the image of God as a network of human capacities (latent or actualized) that enable one to relate to God in special ways, and those who view the image of God as a special status, sovereignly conferred upon humans by God. Let me say a word about each of these views and then transfer this distinction back to our discussion of animals.

The first view construes the image of God as the capacity to exercise rational, moral, and spiritual agency, which in turn enables one to re-

9. Linzey, *Christianity and the Rights of Animals,* p. 76.

spond to God, to enter into a personal relationship with God, and to be morally and spiritually accountable to God. As Alan Richardson put it, there is that in "man" that enables "him" to "answer God's address, hear his law and make or withhold his conscious and deliberate response. There is that in man which is capable of responding to the divine Word; man is akin to God in this respect at least, that he hears God's word: as we say, like speaks to like. . . ."[10] It is this special capacity of which Richardson speaks that makes humans uniquely valuable.

The problem that some, including Linzey, would see with this way of putting matters is that it invests value in us, not in God. We humans are valuable because of what we are, our value residing in our own nature. But does this unacceptably exclude God from the moral picture? I don't believe that it does, for this human capacity with its inherent value has, after all, been created by God, who still remains the Creator and source of this value. Surely we do not wish to say that God cannot create what has inherent value, place it in the world, and expect that inherent value to be recognized and respected — exactly what, it might be suggested, God has done. Praise would continue to go to God as creator of this inherent value, praise to God for those he has created with capacities for rational, moral, and spiritual agency. Further, the inherent value attaching to these special human capacities would be increased immeasurably because of the purposes that God has for those who are so endowed: to come to know God, to serve God, and to be transformed into God's moral likeness.

A contrasting view sees the image of God not as a network of capacities but as a special status conferred by God. Thus, individual humans are valuable not because they have certain capacities (say, the capacity to respond to and know God) but solely because they are declared to be valuable by a sovereign act of God. This declaration of value is not based on inherently valuable capacities; rather, this value is created by a sovereign act of divine valuation. No feature attaching to human nature requires this conferral of value and status, so no appeal to what we are or what we inherently possess can be made as a basis for a special respect or for the possession of any set of rights. Therefore, to declare that humans are in the image of God is to assert that they have a special status which is the sole product of a divine act of valuation. It is not based on anything that humans are in and of themselves.

The difficulty I have with such a view, even though I may sympathize

10. Alan Richardson, *Genesis I–XI* (London: SCM Press, 1953), pp. 53-54.

with its motivation (i.e., to retain God as the basis for value and to undercut any basis for human pride), is that it renders the divine valuation essentially arbitrary. We can receive no answer to the question, "Why does God confer this special status on humans rather than on butterflies and ladybugs?" If we answer, "Because humans, unlike butterflies and ladybugs, are rational, moral, and spiritual agents capable of coming to know, love, and serve God," then we have returned to the first understanding of the image of God as a network of human capacities that render humans more valuable than butterflies and ladybugs. It is this first understanding, I judge, that is to be preferred.

Much more could be said about this debate, but let us, with these considerations in mind, return to our discussion of animals. As with humans, so with animals: we can understand their value either as a product of their natural capacities or as a sovereignly conferred status bestowed upon that which has no value apart from that act of bestowal. I suggest, for the same reasons given in the discussion of the image of God, that we should choose the first alternative over the second. For if animals have value and possess theos-rights solely by virtue of a sovereignly conferred status, then there is no reason at all why God should confer such status on mammals one year of age and older rather than on turnips and carrots. To be sure, on this view of matters – what I understand to be Linzey's view – God has chosen to confer value on the inner psychic life of animals and consequently animals have value because that divinely conferred value attaches to their psychic life, but again there is no reason on this view why God should have conferred that value on the psychic life of animals rather than on the vegetative life of turnips and carrots. The superior value of animals over turnips and carrots becomes arbitrary, for matters could have been just the reverse, with the superior value being conferred by God on vegetative life. The price paid, then, for denying inherent value to animals (or humans) is that the divine conferral of value becomes arbitrary.

To avoid such an arbitrary bestowal of value, we must return to the first alternative and assert that animals have a value that exceeds that of turnips and carrots because their inner psychic life is in fact inherently more valuable than the vegetative life of turnips. We should not, I suggest, find this troublesome, as if by lodging the value of animals (or at least part of their value) in their own natural capacities we render God morally peripheral, as Linzey fears. It remains the case that it is God who creates this inherently valuable psychic life. It is God's special purposes for such life that give it an enhanced value, and it is the God who has created this inherent value with his special purposes for it who wants it appropriately respected and who holds us accountable for our treatment of it. Therefore, to speak of the inherent value of the inner subjective or psychic life of animals does not banish God from the moral scene, and it avoids the charge that animals (and humans) are rendered valuable by an arbitrary divine decree.

If this line of reasoning is found persuasive, then, contrary to Linzey, even for the Christian, rights can be understood as guarding what has inherent value, though indeed a value created by God and enhanced by God's purposes for it. To honor such rights is, therefore, on this account, simply to respect this inherent value, treating it in a manner appropriate to that value, and to respect the purposes for which it was created; to violate such rights is, contrariwise, to fail to respect this inherent value and the purpose for which it was created. This means, among other things, that the writings of a Tom Regan, should they be found cogent, can be understood not as an account antithetical to a Christian vision and to which an alternative account such as Andrew Linzey's must be devised, but rather as a careful analysis of what those in the Christian tradition take to be a divinely created inherent value. To be sure, in addition to what Tom Regan has to say, those in the Christian tradition will wish to underscore the role of God as Creator of this value, God's value-enhancing purposes for this value, and, finally, our accountability to God for our treatment of this value. These, of course, are not incidental additions.

VIRTUE THEORY: AVOIDING CRUELTY

There is yet another ethical standpoint from which to seek an account of the immorality of mistreating animals, the standpoint of virtue theory. When C. S. Lewis observed, "We might think that God wanted simply obedience to a set of rules: whereas He really wants people of a particular sort,"[11] he was giving expression to a vision of the moral life that gives central place to character development, to the acquisition of a set of virtues, and not merely to the application of moral rules to particular cases or to the invoking of rights to settle disputes. This approach to morality is known as virtue theory and has a long and ancient heritage, going back at least to Aristotle. It finds expression in the biblical tradition with its emphasis on the believer being transformed into the image of Christ (Rom.

11. C. S. Lewis, *Mere Christianity* (New York: Macmillan, 1960), p. 77.

8:29) who in turn is the image of God (2 Cor. 4:4; Col. 1:15). The believer is to be inspired and transformed by Christ's own example of self-giving love, compassion, and humility (Phil. 2:1-8). And throughout the Scriptures the believer is warned against a range of vices and encouraged to embrace a range of virtues (Rom. 1:29-31; Gal. 5:19-23).

In the modern era, among both philosophers and theologians, virtue theory was eclipsed by an approach to ethics that viewed ethical theory as teaching one how to make correct moral decisions by applying the relevant principles or rules to situations calling for choice. And when one thinks of taking a course in ethics one tends to think of a course that will evaluate various ethical decision-making procedures. Indeed, when one examines books on ethics this is often what one finds. One enters a world dominated by discussions of principles and rules. Which set of principles and rules should guide one's conduct? How does one rationally justify those principles and rules? Do they have exceptions and how does one decide what those exceptions are? Do they ever conflict, and, if so, how does one resolve those conflicts? And so forth. What one does not find (up until quite recently) is much discussion of virtue. For example, what is a virtue? What virtues should shape and give direction to our lives? How do we rationally justify those virtues? What is courage or gratitude or modesty and how do they give moral shape to a life? These and other questions relating to virtue theory were largely ignored, for ethicists were basically about the business of solving moral dilemmas by the appropriate application of principles and rules. The emphasis was on *acting* rightly, not on *being* virtuous. In recent years, however, there has been a renewal of interest in virtue theory by both theologians and philosophers. This is a salutary revival, because principles and rules, problems and decisions, are not the whole of the moral story, and may even be only a small part of the story. Though virtue is not the whole story either, it is at least a part of that story and a neglected part, and therefore deserves serious attention because of its long eclipse.

Of course, all moral theorists, even those who are not virtue theorists, believe in some sense in virtue. At issue is not whether virtue is good and vice is bad, or whether a person should be good or bad. At issue in the debate over virtue is whether virtue is a basic moral notion, as virtue theorists insist, or whether it is a secondary notion, deriving all its point and value from its usefulness on behalf of those principles that *are* morally basic. Thus, for example, a utilitarian views as virtues those traits of character that prompt one to behave in such a way that happiness and welfare are maximized. In contrast, vices are character traits that have the reverse effect, prompting one to behave in ways that either reduce or fail to maximize happiness. Thus, a person who is cruel, dishonest, selfish, ungenerous, and unsympathetic will not be the sort of person who will contribute to a happier world but, on the contrary, will contribute to the diminution of happiness. On the other hand, a sympathetic, generous, caring, and honest person will be the sort of person, it is argued, who contributes significantly to the goals mandated by the principle of utility: reducing suffering, contributing to the welfare and happiness of family, friends, and community. On such a view of matters, traits of character become vices or virtues, depending on their tendency either to serve or impede utilitarian goals. Thus, character traits derive their moral significance from the principle of utility, which, for the utilitarian, is morally basic. A utilitarian, then, is not a virtue theorist.

If one is not a utilitarian with a single basic moral principle to guide one's conduct but is instead committed to a more complex ethical theory, a theory that affirms a *number* of basic moral principles, including fundamental considerations of justice and a range of rights, then virtues are those character traits that prompt one to behave in accord with those principles, to serve justice and to honor rights. Vices, of course, would be character traits that prompt one to violate those principles, ignore considerations of justice, and disregard rights. Again, as with utilitarianism, virtues and vices derive their moral significance from something else that is morally basic, in this case, principles, duties, and rights.

In contrast to this, virtue theorists argue that virtues (or at least some virtues) are themselves morally basic and do not derive their significance from principles, duties, or rights. Thus, when I am in a situation calling for a moral response, it is not merely that I ought to make the right decision (via application of the appropriate principle or rule) but that I also ought to be the right sort of person in that situation (by giving expression to the appropriate virtue). Thus I might be advised not to be vengeful or boastful or arrogant or cowardly or cruel or dishonest or disloyal or selfish, thereby being directed *how not to be* in that situation; or I might be advised positively to be modest or compassionate or kind or friendly or courteous or loyal or forgiving, thus being directed *how to be* in that situation. Here the moral life gets its direction from virtues that are to be cultivated and expressed in one's living, and from vices that are to be eliminated and not allowed to find expression in one's life.

The moral life for the virtue theorist is more than acting properly and preparing oneself to act properly when the time for decision comes. This is too narrow a conception of the moral life, for it equates the moral life with isolated moments of decision-making. To remedy this, virtue theorists insist (and I think rightly) that morality must focus on "being," not merely on "acting." "Being" encompasses "acting" but also much more than this, for virtues are those desirable traits of character that will manifest themselves not merely in action but in one's intentions, feelings, emotions, desires, hopes, attitudes, interests, and thoughts. All of this is part of the moral life, and although there may be an intimate connection between these facets of one's character and how one acts, their moral significance is not exhaustively accounted for in terms of their giving rise to particular discrete acts or behaviors. Virtue theory thus endows much more of life with moral significance than would be the case were life construed, according to the principles-decisions approach to ethics, as long periods of living punctuated by infrequent moral "moments" when one is called upon to make a choice guided by moral rules.

Thus, the virtue theorist insists, the bulk of my living is to give expression to virtue, even when I am not confronted by a moral problem calling for solution or a conflict between duty and temptation calling for a resolute decision in favor of duty. Thus, our speech is to be civil, polite, decent, modest, tactful, etc.; our attitudes toward people are to be caring, compassionate, concerned, respectful, appreciative, etc.; our reasoning is to be fair-minded, respectful of truth, open to ideas that come from others, etc.; our personal evaluations of others are to be honest, charitable, understanding, etc. None of this needs to be translated into rule-mandated conduct in order for it to be morally significant. Even when it does come to acting appropriately we may not have enough principles or rules to guide all our conduct. When we do run out of principles and rules, after all, we still ought not do certain things, because to do so would be disloyal or cowardly or cruel, and we ought to do other things because this would be kind or gracious or modest. Thus, even when seeking to act correctly we need more guidance than rules can offer us.

And when it comes to abusing animals, we can say that would be cruel, expressive of a vice, and incompatible with the virtue of compassion, and therefore to be condemned. This may be exactly what is captured in that Old Testament text: "A righteous man has regard for the life of his beast, but the mercy of the wicked is cruel" (Prov. 12:10). To be cruel to an animal is to give expression to a bad character and to contribute to the formation of that bad character. Indeed, it is expressive of "wickedness." Thus, one need not ponder the complexities of rights or compute utilitarian outcomes but simply see such an act for what it is, the sort of act a cruel and wicked person would do.

The kind of cruelty that is of appropriate concern here is what might be termed "animal cruelty," a disposition to inflict pain or suffering on animals, to be insensitive to their suffering. Animal cruelty may have no carryover in terms of one's treatment of and concern for humans; there may be a complete psychological separation between one's attitude toward humans and one's attitude toward animals — but it remains a vice all the same.

But what is it that qualifies a particular character trait for virtue status? What is it, in other words, that virtues do that renders them virtues rather than vices or merely optional personality traits? And how should we judge new proposals for virtue-standing, proposals to the effect that a particular trait, say, "animal concern," be embraced as a virtue? Is there some single feature that unites all virtues and would enable us to recognize them as virtues? Or are there multiple features that qualify character traits as virtues, some traits satisfying certain of those features, other traits satisfying yet other features? This, no doubt, is a complicated issue. But reflecting within a Christian context one might at least begin by suggesting that virtues are those traits of character that help create and enrich what Nicholas Wolterstorff has called "shalom" (the Hebrew word for "peace").

Shalom is a vision of a way of life that is first articulated in the Old Testament and finds further expression in the New Testament. Shalom involves, first, "right, harmonious relationships to God and delight in his services"; second, "right, harmonious relationships to other human beings and delight in human community"; and, third and finally, "right, harmonious relationship to nature and delight in our physical surroundings."[12] The stress on right, harmonious relationships is, in part, a stress on justice and appropriate respect. As we relate to God, to other humans, and to our physical surroundings, our relationships are not to be marred by injustice and lack of due respect. But shalom involves more than this, for shalom, as Wolterstorff comments, "is not merely absence of hostility, not merely being in right relationship. Shalom at its highest is enjoyment in one's relationships."[13] This is a helpful picture, but we might wish to add to it, rendering explicit what may be implicit in the third item in Wolterstorff's litany of harmonious relationships and delights. That is, shalom also includes "right, harmonious relationships with *animals* and

12. Nicholas Wolterstorff, *Until Justice and Peace Embrace* (Grand Rapids: Eerdmans, 1983), p. 70.

13. Wolterstorff, *Until Justice and Peace Embrace,* p. 69.

delight in their existence." (We might also, to complete our list, add "right, harmonious relationships with ourselves and an appropriate delight in what one has been called to be by God.") Something like this, then, is shalom, and virtues can be understood as those character traits that help create, preserve, and enrich shalom.

Compassion would be extended, then, to include the suffering of animals. There might also be, in addition to extending the scope of this already existing virtue to include animals, the creation of new virtues (new at least for some of us) that should be part of the character of the good person, "animal concern" and "animal delight" being excellent candidates. If, as Wolterstorff says, shalom is "both God's cause in the world and our human calling,"[14] then we are called to be people of shalom and therefore called to be certain kinds of people possessed of a range of appropriate virtues, including those that relate to animals and the world of nature.

STEWARDSHIP: CARING FOR WHAT BELONGS TO ANOTHER

As soon as one begins talking of accountability to God for our treatment of animals, one is quickly drawn to another ethical framework as a way of understanding that accountability, the framework of stewardship. To place active concern and care for animals, indeed active concern and care for the whole natural order, in the context of stewardship is to offer a moral and spiritual vision that will be attractive to many in the Christian community. And this is understandably so, for it is to appropriate a theological theme found in Scripture, one already familiar to the Christian community and one that gives central place to God, who assigns to the stewards their responsibilities and holds them accountable for the faithful discharge of those responsibilities. Talk of stewardship in the care and protection of animals will not, like talk of animal rights or utilitarianism, strike the Christian as an alien form of discourse in need of a defense. Therefore, a look at the theological theme of stewardship and its application to the animal world is crucially important.

First of all, what is a steward? A steward "in the basic sense (is) a person who manages the affairs of a large and wealthy household. The tasks of a steward in different cases include supervision of the service at the master's table, oversight of other household servants, or management of

14. Wolterstorff, *Until Justice and Peace Embrace,* p. 72.

the master's finances."[15] A steward, then, is a servant but not an ordinary servant. He is "a superior servant, a sort of supervisor or foreman who must make decisions, give orders and take charge."[16] As a manager, the steward has been put in charge of the possessions of another. These are the master's possessions and it is to the master that the steward must give account. So although the steward is a superior servant who is given great authority, even to the point of representing the master as his deputy in the latter's absence, it remains nevertheless the case that the steward is a servant who only manages what belongs to another and therefore must not arrogantly assume, on pain of punishment, that those possessions belong to the steward himself (Isa. 22:15-21).

In Scripture, the steward-master relationship becomes a metaphor for the relationship between the believer and God, the believer being assigned the role of steward and God the role of master (Matt. 25:14-30; Luke 12:35-38; 16:1-8; 19:12-27). It is a metaphor for the whole Christian life: as Christians we are to live our lives as stewards, taking the gifts and talents God has given us and using them faithfully and to their fullest in God's service. More specific application of this metaphor is made to the apostles, who are said to be stewards of God's mysteries (1 Cor. 4:1, 2) and to bishops, who are said to be stewards entrusted with oversight of God's people (Titus 1:7).

Inspired by the ecological crisis and a growing sense of responsibility to care for the natural order, Christians have begun to see their role on the planet earth as one of being stewards of God's creation. The earth, with all its nonhuman life, belongs to God and is to be used by humans only in ways that recognize the divine ownership; we are thus to discard any notion that the earth is ours to do with as we please. If, as Douglas Hall observes, "stewardship does not describe any one dimension of the Christian life, it describes the whole posture called 'Christian,'"[17] then it is understandable that Christians will seek to illuminate their relationship with nature (and animals) in terms of the metaphor of stewardship. More precisely, stewardship is a triadic relationship: "X is steward for Y over Z."[18] For present purposes, then, that would mean that *humans* (or possibly

15. Allen C. Myers, ed., *The Eerdmans Bible Dictionary* (Grand Rapids: Eerdmans, 1987), p. 970.

16. Douglas John Hall, *The Steward: A Biblical Symbol Come of Age* (New York: Friendship, 1982), p. 17.

17. Hall, *The Steward,* p. 124.

18. Alastair S. Gunn, "Traditional Ethics and the Moral Status of Animals," *Environmental Ethics* 5 (1983): 152.

Christians) are stewards *for God* over *nonhuman animals.* Despite the fact that this metaphor of stewardship is sometimes used outside a theistic context, it does not seem that this analysis can be qualified so as to fully make sense outside such a context. A steward is, after all, accountable to someone, but to whom if not to God? To society at large? To human posterity? Such suggestions seem not only morally anemic, but to go contrary to one of the purposes for introducing the stewardship metaphor to begin with, namely, to introduce standards for the treatment of animals and an accountability that transcends both mere usefulness of animals for the human community and accountability to that community.

Alastair Gunn in his own advocacy of the stewardship model for the construction of an enviromental ethic, including an ethic for the treatment of animals, argues, contrary to what we have just suggested, that even secularists who have no place for God in their moral vision can adopt the stewardship model, acting *as if* they were stewards.[19] One may wonder, does acting as if one were a steward also mean acting as if there were a God to whom one was accountable? If so, then all of this seems to be mere pretense and does not constitute an actual moral/spiritual vision but is only an inspiring bit of make-believe. So it would seem that the stewardship model, if it is to be a substantial proposal, must, contrary to Gunn, be a proposal that takes seriously God's reality. Whereas the other bases for an ethic of animal concern (e.g., animal rights) can be placed in a theistic context, but need not be, the stewardship model *requires* such a context.

So, on this model, humans are to be stewards for God, but stewards for God over . . . what exactly? How extensive is that category over which we are to exercise our stewardship? Would it make sense, for example, to speak of our being stewards for God over other adult humans? As a general suggestion this seems a bit awkward. Perhaps this is because the steward is to exercise *authority over* that which has been entrusted to the steward's care. Other human beings, because they are of equal standing and are also called to be stewards, do not seem to be fitting objects of such authority. One can exercise stewardship over nature, indeed over plants, trees, animals, and ecosystems. All these are legitimate objects of stewardly authority, it would seem, because the steward is making decisions on behalf of those who have no capacity to make decisions for themselves. To be sure, bishops, who have a special spiritual authority, are to be faithful stewards of the people of God (Titus 1:7), and this does represent a case of stewardly authority being exercised over other humans who have in this

19. Gunn, "Traditional Ethics and the Moral Status of Animals," p. 155.

case subjected themselves to that authority. In general, however, we do not stand in any such authoritative relationship to other adult human beings. Indeed, where we observe such a relationship, such as in a slave society or in a patriarchal society, what is needed is not stewardship faithfully exercised over the subordinate party but liberation from the conditions that create this subordination. In the case of parents and their children, the stewardship motif might be illuminating, but as the child grows up the parents progressively relinquish their stewardly role; parents and their grown children do not stand in a stewardly relationship.

Perhaps, contrary to what I have suggested, the notion of stewardship could be enlarged and its contours reshaped so that we can speak meaningfully of stewardship directed at the welfare of other adult humans. Possibly the notion of "authority over" could be tempered, being replaced by "responsibility for," thus enabling the notion of stewardship to embrace care for humans without denying the equality of those entrusted to our care nor giving them a subordinate status. If so, stewardship would then embrace a wide range of concerns from humans to animals, to trees, to rivers, all of which are God's possessions to be cared for by us in ways that God deems appropriate. But then it becomes apparent that stewardship is such a wide-ranging notion that appropriate stewardship will vary greatly depending on whether we are dealing with ourselves or others, humans or rivers, the gospel or personal talents, animals or ecosystems, and the concept of stewardship will not by itself tell us how we are to exercise our care and concern in particular cases. Even if we conclude that humans are not fitting objects of stewardly concern, other metaphors being more appropriate to describe and give direction to our concern for humans, stewardship would still remain a wide-ranging notion, calling for sensitivity and discrimination in its exercise.

To understand respect for nature (i.e., for animals, vegetation, ecosystems, etc.) in terms of the stewardship model may, if that model is pressed with a single-minded literalness, yield a moral vision that is shallow, lacking in appropriate nuance and insensitive to the varied character of the natural environment. For to view a steward as nothing more than a caretaker of what belongs to another will reduce everything placed in one's care to this single, broad, undifferentiated category of property. When applied to animals, it might be taken to mean only that I must not brutalize a dog because the dog belongs to another and only the owner has a right to brutalize his dog — not that there is anything wrong by itself with brutalizing the dog.

Moreover, reducing concern for nature to concern for property rights by itself provides no basis for distinguishing how we should treat trees from how we should treat tigers. This is but to say that the stewardship model is a call for moral reflection, not so much an answer to that call. To recognize that we are stewards of God's good creation is to recognize that we have an obligation to secure for the environment (including animals) morally appropriate care. This is thus a call for both ethical and theological reflection, and a call to come to the best understanding of the environment that science can give us.

What the notion of stewardship will do, at the very outset, is to exclude exploitation, denigration, and neglect as appropriate stances for the Christian toward the natural order. It underscores the fact that the value of the natural order is not exhausted in terms of its instrumental value in meeting human needs and satisfying human desires. Indeed, nature has a value that transcends its usefulness for the steward, who is only caring for what belongs to Another. In saying this, we do not want to deny that nature can be used for human benefit. For humans cannot survive, let alone prosper, without using nature as a source for food, clothes, and shelter. But while there is a place to use nature for the meeting of human needs, there is also a dimension to nature that is to be respected and cared for as God's good creation, apart from any possible usefulness for humans. The stewardship model captures this while allowing us to use nature responsibly for human benefit.

Thus the call to stewardship will not by itself answer all our questions. It does not tell us exactly at what point we transgress the line that demarcates legitimate use of nature for the meeting of human needs from the exploitation of nature. But it does declare that this is a crucial concern for the believer. The concept of stewardship raises the right questions, setting an agenda for us — one that says, in effect, that the Christian community must think seriously about a range of matters and begin to work through to satisfactory answers. It is in this sense that the Bible, which is too often viewed solely as an answer book, must also be viewed, significantly, as a question book, raising issues for us, giving us agendas, calling us to think about important matters and work through to answers that, if not final for all times and places, are at least theologically, morally, and factually informed.

Unfortunately, some Christians may be attracted to the notion of stewardship for what may be the wrong reasons. They may be attracted partly because it enables them to speak of concern for animals without invoking the notions of animal rights or duties to animals or without applying to animals moral principles that we also apply to humans (e.g., the principle of non-maleficence). This in turn may be attractive because these latter notions may strike them as odd in a way that talk of stewardship does not. Stewardship can provide an escape from such talk. But the escape may not merely be an escape from what is taken to be odd moral grammar but an escape from what is judged to be an excessive concern for animals that is expressed with that grammar. Therefore, whereas moral concern for humans, according to their view, is to be grounded in the more demanding notions of rights and duties and in the appeal to moral principles, animals, on the other hand, are embraced by the supposedly less demanding notion of stewardly concern. So appeal to the biblical image of stewardship may, in some cases, be motivated by a desire to move away from moral categories that seem to intensify moral concern for animals, to a category that, despite its inspirational character, may be thought to be less demanding. None of this, however, need be so. The stewardly concern for animals does not have to be a substitute for animal rights or for an acknowledgement of direct duties to animals or for the application of moral principles to animals. Could not God entrust to our stewardly care that which has rights and to which we have duties and to which moral principles apply? Not only is the notion of stewardship not incompatible with the appeal to moral principles, rights, intrinsic value, and so forth, but it may actually require it. For how else can the good steward, who desires to do the will of the Master, determine what that will is except by coming to understand the nature of the things entrusted to the steward's care?

And why, to return to the central question of this chapter, is it wrong to cruelly abuse an animal? Because it is a gross failure in faithful stewardship. As a steward, one is to be a caretaker of the natural order, a caretakership that includes the world of animals, who are to be treated in a way that respects the purpose for which they were created.

SUMMARY AND CONCLUSIONS

In asking why it is wrong to gratuitously impose great pain and suffering on an animal, we have looked at a number of moral theories and have seen that each one of them can provide a basis for condemning such brutality. Indeed, we may be so confident to begin with that such brutality is wrong, that any theory that fails to account for its wrongness is to be judged seriously flawed and inadequate as a complete moral theory. Although Aquinas and Kant may be correct that a part of what makes brutalizing animals wrong is that it may incline us to brutalize humans, they are mistaken in concluding that this is all that is wrong with such brutality, as if the animal's own pain and suffering by itself counts for nothing in our moral calculations. We have thus concluded that animals have some moral consideration due them directly — they are a part of the moral universe.

We indeed have seen that there are a number of ways to morally condemn the torture of an animal. Let us briefly review them, and keep them in mind as we explore the extent of our obligations to animals, obligations that may extend beyond the mere refraining from torture. First, we can view the torture of an animal as a violation of the principle of beneficence, which in effect says that we have a general duty to minimize pain and suffering, as well as to further the interests and happiness of others. That is, other lives are to be better off because of our presence in the world, as we seek to refrain from conduct detrimental to the well-being of others and to perform those actions that will enhance their well-being. This means that animals as well as humans (even if in varying degrees) are to come within the purview of the principle of beneficence. Though the suggestion that animals are to be embraced by this principle may be strange and new to many, it should not take too much reflection to conclude that the real oddity is the complete exclusion of animals from concern based on this principle. To the extent that animals experience pain, their exclusion would constitute complete indifference to the suffering of a sizable segment of God's creatures, an indifference completely at odds with the God of Scripture whose own concern extends to all his creatures. We also emphasized in our discussion the importance of the principle of non-maleficence, that is, a principle prohibiting harm to others — not to cause them pain, not to disable them, not to deny them pleasure, not to deny them freedom, and not to kill them without an overriding justification. To apply the principle of non-maleficence to animals is to call for a reversal of our moral attitude toward animals, a shift in the burden of proof from "show me why I should not harm this animal" to "I must offer a substantial reason why I can proceed to harm this animal."

A second way to condemn the act of torture is to appeal to rights: the animal's right not to be tortured. The appeal to rights underscores something important, namely, that the possessor of the right is entitled to a certain moral consideration, that it is not merely a matter of moral discretion when we refrain from torturing or brutalizing animals. Further, to invoke a right not to be tortured means that we cannot torture a possessor of the right even if that torture would secure some small benefit or pleasure for such a large number of others that this benefit or pleasure when multiplied by this large number of beneficiaries will be greater in total than the amount of suffering that the victim undergoes. Rights also serve the important function of providing a strong reason for legislation, legislation that will prevent the violation of that right. So there are understandable reasons for wanting to speak of rights for animals, even if this mode of moral discourse will not resonate with everyone.

A third way to understand moral concern for animals is to see it as generated by certain virtues. I expressed considerable sympathy for virtue theory (though I doubt that all of morality can be reduced to virtue) and argued that to be cruel and uncaring in one's attitude toward, and treatment of, animals is to repudiate the character of God as the norm for virtuous living. Rather, the appropriate virtues in dealing with animals are care and compassion.

Finally, we looked at the notion of stewardship: we are to be good stewards in our treatment of the world of nature and animals, a world that belongs not to us but to Another, to whom we are responsible and ultimately accountable. This precludes attitudes toward animals that involve exploitation, denigration, and neglect, and certainly the suggestion that we can use animals in just any way we choose. But the notion of stewardship, while it provides a framework within which we are to understand our treatment of animals, does not tell us what it is to be a good steward. To fill out this notion we need, I suggest, to appeal to notions of beneficence, rights, and virtue. In other words, a good steward is one who, among other things, applies the principle of beneficence to animals, honors their rights, and expresses the virtue of care and compassion toward them.

CHAPTER 7

Respecting Animal Life

INTRODUCTION

It is one thing to claim that animals are to be objects of moral concern and ought not to be treated cruelly. It is something quite different to argue that animal *life* ought to be respected and therefore that killing animals is morally wrong, possibly even a violation of a right to life. Or to put matters bluntly: if an animal is painlessly killed, why should we think that anything wrong has been done? Certainly not everyone thinks so. Consider the following exchange from a 1974 television program between Harvard philosopher Robert Nozick and a number of scientists, including David Baltimore, a Nobel laureate:

> Nozick asked the scientists whether the fact that an experiment that will kill hundreds of animals is ever regarded, by scientists, as a reason for not performing it. One of the scientists answered: "Not that I know of." Nozick pressed his question: "Don't the animals count at all?" A scientist countered: "Why should they?" At this point Baltimore interjected that he did not think that experimenting on animals raised a moral issue at all.[1]

In this exchange two distinct issues emerge: first, whether killing animals ought to be of any moral concern and, second, whether experimenting on

1. Peter Singer, *Animal Liberation,* revised ed. (New York: Avon Books, 1990), p. 75.

animals (possibly in painful ways) raises any moral issues. Certainly, there is reason to believe that since 1974 professional researchers have become more sensitive to the pain that is often involved in their use of animals, but it is less clear that there has occurred a comparable advance in sensitivities about the killing of animals. And so also for society at large. Causing an animal pain may give us moral pause, but there is less likely to be any such pause over the painless killing of an animal.

Why is this? Whereas most people are convinced that animals experience pain (despite a skepticism that may remain in some academic circles), people are less convinced that animals possess those features that invest life with a value that merits the special respect associated with a right to life (even if we speak of a weaker right to life for animals than for humans). In religious circles, for example, it might be claimed that human life is special because of the religious capacities possessed by humans — for example, the capacities to worship, to love and to serve God, and to respond to God's address. But these are not capacities possessed by animals. In philosophical circles, the claim might be that humans are special because they are autonomous rational creatures, capable of adopting personal projects and life plans that they in turn can submit to moral scrutiny and revision. But it is by no means clear that animals can do any of this. To kill an animal, then, is not to end the life of either a worshiper or a creator of life projects. If this is so, then ascribing a right to life to animals is less secure than ascribing to them a right not to be tortured.

SOME INITIAL ASSUMPTIONS

Nevertheless, I would suggest that killing animals ought not to be a matter of moral indifference. Contrary to those scientists with whom Nozick was dialoguing, animals should count. Accordingly, let me propose for our consideration the following propositions and suggest that ultimately our search for a reason why animal life ought to be respected must be able to account for all of these initial intuitions.

(1) Animal life is to be respected and one needs a justifying reason to end an animal's life.
(2) The reason it is wrong to kill an animal (gratuitously or with insubstantial reasons) is to be found in the harm done to the animal or in the value that the animal has in its own right.

(3) Killing a human is a greater evil and a more serious wrong than killing an animal.
(4) Killing an animal is generally, and all else being equal, a greater evil than killing a plant.
(5) Some animals have higher moral standing and a greater claim to life than other animals.

The initial claim (animal life is to be respected and one needs a justifying reason to kill an animal), though not a claim that would be universally acknowledged, would nevertheless receive a sympathetic hearing by many, and if accepted as true would be an important first step toward a genuine and appropriate moral concern for animals. Simply to acknowledge that killing an animal requires a reason and that one bears the burden of proof to show that one's reason is an adequate reason would constitute an end to the virtually complete moral indifference toward animal life that characterizes many, if not most, of us. Moreover, to acknowledge a moral responsibility to respect animal life is to acknowledge that there may be something we may wish to do to animals that we morally cannot do and that there may even be that which it is in our considerable interest to do to animals that we morally cannot do. We should not expect, therefore, that acknowledging a moral respect for animal life will be for us cost free. It is the nature of the moral life that once one recognizes an individual's moral standing, there will be restrictions placed on our conduct toward that individual, restrictions that in some circumstances one might wish one did not have to honor.

KILLING AS AN ACT OF HARM

Our second initial intuition is that it is wrong to kill an animal because of the harm done to the animal. That is, killing an animal harms *the animal* and because the animal has moral standing, we are required to have an adequate reason to justify inflicting that harm. In this regard, killing an animal is like cruelly abusing an animal; it is wrong because of what is done to the animal. Thus, it is not wrong to kill an animal simply because of the negative consequences it might have for species survival or for the welfare of humans. On the contrary, it is wrong because of what is done to the animal that is killed.

But how is painlessly killing an animal an act of harming the animal? One thing we do when we kill an animal is to destroy an intricately functioning living organism, in much the same way that we do when we chop down a tree. Certainly we harm an animal in *that* sense when we kill it; that is, organismic life is destroyed. That, however, is something that happens not only when we kill animals but when we kill plants as well. And what we want, we have claimed, is a form of harm that will enable us to differentiate harm done to animals from harm done to plants, so that we can understand why killing animals is typically understood to be worse than killing plants. Organismic harm will not be adequate to meet this requirement. Nor, obviously, will the kind of harm that is uniquely associated with killing humans serve our purposes. In the case of humans, who undeniably are self-conscious, who are able to conceive of a future for themselves, and who normally have a desire to continue to exist in order to realize plans and projects, killing will involve a form of harm that will not be involved in the case of animals.[2]

So what exactly is the harm done to an animal when it is killed? Lawrence Johnson makes the following suggestion: "If a cow likes to chew her cud, then it is, other things being equal, in her interest to be allowed to do so. She is benefited by having opportunities to satisfy her desires: the more the better."[3] For an animal who has a certain level of sentience, who has a capacity for experiencing pleasure and for having positive experiences, life can be a good (granting a favorable balance of pleasure over pain), and the more life under such circumstances the better. It is the denial of those future positive experiences by death that renders death an evil, even though the cow may have no future-oriented desires as humans do. In other words (I think we would agree), animals are benefited to the extent that they have experiences that they enjoy or find agreeable, and they are harmed to the extent that they have experiences they dislike or find disagreeable. It follows, I should think, that animals are benefited when their lives are prolonged or spared, in circumstances where they are having experiences they enjoy or find agreeable, and they are harmed when their lives are ended in those same circumstances.

2. Although I believe that killing a human is wrong for reasons that go beyond the harm done to the individual who is killed (reasons that have to do with God's purpose for that life), nevertheless it is wrong, at least in part, because of the harm done to the human victim, and this harm is greater than the harm that would be done to an animal by killing it.

3. Lawrence Johnson, "Life, Death, and Animals," in *Ethics and Animals,* ed. Harlan B. Miller and William H. Williams (Clifton, N.J.: Humana, 1983), p. 128.

Johnson in seeking to make his case that killing animals is a form of harm invites us to consider the following imaginative account:

> Let us suppose that one were to buy a puppy to serve as a family pet. The family delights in the companionship of the young dog, playing with it, sharing walks and outings, and enjoying its affection. When it comes time for their annual vacation, they destroy the dog painlessly, since it would be inconvenient to take it with them or otherwise to make provision for it. On their return, they acquire another pet, making this an annual practice. Perhaps they engage the services of "Disposapup Ltd.," a commercial organization that provides well-bred puppies of good disposition, house-trained if one wants them a bit older, and attends to the annual disposal professionally and painlessly.[4]

It does seem that we find this practice objectionable because of the harm we believe is being done to the dog. It does seem to us to be in the dog's interest to continue to live. To be sure, as Johnson points out, we may be tempted to consider this act of killing a kind of "dirty double-cross." For the family to enter into a "relationship of trust and affection" with the dog and then simply destroy it, even if painlessly, is objectionable as a breach of faith. At least we are tempted to see it this way (whether talk of a breach of faith finally makes sense in this context or not), and we might suppose that this is what really prompts us to view this act of killing as wrong. "Still," as Lawrence goes on to observe, "it would be a morally objectionable double-cross only if Disposapup violated the interests of the double-crossed. If the redundant dog does not have an interest in remaining alive, then its interests would not be violated nor the dog betrayed."[5] So it would seem that our common-sense intuition is that these dogs' interests are sacrificed when they are killed, to the extent that their future prospects were judged to be good.

Or, we might argue in the following way in support of the claim that killing animals harms animals by denying them future positive experiences. Most of us believe that an animal that is suffering horribly can be treated mercifully by being "put out of its misery." That is, in circumstances where the pain suffered by an animal is sufficiently great and the animal's prospects are sufficiently dim, then death would be a good and

4. Lawrence E. Johnson, *A Morally Deep World* (Cambridge: Cambridge University Press, 1991), p. 121.

5. Johnson, *A Morally Deep World*, p. 122.

continued life an evil. To kill an animal in such circumstances would be an act of compassion on our part. It would equally well seem, in other more positive circumstances where there is an absence of pain and suffering, and where the life of the animal is a satisfactory one, that *life* is a good and death is an evil. Killing would then be a form of harm. This is but to recognize that in some circumstances killing an animal may be an act that benefits the animal, while in other circumstances it may be an act that harms the animal. So, just as an animal can be "better off dead" when its life has become sufficiently distressing to it, so an animal can be "worse off dead" when its life is sufficiently satisfying. Consequently, an act of mercy can not only take the form of ending the life of an animal when that life has become painfully distressing, but also take the form of sparing an animal's life or helping to preserve its life when there is reason to believe that its life is relatively satisfying. This is not to say that the harm done to an animal when it is killed is as serious as the harm done when a human is killed, but it is to say that when it comes to harm and benefit, killing an animal is never a neutral activity. Indeed, when we kill an animal we may very well harm what we kill. To say that this harm is morally significant is to say that it is something we must take into account in deciding how we ought to act. It is to say that we are not to harm an animal by killing it unless we have an overriding reason for doing so. It is to say that killing an animal is not morally inconsequential, even if it does not approach the moral seriousness that attaches to killing humans.

Finally, to suggest that killing an animal is normally bad for the animal because it is deprived of the future possibility of positive experiences is to understand harm in a way that would seem to restrict its application to vertebrates. For it is reasonable to believe that invertebrates, who *lack* a central nervous system, do not have the capacity for pain and pleasure, and that their death therefore would not deny them the future possibility of positive and pleasurable experiences. This is not to say that killing invertebrates is morally inconsequential (it might very well be wrong for other reasons), but it is to say that such killing does not entail the same form of harm involved in killing a vertebrate, which has, we suppose, an inner conscious life that can go better or worse for it.

GOD'S WILL AND HARM TO ANIMALS

The account that we are proposing identifies a feature related to the animal, namely, the harm that can be caused the animal, as providing the reason why we should abstain from killing unless we have a justifying reason. It is not wrong to kill an animal, as it is not wrong to torture an animal, simply because of the negative consequences it might have for, say, the welfare of humans. On the contrary, it is wrong to kill an animal because of what is done to the animal. In this understanding, life is of value to the animal, and we harm the animal when we deny it this value. I believe if we are insensitive to this point, for whatever reason, including insensitivity generated by theological confusion, we shall not be a people with the appropriate moral concern for animals.

But is this focus on the animal and on its welfare somehow a failure to adequately focus on God? Religious believers may be tempted to think that it is. They may be tempted to view this as a religiously inadequate ethic, rooted in the welfare of the animal and not, apparently, in the will of God. Isn't it God's will, they will ask, that provides us with the reason why we should refrain from killing and torturing animals? To be sure, we need to acknowledge that God has a right to have creation treated and respected in the ways that God desires, because God is the creator of everything and is a good God with good intentions for creation. But nevertheless — very importantly — we need to add that God wants us to refrain from torturing and killing animals because of the harm that is done to the animal itself. God does not want animals (unnecessarily) harmed and wants us to see that the harm we can cause the animal counts as a reason for not torturing and not killing it. And why should we not think this? That is, doesn't the harm caused the animal matter to God and doesn't it matter to God for the animal's sake? If so, should it not matter to us for the animal's sake as well? When we construe torturing and killing animals as wrong because of the harm done to the animal, we are no more leaving God out of the moral picture than when we judge the torture and killing of humans to be wrong because of the harm that is done to them. Invoking God's will is not to be understood as a substitute for this basic moral concern but as the very thing that God enjoins upon us, when, for example, through Christ, we are commanded to love our neighbor as we love ourselves (Matt. 19:19). For to love one's neighbor is to be concerned with the neighbor's welfare for the neighbor's own sake. Far from being a secular ethic or a human-centered ethic, to focus on human needs and human welfare is simply to focus where God focuses and where God would have us focus. And matters are the same with regard to animals, I am suggesting.

If we are not careful, moreover, invoking God's will can be a prescription for moral insensitivity in our treatment of animals. To see how this might be so, consider the philosopher P. H. Nowell-Smith's charge that Christian morality is infantile.[6] Nowell-Smith charges, in other words, that Christians, with their belief that it is God's commands that make conduct right and wrong, are much like the child who believes it is wrong to pull his sister's hair because his father forbids it, not because it hurts his sister. Part of morally growing up, according to Nowell-Smith, is seeing that what is morally basic here is the hurt caused the sister. To charge Christian morality with being infantile, then, is to charge it with encouraging a kind of arrested moral development.

Now, I do not think that this is true of Christian morality rightly understood, nor do I believe that such arrested moral development is characteristic of the Christian community (though, admittedly, it is not unknown among Christians). Most Christians would, for example, rightly see the brutalizing of another human being as wrong because of what is done to the person who is brutalized. They would also understand that God, in commanding us not to treat human beings in this way, wants us to care about people and about their welfare for the sake of the people themselves. After all, we are called to love our neighbors and to feel their suffering as our own. So, no, Christian morality is not infantile nor are Christians typically infantile in their understanding of the moral treatment of humans. When it comes to our understanding of the moral treatment of animals, however, the charge of infantilism may be more to the point. Here we may be back with the child who believes it is wrong to pull his sister's hair only because father forbids it or (to change the example) believes it is wrong to kick the dog only because his father forbids it, not because it hurts the dog. In contrast, I am suggesting that it is because kicking the dog hurts the dog that it is wrong, and that it is because killing the dog also harms the dog that it is wrong. Indeed, to kill the dog is more serious than kicking it because it causes more harm.

PLANTS, ANIMALS, AND HUMANS

It does seem, as we have stated at the outset of this chapter, that killing humans is more seriously wrong than killing animals and that (at least in general) killing animals is more serious than killing plants.[7] If so, then

6. P. H. Nowell-Smith, "Morality: Religious and Secular," in *Christian Ethics and Contemporary Philosophy*, ed. Ian Ramsey (New York: Macmillan, 1966), pp. 95-112.

7. The assumption that animal life merits higher moral standing than plant life

the reason for respecting animal life must be different in some way from the reason given for respecting either human life or plant life. For should they be the same, then it would follow that killing humans, killing animals, and killing plants would all be *equally* wrong, and the death of each would be an evil of equal proportions. Therefore, the reason why killing animals is objectionable must be a weaker reason than that given for respecting human life; it also must be a stronger reason than that given for respecting plant life. This would mean that for someone simply to observe that humans, animals, and plants have all been created by God, and therefore that each must be respected as God's creation, does not by itself provide an adequate basis for the kind of differential treatment of humans, animals, and plants that we judge to be appropriate. This would give us no reason for viewing the death of a human as a greater evil than the death of an animal or a plant. Each, after all, has been created by God. For the same reason, talk of being good stewards of God's creation does not by itself give us any help in determining the kind of stewardly care appropriate to animals in contrast to plants or ecosystems. As we concluded in the last chapter, to be a good steward is to treat the great diversity found in creation in ways morally appropriate to each kind. There is the need, then, to morally discriminate among various forms of life. It is not sufficient to simply talk of respecting "the telé of living organisms — the patterns of development and activity they are structured or designed to manifest and in terms of which they can be said to flourish or languish."[8] To be sure, to kill any living organism is to frustrate its particular telos and therefore requires, we might reasonably suppose, a justification. But unless we can discriminate between various telé, we are not able to discern why frustrating the telé of some living things is worse than frustrating the telé of other living things, why killing a chimpanzee is worse than uprooting a weed. In seeking, then, to understand why killing animals is objectionable, we need to do more than observe that this is an assault on God's creation or that it is to frustrate the organism's telos.

---

stands in need of some qualification. For we would not want to say that a mosquito is more valuable in its own right than a sequoia is in its own right. Indeed, the sequoia might even be equal in value with more cognitively advanced animal species, though the age of the sequoia, the interest it has for humans, the time it takes to grow, along with its not being in plentiful supply, may all influence our judgment that this is so. Still, for the most part, animals are to be given a higher moral standing than plants, especially as we think of those animals that clearly possess consciousness and are cognitively more developed, such as mammals.

8. This is John Kleinig's characterization of Albert Schweitzer's ethic of reverence for life. See John Kleinig, *Valuing Life* (Princeton, N.J.: Princeton University Press, 1991), p. 50.

What we have suggested in this chapter is that killing animals is wrong because of the harm done to the animal and that this harm takes the form of denying to the animal a future life of pleasant and desirable experiences. This is not something that can be said of plant life since plants are not sentient and cannot be denied future positive experiences. This enables us to see a wrong attaching to killing sentient animal life that does not attach to the killing of plant life. This provides a basis for our conviction that killing animals — at least vertebrates — is more serious than killing plants. It also provides us with a reason for refraining from killing animals that is not so strong as the reason why we should abstain from killing humans, who, unlike animals, are autonomous moral and spiritual agents with future plans and projects. Moreover, because sentience is a matter of degrees and some animals are more sentiently developed than others, this means that the harm done by killing the more sentiently developed would be greater than the harm done the less developed. That is, as we ascend the phylogenetic ladder, there is an expansion of consciousness with more and varied ways to experience pleasure and pain. Those animals with a more varied and a deeper sensitivity have more to lose by death, and hence killing them causes more harm and therefore needs a stronger justifying reason.

THE POSSIBILITY OF AN ANIMAL RIGHT TO LIFE

Certainly to speak of a right to life is a standard way of articulating the wrongness of killing. And it would be one very important way to connect the harm done to the animal to standard moral categories used to condemn the deliberate infliction of such harm. It is wrong then because it violates a right to life. But what notion of rights should we operate with? We might borrow from the philosopher Joseph Raz, who says that "X has a right" means "other things being equal, an aspect of X's well-being (his interest) is a sufficient reason for holding some other person to be under a duty."[9] To say, for example, that an animal has a right not to be tortured would mean that an animal's capacity to experience pain is a sufficient reason to render us duty-bound not to inflict pain on that animal. To say that the animal has a right to life would be to recognize that life is essential to that animal's well-being and that taking its life would harm the animal, and that renders us duty-bound to forego such acts in the absence of

9. Joseph Raz, "The Nature of Rights," *Mind* 93 (1984): 194.

a justifying reason. To speak of a right to life is an invitation, then, to understand in a certain way the evil of killing. It is to focus on the animal, to focus on its welfare and its interests. To speak of an animal right to life fits quite well with our claim that central to the wrongness of killing an animal is the harm done to the animal itself. Killing an animal would be wrong, then, because it is a violation of the animal's right not to be harmed by being deprived of its life. Additionally, this right to life need not be construed as absolute but as overridable in certain circumstances. Thus, if one had a strong enough reason to kill an animal, its right to life could then be overridden. It is being suggested, in other words, that it is *sentient* creatures that have a right to life, since it is sentient creatures that have the capacity to suffer and to enjoy. This enables them to be harmed not only by being tortured but also by being killed. And since sentience admits of degrees, this means that those animals whose sentience is more advanced can be viewed as having a stronger claim to life since the harm done to them by being killed is greater than would be done to the sentiently less developed.

This idea that rights have varying strength is, at a certain level, a commonplace. Certainly, to violate a person's right to life is more serious than violating their right to property. Thus, murder is more serious than theft, and it is more serious, one might well suppose, because it violates a stronger right. Even within the same right there may be degrees of stringency. Thus, some have argued that although the right to life begins at conception, infants have a stronger claim to life than a conceptus because the infant has a stronger right to life than the conceptus, the right to life gaining in strength as the fetus grows and develops. Moreover, to use another example, we generally think that a child's right to self-determination (i.e., its right to make its own moral and prudential decisions, as well as to make choices on matters of personal taste) becomes stronger as the child grows older. We assume that parents and others have an increasing obligation to honor the child's right to make her own decisions and that considerations which might justify an imposition of parental will on the child at an earlier age may not be sufficient later on. So talk of various animals possessing a right to life in varying degrees is not so peculiar as to be without any precedent. Nor should it strike us as strange that animals might possess rights even though they cannot do the kinds of things that are done with rights, that is, invoke them and waive them – for, as we have seen earlier, this would also be true of certain categories of humans, such as infants or individuals suffering from advanced stages of senility.

HESITANCY OVER "ANIMAL RIGHTS"

Despite the fact that talk of a violation of a right to life is the standard way to speak of the wrongness of killing, we may nevertheless be hesitant to speak of animals having a right to life, even while we are willing to recognize that they can be harmed by being killed. Mary Midgley has said that "rights" is a "desperate word."[10] And perhaps to speak of an animal right to life is a desperate move. Certainly to speak in terms of rights and their violation is to say that there is something that urgently needs attention and that to delay in rectifying matters is to condone what is seriously wrong. It is also to suggest, more than any other word in our moral vocabulary, that the use of force is justified in order to stem the violations in question. But some may wonder, as John Kleinig does, whether animal "survival and flourishing is of such importance that we should grace those welfare interests with the language of rights."[11] And I think this is just the question that must be faced.

It is not a matter of whether we can or cannot make sense of ascribing rights to animals. For where there is a moral will, there is usually (though not always) a philosophical and conceptual way. Indeed, we have already seen in an earlier chapter that talk of rights in the case of animals can make moral sense. Animal rights advocates are not going to be defeated by conceptual moves that argue that animal-rights talk is not sensible talk or that it is conceptually confused, like speaking of married bachelors. Rather, it is a moral point that is really at issue here: Do we want to attribute to animals the kind of importance that talk of rights is used to safeguard? For it is not, as Kleinig also observes, that we really justify the use of coercive protection for certain interests by the appeal to rights, but rather that once we judge that certain interests are worthy of coercive protection, we then engage in rights-talk to embrace and communicate that conclusion.[12] Kleinig himself, though appreciative of the value of animal life, is not prepared to invoke rights talk on behalf of animals. Animals are not, after all, moral and spiritual agents, capable of exercising rational autonomy as humans are. We may judge that "right to life" talk should be reserved for those who have these special capacities. Again, this will not be a conclusion based on conceptual claims that talk of an "animal right to

10. Mary Midgley, *Animals and Why They Matter* (Athens, Ga.: University of Georgia Press, 1983), p. 61.

11. Kleinig, *Valuing Life,* p. 187.

12. Kleinig, *Valuing Life,* p. 250, n. 20.

life" is senseless and incoherent. Rather, it is a judgment about the importance of the animal's interest in continuing to live and the appropriateness of extending to it coercive protection.

Yet there is also something problematic about the *denial* that animals have rights or, in this case, the denial that they have a right to life. Mary Midgley raises for us the problems attending any such denial: "to say 'animals do not have rights' does not sound like a remark about the meaning of the word *rights* but one about animals – namely, the remark that one need not really consider them. Subsequently saying that they have some other nebulous thing instead will not get rid of this effect."[13] Indeed, even someone like Peter Singer, a utilitarian who has no place for rights in his moral theory, finds it necessary to engage in the rhetoric of rights talk when seeking to communicate with a more general audience. To publicly *deny* rights to animals would simply be understood by such an audience in the wrong way.

Still, do we want to "grace" animal life with the rhetoric of "rights"? To ascribe a right to life to animals may be misunderstood as placing animals on the same moral plane as humans, as if they have the same strong right to life that humans have, as if animal life is as significant as human life, hence equally deserving of the concern expressed by rights talk. It would therefore seem that if we choose to use right-to-life rhetoric, we must couple that rhetoric with the emphasis that when used of animals such language is intended to protect what has less value and less importance than human life, and therefore that less coercive intervention is appropriate to protect it.

ALTERNATIVES TO A RIGHT TO LIFE

Though I wish to stress that killing animals is wrong because of the harm done to the animal, appeal to a right to life is not the only way to capture this. For example, instead of appealing to a right to life, one could simply claim that it is wrong, as a matter of moral principle, to kill animals without justifying reason because of the harm done to the animal itself, and that God wants animals treated in such a way that their welfare is taken into account for its own sake. In putting matters this way, we capture much of what is also captured by right-to-life talk but without the same emphasis on coercive intervention that rights talk

13. Midgley, *Animals and Why They Matter,* p. 63.

brings with it. Nor is this way of putting matters as likely to be understood as placing animal life on a moral par with human life, though it still remains consistent with this and does not by itself rule this out. Further, the appeal to moral principle, unlike the appeal to rights, leaves the matter of coercive intervention less overt. We can also qualify this principle, indicating that the more sentiently developed the animal is, the more objectionable the killing is and the stronger one's reason has to be in order to justify it. With this principle in hand, the animal advocate would seek to create a community that believes that a good reason is required before one kills an animal, a community that would engage in an ongoing dialogue over what those justifying reasons might be. And the simple recognition that one must possess a good reason in order to end the life of an animal would be to grant animals moral standing and would represent a substantial advance over prevailing beliefs about the significance of animal life. We will have begun a process of moral reflection that, it is to be hoped, will lead many to increasingly appreciate how strong those justifying reasons have to be.

Instead of either principles or rights as the moral vocabulary of choice one could appeal to the virtue of compassion. To kill is to harm, and to have compassion is to be possessed of attitudes and sensibilities that will prompt one to draw back from inflicting that harm (or being implicated in inflicting harm). To proceed with no such hesitancy would constitute a lack of compassion and an unacceptable insensitivity to the harm one is causing. Here our concern is not with honoring rights and adhering to principles but with being the right kind of person. Here the right kind of person is one whose compassion embraces animals as well as humans. The task of the animal advocate would then be one of nurturing in oneself and in others compassion, care, and concern for animals.

For the Christian these three approaches (rights, principles, compassion) would represent differing moral styles whereby one could fulfill one's call to be a good steward. There are, then, different ways that stewardly concern for animal creation can find expression in a person's life. One can become a proclaimer of animal rights that one seeks to have supported by legal means, one can become an annunciator of principles that call for serious dialogue over justifying reasons for killing, or one can become a nurturer of a compassion for animals in oneself and others. Thus, while there are different paths one can follow and different moral styles one can adopt, it would certainly seem that the good steward will choose one of them.

ANIMALS AS INTRINSICALLY VALUABLE

There is yet another moral vocabulary available to us that might be employed to capture the significance of animal life. We might argue that animal life has "intrinsic value." To say that something has intrinsic value is to say that it is worth preserving in and of itself. It is to say that it is better that it exist than that it not exist. This is to say something more than that it has instrumental value, which would be to say that it has value because it is good as a means to preserving or fostering something else that is valuable. Thus if we said that animals have value only because we can use them as beasts of burden or because we can eat them, that would be to say that they have only instrumental value. In contrast, to claim that their value is intrinsic is to say that even if they served no purpose outside themselves, their mere existence would be a good, would make the world a better and more significant place. To say, then, that animals have intrinsic value is to say that it is better that they exist rather than not exist, and that they are to be valued, cherished, and felt positively about for their own sake.[14]

Intrinsic value is sometimes contrasted with inherent value, though sometimes these terms are used interchangeably. When they are contrasted, "intrinsic value" is used to designate that which has value apart from anyone valuing it, while "inherent value" is used to designate what has value because it is valued or appreciated *by someone* for its own sake. Something, then, that has inherent value has value conferred upon it by being appreciated for its own sake, whereas that which is said to have intrinsic value has that value whether or not it is recognized or cherished for its own sake. To say, then, that animals have intrinsic value is to say that they have value apart from their being appreciated by us for their own sake. And it is because they have intrinsic value that we ought to come to cherish and appreciate them for their own sakes. Moreover, the notion of intrinsic value also lends itself quite readily to talk of degrees. Thus animals might be intrinsically valuable in varying degrees, depending upon how cognitively and sentiently developed they are. Among nonsentient animals and plants and ecosystems there could also be intrinsic value to varying degrees.

If we employ the notion of intrinsic value, then killing animals is wrong because it subtracts from the amount of total value in the world.

14. For a helpful and careful discussion of intrinsic value, see Noah M. Lemos, *Intrinsic Value: Concept and Warrant* (Cambridge: Cambridge University Press, 1994).

But something important is lost when we view the evil of killing animals in this way, especially when we think of more cognitively and sentiently developed animals. What is lost is the awareness that when we kill a mammal we harm it, not merely subtract from the world's sum of intrinsic value. What we need to recognize — as we have been emphasizing — is that the value of an animal's life is the value it has for the individual animal whose life it is. If life is a good for the animal, killing is an act of harming that animal, and that is where our moral focus ought to be. Talk of "intrinsic value" may not be as well suited to capturing this as other moral notions at our disposal.

As we have already emphasized, we should see the evil that has been done in terms of the harm done to the individual whose life has been taken. In this regard, killing an animal ought to be viewed as we view the blinding of an animal. It is wrong to blind an animal because of the harm done to the animal — not because there has been a reduction in the amount of visual consciousness in the world and therefore a reduction in the amount of intrinsic value in the world. Talk of animals having intrinsic value may unacceptably shift our focus from the animal itself and the harm it suffers when killed to some abstract aggregate of intrinsic value.

MORAL VEGETARIANISM: SOME BRIEF COMMENTS

A moral vegetarian is someone who abstains from eating meat on moral grounds. Typically what is found objectionable about eating meat is that animals have to be killed in order to provide that meat. I shall discuss moral vegetarianism at greater length in the chapter on factory farming, where I believe perhaps the best case for moral vegetarianism can be made. There the objection focuses not on the fact that animals are killed, but on the treatment they receive under intensive farm conditions, conditions far removed from those that exist on the idyllic farms of our imagination. I shall also discuss vegetarianism in connection with a biblical analysis in chapter 11. Here I only wish to suggest that we should not be dismissive of moral vegetarianism, as if it is reflective of an overly scrupulous conscience and nothing more.

If, as we have argued, a justifying reason is required in order to kill an animal, then we may well ask: what is our justifying reason in the case of killing animals for food? If killing animals for food were necessary for either survival or a healthy life, then it would seem to be justified. That would be our reason. But survival and good health can be secured, as we know today, on a vegetarian diet. Indeed, the healthier diet is most likely a vegetarian diet. So what, then, is our justification for having animals killed for food? We might suspect that it simply comes down to this: we like the taste of meat. We kill or have animals killed because we have a preference for certain taste sensations. One might well wonder whether this is much by way of a justifying reason. One might even suspect that it is among the weakest of reasons that one could possibly offer. For suppose I sought to justify my killing animals on a regular basis by saying that I simply enjoy killing them. In response, one would be strongly inclined to say that my reason is not at all good enough. If one can be justified in killing animals merely because one enjoys killing them, then one is in essence denying that a reason is actually required. One is, in effect, denying that animal life must be respected. But when our reason for killing and eating animals is that we like how they taste, we seem not to have progressed much beyond this. Killing animals because we enjoy eating them seems very much on a par with killing them because we enjoy killing them. To be satisfied with such "reasons" is in effect to say that animals really don't count at all. Or we might put it this way: if killing animals for food is a morally unobjectionable activity when there are healthy alternative diets, then virtually any reason we might offer to justify killing an animal will be good enough.

When matters are put in this way, it does seem that killing meat for food or, in other words, for certain enjoyable taste sensations, is hardly justified. I think, however, that we need to put matters in a larger context, and when we do so matters become a bit more ambiguous. Reflect on the fact that it does seem that killing in the wild is a more serious affair than killing animals that we have raised (let us suppose with decent care) for human consumption. This in part may be because animals that live in the wild are embedded in an ecosystem in a way that domesticated animals, who live in human-created and controlled habitats, are not. To kill the animal in the wild is not only to kill an individual animal, but perhaps constitutes a potentially disturbing intrusion into a functioning ecosystem; this may in turn have unanticipated consequences for other members of that ecosystem and for the ecosystem itself, which we might suppose merits a certain measure of respect. Further — and more importantly for our purposes — when we kill domesticated animals that have been raised for food, we kill that which we have brought into existence and which need our ongoing care and provision for their survival. Not to kill those domesticated animals raised for food would impose on us the burden of either continuing to care for them at our own expense or turning them loose (if possible) to fend for themselves, much to their own detriment and the detriment of others. In contrast, killing wild animals is to kill that which lives and flourishes without any effort or contribution on our part. To refrain from killing an animal in the wild will (typically) impose no burdens on us.

So, to stop killing animals for food would be to impose on us the burden of caring for those animals which we have brought into existence for human consumption but have not yet slaughtered. Here we might wonder: Is the value of cattle, pigs, and chickens sufficiently strong that in order to preserve that value we must continue subsidizing their existence at our own expense? It is not obvious that the answer is "yes." Then may we painlessly kill them? Possibly so. For it is not unreasonable to suggest that the considerable expense of a typical farm operation need not be maintained simply to provide for the continued existence of these animals. But reflect: if we can justifiably kill them, rather than bear the uncompensated financial burden necessary to maintain their existence, why can we not bring them into existence (an existence they would not otherwise enjoy save for our efforts) and then "sacrifice" them for human consumption in order to be compensated for the burden that we (farmers, ranchers, and others) have borne in order to make their existence possible?

In essence there is a kind of quid pro quo operative here. We give the animal life itself along with a relatively satisfactory existence, neither of which it would enjoy apart from us and our efforts. We do this at our own, at times considerable, expense. Without our incurring that expense, the animal would simply not exist. So, to recover our cost and make future animal existence possible, the animal is used (but not abused) in various ways, including being painlessly killed and used for food. This is the price that the animal pays for a relatively decent existence. A successful vegetarian program, on the other hand, would mean not that animals would enjoy a prolonged life by not being prematurely slaughtered but that they would either not have existed at all or they would be killed when their subsidized existence was no longer economically feasible. And there we may simply ask: Can a serious protest be made on behalf of the animal, that it has a right to be brought into existence and to be given a subsidized existence gratis? This does not seem to be an occasion for protest and moral outrage.

This argument, it should be noted, is not open to a certain *reductio ad absurdum,* as if we could apply this line of reasoning to humans, bringing them into existence and requiring a similar quid pro quo for them. The difference between humans and animals is that human life is of greater value and makes more substantial demands on us than animal life. Human life *ought* to be subsidized by the community should that be necessary but a similar moral requirement does not apply to animal life or does not apply with the same stringency.

SUMMARY AND CONCLUSION

In this chapter we have argued that animal life is to be respected and that in order to kill an animal one needs a justifying reason. Killing an animal is an act of harm and is wrong because of the harm that is done to the animal by denying it a future existence that it would find satisfying (i.e., one in which there is a favorable balance of pleasure over pain). Just as killing an animal can be an act of mercy when an animal's existence becomes sufficiently distressing and its prospects sufficiently dim, so killing an animal can be an act of harm when its existence is sufficiently enjoyable and its future prospects sufficiently positive. This reason also serves to distinguish the wrongness of killing animals from the less serious act of killing plants (which are not sentient and where one can only cause organismic harm) and from the more serious act of killing humans (who are more than sentient, additionally being moral and spiritual agents). We also explored the connection between not killing animals because it harms the animal killed and not killing animals because God prohibits it. We argued that these are not competing explanations; rather, it can be argued that God doesn't want animals killed (without a justifying reason) because of the harm done to the animal. To respect animal life is in essence to share God's attitude toward animals – that for their own sake they not be harmed.

This reason for not killing animals can be embraced in a range of ways, depending on the moral vocabulary we choose to use: rights, principles, or virtue. We briefly explained the pros and cons of speaking of an animal right to life (i.e., a right not to be harmed by being denied a future satisfying life). We observed that whether we choose to speak of an animal right to life or reject such talk depends on how much coercive intervention we judge is appropriate in support of preserving animal life. The more we are convinced of the appropriateness of such intervention the more we will judge the use of rights talk to be appropriate, since it is quintessentially the moral vocabulary used to solicit coercive intervention. We suggested that invoking a principle that prohibits killing an animal without a justifying reason or invoking the virtue of compassion are equally plausible alternatives to talk of an animal right to life. Good stewards may see their call to respect animal life by not harming in terms of rights, principles, or virtues, but they will see it in terms of one of these. Talk of animals having intrinsic value, though not rejected, might, we warned, unacceptably shift our focus from the animal and the harm it suffers when killed to some abstract aggregate of intrinsic value that is depleted when animals are killed.

Finally, we commented on moral vegetarianism. We initially provided some reasons to think that killing animals in order to have certain desirable taste sensations, when there are available healthy alternative vegetarian diets, is to provide an insufficient justifying reason. On further reflection and placing matters in a larger context, we provided a line of thought that seemed to justify eating meat but only on the assumption that animals are raised in relatively decent conditions before being humanely slaughtered. In our subsequent chapter on factory farming we shall further explore the case for moral vegetarianism.

CHAPTER 8

A Special Moral Status for Humans

INTRODUCTION

Here we shall explore the notion of human superiority and the implications for animal advocacy of granting to humans a special moral status. The notion of human superiority has been attacked for a range of reasons. Crucially, it has been argued that there are no human capacities not possessed by some animal, somewhere and to some degree, and, therefore, that there is no basis for a special moral standing for humans. Moreover, it is feared by animal advocates that a special moral standing for humans will license a free-for-all toward animals. In contrast, I shall argue in support of a special moral standing for humans rooted in unique human capacities. This will fully preserve the biblical notion of humans as a special creation and will at the same time be consistent, I shall argue, with a robust moral concern for animals.

We shall also see that many attacks on human uniqueness may well be not primarily attempts to secure a decent moral place for animals, but rather, more fundamentally, expressive of a hostility toward Christian claims that humans are a special creation who are called to fulfill a special role in the created order.[1] In this connection, I wish to hold out my hand

1. It is not only Christian claims, of course, that are found objectionable; Muslims and Jews, for example, also believe in special creation. In the West, however, it is the Christian church that is primarily associated with such beliefs and therefore it is the church's teaching that principally comes under attack.

to those seeking a serious and extensive moral recognition of animals while at the same time resisting those attempts to deny that humans are, as the Christian tradition affirms, a special creation.

DEFINING A SPECIAL MORAL STATUS

What precisely do we mean when we speak of humans having a special moral status? If we mean that *only* humans have significance for God, that *only* humans count morally, and that animals are nothing more than objects for human use and enjoyment, then this is a sense of "special" that the Christian community should not be interested in defending for a wide range of theological and moral reasons. This sense of "special" is incompatible with any direct moral concern for animals. But if we reject *this* notion of "special," then we must ask ourselves, in what ways are humans morally special?

Humans are special, first, in that killing a human is a much more serious affair than killing members of any other species. As Mary Warnock has commented, "to kill a member of our own species is a different thing from killing a member of another species, and requires a quite different moral justification, which may often not be forthcoming. No one who seriously imagines himself afloat on a raft and short of food and water, debating whether to kill a human or another animal, can doubt this."[2] To argue that human life is more valuable than animal life does not entail, however, that animal life has little or no value. At some point the human benefit can be sufficiently great to justify acts of killing animals, but human superiority does not give us carte blanche to dispense with animals for just any advantage that we may want for ourselves. Indeed, attaching greater value to human life would be quite consistent with being a moral vegetarian, for example. Thus one might contend that eating meat would be justified should it be necessary for human survival and health, reflecting thereby a belief in the greater worth of human life, but argue that otherwise eating meat cannot be justified. That is, killing animals does not have to be as serious as killing humans in order for a case for moral vegetarianism to be made. And we might also conclude, on the other hand, that vegetarianism is not morally incumbent upon us, but that would not be simply because we believe that human life is more valuable than animal life. That is something we can consistently believe whether or not we are moral vegetarians.

2. Mary Warnock, *The Uses of Philosophy* (Oxford: Blackwell, 1992), p. 24.

Second, animals can be used for human ends in ways that humans cannot. Again, Mary Warnock's comments are pertinent: "to use a member of our own species to subserve our own ends is now generally regarded as unjustifiable in a way that using a horse or a dog for our own purposes is not."[3] This is *not* to say that animals are available for any use to which we may wish to put them. No doubt there are many restrictions that we ought to place on our treatment of animals that we have hitherto failed to observe. Nevertheless, these restrictions, though they may very well be substantial, are not as severe as the restrictions that ought to apply to our treatment and use of humans.

Third, human flourishing is more important than animal flourishing. The spiritual, moral, aesthetic, and rational lives of humans are worth greater sacrifices to preserve, protect, and support than are the lives of animals. Again, this does not mean that an "anything goes" approach to animals is thereby sanctioned. It does not mean that we can do anything to animals, no matter how abusive, in order to assist our own flourishing. But human flourishing, in the sense that God calls humans to flourish and grow, has greater significance than animal flourishing, though the latter is not to be considered inconsequential, and it too is desired by God.

Now, these are very general convictions, and they can be understood in a range of ways, depending upon how strictly one interprets them. Thus, quite consistent with these three affirmations one could be a strict moral vegetarian and committed anti-vivisectionist, for example. Or one could have more modest moral concerns for animals, eating meat but calling for humane treatment for animals raised for food, and approving painful research on animals but calling for stricter regulations to govern such research. Nevertheless, these three moral convictions — that killing humans is much more serious than killing members of any other species, that animals can be used for human ends in ways that humans cannot, that human flourishing is more important than animal flourishing — are not to be abandoned in the course of articulating and defending an ethic of animal concern.

It is important to emphasize that some people erroneously conclude that animal liberationists are assigning to animals an equality with humans simply by the fact that they deny to humans the right to eat animals, to use them for research tools, and to hunt them for sport. The assumption that leads to this conclusion seems to be that if humans have a

3. Warnock, *The Uses of Philosophy,* p. 24.

superior moral standing, that is, their life and their flourishing is more important than the life and flourishing of animals, then there are no limits or no serious limits on what can be done to animals for human advantage. Those who ascribe to this position think, in other words, that to give a moral priority to human life and flourishing over animal life and flourishing is in essence to give humans carte blanche to do with animals what they will (apart, possibly, from extreme cruelty). This would not be merely to give superior moral standing to humans; it would be to deny any moral standing to animals in the process. This is not what is here being conveyed when acknowledging a superior moral standing for humans.

To say that human life is more valuable than animal life is to say that a stronger reason is required to end human life than is required to end animal life. But how good the reason has to be in order to end animal life is what calls for discussion. It might be concluded that the fun of hunting or the enjoyable taste sensations of eating meat are not good enough to justify killing animals, though killing animals for human survival or to avoid a marginal human existence are good enough reasons. Thus, granting a moral priority to humans does not mean that animals don't count. They do count. It is just that humans happen to count more.

This is to deny what Arne Naess, the distinguished Norwegian philosopher and deep ecologist, claims when he says that each species has "an equal right to live and bloom."[4] On the contrary, to build an animal ethic (or an environmentalist ethic) on the denial of the three propositions articulated above, which is just what would be done by giving to all species an equal right "to live and bloom," would be a serious mistake and would only place animal advocacy outside the pale of serious moral consideration by all but a tiny, dedicated minority. Indeed, a major reason why many people are deeply offended by the animal rights movement is that it often appears to be doing just that, as when activists label the killing of animals for food "murder," thereby blurring the difference between killing animals and killing humans, or when they draw analogies between factory farms and Nazi concentration camps. Such exaggerated rhetoric both offends and invites ridicule. In contrast, I am arguing that humans possess a superior moral standing which is both important to recognize and consistent with deep moral concern for animals.

4. Arne Naess, "The Shallow and the Deep, Long-Range Ecology Movement," *Inquiry* 16 (1973): 96.

THE CHALLENGE TO HUMAN SPECIALNESS

In calling into question human specialness, it is often argued that the difference between humans and animals is one of degree and not one of kind.[5] This is almost a standard line of argument offered by those who wish, laudably, to elevate the moral standing of animals. It is thought to pose a successful challenge to the kind of uniqueness required to support a theory of human specialness, which is judged to be a threat to an adequate moral standing for animals.

James Gould, a Princeton University ethologist, has argued in just this way, contending that the differences between the higher primates and human beings and differences of degree and not of kind, and that this has important implications for the status of humans.[6] He argues that the distinctly human behaviors that at one time were confidently pointed to in order to sharply demarcate humans from the lower animals have one by one fallen by the wayside: *tool-making* (but chimpanzees select and prune sticks in order to dig out ants and termites); *social learning* (but a single Japanese monkey, a macaque, discovers that sand on a sweet potato can be removed by washing it in a stream, a skill that is "transmitted culturally through the troop, first to playmates, then to sisters, then mothers, and so on from the bottom of the hierarchy to the top"); *creative problem-solving* (but chimpanzees pile boxes on top of one another to reach bananas hanging out of reach from the ceiling); *a species-specific language* (but the vervet monkey has acoustically distinct warning calls for different predators – leopards, eagles, and pythons); and *self-consciousness* (but chimpanzees who were anesthetized and had spots placed on their foreheads then, when subsequently placed before mirrors, began to rub the spots in order to remove them, thereby indicating an awareness that the image in the mirror was an image of themselves). Thus, Gould triumphantly concludes that the "final bulwark of those who want to believe Homo sapiens to be a special creation" has crumbled. To Gould's crumbling bulwark we might add *altruism* (for rhesus monkeys will consistently suffer hunger rather than operate a device that secured food at

5. When we speak of differences in degree we have in mind two entities, both of which have a common property or capacity, the one having more of it and the other less. When we speak of a difference in kind we have in mind two entities, one of which has a property or capacity totally lacking in the other. Thus, the difference between a mosquito and an elephant in terms of weight is a matter of degree, but the difference in terms of the ability to fly is a matter of kind.

6. James Gould, *Ethology: The Mechanism and Evolution of Behavior* (New York: W. W. Norton and Company, 1982), pp. 482-83.

the expense of shocking another rhesus monkey[7]). The assumption behind Gould's argument is that in order for humans to be a special creation it must be the case that the differences between animals and humans are ones of kind, not only ones of degree.

But why should one think this? John Kleinig, we might initially note, has made two observations about the kind of argument offered by Gould.[8] First, it has a "lack of general application." That is, animals vary enormously in their capacities and these purported affinities with humans can be ascribed only to a few species of the higher mammals. Second, there is in this kind of cataloging "a misleading aggregation of affinities," suggesting that "some, many or most" of the higher species possess all or most of these features, which, of course, they do not.

That any animal can do the things that Gould presents for our consideration is impressive — for an animal, that is. In contrast, however, it would be considered a tragedy for a human family to have a child who could function only at the level of those primates referred to in Gould's account — selecting and pruning sticks to dig out ants and termites, piling boxes on the top of one another to get to bananas, recognizing that an image in a mirror is oneself. When we hear of animals doing the kinds of things described by Gould we are genuinely impressed, but should humans be limited in this way, they would be institutionalized. And the tragedy would be that an individual with such severe limitations would not be able to join in the human community and engage in those activities that we associate with a normal human life. When we look at animals, wonderful in their own way and to be admired and respected for what they are, and to whom we have very real obligations, we do still, and despite Gould's line of argument, see a dramatic and massive divide between them and humans. If one sees nothing special and unique about human life in contrast to the life of animals, one would be simply denying the obvious. As Peter van Inwagen has said, "it is blindingly, boringly obvious that humanity is radically different from all other species. . . ."[9]

There are, of course, rich and significant affinities between humans and animals, but there are also vast differences. These differences may be either differences of kind or differences of degree, and if the latter, they

7. Jules H. Masserman, Stanley Weckin, and William Terris, "'Altruistic' Behavior in Rhesus Monkeys," *American Journal of Psychiatry* 121 (1964): 584-85, and "Shock to a Conspecific as an Aversive Stimulus," *Psychonomic Science* 1 (1964): 46-48.

8. John Kleinig, *Valuing Life* (Princeton, N.J.: Princeton University Press, 1991), p. 98.

9. Peter van Inwagen, "Non Est Hick," in *God, Knowledge and Mystery: Essays in Philosophical Theology* (Ithaca: Cornell University Press, 1995), p. 207.

may be differences of degree compounded to the point where the overall difference turns out to be staggering. But one need not deny the affinities in order to preserve these substantial differences. Indeed, as Mary Midgley puts it, "if the talk is of elephants, we can do justice to the miracle of the trunk without pretending that nobody else has a nose."[10] That is, there may be a capacity which is possessed by two entities but which is possessed by the one to such a degree that it enables one to do something, possibly something of profound significance, that the other cannot do at all. To secure that difference one need not deny the lesser abilities of the other. Whether this difference is finally labeled one of "kind" or one of degree would not seem to matter very much.

Still there are those who are greatly concerned that if the difference turns out to be one of degree this will seriously threaten a special moral standing for humans. The popular philosopher Mortimer J. Adler, a staunch defender of the special status of humans, has claimed that if there is no significant difference in kind but only in degree between animals and humans, then this will have catastrophic implications, threatening the very basis of morality itself. He claims that if it is the case that humans differ from animals only in degree and not radically in kind, then we would have no moral basis for treating humans differently from animals. It would destroy, he argues, the moral basis for affirming that all humans have basic rights and an individual dignity.[11]

Surely Adler goes too far here. He goes too far in claiming that if the difference between humans and animals is only one of degree, then there is no basis for human rights and no basis for treating animals differently than humans. For should the difference be one of degree that would only mean, at most and counter to Adler, that some animals (surely not all animals) will join humans as members of the moral community and become legitimate objects of moral concern. The result would be a larger moral community, with more individuals possessing rights, not the elimination of the moral community and the end to moral rights.

Nor is it the case, contrary to Adler, that a difference in degree between humans and animals entails that we have no moral basis for treating humans differently than animals. Quite the contrary, that there are differences of degree may provide the very basis for differential treatment. For it may be that whereas animals have rights, these rights are weaker and fewer

10. Mary Midgley, *Beast and Man,* revised ed. (London: Routledge, 1995), p. 206.

11. Mortimer J. Adler, *The Difference of Man and the Difference It Makes* (New York: Holt, Rinehart and Winston, 1967), chapter 17.

than those rights possessed by humans, and that our obligations to animals are neither as strong nor as extensive as our obligations to humans. So animals could very well have rights and be members of the moral community, but because these would be weaker rights, there would be a firm basis for differential treatment. Moreover, differences of degree, if the differences – either alone or in combination – are of sufficient magnitude, may invest human life with a greater value than that which attaches to other forms of life. So it is not the case that the end result of accepting the difference of degree thesis is that humans automatically lose their individual dignity and can no longer be considered of greater value than animals.

THE HUMAN DIFFERENCE

The attempt to make a case for a special moral standing for humans usually takes the form of a search for a single capacity or ability possessed by humans that sets them apart from animals and provides the basis for a special moral concern. There may, however, be something misguided about the search for a single defining property that sets humans apart from animals and confers on them a special status. Mary Midgley perceptively observes, "What is special about each creature is not a single, unique quality but a rich and complex arrangement of powers and qualities, some of which it will share with its neighbors."[12] For neither animals nor humans are like triangles, whose essence can be neatly captured in a simple definition (Midgley's example). Without three sides we no longer have a triangle, but matters are more complicated with animals, for a flightless bird is still a bird and a flying fish is still a fish. And the difficulty of trying to do with birds and fish what we do with triangles – identify a simple differentiating property – becomes all the more difficult the more complex the species. With humans, it becomes the most difficult of all. "To expect a single differentia is absurd. And it is not even effectively flattering to the species, since it obscures our truly characteristic richness and versatility," states Midgley.[13] So it is not the case that the greatness and the grandeur that attaches to being human, nor the distinctiveness of being human, is threatened by our failure to demarcate humans from all other animals by a *single* differentiating property that confers praise.

But if one were searching for a single difference of kind, then there are a number of places where one might plausibly begin such a search. One

12. Midgley, *Beast and Man,* p. 207.
13. Midgley, *Beast and Man,* p. 207.

might think in terms of language, conceptual thought, moral understanding, morally responsible behavior, second-order desires (i.e., desires about one's desires), second-order beliefs (i.e., beliefs about one's beliefs), and so forth. I am going to suggest that a fundamental difference in kind can be found in the religious capacity possessed by humans. This capacity is reflected in our ability, for example, to respond to and to worship God. This capacity is not an isolated and independent capacity, but rather it presupposes other basic human capacities, some that have just been mentioned, capacities which themselves may or may not represent differences of kind. Certainly religious engagement presupposes a certain level of conceptual ability sufficient to comprehend basic religious ideas, including the idea of God; it presupposes moral understanding sufficient to understand the ascription of goodness to God, sinfulness and guilt to ourselves, and so on; it presupposes the capacity for moral choice and commitment to spiritual ideals; it presupposes second-order desires and beliefs, which are necessary for our wanting to be a different people and for our wanting to enter into a redeeming and transforming process that will turn us into what we judge we ought to be. No doubt these capacities overlap and no doubt others would need to be added in order to fully comprehend our capacity for religious engagement. Just as Mary Midgley says that it is a "rich and complex arrangement of powers and qualities" that makes us the distinctive beings that we are, so also it is a "rich and complex arrangement of powers and qualities" that makes us the religious beings that we are.

The sociologist Alan Wolfe has argued that what distinguishes humans from other species is what he calls our "meaning-producing abilities." That is, we do not simply live our lives, doing so more or less intelligently, but we seek to interpret our lives, to make sense of them, and thereby we struggle with issues of ultimate meaning. Indeed, humans and only humans raise such questions as: Why do I exist? Why does anything exist? Is there a God? How should I live? Why is there evil? How should we understand suffering and pain? In seeking answers to such questions we seek meaning. In doing so, we may be either discovering meaning or possibly creating meaning, but either way we are exercising a unique human capacity. Wolfe himself puts it this way: "No other species shares the sacred with us. . . . the world of other species is entirely profane, they strive to satisfy basic needs without attributing importance to the ultimate goods these very needs seek to serve."[14]

14. Alan Wolfe, *The Human Difference* (Berkeley and Los Angeles: University of California Press, 1993), p. 110.

A crucial aspect of this "meaning-producing capacity" is our ability to understand the world and our place in it in religious terms, to interpret who and what we are by reference to the transcendent. For the religious believer, this capacity is absolutely fundamental, and it is a capacity that is not shared with animals. It is not that animals have a less developed religious capacity while humans have a more developed and sophisticated religious capacity. Rather, the capacity is uniquely human. And this capacity is found in all peoples, in all times, and in all cultures. It is not a capacity reserved for the highly trained or the intellectual elite. There may be nonparadigmatic humans (say, the massively retarded) who lack this capacity, but this raises a different problem for us. The issue before us is whether there are differences of kind between animals and *normal* adult humans. This is just what is typically denied by those who contend that all such differences are a matter of degree only. So, I suggest, the meaning-producing capacity to which Wolfe refers and more specifically our ability to interpret the world religiously is one identifiable difference between animals and paradigm humans, though this in turn, no doubt, presupposes a "rich and complex arrangement of (other) powers and qualities."

Alan Richardson articulates a biblical version of this difference when (in pre-inclusive language) he observes:

> The Bible makes it clear that there is an essential difference between man and even the highest mammals. It is well aware that man shares with the animals certain characteristics, chief of which is his mortality (cf. Ps. 49:12: "Man is like the beasts that perish"; also Ps. 144:3f.). But he differs from the animals in that God "visits" him, i.e., holds conversation with him (Ps. 8:4): there is that in man which animals do not possess, namely, man's responsibility before God, the fact that he can answer God's address, hear his law and make or withhold his conscious and deliberate response. There is that in man which is capable of responding to the divine Word; man is akin to God in this respect at least, that he hears God's word: as we say, like speaks to like. . . . To man alone is given the responsibility of conscious choice; man alone of all created things is free to disobey the Creator's will. Thus it is that man alone is conscious of his responsibility before God, is aware that he stands in the presence and under the judgment of God.[15]

15. Alan Richardson, *Genesis I–XI* (London: SCM Press, 1953), pp. 53-54.

Speaking, then, within the context of faith, the human "difference in kind" is this capacity to respond to God's call for our total allegiance; to repent of past wrongs, including our previous indifference to this call; to worship God, engaging in acts of adoration, contrition, thanksgiving, and supplication; to intentionally participate in the process whereby we are to be transformed into the moral likeness of Christ.

It is in this context that the notion of the image of God can most helpfully be understood. As theologian Geoffrey Wainwright has said, "The first meaning of humanity's being in the image of God is that God has made humanity sufficiently like himself for communion between God and humans to be possible."[16] Wainwright goes on to observe that the Greek fathers, following Irenaeus, made "an exegetically improbable but doctrinally valuable distinction between 'image' and 'likeness' in Genesis 1:26." The difference is this: *image of God* "expresses the ontological or structural possibility of human communion with God" where *likeness of God* "stands for the existential or moral similarity with God into which humanity is to grow as it actually lives in communion with God."[17] So humans "image" God in that they are so constituted that they can commune with God, and consequently they can be transformed into the moral "likeness" of God. On the assumption that there is a God, this would confer on humans a special place in the moral universe.

For humans to be special in this sense does not mean that other animal species are denied moral standing. That set of capacities that gives humans a special moral standing need not be a necessary condition for having moral standing, as if this were the only way to qualify as a legitimate object of moral concern. Though animals are not capable of religious response, many of them are members of species who nevertheless have an inner life that can go better or worse for them, who can experience pain and suffer, who have interests, who have varying degrees of intrinsic worth, and who are valued by God apart from their contribution to human well-being. Therefore, they qualify as objects of moral concern.

Finally, for humans to have a special moral significance also carries with it special responsibilities. Among those responsibilities are caring for God's creation, respecting the developmental telos of animal and plant life, and working for humane and stewardly treatment of animals. Indeed, Andrew Linzey identifies human uniqueness in our call to be a "servant species." He comments, "Drawing upon the idea of a God who suffers, I

16. Geoffrey Wainwright, *Doxology* (New York: Oxford University Press, 1980), p. 16.
17. Wainwright, *Doxology*, p. 17.

argue that human uniqueness can be defined as the capacity for service and self-sacrifice. From this perspective, humans are the species uniquely commissioned to exercise a self-sacrificial priesthood, after the one High Priest, not just for members of their own species, but for all sentient creatures."[18] This is a valuable suggestion, even if it is in need of some qualification.[19] Nevertheless, that humans are called to be a servant people whose service is to be directed beyond their own species to other inhabitants on this planet is a salutary emphasis. Indeed, our "participation in God's redeeming presence in the world"[20] is not limited to service on behalf of Homo sapiens, though we are not, in the course of this participation, to abandon our recognition of a privileged moral standing for humans.

SPECIES EQUALITY WITHOUT DENYING THE HUMAN DIFFERENCE

There are those who are quite willing to acknowledge substantial differences between humans and animals, indeed even dramatic differences in kind, but who simply are not convinced that these differences yield a preferred moral standing for humans. Here there is no attempt to close the gap between humans and animals by arguing that the gap is one of degree and that this gap is not so great as many people have thought. Here the gap is acknowledged, but its significance is denied. For example, Jana Thompson, who takes her feminist anti-hierarchicalism to an extreme, says, "there is no reason in nature why we should regard the qualities that human beings happen to have as making them more valuable than living creatures that do not have these qualities – no reason why creatures who can think or feel should be regarded as more valuable than plants and other nonsentient creatures."[21] Here, humans are not only not given a su-

18. Andrew Linzey, *Animal Theology* (Urbana: University of Illinois Press, 1995), p. 45.

19. One might wonder, among other things, about the role of material delight and flourishing in the lives of those sacrificially seeking social justice for humans or better treatment for animals and the environment. As Professor John Schneider has said, "They both [i.e., material flourishing and justice] turn out to be expressions of the redeemed and redeeming life before God. There is no true prosperity or delight without compassion and justice; but likewise, there is no real justice or liberation, no shalom, without material delight and flourishing" (*Godly Materialism* [Downers Grove, Ill.: InterVarsity Press, 1994], p. 17).

20. Linzey, *Animal Theology*, p. 57.

21. Jana Thompson, "A Refutation of Environmental Ethics," *Environmental Ethics* 12, no. 2 (1990): 150.

perior standing to higher mammals, they are not even given a higher standing than nonsentient animals and plants. On this view, the pursuit of human good, that is, the development and exercise of moral and spiritual capacities, has no more inherent value than the pursuit of the good of plants, which is simple biological growth. This is certainly an astounding conclusion, seriously complicating, one would suppose, the weeding of one's garden.

The philosopher Paul Taylor also argues for moral equality among species.[22] Taylor observes that rationality may be essential to human self-realization or the achievement of human good. But, then, visual acuity and flight may be essential to the realization of the hawk's good or speed and agility may be essential for the realization of the cheetah's good. Ground speed isn't more valuable than flight, though it is for the cheetah, and flight isn't more valuable than ground speed, though it is for the hawk. Similarly, rationality is not more valuable than ground speed, though it is for humans whose good is linked to and partly defined in terms of rationality. To insist, in response, as we may be strongly inclined to do, that rationality is more valuable and of greater worth than ground speed is only to say, according to Taylor, that it is more valuable for humans whose good it is. Thus, the value or worth of all goods – ground speed, flight, and rationality – is thereby relativized to cheetahs, hawks, and humans, respectively. Again, to insist that rational-moral-spiritual beings are more valuable than cheetahs or hawks is simply, Taylor would argue, to take the human good, which undeniably is an affirmative value for human life, and to arbitrarily view it exclusively from the human vantage point.

In response, we continue to insist that the exercise of human rational, moral, and spiritual capacities is intrinsically more valuable than a cheetah's exercising its speed and agility in running down a prey. Thus, it would be a greater tragedy to eliminate all humans from the world than to eliminate all cheetahs because humans are intrinsically more valuable (we still continue to insist) than cheetahs. Their presence in the world constitutes a greater good than that of cheetahs. This is to make a judgment of intrinsic worth, and it is obviously a human judgment, but then all our judgments will always be judgments made by humans. This does not beg the question in quite the sense that Taylor charges that it does,

22. See especially *Respect for Nature* (Princeton, N.J.: Princeton University Press, 1986), chapter 3; and "Are Humans Superior to Animals and Plants?" *Environmental Ethics* 6 (Summer 1984).

because Taylor's own judgments to the contrary are also, every bit as much, human judgments. It is true that this human judgment can perhaps best be supported in a theistic universe. In such a universe, humans, because of their rational, moral, and spiritual capacities, are in the privileged position of being able to serve and worship the one who is the Creator and Lord of the universe and who is the ultimate source of all that is true and good and beautiful. Further, these special human capacities enable humans to consciously and intentionally share in those good purposes that the Creator-Lord has for the universe and for all its inhabitants. Granted the sort of universe that Christians believe ours to be, we can support the claim that humans are special and worthy of a preferred status in the universe, though admittedly a preferred status that has too often been misinterpreted to justify dismissing serious moral concern for animals.

Animal advocates are understandably concerned that the establishment of human superiority will give humans carte blanche to do with animals whatever they want and will allow human interests, no matter how trivial, to override animal interests, no matter how substantial. No doubt this is why many animal advocates become nervous when confronted by claims of human superiority. Paul Taylor fully shares this concern. He says that granting to humans a superior moral standing means "that whenever a conflict arose between [animals'] well-being and the interests of humans, human interests would automatically take priority."[23] But John Kleinig rightly labels this a non sequitur, pointing out that it doesn't even follow with regard to plants, let alone animals; to quote again his pertinent remark, "A person's desire to barbecue his steak over sequoia coals would not justify felling a thousand-year-old tree."[24] Indeed, as I have argued throughout this book, because something has a lesser value, it does not follow that it has no value or no significant value; it doesn't follow that because animals have a lesser moral standing than humans that our obligations to animals can always be subordinated to human interests. Certainly the animal's interest in not being cruelly treated will override the human's interest in being entertained — and that despite the human having a higher moral standing than the animal.

It is right here that confusions and misunderstandings may seriously hurt animal advocacy, causing unnecessary alienation, especially among people of religious persuasion. On the one hand, animal advocates

23. Taylor, *Respect for Nature,* p. 136.
24. Kleinig, *Valuing Life,* p. 86.

may, wrongly, see all defenses of a superior moral standing for humans as expressing and entailing a dismissive attitude toward animals, and in their enthusiasm for animal advocacy they may rigorously attack all such claims. This, in turn, may evoke a strong counter response, and possibly an overreaction, from sympathetic "outsiders" who then dismiss all talk of animal advocacy as nothing other than a brutal assault on what is human; they will view animal advocates not merely as eccentric but as dangerous. Battle lines will be drawn and then harden, each side in the controversy seeing itself defending something of vital importance, and we end up with combat rather than mutual exploration and growth. Animal advocates need to see that an appropriately qualified special moral standing for humans is not a threat to serious, far-reaching, even revolutionary, moral concern for animals. Defenders of human superiority need to see that serious moral concern for animals does not threaten an appropriately qualified special moral standing for humans.

It is not unreasonable to fear that talk of a superior moral standing for humans will encourage a morally lax attitude toward animals. That is, granting humans a superior moral standing may encourage (even if mistakenly) the view that any human interest (no matter how trivial) overrides any animal interest (no matter how substantial). And no doubt there is such a danger. But the corrective for this is not to attack sensible notions of human moral superiority. The cause of animal advocacy is not going to be helped by such an attack. It will only alienate large numbers of potential sympathizers and will never prove convincing, I believe, to any substantial body of opinion. Whatever careless attitudes toward animals may be encouraged by claims on behalf of the moral superiority of humans, the negative effects for animal advocacy will, I believe, be even greater with its denial.

ATTACKS ON HUMAN SUPERIORITY AND THE ENLIGHTENMENT AGENDA

Christian defenders of human superiority not only may see human superiority (rightly understood and appropriately qualified) as something important to defend, but, at times, may see attacks on this claim as something more than a simple expression of moral concern for animals. They may rightly see criticisms of human superiority as an extension of the larger "Enlightenment agenda" — Peter van Inwagen's term for a continuation of certain Enlightenment attacks on fundamental teachings of the

Christian church. Here the notion of humans as a special creation is *itself* found objectionable, not merely objectionable because it is used (or misused) to support a moral disregard for animals. That is, even if an understanding of humans as a special creation were offered that is consistent with a fully satisfactory moral concern with animals, the notion of a special creation would still be found objectionable. And why?

It is in the context of the Enlightenment agenda, I believe, that one can view James Rachels's book *Created from Animals: The Moral Implications of Darwinism.*[25] This book is much more than a plea for moral concern for animals. Rachels views his work as a criticism and a rejection of "the idea of human dignity," which is the belief that "human beings are in a special moral category: from a moral point of view, human life has a special, unique value, while non-human life has relatively little value. . . . morality is conceived to be, primarily, the protection of human beings and their rights and interests."[26] Not only will animals be elevated in our moral thinking as a result of rejecting the idea of human dignity, he argues, but we will no longer view human life with the "superstitious awe" which has characterized past moral thought.[27] This in turn will enable us to revise our attitude toward suicide and euthanasia, since there will no longer be a special value attaching to human life above and beyond the value that it has for the individual whose life it is. This, in turn, will yield a more permissive moral stance toward suicide and euthanasia.[28]

The idea of human dignity, Rachels says, is supported by two pillars, the philosophical claim that humans are uniquely rational and the theological claim that humans are made in the image of God. Darwinism undercuts both of these claims, Rachels argues. The first pillar is rendered doubtful by Darwinian evolutionary theory, which "makes us suspicious of any doctrine that sees large gaps of any sort between humans and other creatures."[29] Rather, because humans have evolved from other animals and share a common developmental ancestry, one would expect to find many close affinities between humans and other animals. Further, Darwinism encourages us, we are told, to look and see what animals are like,

25. James Rachels, *Created from Animals: The Moral Implications of Darwinism* (New York: Oxford University Press, 1990).

26. Rachels, *Created from Animals,* p. 4.

27. Rachels, *Created from Animals,* p. 5.

28. See especially Rachels, *Created from Animals,* chapter 5, "Morality with the Idea that Humans Are Special."

29. Rachels, *Created from Animals,* p. 172.

not to come with preconceived ideas about what animals should be like. (Though one may wonder if the Darwinian expectation that there will be no large gaps between humans and animals is not itself a preconceived notion.) And when we look carefully, Rachels claims, we see that the difference between animals and humans is one of degree, which undercuts the notion that humans and animals are distinguished by differences in kind. (We earlier examined this kind of attack on human uniqueness and did not find it persuasive.)

In the case of the second pillar of human dignity, the claim that humans are in the image of God, Darwinism discredits the very idea that humans are products of the superintending design of a Creator. Rachels comments, "After Darwin, we can no longer think of ourselves as occupying a special place in creation — instead, we must realize that we are the products of the same evolutionary forces, working blindly and without purpose, that shaped the rest of the animal kingdom."[30] Thus Darwinism, according to Rachels, significantly weakens the claim that God has created humans in such a way that they could have been endowed with those special capacities that would enable them to assume a special role in the world and to enjoy a unique moral status. Since the forces at work are blind and without purpose, such a process cannot yield a special creation, one designed for some unique role and endowed with special capacities. This point of view would even clash with Andrew Linzey's generous notion that humans are endowed with special capacities for the task of being a servant species. For what would be judged objectionable here, according to Rachels, is that humans have a divine endowment for whatever purpose, even one generously disposed to all animal species.

It is interesting that this is just what has emerged from this supposedly blind and purposeless evolutionary process — individuals who do have special capacities not shared with other animals. For out of the evolutionary process have emerged beings who are capable of religious response and religious engagement, something unique to the human species. And isn't this just what one would expect if humans were a special creation, made to relate to God as worshipers and servants and stewards, as Christians and many other religious believers claim? For only humans have the endowments necessary for this. And the reality of what humans are actually like is not altered by talk of blind and purposeless evolutionary forces. Indeed, if the outcome is something special or unique (as I judge it to be), then one might wonder whether the forces that brought

30. Rachels, *Created from Animals,* p. 1.

humans into existence were so blind and purposeless after all. At least the outcome is consistent with Christian expectations.

MORE ABOUT THE ENLIGHTENMENT AGENDA

Peter van Inwagen characterizes the "Enlightenment agenda" as follows: "Its main intellectual goal is twofold: first to show that there is no God, or at least no providential God who acts in history (and hence that all that the church teaches is false), and, secondly, that the church not only is wrong about history and metaphysics and eschatology, but is a socially retrograde force." An important part of the strategy of such opponents of the church "is to exhibit those things that the church sees as unique as very much of a piece with lots of other things."[31] In this way the special character of the claims made by the church is called into question. Because the church's claims are rendered less special, they are also supposedly rendered less likely to be of divine origin. An example, given by van Inwagen, of this Enlightenment strategy is the attempt to show that there is nothing special about the creation-and-flood story found in the book of Genesis.[32] It would be argued that the same sort of thing is found in the Sumerian, Akkadian, and Iranian creation-and-flood stories. Thus, the Genesis story has nothing more to recommend it than do similar stories found in other cultural and religious traditions. These stories are all very much the kind of thing that humans, sitting around and reflecting about various matters, would likely come up with, which is demonstrated by the fact that this is just what many of them did come up with (unless, of course, they all borrowed from a common source). The suggestion is that this points to something other than a divine origin for the biblical story.

More significantly, what has been done to the Genesis creation-and-flood story can also be done to the claim that humans are a special creation: we can question their uniqueness and therefore cast doubt on their divine origin. Whereas the church has taught that humans are "radically different" from all other animals, the Enlightenment agenda denies this, van Inwagen argues. It claims that humans are not at all that different from other animals. This attack is not prompted so much by a desire to get a better "moral deal" for animals as it is by a desire to discredit the

31. Van Inwagen, *God, Knowledge, and Mystery,* pp. 206-7.
32. Van Inwagen, *God, Knowledge, and Mystery,* p. 207 fn. 10.

church's version of a Creator-God who brings into existence humans with a preferred moral standing and a special calling. Instead, an alternative vision is proposed, one that does not see and understand humans in terms of divine purposes and action, but exclusively in terms of natural process and causes. In this spirit, James Rachels quotes, with enthusiastic approval, Darwin's words: "Man in his arrogance thinks himself a great work worthy of the interposition of a deity. More humble and I think truer to consider him created from animals."[33] Notice in this quotation the contraposition of two different visions. One understands humans as a "great work," requiring the creative interposition of a god; the other sees humans as nothing more than an extension of earthly and natural processes. The first vision, impressed with human capacities (indeed capacities for great good and great evil), finds expression in the words of the Psalmist: "Thou hast made him little less than God, and dost crown him with glory and honor" (Ps. 8:5). The other vision, when it contemplates humans, has its attention drawn not to God but to apes, dolphins, and whales, where, it is judged, their true kinship lies. So, rather than humans being seen as a little less than God, they are seen as a little more than apes.

But, as van Inwagen has said, it is "blindingly, boringly obvious that humanity is radically different from all other species." Those who seek to deny this fly in the face of the obvious and end up having to argue, van Inwagen claims, by misdirection.[34] An example of such misdirection is the use to which the following biological fact is often put (van Inwagen's example): human DNA is closer to chimpanzee DNA (they differ in fewer base-pairs) than grizzly bear DNA is to the DNA of Kodiak bears. This is meant to somehow impress us with our closeness to chimpanzees, that we are actually closer to chimpanzees than grizzlies are to Kodiak bears. But one would think that the argument should run in reverse: since – clearly – grizzly bears are closer to Kodiak bears than chimpanzees are to humans, it follows that the DNA facts cited are not good indicators of those differences that we judge to be important.

On the other hand, those who see humans as a special creation do not need to deny nor feel apologetic about the fact that we humans are animals and that there are significant affinities between us and these other inhabitants of our planet. Indeed, the biblical texts do just this; they affirm both dimensions, the affinities that humans have with animals and those they have with God. As John Austin Baker notes, Old Testament

33. In Rachels, *Created from Animals,* p. 1.

34. Van Inwagen, *God, Knowledge, and Mystery,* p. 207.

writers see "man" as "part of the panorama of nature. Psalm 104, for example, places him firmly, and with great artistry, in the context of all the other teeming life of the earth. Nothing is done to highlight him; he is just another figure in the landscape."[35]

> Thou makest darkness, and it is night,
>   when all the beasts of the forest creep forth.
> The young lions roar for their prey,
>   seeking their food from God.
> When the sun rises, they get them away
>   and lie down in their dens.
> Man goes forth to his work
>   and to his labor until the evening.
> O Lord, how manifold are thy works!
>   In wisdom has thou made them all;
>   the earth is full of thy creatures. (104:20-24)

Moreover, both humans and animals are, in the Genesis account, formed from the dust of the ground (see Genesis 2:7 and 2:19), both being made from the same earthly stuff and kin in that sense. And yet there is that crucial difference: humans alone are said to be in the image of God; humans alone possess "a rich and complex arrangement of powers and qualities" that enables them to hear and respond to God's address and to assume special responsibilities for the planet and to them alone therefore it makes sense to attribute a privileged moral standing.

THE ARGUMENT FOR ANIMAL LIBERATION FROM MARGINAL CASES

Humans are special, we have argued, because of their capacity for moral and spiritual agency. But not all humans possess this capacity (actually or potentially). There is a subclass of humans – not numerous, sequestered from contact with the larger population, but there all the same – whose cognitive capacities are sufficiently limited that they neither have this capacity nor have the natural potential to develop it. Here we have in mind the massively retarded and not, say, participants in the Special Olympics, who typically possess this capacity for moral and spiritual agency, limited though it may be.

35. John Austin Baker, "Old Testament Attitudes to Nature," in *Animals and Christianity,* ed. Andrew Linzey and Tom Regan (New York: Crossroad, 1988), p. 11.

We do commonly grant massively retarded individuals full moral standing. But how can we grant to these individuals full moral standing while denying this same standing to chimpanzees, who may be more intelligent than some severely mentally deficient humans? These are more than perplexing and interesting theoretical issues, for they have practical implications for the issues central to this book. For the argument can and has been pressed: we would not hunt severely mentally deficient humans for sport, use them in painful research experiments, or slaughter them for food; therefore, we ought not to do the same with the animals that we subject to pain and death, who are, after all, intellectually superior to some mentally deficient humans who would *not* be subjected to such treatment. To give preferential treatment to intellectually deficient humans over against the more intelligent animal, as we in fact do, is labeled by various animal advocates as "speciesism," an arbitrary and unwarranted preference for one's own species, akin to racism and sexism. This argument is called "the argument from marginal cases," appealing as it does to the special treatment given to "marginal" humans, which it is claimed must be extended to animals (or some animals) on pain of gross arbitrariness.

This argument presupposes what James Rachels calls (and endorses) "moral individualism." That is, the moral standing of individuals is to be determined on a case by case basis; it is not something automatically bestowed because of one's membership in a group or species. And the point is a persuasive one. Rachels puts it this way:

> Moral individualism is a thesis about the justification of judgments concerning how individuals may be treated. The basic idea is that how an individual may be treated is to be determined, not by considering his group memberships, but by considering his own particular characteristics. If A is to be treated differently from B, the justification must be in terms of A's individual characteristics and B's individual characteristics. Treating them differently cannot be justified by pointing out that one or the other is a member of some preferred group, not even the "group" of human beings.[36]

So, if we are puzzling over whether or not to engage in painful research on a chimpanzee after which it will be painlessly killed, we must ask ourselves whether we would be willing to submit a severely mentally deficient human being to the same treatment. Moral individualism dictates that only individual characteristics may be taken into account in de-

36. Rachels, *Created from Animals,* pp. 173-74.

ciding this, not group memberships. That one of these individuals is a member of the species Homo sapiens and that the other is a chimpanzee is not relevant. That the chimpanzee has the same cognitive capacity and the same capacity to experience pain would be relevant. This means that, regarding their possible use as experimental subjects, they both must be accorded the same moral standing and given the same treatment. But to be assigned the same moral standing and to be given the same treatment is not, however, to decide what that treatment should be. It is just to say that they should be treated in the same way. Should that which we are willing to do with chimpanzees – use them in painful and sometimes lethal experiments – be viewed as normative? If so, we can conclude that since there is no relevant moral difference between the chimpanzee and the massively retarded human, we can experiment on both of them. (In point of fact, the chimpanzee would be cognitively superior and just as sensitive to pain as the massively retarded individual.) Or should our treatment of the massively retarded human be viewed as normative, forcing the conclusion that using chimpanzees as research subjects is wrong? The animal advocate who uses this argument is confident that we will find the suggestion of using mentally deficient humans for painful research projects, or for food or game for hunting, sufficiently repellent that we will capitulate to their contention that animals ought not to be used in these ways.

Even if one finds Rachels's individualism convincing (as I do), one may still not be convinced that this argument for better treatment for animals works. There may still be reasons for giving to mentally deficient humans a moral standing on a par with that of normal or paradigm humans – reasons that are not available to animals. (Though to suggest that this particular argument does not work is not also to suggest that there are no other arguments that do work, arguments that will succeed in making a case for a radical revision of our attitudes toward and treatment of animals.) Even Steve Sapontzis, himself an animal liberationist, is unconvinced by the Rachels-type argument and has granted that there are reasons to extend full moral standing to the severely, incurably retarded that do not apply to animals. He comments, "This small, isolated group can plausibly be treated as 'honorary rights-holders' out of deference to the feeling of species affinity most all of us share."[37] Indeed, there does seem to be a natural sympathy and identification with all who share our hu-

37. Steve Sapontzis, *Morals, Reason, and Animals* (Philadelphia: Temple University Press, 1987), p. 141.

man form. To deny full moral standing to the severely retarded and to act accordingly would not only offend deeply embedded sensitivities but might (in time) erode those sensitivities to the detriment of our treatment of those humans who are paradigmatically human. Moreover, it does seem that we humans (like other animals) do care intensely for our own offspring, no matter their cognitive deficiencies. And out of respect for the feelings and sensibilities of those who love them and are related to them a special standing seems appropriate for the full range of the retarded. Further, to withhold moral standing from some humans is inherently dangerous and open to abuse. For then we are involved in drawing lines — "here rationality is adequately developed, but there it is not." These are all reasons for extending full moral standing to massively retarded humans that do not have application to animals. So from the fact that a chimpanzee may be as intelligent as a particular massively retarded human, it does not follow that they share the same moral standing and are to be treated in a similar way.

SUMMARY

In this chapter we have examined and defended a particular notion of a privileged moral standing for humans. This special standing is captured by the following three affirmations: first, killing humans is more serious than killing animals; second, animals can be used for human ends in ways that humans cannot; third, human flourishing is more important than animal flourishing. Part of what we mean by saying that humans are a special creation — in addition to their being called to fulfill a special role in the created order as worshiper, servant, and steward — is that they have this privileged moral standing.

We argued that this notion of a special moral standing for humans is consistent with a serious, even revolutionary, moral concern for animals. That is, this privileged standing does not have to be rejected by animal advocates out of a fear that it is incompatible with substantial moral concern for animals. In fact, linking animal advocacy to a rejection of a special moral standing for humans may only evoke ridicule and hostility toward animal advocacy. In practical terms, I argue, it is bound to be counterproductive. In fact, to be effective in the battle for the hearts and minds of people, it needs to be made quite clear that a robust moral concern for animals does not require a relinquishing of a special moral status for humans.

We defended the claim that there are unique human capacities that provide a basis for this special moral standing. The contention that humans are different from animals only in degree was judged to be insufficient as a basis for rejecting a human uniqueness, the kind of uniqueness required to ground a special moral standing for humans. Very simply, the reason for this is that differences of degree, if the difference is great enough, can constitute a difference of monumental proportions. We also argued that a difference in kind between animals and humans is found in the capacity for religious engagement, in particular the capacity to hear God's address and "make or withhold a conscious and deliberate response."

We distinguished between attacks on human uniqueness that are motivated by a desire to secure a fully satisfactory moral standing for animals and those motivated by a desire to discredit the doctrine that humans are a special creation. Individuals in the former category can, in principle, be satisfied by being assured that the doctrine of humans as a special creation poses no threat to a fully adequate animal ethic, whereas the latter, opponents of special creation, will not be satisfied by this. In this chapter, then, we have sought to reassure the animal advocate that the doctrine of special creation is no enemy, while defending the doctrine of special creation from attacks by those who simply object to a Creator at work in the world, providentially shaping and endowing humans and other species for particular purposes. Finally, we examined the argument for animal liberation from marginal cases. Reasons were offered for giving mentally deficient humans a moral standing equivalent to that of normal or paradigm humans, reasons not available to animals.

CHAPTER 9

A Case Study: Factory Farming

INTRODUCTION

The charge leveled at society by animal activists is that we humans systematically engage in socially accepted but morally unjustified practices that cause massive numbers of animals unnecessary pain, suffering, and death. To correct this, we are told, we need to radically alter how we view animals and how we use them. Objects of criticism include painful animal experimentation, the farming methods associated with "factory farming," trapping animals by means of leg-hold traps, the fur industry, hunting, and the use of animals for entertainment in circuses, rodeos, and zoos. It is to areas such as these that animal welfarists and animal liberationists direct their practical attention. They do not always agree on the nature of the problem nor on the solution. Thus, the welfarist may call for reform or even "radical" reform of the practice under criticism, while the liberationist, more typically, will call for its complete abolition. I would argue, minimally, that all these practices are legitimate objects of moral scrutiny and that all of them raise, in varying degrees, disconcerting moral problems — "disconcerting" because the problems raised are real, because they concern customs and practices deeply embedded in our way of life, and because realistic solutions are not always easy to find.

In this and the succeeding chapter, then, I shall look at some of the uses to which animals are put that are found objectionable by animal advocates. There is no attempt to be exhaustive; rather, we shall look at only two such uses — laboratory research and factory farming. The discussion, it is hoped, will model a strategy that can be applied to other practices as well, for all ethical theory — including, as in this case, ethical theory about animals — must have practical application if it is to be more than an esoteric undertaking remote from our moral lives. If animals do have moral standing, then that fact must be recognized in practice as well as in theory. Concluding, as we have done, that animals have moral standing, is not like concluding that extra-terrestrials have moral standing. The difference is that our lives actually interconnect with many of the billions of animals with whom we share this planet, and, if these creatures can be said to have moral standing, that conclusion must have implications for our interaction with them. The moral recognition of animals, like the moral recognition of anyone, means that there are some things that it may be in our power and our interest to do with them that we are morally obliged *not* to do. Thus, we may very well be obliged to forego certain advantages and benefits that could be ours by using animals in certain ways. It is at this point that matters may become uncomfortable for us, for historically we have used animals in ways that have not taken seriously their moral standing. And we have subsequently become accustomed to the benefits that such use has brought us. We are reluctant to change our ways, for there may be a price in doing so, both financially and in terms of convenience — a price we are not eager to pay.

As I present these issues of vital concern to animal advocates, I may not always do so with a zeal and definitiveness that they will find fully satisfactory, nor do I expect that defenders of these practices will be fully pleased. The tone of these chapters, then, is not that of the convinced crusader, though I have my sympathies and that shows. Rather, I seek to embody the tone and style that Austin Farrer referred to as a "slow exploratory wisdom." These chapters are an attempt to look at some of the present realities of our use of animals and to consider what it would mean to bring these realities under the scrutiny of moral reflection. In this chapter we shall look at the practice of factory farming and in the following chapter we shall explore issues surrounding the practice of painful animal research.

First I shall make some preliminary observations about animals as legitimate objects of sympathy and compassion, for it is just such sympathy and compassion that animal advocates seek to evoke by directing our attention to these practices that they judge to be objectionable. After looking briefly at the practices of factory farming, we shall reflect on what our personal response to these practices ought to be. It is right here that many believe the best case can be made for vegetarianism or what we shall refer to as "conditional, selective vegetarianism," which is more in the nature of a boycott of certain meats. We shall be confronted here with the important questions of what our own moral beliefs commit us to by way of action and response. If we do judge certain practices to be objectionable, factory farming in particular, what does moral consistency and our own personal integrity then require of us? Here there is some controversy and some uncertainty, but this provides us with an opportunity to reflect on questions that apply to the whole of our moral life, and may help us begin to understand something about the nature of moral integrity.

ENGAGING THE EMOTIONS

Serious moral concern for animals is not simply the product of abstract ethical theorizing. More often than not in the moral life, moral concern grows and encompasses new areas as we are exposed to concrete instances of injustice or of cruelty or of just plain suffering that strike us with new force and evoke in us a recognizable moral response. Accordingly, activists on behalf of virtually any moral cause seek to win us to their side by engaging our moral emotions (e.g., love, compassion, sympathy), and they seek to do this by explicitly portraying those evils they believe need to be eliminated. Such presentations are attempts to overcome our indifference and to secure our active support. Animal advocacy groups are no different in this regard. They wish to convince us that bad things are happening to animals and that those bad things need to be stopped. Often they attempt to do this by graphically portraying those bad things. Where possible, photographs are used, not so much to prove their allegations but, more importantly, to help us see and feel the reality of animal suffering. Unquestionably "one picture is worth a thousand words." Indeed, what better way to effectively condemn the use of leg-hold traps to capture animals than to present us with a photograph of an animal in just such a trap, in pain, vainly seeking to escape.

Here the charge of emotionalism is frequently raised, but often somewhat disingenuously, I believe. For no doubt we are more diligent in noticing and objecting to an appeal to the emotions in areas where we are simply unsympathetic with the cause being represented in the first place. In fact, we may operate with a double standard, not objecting to putting emotions in the service of our own favorite causes. The charge of emotionalism is no more appropriate in the case of suffering animals than it would be were it directed at pictures of starving children used in a campaign to raise funds for food and medicine. Emotion has a legitimate place in the moral life. Certainly this is true of the altruistic emotions, which, as philosopher Lawrence Blum observed, are "directed toward others in light of or in regard to their weal and woe."[1] Prime examples are love, sympathy, and compassion, which are certainly no strangers to the Christian tradition. Far from being objectionable, engaging our altruistic emotions is what it means for moral reality to register with us. Not to feel in the moral realm is tantamount to not seeing; it constitutes a form of moral blindness. It is simply not true that we can conduct our moral lives with the same cold detachment that we associate, say, with doing geometry. The altruistic emotions help us to notice features of the world, bringing them forcefully to our attention — the starving child, the wounded animal — features that need to be taken into account as we decide what we ought to do. Crucially, the engagement of these emotions provides us with motivation to act, in contrast to mere conclusions reached by a kind of moral geometry, which will no more prompt us to act than conclusions reached by geometry itself. Whereas this is exactly what love and compassion, sympathy and pity, will do: generate action.

Precisely because the engagement of our emotions does prompt action, there is often the fear that in these cases we will necessarily be led to act rashly or thoughtlessly. But the altruistic emotions have a rational component. They are not raw feelings or objectless moods, and therefore they can be subjected to rational criticism. Thus to have sympathy is to have sympathy for someone in light of his or her perceived unfortunate circumstances. Sympathy can be inappropriate and criticizable should the situation not in fact be unfortunate. Thus, should it be the case that animals experience no pain and never suffer, then sympathy directed toward them would be as unsuitable as having sympathy for a toy animal. Indeed, once one comes to believe that a situation is not what one supposed, that there actually is no pain and suffering, sympathy will simply vanish. Sympathy, then, logically depends on having certain beliefs, and morally appropriate sympathy depends on those beliefs being true. But if animals can, on the contrary, really feel pain and suffer, then sympathy cannot be judged inappropriate for that reason. Of course, sympathy might be inappropriate when the individual deserves to suffer, a consideration that is not relevant in the case of animals. But even supposing that the infliction of pain is actually morally justified, sympathy for those who

1. Lawrence Blum, *Friendship, Altruism, and Morality* (London: Routledge and Kegan Paul, 1980), p. 24.

suffer it may still be appropriate. In wartime, for example, it has often been judged morally permissible in certain circumstances to place innocent civilians at risk; but should those civilians be killed or maimed, that will be regretted and they will continue to be appropriate objects of sympathy. Having such sympathy is part of what it means to be morally alive, even though sympathy may make what one does harder to do. After all, inflicting pain and suffering on innocent individuals (even if only foreseen but unintended) ought to be hard to do. Similarly, should a painful experiment on an animal be justified by reference to some greater good, that animal is not thereby rendered an unsuitable object of sympathy. Indeed, it is morally dangerous to allow the justified infliction of pain on animals to extinguish our sympathy for their plight. In doing so we are also extinguishing that all-important human barometer whereby moral reality registers with us.

SYMPATHY, SENTIMENTALITY, AND A GOOD WORD FOR RATS

Of course, sympathy for animals can be sentimental, grounded in factors other than the fact that the animal feels pain and suffers. Thus, one may feel more sympathy for the suffering of a dewy-eyed harp seal pup or a "cute and cuddly" rabbit than for a rat. But if the suffering is equivalent, then should not that sympathy also be equivalent? It would seem so, though often, of course, it is not. This sort of problem with our sympathy – the fact that it irrationally discriminates – is not unique to our relationship with animals. Some people, for example, experience more sympathy toward people of their own race than toward others. Or one also thinks of the grossly deformed "Elephant Man" and the insensitivity that was shown his plight. Whereas there was every reason to extend to the Elephant Man the same sympathy that we would extend to other suffering humans (maybe even more), nevertheless, there was something about the grotesqueness of his form that blocked the kind of sympathetic response that was morally appropriate.

It may be that we respond more sympathetically to the harp seal pup and the rabbit than we do to the rat because the former are viewed as more vulnerable. In general, vulnerability encourages sympathy – witness how the suffering of babies and children can evoke especially strong feelings of sympathy. Or it may be that the "Bambi syndrome" is at work here. That is, à la Walt Disney or Beatrix Potter, we engage in acts of anthropomorphizing fantasy when it comes to animals – they virtually become little humans living out their lives in animal bodies. And certain animals can be special beneficiaries of this fantasy as we portray them in a favorable light and extend to them favored treatment based on half-believed illusions about them. On the other hand, animals such as the snake and rat can be objects of negative fantasy, as we attribute to them sinister intentions and maliciously deceptive behavior, which in turn may limit our capacity for sympathy. Indeed, it may even seem, in our distorted thinking, that they deserve to suffer.

Consider how different our reactions would be to the thought that rabbits were used in the following experiments rather than rats, as was actually the case: (1) "animals" were dropped into specially designed cylindrical tanks filled with water and from which they could not escape. Some of the "animals" gave up almost immediately, seeing their situation was hopeless, while others swam up to sixty hours before finally drowning; (2) "animals" were subjected to intense electric shocks at irregular intervals, the experimenters observing that this evoked squealing, defecation and rigorous attempts to jump out of the compartment. To think of this happening to rabbits does evoke in many of us a far stronger sympathetic response than the thought that it happened to rats. Indeed, "animal lovers" themselves are often not consistent, and those who are just beginning their journey to greater respect and moral concern for animals may be especially guilty of this.

Surely we ought to be consistent. But what does that mean? Should we seek to extend the generous attitudes we have toward rabbits to rats, or should we extend the unsympathetic attitudes we have toward rats to rabbits? I suggest that we seek what philosopher John Fisher calls "enlightened sympathy," in contrast to "folk sympathy."[2] Whereas folk sympathy is based on "a culturally bound set of ideas about animals, enlightened sympathy is based on the far more adequate description of animals by ethologists and biologists."[3] Various "folk prejudices" that distort our sympathetic response to animals need to be replaced by a more firmly grounded empirical understanding of their lot. Folk prejudice would include not only the Disney-like characterization of animals but also our preference for the cute and cuddly — for example, our preference for the rabbit over the rat. For the rat, no less than the rabbit, is — dare we say it — God's crea-

2. John Fisher, "Taking Sympathy Seriously: A Defense of Our Moral Psychology Toward Animals," in *The Animal Rights/Environmental Ethics Debate,* ed. Eugene C. Hargrove (Albany: State University of New York Press, 1992), p. 235.

3. Fisher, "Taking Sympathy Seriously," p. 235.

ture; the rat no less than the rabbit can feel pain and suffer. And, therefore, the rat, no less than the rabbit, is a suitable object of sympathy.

SYMPATHY AND ANIMALS: A CAUTIONARY NOTE

Having put in a good word for the rat and for the altruistic emotions (such as sympathy), one is still forced to admit that there are difficulties attaching to the suggestion that rats (or chickens or dogs or any animal) can be the object of sympathetic concern. Professor John Kleinig identifies the problem for us when he observes that "the sympathetic identification that is called for does not involve 'putting oneself in another's shoes' so much as coming to appreciate what it is to be from the other's standpoint."[4] And it is "putting oneself in another's shoes" that is the much easier task of the two, for in doing this I simply project my own mental states and subjective feelings onto the animal. Here we do not need knowledge of the animal but only knowledge of ourselves. How would I like to be caged like that? How would I like to be carted off to be butchered for meat? Thus, I simply imagine what it would be like for me in those circumstances and conclude that this is how it is for the animal. It is here that we would be guilty of anthropomorphizing, that is, illicitly attributing to animals our own mental and emotional states. Putting ourselves in their shoes, then, just won't do. More is required than this.

What is needed is "coming to appreciate what it is to be from the animal's standpoint," and this is a far, far more difficult task. This requires knowledge of the animal, not simply knowledge of ourselves. New York University philosophy professor Thomas Nagel has perplexed and intrigued us with his fascinating article, "What Is It Like to Be a Bat?"[5] Indeed, what is it like for a bat to be a bat? What would it be like to experience the world embodied in the bat's unique physiology, finding one's way around in the dark using echolocation? Here, I believe, we must confess that all this is very mysterious. No doubt we could do much better should we try to imagine what it is like to be a chimpanzee, because of their phylogenetic closeness to humans. But even here there is mystery enough.

Perhaps what we have to do is to think analogically, that is, to view

4. John Kleinig, *Valuing Life* (Princeton, N.J.: Princeton University Press, 1991), p. 100.

5. Reprinted in Thomas Nagel, *Mortal Questions* (Cambridge: Cambridge University Press, 1979), chapter 12.

animal experience as like ours, as similar to ours in certain respects, but also as different from ours. Those analogies will, in part, be based on similarities between our behavior and theirs. Thus, observing a locust continuing to feed while it itself is being eaten by a mantis may signal that here there is no basis for sympathetic concern, in contrast to the dog whimpering at the side of the highway, having been hit by a passing automobile. And there are other things we know about dogs, in addition to analogous behavior — analogous brain structure, analogous response to analgesics, etc. — that bolster our conviction that dogs experience pain much like we do, that is, that their pain is analogous to ours.

So it might be suggested that when we say of an animal that it is afraid or bored or enjoying itself or in pain we are doing something very much like certain theologians (such as Thomas Aquinas) have argued we are doing when we make predications of God: we are taking terms that have their home in a human setting and that take on their primary meaning from that setting, and we are applying them analogically. That is, the terms are not being used univocally (i.e., with the very same meaning, for God is radically different from us) nor are they being used equivocally (i.e., with a totally different meaning, for God does have certain similarities with us). Interestingly, John Hick, in seeking to clarify what analogical prediction of God might mean, illustrates by reference to what he calls analogy "downwards" — for example, by predicating "faithfulness" of a dog. Hick comments,

> We are using it ["faithfulness"] analogically, to indicate that at the level of the dog's consciousness there is a quality that corresponds to what at the human level we call faithfulness. There is a recognizable likeness in structure of attitudes or patterns of behavior that causes us to use the same word for both animal and man. Nevertheless, human faithfulness differs from canine faithfulness to all the wide extent that a man differs from a dog. There is thus both similarity within difference and difference within similarity. . . .[6]

In trying to fill out the meaning of these analogical predications as applied to animals we shall need the assistance of knowledgeable experts because animals differ so greatly in their physiology, both from us and from each other. As Marian Stamp Dawkins puts it,

6. John Hick, *Philosophy of Religion,* second ed. (Englewood Cliffs, N.J.: Prentice Hall, 1973), p. 70.

> It takes a certain amount of humility to accept that other animals besides ourselves may suffer and feel pain. Here drawing analogies with ourselves can be most valuable. But it takes even more humility to recognize that the subjective experiences of other species may not be exactly or even remotely like our own. Here analogies with ourselves may be misleading unless firmly tied to evidence from all possible sources about species.[7]

Scientifically informed analogies can, then, provide a possible basis for sympathetic concern for animals, though this is not to deny that there are also credible common-sense analogies based simply on our own experience with animals. It is to say, however, that we should always be open to that scientific input, for in many circumstances it will prove crucial if our sympathy is to have a secure basis in reality. With these observations in mind, let us turn to an important practical issue that concerns animal advocates: factory farming.

FACTORY FARMING

In 1964, Ruth Harrison's book *Animal Machines*[8] raised for us the moral issue of factory farming. It also began the public campaign for more humane treatment of animals by agribusinesses that employ "confinement" or "intensive" farming methods or what critics call "factory farming." Here the issue is not one of moral vegetarianism, that is, opposition to raising and killing animals for food; rather, it is opposition to the suffering presumed to be caused by factory farms, which have increasingly replaced the traditional, diversified farm — the farm most of us have in mind when we think of farms. As Jim Mason says in the introduction to his book on the subject,

> The reality of a modern animal factory stands in sharp contrast to the farm of our fantasies. The farm in our mind's eye is a pleasant, peaceful place where calves nuzzle their mothers in shady fields, pigs loaf in mudholes, and chickens scratch and scramble about barnyards. The farm animals in our fantasy live tranquil, easy lives. So we like to be-

7. Marian Stamp Dawkins, *Animal Suffering* (New York: Chapman and Hall, 1980), pp. 106-7.

8. Ruth Harrison, *Animal Machines* (London: Vincent Stuart, 1964).

> lieve — because if they have fresh air, good food, exercise, and rest, we have more wholesome and delicious meat, eggs, and milk.[9]

But increasingly this mode of farming is being replaced by high-production factory farms. Here animals are crowded into pens and cages inside massive farm buildings; the animals never see the light of day and are fed and controlled under automated conditions that resemble factories more than farms. This appears to many to be far from ideal for the animals that must live out their lives in these conditions. Indeed, defenders of behavioral research on animals have even argued that the misuse of animals is far more severe on factory farms than it is in their own research laboratories.[10]

IT BEGAN WITH THE CHICKEN

Factory farming began with chicken and egg production after World War II. The chicken, being a small animal, lent itself more readily to being placed in automated factory buildings. Family egg farms were forced out of business, and today 95 percent of all egg production is from chickens housed and kept in these buildings. (In 1967, 44 percent of all layers were caged; in 1978, the figure had grown to 90 percent.) Typically, there are 80,000 chickens per building, kept in wire-mesh cages suspended over trenches to collect excrement; conveyor belts bring in food and water and carry away the eggs. The cages are often stacked three and four levels high; sheet metal coverings catch the droppings from the cages above, and power driven scrapers remove the excrement from the metal coverings and push it into a pit below. The cages in which these chickens are confined, known as battery cages, are made of wire mesh and are very small, 45 × 50 cm (or approximately 17½ × 19½ inches) for five hens. Indeed, the wing span of a chicken is about thirty inches, almost twice the width of the cage in which these five chickens are confined.[11] Whereas, in natural conditions, chickens will live for fifteen to twenty years, in the apparently stressful circumstances of the factory farm, they remain economically

9. Jim Mason and Peter Singer, *Animal Factories* (New York: Harmony Books, 1990), p. xiii.

10. G. G. Gallup Jr. and S. D. Suarez, "On the Use of Animals in Psychological Research," *Journal of Psychological Research* 30 (1980): 211-18; N. E. Miller, "The Value of Behavioral Research on Animals," *American Psychologist* 40 (1985): 423-40.

11. Andrew Johnson, *Factory Farming* (Oxford: Basil Blackwell, 1991), p. 26.

productive for about one and a half years, at which time they are taken away, slaughtered, and used in soup and processed foods. About 20 percent of the chickens die before they run their year and a half term, but because the overall production is sufficiently high this does not defeat the economic advantages of the system.

The raising of broiler chickens has followed a similar pattern, with over five billion chickens and other poultry being raised each year in these automated factory farms in the United States alone. Crowding massive numbers into small quarters (one chicken per space the equivalent of a standard sheet of typing paper) caused a number of problems, including fighting and cannibalism (some chickens would be pecked to death and eaten by the others) because of their inability to establish a pecking order. To solve this problem chickens are debeaked, using a specially designed machine called a "debeaker" that slices off the beak with a hot blade. Broiler chickens are debeaked only once, shortly after birth, since they are sent off to market before the beak can grow back, but egg layers are debeaked a second time when they are between twelve and twenty weeks of age. Debeaking thousands of chickens, at the rate of fifteen birds per minute (as recommended by experts), is a monotonous activity that can yield sloppy work with undesirable consequences for the chicken. So as one professional source warns,

> An excessively hot blade causes blisters in the mouth. A cold or dull blade may cause the development of a fleshy, bulb-like growth on the end of the mandible. Such growths are very sensitive and will cause below average performance. . . . Incomplete severance causes torn tissue in the roof of the mouth. The bird's tongue must be held away from the blade. Burned or severed tongues result in cull (worthless) hens.[12]

Granting that debeaking may not always be done properly, is it a painful experience when done properly? "No," says the poultry industry, "it is no more painful than clipping our own toenails." "Yes," says the Brambell Committee, appointed by the British parliament to explore factory farming in the British Isles and consisting of veterinarians and other experts. Referring to the toenail claim, they respond, "There is no physiological basis for this assertion. . . . The hot knife blade used in debeaking cuts through the complex horn, bone and sensitive tissue causing severe pain."[13]

12. *Poultry Digest* (May 1975), quoted in Mason and Singer, *Animal Factories,* p. 39.

13. Quoted in Mason and Singer, *Animal Factories,* p. 40.

All broiler chickens are of course destined for slaughter. Andrew Johnson describes it this way:

> Long vehicles draw up beside vast dimly lit sheds, where teams of boiler-suited workers are stuffing crates with chickens in their thousands and their tens of thousands. Many of the birds suffer broken bones or dislocated hips, and if the journey to slaughter is long, more will die from cold or thirst on the road. At the abattoir the birds are attached by their feet to an overhead conveyor which takes them hanging upside down, to be stunned, bled and scalded. In theory, they lose consciousness in the electric stunning booth, but in practice many birds go to the knife inadequately stunned, and the unlucky few who escape having their throats cut are boiled alive in the scalding tanks.[14]

CHICKENS: HOW CONCERNED SHOULD WE BE?

As one looks at photographs of massive numbers of factory farm chickens so crowded together that they only have a small space in which to move about, unable to stretch their wings nor do the many other things that chickens naturally do – scratch the ground (there is only wire mesh flooring), peck and establish a pecking order – one wonders, "How concerned should one be about all this?" Unfortunately the chicken may be at a disadvantage when it comes to our personal attitudes, for we may view it, as people often do, as "brainless, cowardly, mean-tempered and filthy."[15] Indeed, with its little brain, we skeptically wonder, might the chicken simply be oblivious to everything that is happening to it? But to downgrade the chicken merely because of its small brain would be a mistake. For birds, small brains and all, have been taught quite complicated tasks. Marian Stamp Dawkins (Mary Snow Fellow in Biological Sciences, Somerville College, Oxford) has noted, "Birds equal and sometimes surpass mammals in their ability to learn."[16] Indeed, rather impressive research has been done with pigeons which, though not uncontroversial in all of its claims, has been offered in support of the conclusion that pigeons have the concept of number, could recognize the picture of a particular person, and even distinguish "man-made" from "natural" objects.[17] Euan MacPhael of the Univer-

14. Johnson, *Factory Farming*, p. 103.
15. Mason and Singer, *Animal Factories*, p. 1.
16. Dawkins, *Animal Suffering*, p. 104.
17. For references to the literature on pigeons see Dawkins, *Animal Suffering*, pp. 18-21.

sity of York, after reviewing recent work on complex learning by psychologists, concludes that "it is not currently possible to reject the hypothesis that there are neither qualitative nor quantitative differences in intellect between birds and mammals."[18] So we should not be too quick to dismiss the chicken as an object of sympathetic concern simply because of its small cranium or its being a bird.

Having said this, it should be noted that Dawkins cautions us not to automatically assume that animals suffer if they are prevented from behaving naturally, that is, if they are prevented from doing everything that is in the repertoire of their species, which, in the case of chickens — crowded into battery cages — means not moving about, not flapping their wings, dust bathing, or roosting. Though this does not *necessarily* cause suffering, it should, Dawkins argues, alert us to the possibility that suffering is occurring. It "can be used as a kind of warning system: 'Here is an area which needs looking at.'"[19] Thus, rather than assume immediately that what is not natural for animals is painful, Dawkins argues that treating animals in ways that prevent natural behavior should be viewed as a warning sign, alerting us to potential dangers. Then Dawkins suggests two further danger signals. The first of these is abnormal behavior; in this instance, the cannibalism that necessitated the debeaking, which might be an expression of frustration on the part of the chicken, especially in view of the extreme nature of this behavior. The second of these signs is the health of the animal. Thus, the death rate of chickens kept under factory farming conditions may be suggestive of suffering. Cumulatively, at least, these factors point to an object of legitimate concern.

The philosopher Andrew Johnson has commented, "It is still possible to find people who believe that battery chickens are quite happy, and that the cages are good for the birds; but reputable scientific opinion is now overwhelming against this."[20] Indeed, the Nobel-prizewinning ethol-

18. Quoted by Joe Crocker, "Respect your Feathered Friends," *New Scientist* (October 10, 1985), p. 49. Crocker discusses a range of interesting studies done with birds. He refers to Irene Pepperberg's work at the University of Indiana. She taught an African grey parrot to name more than forty objects, recognize five colors and four shapes, and answer, with considerable accuracy, the questions "What color?" and "What shape?" He also refers to Epstein's work at Harvard with pigeons who were able to engage in the following purposive behavior: push a box to a spot where bananas were hung out of reach, then jump on the box to reach the bananas. In this case the pigeons had been trained to reach the bananas from an appropriately placed box and they had been trained to push boxes; then, when the box was displaced, the pigeons pushed it back into place.

19. Dawkins, *Animal Suffering*, p. 54.

20. Johnson, *Factory Farming*, p. 123.

ogist Konrad Lorenz describes the ordeal of chickens living in such conditions as "heart-rending."[21]

FACTORY FARMING SPREADS: PIGS AND VEAL

The poultry industry was just the first to introduce factory farming and unquestionably it continues to be the leader. But now we have not only "factory-made" chickens but "factory-made" pigs. In fact, two-thirds of the pigs produced in the United States (fifty-three million pigs) are raised in total-confinement operations. The animals are confined in wire mesh cages that in some cases are three levels high. Here the pigs "are conceived, born, weaned, and 'finished' (fed for market) in specialized buildings loaded with automatic feeding, watering, manure removal, and environment control equipment."[22] Once more we have an operation more akin to a factory than a farm. The animals are raised in semi-darkened conditions, which seems to provide a measure of calm. Sows are continually bred with boars or artificially inseminated in order to produce a maximum number of offspring and are placed in narrow steel stalls (gestation crates) during their pregnancy where they can stand or lie down but cannot walk or turn around. Confinement continues after birth for a period of three weeks, efforts being made to reduce the time the new offspring spend with their mothers, in order to speed-up the reproduction cycle. The sow is then returned to the breeding area and her offspring are taken off to a "finishing building" where they spend about twenty weeks before reaching market weight and being shipped off to slaughter. Here one can ask the same questions about the meaning of the pig's suffering that we asked about the chicken's suffering. We do know that, as with chickens, so with pigs, abnormal behavior results from the crowded conditions, such as "tail-biting" that can result in mutilation and death. Also, the pigs can be seen chewing on the wire-mesh, a stereotypic behavior that critics claim reflects the stress and boredom of confinement. By Dawkins's standards we again have something that needs to be looked into.

Factory farming techniques have also been applied to veal production. Accounts of the production of veal, a tender white meat from calves slaughtered at fourteen to sixteen weeks of age, often evoke a strong, immediate, and negative response when presented to people. Two factors

21. Quoted in Johnson, *Factory Farming,* p. 124.

22. Mason and Singer, *Animal Factories,* p. 8.

perhaps account for this: first, the confinement of veal calves is arguably the harshest of those associated with factory farming, and, second, we tend to be more warmly disposed to calves than to chickens and pigs. In the United States, 1.2 million calves are raised annually in apparently unpleasant circumstances in order to produce this special pale-pink meat that is noted for its tenderness. Taken from their mothers shortly after birth, these calves are placed in small confining stalls; they are tethered, at first, so they cannot turn around (the tether can be removed when the calf grows to the point where it is physically impossible for it to turn around); they are provided with no straw or other bedding material to cover the hard slatted floors on which they must stand or kneel. They are fed twice a day from a plastic pail containing a special liquid diet. At fourteen to sixteen weeks, when they weigh about 330 pounds, they are taken away for slaughter. Before the introduction of this method of raising veal, the newborn calf would simply be taken to slaughter immediately after birth, when it weighed only about 90 pounds. The new method produces a similarly tender meat but in much greater bulk.

Why all these special measures? The calves are confined because freedom of movement to romp and play would unacceptably toughen the meat. The lack of straw bedding is to prevent the intake of the iron, which is found in the straw and which would be eaten by the calf; the intake of iron is in turn objectionable because it results in the darkening of the meat, something considered undesirable by consumers. The animal is tethered so that it will not turn around and lick its own urine (normally repugnant to calves), which it does because it craves the iron that it contains. The slatted floors enable the manure to fall through to a pit below, though the exclusively liquid diet makes for loose bowel movements and diarrhea. As a consequence of all this, the animals are prevented from engaging in a number of natural behaviors: they cannot turn to groom themselves, chew cud, or suckle. Further, the peculiar iron-free diet provided the calves results in anemia, a generally weakened physical condition, various other health complications, and a mortality rate of 10 to 15 percent. Here, again, features are present that point to the possibility of suffering: (1) the prevention of natural behaviors that are part of the repertoire of their species, (2) the presence of abnormal behavior (species defined), and (3) associated health problems. This suggests, once more, in Dawkins's words, "Here is an area that needs looking at."

Apart from their concern for the existing practice of factory farming, animal advocates are concerned about its spreading into other areas. Thus there is concern over "factory-made milk," confinement systems being used with an increasing percentage of the nation's ten million milking cows. "Factory-made beef" has also been an object of concern, but the problems there do not seem to be quite so acute, though this is not to say that no problems exist. Also, there is concern that factory farming will spread to the raising of sheep, rabbits, and other animals.

COMMERCIAL INTERESTS AND ANIMAL INTERESTS

One might hope that there would be a happy congruence between economic advantage for the factory farmer, and the health and well-being of the factory animal, so that it would turn out to be in the factory farmer's interest to take good care of her animals. In the abstract, one might reason that healthy and "happy" animals will be more productive, yielding more eggs and gaining more weight, thereby better serving the owner's economic self-interest. Consequently, well-informed factory farmers will see to it that their animals are well taken care of. So perhaps we should leave matters there.

Unfortunately, this is not always so. As Dawkins points out,

> There may be some circumstances in which it is actually more profitable for a farm unit as a whole if the animals are kept in conditions in which their individual productivity is less than maximal. Economies of space, for example, putting more hens into a battery cage, may lower individual productivity, but enable larger numbers of animals to be kept in the same area. This may more than compensate for the losses on each individual.[23]

Thus, a single farm worker may care for twenty thousand chickens, and it may be that the birds would be better cared for and more productive both if they had more space and if there were more workers to care for them. But that does not mean it is economically advantageous to do so, for as Dawkins observes, "Considerable losses of growth rate, food use and even death in some animals can be tolerated before it becomes worthwhile to employ more men or to increase the space allowed to each bird."[24] So it is not, I suggest, that those individuals in charge of factory farms are especially prone to greed and driven by profit in a way that traditional farmers (and the rest of us) are not, but rather it is that economic realities are dif-

23. Dawkins, *Animal Suffering,* p. 30.
24. Dawkins, *Animal Suffering,* p. 30.

ferent on a factory farm. That is, on a factory farm, with its larger number of animals, it is more likely that the strategy that renders the whole farm unit maximally efficient is not one that also renders each of its animals maximally healthy and therefore maximally productive. In the case of the smaller traditional farm there is more likely to be this happy congruence between the health of the animal and the economic interest of the farmer.

A BETTER WAY

The Europeans have traditionally been more sensitive to the issue of factory farms and have already placed restrictions on this mode of farming that have yet to find political favor in the United States. In Europe, the political will necessary to do this is partially a product of a much stronger opposition to factory farming on the part of the consumers. Sweden, Switzerland, the Netherlands, West Germany, and the United Kingdom have all passed legislation that has addressed (in varying degrees) the problems posed by factory farms. For example, "In 1987, the European Parliament by an overwhelming vote, passed recommendations that, if enacted by the European Economic Commission, would effectively eliminate factory farming."[25] But the most advanced laws affecting factory farming that have been passed were enacted by the Swedish parliament in 1988. A Swedish ministry of agriculture press release indicated that the following measures were to be phased in over a ten-year period:

- require that animal facilities provide enough space to allow all animals to lie down and move freely and that they be designed to allow for animal's natural behavior;
- require that dairy cows and young pigs be released to pastures in the summer;
- require that dairy cows and young pigs be provided straw or other suitable bedding material;
- forbid that any animal be kept tied or held in a way that does not allow freedom of movement.[26]

No doubt, this means consumers will be confronted with higher prices for dairy products and meat. But this may be the very sort of sacrifice that is

25. Dawkins, *Animal Suffering,* p. 196.
26. Dawkins, *Animal Suffering,* p. 195.

required if we are to bring our treatment of animals into line with our moral sensitivities.

CONDITIONAL VEGETARIANISM AS A RESPONSE TO FACTORY FARMING

The "better way" described above is an attempt to improve the lot of animals who are raised and slaughtered for human consumption. It is an attempt to change, by political and legal means, those more objectionable features associated with factory farming. But one need not wait for political or legal action to address this concern. At a personal level one might consider becoming a vegetarian, that is, simply refusing to eat meat (or consume dairy products) produced under what one judges to be the objectionable conditions of intensive farming. In which case, one would have become what R. G. Frey has called a "conditional vegetarian" – a vegetarian only until such time as animals are raised and slaughtered in ways that are humane and painless.[27] And if, as Peter Singer contends, the "case against using animals for food is at its strongest when animals are made to lead miserable lives"[28] then with conditional vegetarianism we may have the most defensible form of vegetarianism. If a case for vegetarianism can be made anywhere, it can be made here, one might very well suppose.

Thus, one might purchase only "free-range" eggs, that is, eggs produced by hens that are free to range over a normal territory, hens that would be living in relatively humane circumstances, not subject to the apparent stress of battery cages and therefore not subject to the necessity of debeaking. When such eggs are not available, one would simply not consume eggs. Further, one would abstain from certain meats, but one would not have to abstain from all meat. It is chickens, pigs, and veal calves that are primarily subjected to the unpleasantness of factory farming, whereas cattle and sheep graze freely outdoors and are not subject to the rigors of factory farming. So it is "selective" vegetarianism – giving up some meat (chicken, pigs, veal calves) but perhaps not all meat (cattle, sheep, and fish) – that might be prompted by a moral critique of factory farming.

The rationale for such vegetarianism, according to some, is simply practical and utilitarian: by boycotting certain meat we reduce the de-

27. R. G. Frey, *Rights, Killing, and Suffering: Moral Vegetarianism and Applied Ethics* (Oxford: Basil Blackwell, 1983), p. 31.

28. Peter Singer, *Practical Ethics* (Cambridge: Cambridge University Press, 1979), p. 55.

mand for that meat and thereby reduce the number of animals being subjected to the painful conditions of factory farming. As Peter Singer comments, "George Bernard Shaw once said that he would be followed to his grave by numerous sheep, cattle, pigs, and a whole shoal of fish, all grateful at having been spared from slaughter because of his vegetarian diet."[29] By reducing the demand for factory farm products and thereby reducing the number of factory farm animals, however, we do not thereby free those animals to live in alternative, more humane conditions. Rather, meat producers will simply reduce the birth rate of these animals (or, more likely, slow the growth of the birth rate). So the result of the vegetarian's boycott will be fewer chickens and pigs in the world, not more chickens and pigs living in better conditions. Shaw, then, did not save animals so that they could go into the grave with him, as he thought; most likely, if his vegetarianism did anything, he prevented them from coming into existence so that they could then be killed for food. Likewise, the factory farm boycotter, even if successful, does not secure a better existence for some animals but rather prevents some animals from being brought into existence.

So the question that then confronts us is this: do we make the world a better place by preventing chickens and pigs from being brought into existence, chickens and pigs that otherwise would be subjected to the abuses of factory farming? The answer would be "yes," if on the whole their existence is a miserable one, sufficiently bad so that living is more of a curse than a blessing. But is it? This, of course, is a judgment call. And if a kind of computational accuracy is required here for knowledge, then admittedly we don't know. But, then, many issues in life come down to making common sense judgments in just such circumstances. We frequently must decide between courses of action that require an informed but not precise weighing of pleasures and pains, positive and negative experiences, in order to decide which result will on the whole be better. We do this by becoming as well acquainted with the situation before us as we can. And in the case of factory farming, the picture presented, at least by critics, is sufficiently bleak that one would not be unjustified in judging that life for these animals is, on balance, a negative one. One might be assisted in one's reflections by considering the following: if one were presented with the choice of having a pet animal of ours subjected to the same conditions to which factory farm animals are subjected or having the pet "put down,"

29. Peter Singer, *Animal Liberation* (Berkeley and Los Angeles: University of California Press, 1978), p. 163.

would we, out of compassion, choose the latter? One could imagine the answer being "yes."

One might wonder, of course, whether a personal boycott of selected meat products will actually make any difference, even if our goal is simply to have fewer animals brought into existence for purposes of factory farming. My vegetarian diet, by itself, might not affect the commercial demand for meat sufficiently to reduce in any way the numbers of animals raised in factory farms. Therefore, the difficulties and the inconvenience of my foregoing meat might turn out to have no effect whatsoever on reducing the number of the chickens, pigs, and calves subjected to the rigors of factory farming methods. Possibly, no matter what I do, exactly the same amount of meat will be produced, under exactly the same conditions. One may subsequently wonder, why give up the pleasure and convenience of particular meats when there is no substantial reason to believe I can thereby make a difference? So the attempt to decide matters, as the utilitarian would urge us to do, by adding up all the pleasurable and painful consequences of my becoming a selective vegetarian (for all concerned, including myself) may leave matters in an uncertain state and tempt one in the context of this uncertainty to favor oneself, deciding to go with the convenience and pleasure of meat eating.

Nevertheless, it is still arguable that there are good utilitarian reasons for my becoming the sort of person who will, in contexts of utilitarian uncertainty, act and live in ways that favor such larger good causes, willingly accepting personal inconveniences for myself. Such people, it is reasonable to suppose, make the world a better and happier place, whether or not, in a particular set of circumstances – for example, becoming a selective vegetarian – they succeed in doing so. Overall, such people are utilitarian contributors, whose pattern of conduct serves to maximize happiness and welfare, thus meeting the test of the principle of utility. In contexts of uncertainty they give the benefit of doubt to the good cause they seek to serve, and overall – if not in every instance – they make the world a better and happier place.

But there is another way to look at this. It is common for individuals to band together to achieve important goals that they can achieve only as a group. Typically, in those cases, no one individual in the group is indispensable. Thus, for example, in seeking victory in war or in an election, no individual soldier and no individual voter is indispensable. That is, the outcome of the war or the outcome of the election will be the same, whether or not I fight, whether or not I vote. It is always tempting, in such circumstances, to conclude that because I am dispensable –

"they can get along without me" – that consequently I have no obligation to participate.

But aren't we obligated to vote even in circumstances where our vote, taken by itself, will not determine who wins and who loses? However we ultimately account for it, circumstances where we are, as individuals, dispensable often do generate obligations and duties that fall upon all of us "dispensable" individuals. That the war can be won without my participation and the election outcome remain the same without my vote, does not, we judge, serve to remove from me my obligation to vote and to fight. If it did, then none of us would be obligated to vote in an election or to fight in a just war (considerations of pacifism aside). The moral logic is the same with regard to a boycott of meat produced by factory farming methods. I may be quite dispensable – that is, my refraining from purchasing factory farm meat may, by itself, achieve nothing. But the aggregate impact of all vegetarians and other boycotters can and does make a difference. Together our abstinence from select meat will achieve a reduction in the demand for factory farm products (from what it otherwise would be) and therefore a reduction in the number of animals subjected to factory farming methods. So, as a group, we may do what as individuals we cannot do, and I may have an obligation to be one among many, doing my fair share, if the practice of factory farming is, as many believe, seriously objectionable.

CONDITIONAL VEGETARIANISM: ADDITIONAL JUSTIFICATIONS

Suppose one is not a utilitarian at all; suppose one has an approach to ethical decision-making that does *not* place an exclusive stress on producing good consequences (as utilitarianism does). One may very well judge that one is obligated to participate in a boycott not only if one's own efforts made no difference but even if the efforts of all boycotters (in aggregate) made no difference (though one would hope that they would). In the case of utilitarianism one has an obligation to refrain from eating meat only if refraining from eating meat yields the best overall results. In contrast, with a duty or rights approach to ethics, one will recognize obligations that hold even when no net gain in good consequences is achievable (indeed one may even have some obligations to act in ways that decrease overall good consequences).

Suppose that we lived in a society with a cruel system of permanently entrenched human slavery. Suppose that nothing could be done to abolish this offensive practice. It would, nevertheless, seem wrong to purchase goods produced by slaves simply because they were cheaper than goods produced by free workers. (This is on the assumption that my boycott would not cause the slaves additional unacceptable suffering and that one had a choice between goods produced by free individuals and those produced by slaves.) Arguably, to see economic advantage for myself in this way would be wrong. In contrast, on utilitarian grounds, I might actually be obliged to purchase the cheaper goods produced by the slaves, if I thereby bettered my own situation without harming anyone else, thereby maximizing overall happiness. But from the perspective of a non-utilitarian duty theory, one might judge that respect for the personhood of these slaves requires that one not seek personal advantage from the evil system that exploits them, especially when the burdens one assumes by refusing that advantage are relatively light. Similarly, one could argue, there is an obligation not to take advantage of animals who are made to suffer by intensive confinement farming. If the system is abusive, and to that extent evil, then benefits of such a system should be rejected when offered, unless there is some overriding reason for not doing so. So although we may achieve nothing by way of helping animals, nevertheless our duty, out of respect for their moral standing, may be to refrain from complicity in practices that exploit them.

If one embraces a virtue theory, one could invoke considerations of character to justify a boycott of factory farm meat, doing so independently of a consideration of practical success. Here the focus is not on utilitarian calculations nor on principles of duty to be honored, but on being the right kind of person. Thus, personal integrity might require, in order to be true to the virtue of animal concern, that one not subvert that virtue by making peace with practices that are cruel to animals. Or one may simply steadfastly refuse to be the kind of person that takes advantage of the unjustified suffering of others, be they humans or animals. One simply declares, "I am not going to be that kind of person." The words of Alice Walker perhaps capture something of what is involved here: "I know, in my soul, that to eat a creature who is raised to be eaten, and who never has a chance to be a real being is unhealthy. It's like . . . you're just eating misery. You're eating a bitter life."[30] This, it would be argued, is how a person with those sensitivities associated with the virtue of animal concern will respond to the invitation to eat factory-farmed meat.

30. Quoted in Anna Sequoia, *67 Ways to Save the Animals* (New York: Harper Collins, 1990), p. 46.

If, finally, one sees the stewardship model as providing a helpful ethical and spiritual vision, one might first ask whether the good steward could faithfully serve the Creator and Lord of all life in the role of factory farmer. If not, then one might also conclude that one ought not to take advantage of benefits secured at the cost of violating a stewardly trust. Indeed, if we conclude that factory farming is a violation of God's call to faithful stewardship, then it appears we must not only seek ways to change factory farming, making it consistent with stewardly standards, but we must also morally distance ourselves from those practices.

AN ALTERNATIVE TO VEGETARIANISM

R. G. Frey has argued that it is not required that one become a (selective) vegetarian in response to the abuses of factory farming. This is not, he contends, the only way to express one's moral concern with factory farming. Indeed, Frey argues, and at great length, that one can both be opposed to factory farming, be deeply offended by its treatment of animals, and also remain a total meat eater, being all the while "concerned, consistent, sincere, and moral."[31] One might initially wonder how a person can be knowledgeable about the apparent cruelty involved in veal production, for example, indeed be deeply offended by it, and yet, from a large selection of entrees at a restaurant, order veal, and, with complete moral consistency and no regrets, eat it with relish. But this is what Frey argues can occur.

There is, he claims, a perfectly acceptable alternative to selective vegetarianism. One can choose this alternative, remain a total meat eater, and yet be a conscientious opponent of factory farming. "For example," Frey writes,

> if the concerned individual joins various animal welfare organizations and vigorously supports them; if he supports the strengthening of present laws against cruelty and the passage of more stringent ones; if he contributes to animal shelters; if he spreads the word about certain practices on factory farms and lobbies government officials to do something about those practices; if he speaks out on the relevant issues, in order to raise the level of public awareness of them; if he supports research into new and painless breeding, feeding, and killing

31. Frey, *Rights, Killing, and Suffering*, pp. 114-248.

> methods and into other animal related technology; if, in short, he is assiduous in showing his concern over some aspect of intensive farming, then I can see no reason to think he is not making gestures appropriate to his concern.[32]

If one does all of this, according to Frey, then one can in good conscience eat ham sandwiches, enjoy a veal cutlet from time to time, and consume one's share of fried chicken. Indeed, one could well imagine that it would be actually less onerous to be a selective vegetarian than to engage in all the many activities adumbrated by Frey. Certainly one would be giving personal expression to one's moral concern over the cruelties of factory farming by doing what Frey suggests. There is, he is claiming, no single way to express opposition to factory farming consistent with moral integrity. It is essential that one give expression to that concern, but it is not required that the concern be expressed in any particular way.

WHAT DOES MORAL INTEGRITY REQUIRE OF US?

Frey's contention that disapproval of factory farming does not require that one become a conditional vegetarian raises intriguing questions about what it means to be true to one's moral beliefs. This is a concern that extends well beyond discussions of factory farming. In general, what does my moral disapproval of a group, organization, practice, etc., require of me by way of moral response? Granted that others may not share my disapproval, what does my disapproval commit me to? If I am environmentally concerned, deeply so, let us suppose, and if I judge a particular company to be a prime polluter of the environment, do my beliefs, should I desire to be true to them, prevent me from investing for profit in that particular company? Perhaps so, we respond, being inclined to think that this might be required of us. Suppose I strongly disapprove of the Israeli treatment of the Palestinians, does that require of me that I not buy Israeli oranges? Perhaps not, we respond, being less convinced here than in the previous case that this is the form our disapproval should take. But how do we sort out these cases (and a myriad of others) so that we make the response required by our own moral convictions? What exactly is the nature of moral consistency? What is it for us to be people of integrity, which is, as dictionary definitions remind us,

32. Frey, *Rights, Killing, and Suffering*, pp. 191-92.

"the quality or state of being complete or undivided." To believe one way and to act another is to be divided, not, therefore, to have full integrity. But how would our moral beliefs have us act, especially those beliefs that include disapproval of people and practices, organizations, and institutions?

Frey argues that moral consistency does not require that those who sincerely disapprove of factory farming become selective vegetarians. It is sufficient that one become an activist such as Frey describes. One doesn't, then, have to be a vegetarian to retain one's moral integrity. Part of Frey's strategy in arguing his case is to show that one cannot formulate a defensible principle that (a) tells us how to give consistent expression to moral disapproval and (b) will require that the sincere moral opponent of factory farming become a vegetarian. Thus, for example, we cannot condemn this person's decision not to become a vegetarian on the grounds that "if one disapproves of a practice one must have nothing to do with it," for such a principle is clearly mistaken. Consider in this regard (this is Frey's example) an Anglican priest who is strongly supportive of women's ordination, who judges that the church's refusal to ordain women is a terrible failure — a failure of justice, a failure to fully utilize all of God's gifts in the service of the church, a failure to recognize that "in Christ there is neither male nor female," and so on. Over the years he has been an active and tireless spokesman for this cause. Surely, Frey argues, moral consistency does *not* require that the priest leave the church because of his strong disapproval of its ordination policies. Therefore, we cannot condemn the meat-eating opponent of factory farming by appeal to a principle that says we are to have nothing to do with practices that we disapprove of, for that principle won't do, as the Anglican priest example demonstrates.

We might, instead, opt for a more liberal principle, one that allows us to have *everything* to do with practices or institutions that we personally disapproves of, so long as we declares our disapproval. This principle would allow the priest to continue his labors within the church. And it would also, incidentally, allow the opponent of factory farming to continue to eat meat, so long as she gives public expression of her disapproval. But this principle won't work either. Counterexamples abound. For according to such a principle one could be associated with and profit from utterly corrupt groups and organizations (the Mafia, the Nazis, the KKK). So long as one declares one's disapproval, one could, with complete moral integrity, continue one's profitable associations with these groups. But clearly this would be wrong and inconsistent. At some point organizations can become sufficiently odious that declaring one's disapproval is not good enough, but rather one's disapproval requires a complete severing of ties and profitable connections.

So it seems that both the following are unacceptable principles: (a) one must have nothing to do with groups, institutions, practices, etc., that one morally disapproves of, and (b) one can associate in any way one wants with groups, institutions, practices, etc., that one disapproves of, as long as one declares one's disapproval. Our search for a guiding principle, however, need not stop here. One might seek a middle ground between these two principles. Frey suggests the following: if one disapproves of a group, institution, or practice, then, in order to be consistent, one must "not aid, support or help to maintain" the disapproved groups, institutions, or practices. But what constitutes "aiding, supporting or helping to maintain"? If interpreted strictly, it then may amount to "having nothing to do with," a principle which we have seen is unacceptably strict and which wrongly precludes our priest from continuing his ministry in a church whose ordination practices he disapproves of. If we understand "aiding, supporting and helping maintain" as *significantly* "aiding, supporting and helping maintain," then we will have made the principle less strict and perhaps more defensible. But this looser version doesn't seem ultimately to be defensible either. It is simply too loose, for surely "insignificant" contributions to an organization that I judge to be utterly corrupt would be wrong and inconsistent – e.g., a dollar a month to the KKK or some Neo-Nazi group for some small personal benefit.

Frey's point is that a morally defensible principle that condemns as morally inconsistent the person who eats meat and disapproves of factory farming does not seem to be forthcoming. It certainly is difficult to formulate such a principle, at least one that works in a way that a formula, say, is supposed to work, very explicitly guiding our conduct. But principles are not rules or formulas in this way. They are more in the nature of general reminders to seriously consider certain important features of a situation when making a moral decision, as, in this case, asking whether your actions aid, support, or help maintain what you judge to be morally objectionable. So although this is an important consideration, it is not always a conclusive consideration in determining what we should do. There may, in certain circumstances, be other overriding factors present that direct one to act contrary to that principle.

It is, however, important to notice that Frey, in rejecting various proposed principles, does so by appealing to our intuitions. Thus it was pointed out by Frey that these principles either forbid actions that we judge to be permissible or they permit actions that we judge to be forbidden. Therefore, these principles are unsatisfactory. In proceeding in this manner, Frey was asking us to trust our judgments about particular cases without the aid of any principles to guide us. Indeed, we evaluated the proposed principle by reference to our judgment about the particular case before us. For example, we judged that it is morally permissible for the Anglican priest to stay in the church and continue to work for reform. Therefore, one does not always have to remove oneself from morally compromised institutions. But if we can trust our judgments about particular cases in this way, then we can also trust our judgment about the particular case under present discussion: should deep moral disapproval of factory farming find expression in our refusing to eat meat produced on factory farms? And our judgment might very well be (with no infallible principle to guide us) that someone who is seriously and deeply opposed to factory farming as cruel and abusive should, to be true to that opposition, boycott factory farm meat.

Maybe what we have here is as much a case of psychological consistency as it is a case of logical consistency. One might be pardoned for wondering, how could one have all the sensitivities and depth of moral concern sufficient to prompt one to persistently and continuously engage in all the activities listed by Frey, as an alternative to selective vegetarianism, but not also become a selective vegetarian? For to possess integrity and moral consistency is as much a matter of being true to what one is as a person, as it is an abstract issue of drawing the right conclusion from those propositions that constitute one's moral beliefs. It may be that persistent and continuous opposition to factory farming and regularly eating factory farm meat (without regret or remorse) do not reinforce but rather subvert one another, pulling us in different directions, pulling us apart, morally speaking. This may be a matter of psychology, not logic.

PUTTING VEGETARIANISM IN ITS PLACE

We can, of course, be sincerely opposed to factory farming and not be a boycotter or selective vegetarian for the simple reason that we are failing to be true to our own beliefs. Such failures are, of course, a common feature of all of our lives. Too often we fail to act on what we judge to be the requirements of our moral beliefs. Our problem is not merely that we are guilty of discrete violations of the moral law – as, of course, we are.

Rather, our problem is that we struggle and fail to create patterns of behavior in our lives that adequately reflect our commitment to larger moral, spiritual, and prudential goals. We don't, in other words, always live the morally disciplined lives that we feel we ought to live. We don't provide, as we might wish, the kind of consistent, long-term support for goals that we wish to identify with and advance.

It should not be at all surprising, therefore, that there are those who find factory farming objectionable, and who judge that they ought to forego eating meat from factory farms, but who nevertheless continue to consume such meat. Consider our failure to control our intake of food in ways we know to be essential to weight loss, attractive appearance, and good health, which are all things that we desire for ourselves. And if we don't fully control our eating habits when we ourselves are the potential beneficiaries, we should not be too surprised that we do not do so when chickens, pigs, and calves are the beneficiaries. But, of course, it is not only believers in the cause of animal welfare who fail to bring disciplined support to what they believe. People fail in many other areas as well. Consider attempts to fight poverty, overcome injustice, reduce the destruction of the environment, and further the worldwide mission of the church. Here also, we fall short. We simply do not always discipline ourselves in ways that we ourselves judge appropriate, even when what is required of us is not particularly onerous.

Moreover, for many, there is admittedly something off-putting about a call to vegetarianism, something divisive even among people of goodwill and wide moral sensitivities. Indeed, in the present context of factory farming, it might be better to drop the term "vegetarian" and speak instead of "boycotting" certain meat. Discussions of "vegetarianism" polarize people, and the term itself is often a contributor to this. The meat-eater views the vegetarian as morally eccentric; the vegetarian views the meat-eater as either benighted or morally corrupt. And there matters typically remain. As Mary Midgley has commented, "The symbolism of meat-eating is never neutral. To himself the meat-eater seems to be eating life. To the vegetarian, he seems to be eating death. There is a kind of gestalt-shift between the two positions which makes it hard to change, and hard to raise questions on the matter at all without becoming embattled."[33] We need to overcome this division between absolute abstainers and total eaters. We need to open up a middle ground for moral discus-

33. Mary Midgley, *Animals and Why They Matter* (Athens, Ga.: University of Georgia Press, 1983), p. 27.

sion and concern. For as Midgley also says, "what the animals need most urgently is probably a campaign for treating them better before they are eaten."[34]

Regrettably, vegetarianism is often accompanied by an "us-them" attitude — you are either a vegetarian and with us or you are a meat-eater and against us. There is no middle ground that is considered honorable, even as a temporary one for the novice seeking to reconnoiter new moral terrain. The morally inquisitive, who sense that there may be issues worthy of genuine moral concern to be found here, may keep their distance out of a fear of being ensnared in the nets of zealous vegetarian evangelists. The impression "outsiders" can receive is that moral concern with animals, unlike most other moral concerns, is an all-or-nothing affair, comparable to conversion to a religious cult or joining a monastic order, something for only the totally converted, for only the pure in heart. No room here for sinners and slackers; no room for the half-hearted, for the weak or the faint, for those prone to stumble on their moral and spiritual journeys. In other words, it doesn't seem to be a place for people like ourselves.

Vegetarianism, the symbol of total conversion and purity of heart, can, more than anything else, keep many good people from drawing closer and intentionally entering into a life increasingly characterized by growing moral concern and compassion for animals. The problem is not necessarily with vegetarianism itself nor even with vegetarians themselves but with the response that it evokes in many of us as a result of cultural factors and upbringing. Nevertheless, the concerns of vegetarians are legitimate and vegetarian advocacy must continue, recognizing that it will repel as well as attract. Here I offer no further comments, other than to observe that there are many good reasons for the Christian to draw closer and to reconnoiter this new moral terrain. And there are many good reasons for eating more vegetables and less meat.

SUMMARY

In this chapter we did three things. First, we examined the legitimacy of engaging the moral emotions (e.g., love, compassion, sympathy) when responding to the needs of animals. We defended this against charges of sentimentality, irrationality, and inappropriateness due to dissimilarity be-

34. Midgley, *Animals and Why They Matter,* p. 27.

tween animals and humans. In essence, we defended vivid portrayals of animal suffering and abuse made in order to elicit a sympathetic response.

Second, we examined the charge by animal advocates that intensive farming methods, or what is known as factory farming, involve an inhumane and objectionable treatment of animals. We saw that there was good reason to take these charges seriously and much to recommend the European movement toward eliminating factory farming methods.

Third, we explored the case for conditional vegetarianism, both as a practical measure directed against factory farm produced meat and as an expression of moral integrity on the part of the person who judges the rearing of animals in factory farms to be seriously objectionable. Issues of moral consistency were explored, along with the danger that vegetarianism may pose by unnecessarily offending morally serious people who might otherwise wish to take the cause of animal advocacy seriously.

CHAPTER 10

A Case Study: Painful Animal Research

INTRODUCTION

No issue has generated such concern among animal advocates as has the use of animals in laboratory research. The reason for this is that the pain and suffering undergone by animals in the course of this research can be of such a character that it immediately evokes a strong emotional response from people. The philosopher Michael Allan Fox, in the course of his own apologetic *for* animal experimentation, acknowledges that reading through accounts of such research "is a chastening experience for the uninitiated."[1] And most people *are* uninitiated. In other words, they are unaware that this sort of research even occurs. Indeed, there may even be a tendency to believe that opponents of animal research are making up these accounts or that the cases presented for our inspection are bizarre exceptions. What the uninitiated have in store for themselves when they begin to peruse animal research literature is indicated by Fox when he observes,

> there is no denying that laboratory animals are sometimes subjected to unpleasant procedures and manipulations, the following are major examples: burn injuries, electric shocks of varying intensities, radiation, brain stimulation by electrical means or by the injection of drugs, stress (including the induction of seizures, fear, social isola-

1. Michael Allan Fox, *The Case for Animal Experimentation: An Evolutionary and Ethical Perspective* (Berkeley and Los Angeles: University of California Press, 1986), p. 97.

tion, and so on), eye damage, and battering trauma. From published reports it appears that some potentially painful or stressful experiments are carried out without using anesthetics (for example, neurological procedures in which anesthesia would suppress the response being tested for or averse conditioning); and in cases where anesthetics are used (as in experimental surgery), mention is seldom made of the postoperative use of analgesics (painkillers) – although most contemporary ethics codes for animal experimentation prescribe them. The employment of muscle relaxants or paralytics (curariform agents) in place of anesthetics is also quite common, particularly in brain stimulation experiments in which they ensure that the subject animal will remain conscious and alert throughout, though unable to move, struggle, protest, or escape.[2]

Estimates of the number of animals used in laboratory research annually in the United States vary, some being as high as seventy million. The reason we must have recourse to estimates is that the use of animals in research has not been carefully monitored in this country as it has been in Great Britain, where accurate figures do exist. Official estimates put the annual figure in the U.S. at between twenty-five to thirty-five million.[3] Eighty percent of these would be rats, mice, and birds. A 1988 report issued by the Department of Agriculture[4] reported that the number of animals, by species, used in laboratory research was as follows:

dogs	140,471
cats	42,271
primates	51,641
guinea pigs	431,457
hamsters	331,945
rabbits	459,254
wild animals	178,249

This list does not include rats and mice, but it does indicate that a fairly wide range of species is used.

2. Fox, *The Case for Animal Experimentation*, p. 97.

3. U.S. Congress Office of Technology Assessment, *Alternatives to Animal Use in Research, Testing, and Education* (Washington, D.C.: Government Printing Office, 1986), p. 64.

4. Reported in Peter Singer, *Animal Liberation* (New York: Avon Books, 1990), p. 37.

ON NOT TAKING THE ANIMAL RESEARCHER'S WORD FOR IT

To evaluate critically, yet fairly and knowledgeably, the use to which animals are put in the course of scientific research is a daunting assignment. Those who are professionally unfamiliar with the actual practice of animal experimentation and do not have a mastery of the literature and research results to which it has given rise may well judge that they are in no position to arrive at an adequately nuanced assessment. And they may be right in this judgment. Yet this is the position in which most of us find ourselves, for we are part of that general public that animal researchers and animal advocates alike are seeking to persuade. And most of the information and descriptions about animal research to which we are exposed come to us from those who have already made up their minds about such research. Nevertheless, it would seem important to take a brief look at the nature of these competing accounts from which the public must in turn draw its own conclusions about the morality of animal research. On the one hand there is the voice of the animal researcher; on the other, the voice of the animal advocate. Both need to be listened to.

We outsiders can, of course, turn to practicing professional animal researchers and let them alone speak to us. For they, after all, are the experts. Here, however, one has to be careful because assessing the moral justification of animal research is itself not a scientific undertaking. When one asks, "Are the research results worth the pain and suffering undergone by the research animals?" one is not asking a question that can be answered by the scientific method. This is, after all, a moral and not a scientific question. And although animal researchers have important things to say in helping us to answer this question, their answer should not be taken as definitive. In the moral arena, the animal researcher is not functioning in her professional capacity. Moreover, there is no reason to believe that animal researchers are more sensitive about the morally problematic features of their profession than other professionals are about their professions.

It is for this reason that outside scrutiny of the ethical character of a profession's practices is a good thing, even if that scrutiny is not always as fully informed and as sensitive as one might wish; it can nevertheless engender a helpful spirit of self-criticism, awakening any profession from its dogmatic moral slumbers. Indeed, no profession, including the Christian ministry, should be given a kind of carte blanche to proceed on its own, with little sense of accountability to a world outside its own professional borders. So, whereas we must listen to animal researchers, we ought not to conclude that they, any more than other professionals, see their own practice with perfect moral clarity. Indeed, as we dialogue, they will provide insights that only they can provide, but they may also bring certain insensitivities endemic to their profession. Further, if one judges that our society as a whole is not sufficiently sensitive to animal welfare and does not take seriously the claim that animals are to be objects of moral concern, then one may reasonably conclude that animal researchers, who, like the rest of us, reflect larger cultural attitudes, will share some of this insensitivity and lack of moral concern. Moreover, prolonged professional involvement with painful research on animals may desensitize researchers, as they become inured to what has become for them a daily experience. Of course, one can claim that the tough-minded, clinically detached attitude toward animal pain that (we might suppose) characterizes the experienced animal experimenter is the appropriate attitude, not the tenderhearted response of outsiders. But this may amount to no more than the observation that when you do this long enough it doesn't bother you anymore. And surely the relevant question for moral reflection is: should it bother us?

A further difficulty with attempting to settle the question of the moral acceptability of painful animal research simply by turning to the professional experimenter is that they do not all speak with one voice. At least, those who have taken the time to write on the subject do not speak with a single voice, though one might reasonably conclude that practicing professionals would uniformly defend their profession. Nevertheless, one can find severe critics (usually those who have left the profession condemning it as they have left),[5] staunch defenders,[6] and even one prominent defender (though not a professional experimenter) who, within months of his published defense,[7] reversed himself and retracted those very published views.[8] Or if one is attracted to a position that supports an active and rigorous program to promote laboratory animal welfare, while

5. E.g., Richard Ryder, *Victims of Science* (London: Davis-Paynter, 1975); Jeff Diner, *Physical and Mental Suffering of Experimental Animals* (Washington, D.C.: Animal Welfare Institute, 1979).

6. D. H. Smyth, *Alternative to Animal Experiments* (London: Scholar Press, 1978); William Paton, *Man and Mouse: Animals in Medical Research* (Oxford: Oxford University Press, 1984); Fred Lembeck, *Scientific Alternatives to Animal Experiments* (Chichester, Eng.: Ellis Horwood Limited, 1989).

7. Fox, *The Case for Animal Experimentation.*

8. Michael Allen Fox, *The Scientist* (December 15, 1988), p. 10; "Animal Experimentation: A Philosopher's Changing Views," *Between the Species* 3 (1987): 55ff.

at the same time reluctantly accepting the need for continued painful research on animals, one can find that too.[9] The reason they do not all agree is not, of course, merely that they disagree over various technical scientific issues. Rather, it is rooted in other more fundamental differences. Thus, they may differ over how extensive and real animal pain actually is; they may differ about the degree of evil attaching to such pain; they may differ over the legitimacy of animals as objects of sympathy and compassion; they may differ about the strength of, or even the existence of, moral obligation to animals. These differences may not always be explicitly articulated but they will nonetheless be present, determining how one shapes one's case for or against painful animal research. In short, much of the disagreement over the moral justification of animal research arises out of differences of opinion about matters that cannot be settled by the procedures and methodology that are the domain of the professional researcher. So, then, we cannot simply take as definitive the moral word of the professional animal researcher.

THE ANIMAL ADVOCATE AND THE CATALOGUE OF HORRORS

It is not only the word of the professional animal researcher that requires careful assessment; the same requirement applies to the animal advocate. Indeed, criticisms of animal research made by animal advocates have often been characterized as nothing more than "catalogues of horrors." Such a catalogue consists of a series of descriptions of rather horrifying experiments on animals: for example, baboons in their third trimester of pregnancy placed on impact sleds and subjected to crash experiments; animals kept awake by placing them in rotating drums, some surviving up to thirty days without sleep, others dying; animals placed in the Noble-Collip drum, which is much like being placed in a rotating clothes dryer, causing severe trauma including crushed bones, broken teeth, and ruptured internal organs; monkeys placed in restraining chairs with headgear to anchor their heads for periods of time up to 205 days in the course of testing orthodontic procedures; tranquilized but unanesthetized monkeys placed in a stereotaxic apparatus that anchors their heads so that they can be shot in the head in order to create "clean wounds"; electric shocks delivered through electrodes planted in the brains of rats; precipi-

9. Andrew N. Rowan, *Of Mice, Models, and Men: A Critical Evaluation of Animal Research* (Albany: State University of New York Press, 1984).

tating cardiac arrest in dogs by clamping the windpipe and removing the clamp when pulse and blood pressure no longer register, in order to demonstrate resuscitation techniques; studying the sexual response of male cats who, variously, had their penile nerves severed, had electrodes attached to their penile nerves, and had their sense of smell surgically destroyed. The list could go on.[10]

The problem with the catalogue of horrors approach is not that the descriptions misdescribe the research being reported or that the critics are guilty of an excessively vivid prose, though certainly there are instances of this.[11] A catalogue of painful experiments can consist simply of quoting verbatim from the journals in which the research has been reported by the experimenters themselves, devoid of any distortion by the critic, and all carefully documented. Rather, what is problematic with this approach, as Andrew Rowan sees it, is that it is "always vulnerable to the counter argument that, if only the reasons behind the research had been described, then one would understand why the research was necessary and why it had to be done in precisely that manner."[12] And so individuals who are initially skeptical of charges made by critics of animal research and who by disposition are more trusting of the scientific community will look at the catalogue of painful experiments and say to themselves, "There must be some good reason for these experiments, a reason which, if it were known, would make sense out of what, on the surface, admittedly, looks like cruelty." But such suspicions can be dispelled only by placing the research that is being singled out for criticism in the larger scientific context that will help clarify whether or not it has substantial sci-

10. As examples of this approach, one might consult a wide range of literature. At the more popular level there is *The Case Book of Experiments with Living Animals,* a pamphlet published by the Anti-vivisection Society (n.d.). But there is other, more substantial, literature that exemplifies this approach: Dallas Pratt, *Painful Experiments on Animals* (New York: Argus Archives, 1976); Richard Ryder, *Victims of Science: The Use of Animals in Research,* second ed. (London: National Anti-vivisection Society, 1983); Jeff Diner, *Physical and Mental Suffering of Experimental Animals* (Washington, D.C.: Animal Welfare Institute, 1979); Peter Singer, *Animal Liberation* (Berkeley and Los Angeles: University of California Press, 1978), chapter 2.

11. At the more popular level, literature critical of animal research will often describe animal researchers as engaged in "torture" and "murder," strong words indeed. However, the antiseptically neutral language of the animal researcher may be equally problematic. As Mary Midgley comments, "In scientific articles, experimental animals never moan, scream, cry, growl, whimper, howl, snarl or whine; they just discreetly vocalize" ("Are You an Animal?" in *Animal Experimentation: The Consensus Changes,* ed. Gill Langley [New York: Chapman and Hall, 1989], p. 15).

12. Rowan, *Of Mice, Models, and Men,* p. 2.

entific merit, sufficient to constitute a moral justification for the enormous suffering undergone by the animals.

Having acknowledged Rowan's point, I would nevertheless suggest that a "simple catalogue of painful experiments" can serve an important function; at the very least, it can *raise* moral problems for us, even if it does not solve them. That is, it can make clear that we do some very painful things to animals, even if most work with animals is not of this character. This is itself something that many people do not realize: they are unaware that such things occur — justified or not. Granting, then, that animals deserve moral consideration and that inflicting pain on them requires a substantial moral justification, a catalogue of painful animal research is at least a challenge to produce that justification. It is, minimally, a call for moral dialogue.

It may well be that how convincing one finds the catalogue of horrors approach will be determined by what one takes to be an adequate moral justification of painful animal research. If one agrees with Peter Singer, for example, that one is justified in subjecting animals to painful research only if one would also be justified in performing the same painful experiment on massively retarded or brain damaged human orphans, then one will not (assuming more or less traditional attitudes toward these individuals) require a finely nuanced scientific discussion of these experiments, all appropriately contextualized, before reaching a negative conclusion. In other words, the catalogue of horrors approach will do quite nicely, for surely one would not take a long time puzzling about cases of painful research, such as those listed above, had severely retarded or brain damaged humans been used instead of research animals. Thus, when one has a high moral view of animals (as, say, Singer does) one typically will not require complicated scientific discussions to expose most painful animal research as morally unjustified. On the other hand, to the extent that one construes our obligation not to inflict pain on animals as being less stringent than Singer's qualifications, then one will recognize a wider range of considerations that might justify painful animal research and one will consequently be drawn into more extensive scientific discussions to determine the presence of those justifying considerations. Thus the need for extensive and technical discussions of the purpose and result of animal research is partly a product of one's moral perspective on animals to begin with. For some, the description of the experiment speaks for itself; for others, a more nuanced discussion of the research is required. But, in each case, what is required — mere description or nuanced discussion — is in part a product of the moral stance that one has taken toward animals to start with.

SERENDIPITY, CURIOSITY, AND SCIENTIFIC PROGRESS

In the course of defending the claim that the vast bulk of painful animal experiments is morally justified, Michael Allen Fox argues that this can be seen only in the context of the larger phenomenon of scientific progress. Fox points to two factors that have proved essential to such progress: (1) serendipitous discoveries and (2) basic or "curiosity-oriented" research. Serendipitous discoveries are those discoveries that are made accidently. That is, one may be investigating one thing and a quite different discovery is made, one that had not at all been anticipated. Or, one may make a discovery that seems at the time to have little importance and no practical application whatsoever but subsequently, with further advances in other areas, takes on crucial theoretical and practical significance. Fox refers to impressive examples of such serendipitous discoveries as reported by Julius Comroe, for many years director of the University of California's Cardiovascular Research Institute in San Francisco.[13] Comroe identified "the ten most important clinical advances in cardiovascular-pulmonary medicine and surgery" between 1945 and 1975. He surveyed 4,000 scientific publications and from these selected 529 "key" articles, those "that had an important effect on the direction of subsequent research and development, which in turn proved to be important for one of the ten clinical advances." Interestingly, 41 percent of the key articles (217 of the 529), at the time they were done, "had no relation whatever to the disease that it later helped to prevent, diagnose, treat or alleviate."[14] They subsequently became significant, of course — a significance that could not have been anticipated at the time the research was being done. Thus, they were truly serendipitous discoveries. And, presumably, what is true of advances in

13. Fox, *The Case for Animal Experimentation,* pp. 139-40. It is true that Michael Allan Fox has retracted the views found in *The Case for Animal Experimentation,* where he denied that we have moral obligations to animals and judged most experiments on animals to be justified. He now argues, "*No* animal experiments can be morally justified. We act wrongly when we do them. Does this mean that we should all become antivivisectionists or abolitionists? Yes" ("Animal Experimentation: A Philosopher's Changing Views," p. 59). Fox has come to believe in the equal intrinsic value of all living organisms — a radical transformation indeed. But this fact makes his original views and support for animal experimentation no less credible than they were before his change of mind and heart. Indeed, should there be yet another change, back to his original views, that would not somehow magically restore to them a lost credibility. His arguments stand on their own merits, independently of his own post-publication opinion of them.

14. Julius H. Comroe Jr., *Retrospectoscope: Insights Into Medical Discovery* (Menlo Park, Calif.: Von Gehr Press, 1977), p. 12.

cardiovascular-pulmonary medicines is more or less true in other areas of scientific research as well. There is, of course, the other side of the coin. Not only is there research that takes on an increasing significance with the passage of time, but there is also research that, promising when first undertaken, has not been treated so kindly with the passage of time. The important point here is that on an individual basis, we cannot always predict which research will prove to be important. Therefore, as a matter of strategy, we commit ourselves to producing a great deal of reasonably well-designed research which individually may lack strong justification in terms of immediate human benefit, but which is expected on the whole to produce significant benefits.

All this, Fox argues, highlights the need for basic or "curiosity-oriented" research. That is, there is a need for a great deal of research that has no practical goal in sight and that cannot be directly and immediately justified by reference to such goals. Such research, although motivated at the time simply by intellectual curiosity, can be justified indirectly and in the long run by reference to practical human benefit. Such research will have the same motivation that prompts one to do history or philosophy: a desire to know, to satisfy intellectual curiosity. In the course of many scientists doing curiosity-oriented research, discoveries will be made that will, with the passage of time, turn out to have significant practical application and human benefit. But, crucially, there will be such discoveries only if there is a great deal of basic research. So, from this perspective, it is no criticism to point out that a given proposed research project has no ascertainable practical application. It is enough simply to know, first, that this project is part of a quest for knowledge, which has its own justification (it is simply good to know) and, second, that it is one small part of a much larger enterprise that as a whole yields beneficial results for humans. So, at least one implication of Fox's serendipitous defense is that the good that does or does not result from a particular experiment does not by itself serve as a measure by which to assess whether the pain and suffering of the animals involved in that experiment was "worth it."

There will, I surmise, be little disagreement about the value, in general, of basic research. But the appeal in this instance to serendipity and to curiosity-oriented research is made in the context of justifying painful experiments on animals, and one may wonder whether this might justify too much. That is, it sanctions our doing a great deal of painful experimentation on animals, which, on an individual basis, is undertaken to satisfy our desire to know, and which has no identifiable practical benefits but is justified by the serendipitous discoveries that sometimes occur in the course of doing a great deal of this kind of painful research. The research is not morally evaluated on a case-by-case basis but only as a part of a much larger practice that is justified by the beneficial consequences that emerge here and there. This does mean that the following sort of proposal, frequently heard in the course of discussions on animal research, will have to be rejected: "Experiments which cause pain and suffering demand special justification. That special justification cannot merely be that scientists are entitled to do anything that might increase the sum total of knowledge or bring about a medical advance in the remote future. There has to be direct benefit, a good and immediate relevant reason — one which most people would accept as adequate."[15] What this proposal does is apply a cost-benefit analysis to each proposed research project: will the pain inflicted on the animals *in this project* be compensated by a proportionate good? This is to be contrasted with the previous proposal, one that applies the cost-benefit analysis to the *practice* of such research in general: will the pain inflicted on all the animals involved in all the experiments be compensated by an overall proportionate good? Here one might suppose that if a cost-benefit analysis were applied on a case-by-case basis fewer projects would pass muster; while a cost-benefit analysis applied to the entire practice of research would mean that more projects would be judged acceptable.

THE VICE OF CURIOSITY

Curiosity, or the desire for knowledge for its own sake, has not been an unmitigated blessing for the human race. Nor can the satisfaction of curiosity provide a justification for just any and all exploratory activities. Indeed, it is not even clear whether curiosity should be considered a virtue or a vice. In his essay "It Killed the Cat," Gilbert Meilaender draws upon Augustine, Aquinas, Newman, and C. S. Lewis to explicate what he takes to be the vice of curiosity. It is not that curiosity *per se* is a vice but "It becomes vice only when we set no limits to our curiosity, when we can never find reasons why we *ought* not gratify our desire to see and know, when we regard no secrets as closed to our inquiring minds, when curiosity is bounded neither by re-

15. This is a proposal by Dr. Louis Goldman presented in a paper delivered at a symposium at Trinity College, Cambridge, on this subject and quoted by Clive Holland, "Trivial and Questionable Research on Animals," in *Animal Experimentation,* ed. Langley, p. 119.

spect for others nor reverence for God."[16] And to this we might add "nor by respect for God's animal creation" – for to inflict considerable pain on an animal simply to satisfy our desire to know certainly seems like a fitting candidate for the vice of curiosity. But, of course, things are a bit more complicated than this, since the curiosity-oriented research of which Fox spoke, though motivated at the individual level by curiosity, is justified (Fox argues) at the level of practice by benefits that will accrue to other humans. But here also Meilaender has relevant words: "That we seek knowledge that will benefit others does not mean our search should recognize no limits. In such a case, the end – benefit to others – is certainly worthy and justifies some means, but it will not justify *any* means."[17] Indeed, to recognize the moral standing of animals is to recognize just such limits; it is to recognize that good ends do not justify any and all treatment to which we might subject research animals.

In Meilaender's discussion of Augustine, a distinction is made between "the life of wisdom" (which I shall call "the life of virtue") and "the life of power." Curiosity, the desire to know without limits, is an expression of the life of power, the desire to possess and control. In contrast, the life of virtue involves the renunciation of power, for in recognizing moral limits to living our lives, we thereby deny to ourselves the power and the mastery that could be ours, say, by the lie told, the valuables stolen, the life taken, the cruelty exercised, the knowledge (wrongly) secured. And both the life of power and the life of virtue have their "own peculiar threat or risk."[18] In the case of the life of power, the risk is "final foolishness . . . that in the end one will find one's attainment futile or even bitter." In the case of the life of virtue, we must confront the threat of "final resourcelessness." Indeed, it is the fear of resourcelessness, the fear, in other words, that we cannot fully secure our comfort and security, our health and well-being, that prompts us to transgress the moral limits, to gain the power that eluded us when life was lived within appropriate limits. But that is just the risk that one runs when one chooses to live virtuously.

And is it not, in part, the fear of resourcelessness that prompts us to do with animals what we will? For to use animals in painful experiments

16. Gilbert C. Meilaender, *The Theory and Practice of Virtue* (Notre Dame, Ind.: University of Notre Dame Press, 1984), p. 150. Though Meilaender is not discussing virtue in the context of animal research, his comments are nevertheless applicable to the subject at hand.

17. Meilaender, *The Theory and Practice of Virtue,* p. 150.

18. Meilaender, *The Theory and Practice of Virtue,* p. 139. These are quoted remarks of the Augustinian scholar Robert Meagher.

any way we choose is to reach out for increased mastery and power; in contrast to this, to place limits on our painful use of animals is to expose ourselves to this very threat of resourcelessness. Indeed, to recognize the moral standing of animals as God's creatures is to place limits on our conduct and thereby to place ourselves at risk. As Meilaender observes, "Virtue itself can offer no guarantees that all endings will be . . . happy. . . ."[19] That is, we are agreeing to accept the risk of undesirable consequence that may come our way as a result of not using all the available means within our power to realize our human projects. We may, of course, seek alternatives to painful animal experimentation, hoping for a happy ending, but those alternatives may not be there or, if they are there, they may not serve us as well as does the painful use of animals. Virtue may nevertheless have us run that risk; virtue may also have us begin to place limits on the painful use to which we put animals in the course of basic research and to accept the risk of resourcelessness as we do. As we reflect on where boundaries should be drawn around painful laboratory research on animals it might be helpful to consider very tangible areas of such research.

TOXICITY TESTING

One of the major research uses of animals is for the poison-testing of commercial products, known as toxicity testing. This field is subdivided in the following way: (1) acute toxicity testing (determines the toxic effects of a large dose of a particular product or several smaller doses closely spaced in time); (2) subchronic toxicity testing (determines the effects of repeated doses for periods between one week to six months); (3) chronic toxicity testing (determines the adverse effects over still longer periods of time, up to several years). Fifty percent of these animals used in toxicity testing undergo acute toxicity testing. The two most famous examples of this are the LD50 test and the Draize test, each of which has received considerable notoriety through passionate criticism by animal advocacy groups and an energetic public campaign to stop or curtail its use. Reference to the LD50 test and the Draize test is, in a discussion like this, virtually obligatory.

"LD50" stands for Lethal Dose 50 percent, and refers to the testing procedure which seeks to determine the dose that will kill 50 percent of the test group within fourteen days. The substance being tested is put di-

19. Meilaender, *The Theory and Practice of Virtue,* p. 140.

rectly into the stomach of an animal by tube. The products tested are various and include insecticides, pesticides, anti-freeze, brake fluid, ink, suntan oil, floor wax, drain cleaners, oven cleaners, hair sprays, hair dyes, bleaches, kerosene, talc, bubble baths, deodorants, paints, fire extinguisher compounds, and nail polish – in other words, virtually any commercial product. The animals used include rats, mice, rabbits, dogs, and monkeys. The adverse effects on the animals, short of death, include vomiting, diarrhea, paralysis, convulsions, and internal bleeding. Dying animals are not killed since that would distort the results of the test. To find the dosage at which 50 percent are killed a number of sample groups are used with up to one hundred animals being used per test. Andrew Rowan has argued that we could cut the demand for laboratory animals by two to four million per year should the FDA and other regulatory agencies place the burden of proof on those who wish to use sixty to one hundred animals per LD50 test instead of placing the burden of proof, as it now is, on those who wish to use only six to ten animals. This could be done, he argues, without any negative impact on human health and safety.[20] If he is correct, then it would seem to be a proposal that must be taken seriously.

Another test that has received a great deal of notoriety, especially in the 1980s when animal advocates gave it considerable attention, is the Draize test. This involves putting a test substance in the eyes of rabbits to evaluate its safety for commercial use. Rabbits are most often used because they lack tear ducts and cannot shed tears; hence they cannot dilute the test substance (nor, thereby, relieve the pain and prevent harm to the eye). Of course, like most animals, the rabbits would seek to rub their eyes in response to the offending substance and so, to prevent this, the rabbits are immobilized in stocks. The damage to the eye is measured according to redness, swelling, and injury. This is often painful for the rabbit and in some cases the eye will dissolve from its exposure to the test substance. Bred for this purpose, the rabbits are killed after the completion of the tests.

This eye irritancy test, named after its principal creator, Dr. John Draize, was first introduced in Great Britain in the 1930s to evaluate chemicals to be used in chemical warfare weapons. But in 1938, in partial response to a tragic case in which a woman was blinded and disfigured by

20. Rowan, *Of Mice, Models, and Men,* p. 243. For the adequacy of using six to ten animals rather than sixty to one hundred Rowan refers to G. Zbinden and M. Flury-Roversi, "Significance of the LD50 Test for the Toxicological Evaluation of Chemical Substances," *Archives of Toxicology* 47 (1981): 77-79.

a mascara, the U.S. Federal Food Drug and Cosmetic Act (of 1938) was passed, which legally mandated that cosmetics be free of deleterious substances. The cosmetic industry, to satisfy the requirements of the law and to protect itself against potential litigation, began to use the Draize test. Though a major user of rabbits for the Draize test, the cosmetics industry is not the only industry to use the test. A range of other commercial products have also been tested, including oven cleaners, lye, ammonia, ink, and detergents. Figures from the U.S. Department of Agriculture for 1983 indicate that toxicology laboratories used 55,785 rabbits, while chemical companies used 22,034. While not all were used for the Draize test (exact figures are not available), many were.

The Draize test is of interest because it became the object of a sustained and successful public campaign by a coalition of over four hundred animal advocacy groups in the 1980s.[21] It was targeted because the tests caused pain and because there was substantial professional opinion that the development of an alternative testing mode that did not use animals was scientifically feasible. Revlon, the largest cosmetic company, was approached and asked to contribute funds for the development of nonanimal alternatives to the Draize test. Unreceptive at first, Revlon, after being subject to full-page newspaper ads attacking their use of the Draize test ("How Many Rabbits Does Revlon Blind for Beauty's Sake?" the ads asked) and to public demonstrations with protesters dressed in rabbit costumes, finally yielded to this request and donated $750,000 for the development of alternatives to the Draize test. Other major companies subject to similar pressure soon followed suit. In time, a number of cosmetic companies gave up the Draize test and introduced nonanimal alternatives. The successful campaign against the Draize test was a particularly satisfying victory for animal advocates, but considerable headway has also been achieved in reducing the use of LD50. Thus, not only the cosmetic industry but other major industries that use animals in painful research have been affected. One source reports, "Prodded by the animal welfare movement major manufactories of pharmaceuticals, pesticides, and household products have made significant advances in recent years toward the goal of reducing the number of animals used in toxicity test-

21. An interesting account of this campaign is given by Henry Spira, "Fighting to Win," in *In Defense of Animals,* ed. Peter Singer (New York: Basil Blackwell, 1985), pp. 194-208. Spira, an active campaigner for civil rights and democracy in the maritime union, brought his skills as an organizer and campaigner to the fight for animal welfare and led the campaign against Draize testing. He had been influenced by the writings and teachings of Peter Singer.

ing."[22] Thus it appears that the prodding was necessary, and that organized animal advocacy groups did play a significant role in securing animal welfare goals that are widely recognized as good and genuine achievements.

Chronic toxicity testing, as we have already noted, involves exposing the test animal to smaller amounts of the test substance over a longer period of time, up to three years or more. It is far more expensive than acute toxicity testing, and for that reason fewer tests are run and fewer animals are involved. The most well known of these are testing for carcinogens (cancer-causing substances) and for teratogens (fetal deformity-causing substances). Certainly this is a worthy goal: to identify those substances, exposure to which will cause cancer to humans and deformities in human fetuses. But there is some uncertainty about the reliability of these tests, and animal advocates have been quick to pick up on the discussion that has questioned their reliability. It is, of course, fairly common knowledge that thalidomide, perhaps the twentieth-century's most infamous drug, was judged safe after extensive testing on pregnant monkeys, dogs, cats, hamsters, and chickens. When released for human use, however, it caused serious deformities, and the term "thalidomide baby," with all its tragic associations, was introduced into the English language. The drug Opren caused at least sixty-one deaths in Great Britain despite having passed a battery of animal tests.[23]

Not only can drugs that were innocuous to animals prove harmful to humans, but sometimes the reverse can be the case. For example, insulin causes deformities in infant rabbits and mice but is harmless to humans.[24] Of course, this is only to suggest that chronic toxicity testing of animals does not yield perfect results and that extrapolating from studies on one species to another species is not a precise activity; it is not to say that such tests are without some predictive value and have not contributed to human safety. It is argued, however, that *in vitro* testing, which is quicker and less expensive but does not use live animals, holds out some prospect for yielding satisfactory test results. The *in vitro* method involves removing tissue from the animal (in many cases while the animal is anesthetized). The tissue is kept alive for research purposes and in this case is tested in a glass or plastic dish (*vitro* is from *vitrum,* meaning

22. "Industrial Toxicologists" (unsigned editorial), *Science* (April 17, 1987), p. 252.

23. *New Scientist* (March 17, 1983).

24. S. F. Paget, ed., *Methods in Toxicology* (Cambridge, Mass.: Blackwell Scientific Publications, 1970), p. 132.

"glass"). This is to be contrasted with the *in vivo* method where the tissue is studied and tested in its physiological position in the living animal's body. Apparently, the *in vitro* method is more effective in detecting carcinogens than it is for teratogens.[25] More research is required in both cases, but clearly if we acknowledge that animals are legitimate objects of moral concern, then at least a serious search for *in vitro* alternatives is justified. It would seem, then, that at the very least we ought to be using no more animals then necessary for toxicity research, and we ought to vigorously seek alternative means to obtain knowledge about the toxic effects of various substances. One might go even further and suggest that we ought to begin questioning the assumption that it is acceptable to purchase our own safety at the expense of great pain to animals, especially as we think of the safety testing of new products that themselves have only a marginal utility for the human community. Peter Singer challenges us with these words: "Should thousands of animals suffer so that a new kind of lipstick or floorwax can be put on the market? Don't we already have an excess of most of these products? Who benefits from their introduction except the companies that hope to profit from them?"[26]

It might be argued in response, as Michael Allan Fox does, that comments like those of Peter Singer are naive in light of the reality of a capitalist economy, which in large measure is driven by the artificial creation of new "needs." We are simply not going to solve the "cosmetic problem," argues Fox, without fundamental alterations in our economic system, which is unlikely in the extreme.[27] In other words, the "new-and-improved" floor wax and the exciting new lipstick, like the poor, will always be with us. But the significance of Singer's comments is not undermined by Fox's appeal to unchangeable economic reality. There is still the need for the *individual* to act with moral integrity despite pessimistic forecasts about the prospects of changing the economic system for the better. Furthermore, awareness that our economic system, which we might suppose benefits us all, results in considerable animal suffering for the sake of satisfying frivolous human desires should underscore our moral obligation to seek at substantial cost, if necessary, alternatives to toxicity testing with animals.

25. Rowan, *Of Mice, Models, and Men,* p. 240.

26. Singer, *Animal Liberation,* p. 53.

27. Fox, *The Case for Animal Experimentation,* p. 186.

OTHER RESEARCH USING ANIMALS

In addition to toxicity testing there are four additional categories of research that we should identify: behavioral research, pain research, weapons and warfare research, and medical research. There is clearly some overlap among the categories, but it is helpful to note something of the variety existing under the rubric "animal research."

Using animals in behavioral research is largely carried on by departments of psychology at universities and colleges. Even though the amount of published psychological research involving animals is relatively small — in 1979 only 7.5 percent of the articles in *Psychological Abstracts* involved the use of animals[28] — nevertheless some of this research is very painful and much of it, as with research in all fields, is never published, which does mean that the use of animals is much greater than the published research alone would indicate.

Andrew Rowan has pointed out, "The use of animals in psychological research has not usually been perceived as a major ethical problem. The situation is changing now as a result of increasing pressure from animal welfare groups."[29] The focus of concern is on research that involves (1) deprivation of food and water; (2) sensory deprivation: raising animals in total darkness or depriving them of auditory or tactile sensation (e.g., kittens having their eyelids sewn shut so as to prevent all visual experience); (3) social isolation: separating infant animals from their mothers or placing them in solitary confinement in small boxes or soundproof chambers; (4) inducing psychopathology — for example, "learned helplessness," where animals are given electrical shocks in circumstances in which they cannot escape and soon huddle motionlessly as the shock is administered, and "experimental neuroses," where the animal must choose between going hungry or selecting food that brings with it an electrical shock; (5) aggression and punishment studies: fairly severe electric shocks are used to elicit the reflex fighting response; (6) drug studies: animals are used to study the effects of drug addiction and drug withdrawal.

In the case of pain research, the infliction of pain is not incidental but central to the study itself. Pain is induced by a variety of means — *mechanical:* using metal pincers or clamps, tender parts of the body will be pinched or pressed (e.g., the tails and toes of cats have been subjected to

28. G. G. Gallup and S. D. Suarez, "On the Use of Animals in Psychological Research," *Journal of Psychological Research* 30 (1980): 211-18.

29. Rowan, *Of Mice, Models, and Men,* p. 133.

intense pressure and the response recorded, "vocalization, biting, struggling"); *electrical:* strong shocks have been administered to animals by means of electrodes attached to the scrotum, rectum, and tail of the animal (e.g., dogs have had electricity passed through the pulp of their teeth); *heat:* pain produced by radiant heat and by placing animals on hot plates.

A third category of animal research is weapons and warfare research. In Great Britain a distinction is made between using animals to test weapons, which is forbidden, and experiments that are designed to produce better treatment for those wounded by those weapons, which is allowed. But as Clive Holland comments, "The line is a very fine one. . . ."[30] Indeed, one might suppose that submitting monkeys, cats, rabbits, guinea pigs, rats, mice, and pigeons to high explosive blasts (an actual experiment) could be viewed as an attempt to determine the killing and damaging force of the explosive, thus forbidden, or it could be viewed as an attempt to determine the impact of such explosives on those who subsequently would need treatment, thus permitted. But, Holland comments, "In the USA no such distinctions exist. Animals have been shot, gassed, irradiated and subjected to all the horrors of modern warfare."[31]

Consider two examples of subjecting animals to what might be called the "horrors of modern warfare." At the Armed Forces Radiobiology Research Institute in Bethesda, Maryland, thirty-nine monkeys were trained on an "activity wheel"; in essence this was a treadmill that the monkeys were forced, by means of electric shock, to keep moving at a speed of one mile per hour. The monkeys were then subjected to varying degrees of radiation. The radiation sickness that resulted is commonly marked by fatigue, nausea, and vomiting. The monkeys were placed back in the activity wheel, where, in some cases vomiting, they were forced by means of an intense electrical shock (10mA) to continue their work on the treadmill.[32]

At Brooks Air Force Base monkeys were trained to keep a platform, which was known as the Primate Equilibrium Platform and which would pitch and roll, level, simulating flying. The use of a control stick had to be mastered by the monkey and should the platform pitch below horizontal level a shock would be administered. The monkeys were then subjected to various forms of radiation and chemical warfare agents, including the

30. Clive Holland, "Trivial and Questionable Research on Animals," in *Animal Experimentation,* ed. Langley, p. 133.

31. Holland, "Trivial and Questionable Research on Animals," p. 133.

32. Carol G. Franz, "Effects of Mixed Newton-Gamma Total-Body Irradiation in Physical Activity Performance of Rhesus Monkeys," *Radiation Research* 101 (1985): 434-41.

nerve gas Soman, noted for causing considerable agony to soldiers in World War I.[33] And what was the rationale for these studies? Donald J. Barnes, who for a number of years was in charge of this project at Brooks Air Force Base, and under whose direction over one thousand monkeys were so used, commented, "It became my job to determine the probability estimates of air crews functioning following nuclear radiation. If the pilot (co-pilot, bombadiers, etc.) became comatose following the receipt of 5,000 rads, why spend an exorbitant amount of time and money 'hardening' the electronic components to withstand 10,000, 15,000, or 20,000 rads?"[34] But, of course, in all this, we are talking about a business – the military – that is involved in killing and being killed, a business whose goal is to direct lethal destruction at large numbers of other human beings, while seeking to avoid the same for oneself. Granting the lethal nature of this activity, which for the sake of argument we may suppose is morally justified, then how can one object to the use of one thousand or so monkeys in painful and unpleasant research in the service of those ends? The justification of the military enterprise itself may seem to carry with it a justification of what is done to the monkeys.

It is interesting to note that Donald Barnes himself repudiated this project. Indeed, he not only repudiated it, but he subsequently became director of the Washington, D.C., Office of the National Anti-Vivisection Society.[35] Of course, a change so dramatic as this will involve a profound moral reorientation; in this case it involved rejecting the operative moral assumption of the research itself: possible benefits to humans justify the painful use of animals. But even prior to this Barnes began to question the *utility* of the research. He questioned the extrapolation of results from experiments with nonhuman primates in artificial circumstances to hypothetical human situations, but he reasoned "close is better than nothing."[36] As Barnes's own moral respect for the monkeys grew, however, so did his need for a commensurately better justification. Increasingly, for him at least, "close" was not "close enough," and the point came when he felt compelled to repudiate the research that had engaged so much of his professional life. Barnes's own moral development continued to the point

33. See Singer, *Animal Liberation,* p. 272 nn. 1 and 2 for documentation: U.S. Air Force School of Aerospace Medicine, Report no. USAFSAM-TR-82-24, August 1982; Report no. USAFSAM-TR-87-19, October 1987.

34. Donald J. Barnes, "A Matter of Change," in *In Defense of Animals,* ed. Singer, p. 162.

35. The account of Barnes's own conversion from vivisector to anti-vivisector is given in "A Matter of Change."

36. Barnes, "A Matter of Change," p. 163.

where animal research was completely rejected, even to the point where, supposing that one could extrapolate *perfectly* from monkey to human, one would still not be justified in painfully using animals for human ends. One need not be an absolutist in this regard in order to morally question painful research on animals for military purposes. One may at least require that one have *strong* reason to believe that a *substantial* good will result from the research in question before one can justifiably proceed.

When the general public thinks of animal experimentation, they tend to think of experimenting on animals for the purpose of advancing medical knowledge and medical technology, hence furthering the ability of the medical profession to save lives, relieve people of pain and suffering, and overcome illness, disease, and disability. In point of fact, the use of animals for medical research constitutes a relatively small part of the total amount of animal experimentation. Yet those who are identified as opponents of animal experimentation are viewed by the general public as essentially opponents of using animals in *medical* research. This is unfortunate because the general public may consequently be too quick to dismiss what critics of animal experimentation have to say, not listening to the full range of their moral concerns. Some of their other concerns might well find a more sympathetic response from the general public. But too often, to the public, animal experimentation is simply medical research, and a critic of medical research is presumed not to be worth listening to. For whose life is more important, they ask, that of a child who may be saved by such research or a dog who may have to be sacrificed?

But must we choose between the child and the dog? There are opponents of animal experimentation who see the ending of all animal research as benefiting both the dog and the child. Thus the scientist and animal rights advocate Robert Sharp (formerly a research chemist at the Royal Postgraduate Medical School in London) comments,

> But since animal-based research is unable to combat our major health problems and, more dangerously, often diverts attention from the study of humans, the real choice is not between animals and people; rather it is between good science and bad science. In medical research animal experiments are generally bad science because they tell us about animals, usually under artificial conditions, when we really need to know about people.[37]

37. Robert Sharp, "Animal Experiments — A Failed Technology," in *Animal Experimentation,* ed. Langley, p. 111.

So, according to Sharp, the choice is not between the child and the dog, for we don't need to sacrifice the one for the other. (Though one wonders, in partial response, why one couldn't study both animals *and* humans, in ways appropriate to each.) Further, sometimes the charge is made (not only in this context) that modern medicine places too much emphasis on cure and not enough on prevention. Had medicine proceeded without a heavy reliance on animal research, medicine may well have emphasized prevention, and public health would possibly be even better than it is today.[38] Though, again, one wonders, in partial response, why one couldn't stress both prevention and cure.

Another way that some animal advocates have sought to minimize the importance of animal experimentation is by minimizing the importance of medical intervention itself. And indeed medical sociologists have questioned the importance of medical intervention in bringing about the dramatic fall in the death rate that has occurred in the West since the mid nineteenth century. The recent debate on this topic was begun in earnest in 1976 with the publication of Thomas McKeon's book *The Role of Medicine: Dream, Mirage or Nemesis?*[39] McKeon, who was professor of social medicine at the University of Birmingham, attributed the increasing life expectancy not to medical interventions but to social and environmental changes such as better hygiene and sanitation, improved diet, higher standard of living, and so on. Indeed, one physician writing to the British medical journal *Lancet* felt sufficiently confident to write, "The debate has been resolved, and it is now widely accepted that medical intervention had only a marginal effect on population mortality and mainly at a very late stage, after death rates had already fallen strikingly."[40]

A study of the eleven major infectious diseases[41] that caused 30 percent of the deaths at the turn of the century and whose decline accounted for 40 percent of the decline of the mortality rate from 1900-1973 yielded the following rather surprising results: only "3.5% of the fall in the overall death rate can be explained through medical interventions for the major infectious diseases."[42] To whom would this be surprising? To the average

38. Singer, *Animal Liberation,* p. 92.

39. Originally published in 1976, a second edition was subsequently issued: *The Role of Medicine: Dream, Mirage or Nemesis?* (Princeton, N.J.: Princeton University Press, 1979).

40. David St. George, *The Lancet* (August 9, 1986), p. 346.

41. Typhoid, small pox, scarlet fever, measles, whooping cough, diphtheria, influenza, tuberculosis, pneumonia, acute digestive infections, and poliomyelitis.

42. John B. McKinlay, Sonja M. McKinlay, and Robert Beagehole, "Trends in Death and Disease and the Contribution of Medical Measures," in *Handbook of Medical Sociology,*

person on the street, no doubt, but not, apparently, to those with relevant professional expertise, for "it is now generally conceded that medical intervention (as opposed to public health measures) contributed little to the decline in infectious disease mortality."[43] Further, a study of the decline in death due to coronary heart disease and stroke yields similar results, with the overall conclusion being that "medical care has contributed little to the modern decline in mortality and therefore in any improvement in health."[44] This is not to say that life-saving medical intervention does not help a subset of individuals, who have every reason to be appreciative, but it is to say medical interventions have been a relatively minor factor in the overall lowering of the mortality rate. So, it would be argued, if medical interventions have played a relatively small role in increasing life expectancy and if animal research, in turn, makes only a small contribution to the total development of medical interventions, then, had medicine proceeded without animal research we would still find intact the major increases in life expectancy we have seen over the last century. An attack on animal research is not, then, an attack on human life expectancy.

In fairness to clinical intervention, however, it needs to be noted that such interventions also involve the treatment of nonfatal illnesses and disabilities, and the provision of palliative measures, none of which would necessarily affect the mortality rates but which would certainly improve our quality of life. For example, corneal grafting, which was first developed on rabbits' eyes, can save a person's sight but would not save a person's life. Or consider the replacement of the hip joint in a patient with osteoarthritis, who is thereby saved from the consequences of a crippling disease. In part this is made possible by animal research, which determined tissue compatibility with the materials used in constructing the artificial hip. Again, though not life-saving, this clearly has much to do with the quality of a person's life.

These kinds of considerations aside, I suspect that most people would still not be completely convinced by an argument that seeks to minimize the importance of animal research by minimizing the importance of life-extending medical intervention. First, there will be some uncertainty whether we can extrapolate from studies about the past to con-

---

fourth ed., ed. Howard E. Freeman and Sol Levine (Englewood Cliffs, N.J.: Prentice Hall, 1989), p. 16.

43. McKinlay, McKinlay, and Beagehole, "Trends in Death and Disease," p. 16.

44. McKinlay, McKinlay, and Beagehole, "Trends in Death and Disease," p. 39.

clusions about the future, setting limits in advance as to what we will be able to achieve through animal research by way of life-extending advances in the future. Second, even if we grant that clinical interventions have had and will continue to have only a relatively small role in reducing the death rate, nevertheless the contributions of these interventions are real and significant, even if they are not the major factor that some have thought. And animal research has played a not inconsequential role in this. In this regard consider the following: In the 1930s sulfa drugs were introduced, prontosil being the first so-called "miracle drug." It provided cures for bacterial pneumonia, meningitis, gonorrhea, and bowel and urinary tract infections. It was, for example, instrumental in lowering the number of maternal deaths from 400 (in 1930) to 40 (in 1960) per 100,000 births.[45] It was necessary to use mice in developing the drug since it was inactive *in vitro;* subsequently rats and monkeys had to be used to discover the side effects of the drug and to determine treatment modifications necessary to avoid those side effects.

Insulin was discovered after experiments on dogs and is extracted from the pancreas of slaughtered cattle and pigs. And with what results? As Andrew Rowan comments, "insulin injections convert a sentence of an early and unpleasant death to one of a reasonably healthy and prolonged life. . . . In 1974 it was estimated that 130 million diabetics had had their lives prolonged by insulin."[46] In the case of polio, we have a disease that struck large numbers of children (and old people as well), and of these about 25 percent sustained severe permanent disability and 25 percent had mild disabilities, with mortality figures varying from 1 to 10 percent, depending on the kind of polio. In 1955, when the Salk vaccine was introduced, the incidence of polio was 28,985 for that year; the introduction of the vaccine virtually eliminated the disease. It was animal research that significantly contributed to the development of our knowledge of the disease to begin with and the "polio virus could only be grown successfully in primate tissue and monkey cell cultures became the substrate of choice."[47] Further, it has been argued[48] that the importance of animal research is most clearly seen in the development of advanced surgical techniques, along with our understanding of shock and anesthesiology. Row-

45. William Paton, "Animal Experiment and Medical Research: A Study in Evolution," *Conquest* 169 (1979): 1-14.

46. Rowan, *Of Mice, Models, and Men,* p. 182.

47. Rowan, *Of Mice, Models, and Men,* p. 182.

48. L. C. Winterscheid, "Animal Experimentation Leading to the Development of Advanced Surgical Techniques," *American Journal of Public Health* 5 (1967): 1604-12.

an comments, "The fields of surgery and anesthesia demonstrate a steady and sometimes, spectacular series of advances in the last fifty years. Significant credit for these advances must be given to animal research. Without animal studies, it is virtually certain that elective surgery would still be the exception rather than the rule and that mortality rates from surgery would still be high enough to make surgery a life-threatening rather than a life-saving choice."[49]

Aware that animal medical research cannot simply be dismissed as so much cruelty, with no significant human benefits at all, Peter Singer confronts the issue squarely when he declares, "the ethical question of the justifiability of animal experimentation cannot be settled by pointing to its benefits for us no matter how persuasive the evidence in favor of such benefits may be."[50] The reason that it cannot be so settled, according to Singer, is that "the principle of the equal consideration of interests" requires that the animal's interest be counted equally with ours. And nowhere else, so much as in the area of medical research, are convictions like Singer's put to the test. For would we be willing to abandon diabetics to their fate or be willing to have children struggling with the crippling consequences of polio rather than have used animals in the way that we did? We should not think, therefore, that there will be no cost to the human community in ceasing to use animals in painful ways in the course of doing medical research. If this is a moral pill that one has to swallow, one should at least not be misled into thinking that it will be easy to swallow, even if it will not be quite so hard as we might be led to believe by those who have overestimated the significance of medical interventions.

It is often pointed out in the course of defending animal research for medical purposes that animals themselves are the beneficiaries of such research. (Sir) William Paton (Professor of Pharmacology at Oxford University) has observed, "Many of the drugs and procedures that have been of importance for man are of equal effectiveness in animals. The veterinary surgeon has the same antibiotics and antiseptics; the same hormones, tranquilizers, local anesthetics, and general anesthetics; the same surgical procedures and principles of resuscitation or other life support; and many of the same nutritional supplements."[51] Further, more than half the veterinarian's pharmacopia comes from human medicine. Moreover, in 1937 it was calculated that over one hundred million animals had their

49. Rowan, *Of Mice, Models, and Men,* p. 183.
50. Singer, *Animal Liberation,* p. 92.
51. Paton, *Man and Mouse,* p. 71.

lives saved by inoculation against anthrax and rinderpest (cattle plague). Dog distemper, which at one time killed hundreds of thousands of animals, has virtually been eliminated. Elizabeth Baldwin, Research Ethics Officer for the American Psychological Association's Science Directorate, offers us a similar argument, "Animal rights activists often fail to appreciate the many benefits to animals that have resulted from animal research. Behavioral research has contributed to improvements in the environments of captive animals, including those used in research. . . . The list of benefits also includes a host of veterinary procedures and the development of vaccines for deadly diseases such as rabies, Lyme disease, and feline leukemia."[52] The point is: animal research helps animals.

This line of argument is interesting but curious. It is frequently put forth by those who defend painful animal research — that is, by those who in this debate are the ones supposedly less concerned with animal welfare. It is usually rejected by critics of such research, who are the ones supposedly most concerned with animal welfare. There may be a number of reasons for what on the surface appears to be a strange anomaly. It may be that defenders of animal research may offer this particular argument simply to mollify their critics, though what really convinces them that their research is justified is the benefits that accrue to humans. *Critics* of animal research, on the other hand, may not be persuaded because they take seriously the motto of the American Anti-Vivisection Society, "You cannot do Evil that Good may result," a principle that applies, they are convinced, whether the good achieved by painful animal research is a benefit to humans or to other animals. Or, to put this same point differently, the critic of animal research may believe in animal rights, and rights, of course, can be invoked in order to prevent the individual from being used in objectionable ways for the good of others, indeed for the good of many others, be they humans or animals. Moreover, the individual animal who suffers painfully for the benefit of others is no more compensated for its suffering because the beneficiaries of its suffering are nonhuman animals than it would be if they were humans. Whereas there are genuine benefits that have accrued to animals from research on animals and those benefits must be considered in the course of an overall assessment of the value of this kind of research, nevertheless, the fact that animals are the beneficiaries of this research is not a consideration that carries any special weight, as if it were easier to justify suffering imposed on animals for the sake of

52. Elizabeth Baldwin, "The Case for Animal Research," *Journal of Social Issues* 49, no. 1 (1993): 125-26.

other animals. For why should it carry more weight that a rat, for example, suffers for the sake of dogs or cows rather than for the sake of humans? After all, dogs and cows are, as much as humans, members of different species. Nor does it in any way improve matters when the beneficiaries of a rat's suffering are other rats, members of its own species. For why, again, is it preferable for a rat to die or suffer to help other rats rather than to help a member of another species altogether? Certainly it brings the rat no additional consolation. Research on animals may benefit other animals but that does not mean it benefits the animals used in the research, and that, for the animal painfully experimented upon, is the bottom line.

ANIMAL RESEARCH: THREE POSITIONS

Having looked at a variety of modes of animal experimentation – toxicity testing, behavioral research, pain research, weapons and warfare research, medical research – let us look at three approaches that one might take to painful animal experimentation. First, one might argue that the painful use of animals poses no moral problem whatsoever, that the researcher should be free to proceed very much as she pleases, human benefit and the extension of human knowledge alone being controlling considerations. This is effectively to put animals outside the moral community, that is, to put them in the same category as inanimate objects. Second, we can take the position that no animal research is ever morally justified. If finding a cure for cancer or AIDS involves painfully using or sacrificing animals, then we simply must live with cancer or AIDS. Here animals have, in essence, a shared moral status with humans. Third, we can take the position that animals count morally, so that the first alternative is unacceptable, but they count less than is assumed in the second alternative, so that some painful experimentation on animals, but not all, can be morally justified – the position I am inclined to embrace. Laws designed to control the practice of animal experimentation assume something like the third position: animals count but they do not count as much as animal liberationists typically believe. As Judith Hampson comments, "These laws rest on a basic assumption, that it is legitimate and morally acceptable to kill animals and to cause them pain and distress in order to protect human society from illness and environmental hazard and to gain scientific knowledge. Most laws seek to impose limits upon the degree of pain and distress which might be caused and some seek to restrict the purposes for which it is considered legitimate, but none question its legitimacy."[53]

Believing, then, that animals count morally, but that some painful experimentation can be justified, one will insist that animal suffering can be too great and the projected knowledge or benefits sufficiently small or uncertain that many experiments may not be morally justified. One will also insist that we actively promote alternatives to painful experiments on animals, that such alternatives be used when available, that anesthetics and analgesics be used wherever feasible, that redundant experiments be avoided, that research animals be properly housed and cared for, that the animal's post-experimental needs be met, and so on. In all of this, we are saying that animals count morally and that we should pursue these humane goals at some cost to the human community. This latter consideration is, of course, an important consideration because an unwillingness to bear any cost at all is, in essence, to effectively discount the animal's moral standing.

In the course of evaluating research projects, three variables will need to be weighed: the quality of the research, the degree of animal suffering, and the probability of human benefit.[54] These are considerations that may, of course, pull us in opposite directions. Would that we were confronted either with projects in which the quality of the research was high, the degree of animal suffering low, and the probability of human benefit high, or else projects in which the quality of research was low, the degree of animal suffering high, and the probability of human benefit low. In such cases decisions would be relatively easy to make. But often, of course, matters will not be so straightforward and competing considerations will have to be weighed carefully, though necessarily imprecisely. No doubt, these three variables will need to be worked on and rendered more precise. And, although they will never be so precise as to provide easy answers to difficult cases, they at least point to considerations that are to be taken into account in the course of making a judgment. It may also be that we shall wish to extend veto power to extreme animal suffering, so that only under the most extraordinary circumstances could research projects that entail such suffering ultimately be allowed to proceed. Of course, the significance that we assign to animal suffering will be determined by how much moral consideration we believe animals are due in the first place.

53. Judith Hampson, "Legislation and the Changing Consensus," in *Animal Experimentation,* ed. Langley, p. 219.

54. Patrick Bateson, "When to Experiment on Animals," *New Scientist* 20 (February 1986): 3-32.

Once one accepts this third position, a middle way between the other two, one finds oneself embracing a position that does not, like the other two, provide precise guidance. For although animals count morally, one wonders, among other things, how much do they count and how does one weigh the suffering of the animal over against the prospective benefits to the human community? Further, this third alternative is not a single position but a wide spectrum of positions, ranging all the way from one that says that animals count, but just barely, to one that says they count almost as much as humans, but not quite. So within this third alternative one can imagine strong disagreement over the moral justification of particular research projects. Here there are no formulas to adjudicate the differences. Rather, one can only appeal to developing and maturing sensitivities. This is not a fatal flaw, for it does not follow that anything goes nor that any decision on such matters is as good as any other. Indeed, situations of this kind are the norm rather than the exception in living the moral life. It is simply the nature of the moral life to have to balance competing goods or choose between competing obligations.

It is my judgment that this third view is to be preferred to the two alternatives and that, within it, one should stake out a position that gives animals considerably more moral weight than has customarily been the case in the research community or in the larger general community. It is also my belief that the ethics of animal experimentation should be a continuing focus of discussion as we seek to refine our moral sensibilities and begin to discover what serious and appropriate moral concern for animals looks like.

A CASE IN POINT

Here we might look at one famous, perhaps infamous, case of behavioral research and see if our moral sensibilities can give us some direction in helping us morally evaluate it. The work of the late University of Wisconsin psychologist, Professor Harry Harlow, is often presented by animal advocates as an example of the terrible things that can be done to animals by behavioral researchers. Admittedly, it is usually presented without any reference to the expected benefits from these studies, though these benefits would hardly appease most animal advocates, even if elaborated upon at great length. Working with his wife, various collaborators, and graduate students for a period of some twenty years, Harlow studied the effects of maternal and sibling deprivation on rhesus monkeys. Separated from their mothers only a few hours after birth, they were subjected to total social isolation, placed in isolation cages for periods of three, six, and twelve months. The research yielded the following results: Three-month social isolates, though displaying marked fear response, could be fully socialized when united to their peer groups; six-month social isolates were unable to establish bonds of affection, played alone, and did not resist aggressive attacks; twelve-month social isolates were the most passive of all, "crouching and cowering" in the face of abuse that could in some instances be lethal. Variations on social isolation include the creation of "wells of despair." These were narrow pits, devoid of stimuli and social contact of any kind, from which the monkey was unable to escape. There they would collapse into a ball, hiding their faces in their paws, engaging in a constant rocking motion, and even clawing and biting themselves.

An ingenious twist was given to all this by the introduction of various "monster mothers." Placed in isolation with a choice between two surrogate mothers, one a wire mesh supplier of milk and the other a soft, cloth covered, heated "mother," the infant monkey would, it turned out, choose the cloth mother, spending most of its time clinging to it. Then there were variants of the cloth surrogate mother: one that ejected high-pressure compressed air, one that rocked violently, one that ejected sharp brass spikes, one that would go from 99° F to 35° F. In addition, Harlow wanted to introduce a real living monster mother. But how to create these real monster mothers? What Harlow did was to take female social isolates, who had no interest in mating. He then restrained them in "rape racks," there to be impregnated by normal male monkeys. These mothers rejected their offspring, and refused to respond to their cries for physical contact and cuddling. In some cases, the response of the mothers was brutal and deadly, crushing the infant's skull with their teeth or "smashing the infant's face to the floor, and then rubbing it back and forth."[55]

Well, what should we think about all this? Even those who point to the substantial value of this research acknowledge its dark side. Thus the behavioral scientist W. H. Thorpe comments, "Cruel and horrible as these experiments certainly are, they have had results of great value."[56] Michael Allan Fox declares, "Yet even these nightmarish and regrettable experiments, offensive as they are to normal sensibilities, are not without redeem-

55. *Engineering and Science* 33, no. 8 (1970).

56. W. H. Thorpe, *Animal Nature and Human Nature* (Garden City, N.Y.: Doubleday, 1974), p. 236.

ing features of considerable importance."[57] And what are those redeeming features? Observations by Fox include the following: (1) Virtually every textbook on the psychology of child development cites and discusses Harlow's research; (2) the infant's attachment to the mother is shown *not* to be solely a product of the hunger drive (note: the infant prefers the cloth surrogate mother to the wire mesh mother that provides milk); (3) the research provides evidence that the infant's clinging, smiling, and vocalizing is preprogrammed (note: it engages in these behaviors though having had no social contact); (4) the research called into question the claim that mothering is instinctual and does not need to be taught; (5) the research shows that the effects of social isolation are reversible; (6) finally, it shows that normal social development does not require attachment to a single mother.

Granting that professionals in developmental psychology are in a special position to appreciate the significance of these studies as intellectual achievements, nevertheless it is hard not to believe that the price in terms of animal suffering is too high. Here no proof can be offered, for there are no formulas to the effect that X amount of suffering must be compensated by Y amount of human benefit. In lieu of proofs, one can only invite others to view matters from a certain perspective, one that takes seriously both the reality of animal suffering and the moral standing of the animals themselves. One can only invite others to reflect on the observable impact of this research on each of the monkeys subjected to these experiments and ask: Is this not a situation where curiosity and the search for knowledge ought to be checked by the high price to be paid in animal suffering?

Of course, where research has clear practical application in meeting significant human needs, one becomes more sympathetic and accepting of that research. Indeed, one might suppose that Harlow's research has implications for dealing with victims of child abuse. And, for many people, to simply suggest such a linkage is to put to rest all unease they might have experienced over this research. Indeed, their tendency to trust the scientific community is so strong that for them, the mere suggestion of a connection ends all enquiry. At the professional level just such suggestions have been made. Thus D. Horenstein has observed that the work of Harlow and others points the way to possible therapies: teach the abusive mother normal maternal behavior and place the abused child in a supervised setting that provides peer interaction.[58] But as Rowan comments,

57. Fox, *The Case for Animal Experimentation,* p. 104.

58. D. Horenstein, "The Dynamics and Treatment of Child Abuse: Can Primate Research Provide the Answers?" *Journal of Clinical Psychology* 33 (1977): 563-65.

"To the animal welfare advocate, this hardly sounds like a startling innovation (even assuming that one can entice abusive mothers into a training clinic). It sounds a lot more like a common sense approach to the problem than one requiring either animal research or animal suffering to reach."[59]

But the central point is that despite the knowledge and possible human benefit of this research, it still remains morally suspect. Unquestionably, painful research on animals can yield important knowledge that may have significant human benefit. To simply take the line that all such research is pointlessly cruel, arguing that it will yield nothing of worth, is to distort the facts. It is also to mislead us into thinking that all our moral choices in this area will be easy ones. It wrongly suggests that we will not be confronted by moral demands that will require our foregoing something of genuine human value, something that there is reason to regret having had to forego but which is required of us all the same. Harlow's work with rhesus monkeys appears to be in this category. This research is by no means worthless, but it is not worth, it is plausible to suggest, the pain, agony, and suffering inflicted on these monkeys. In saying "no" to this research, we are also regrettably saying "no" to certain benefits that could accrue to humans. Other research may not be so *obviously* objectionable but may be objectionable all the same. Thus one may have to choose between considerable human benefit or considerable animal pain, and one may, in such circumstances, be perplexed as to what should be done. Again, the moral life does not always provide us with completely happy and easily resolvable endings.

But when the decision is made to secure a human good at the cost of animal suffering that must always be a somber choice. In such circumstances, we will be called to a recognition of the great price being exacted to secure human benefit, accompanied by a strong sense of regret that it had to be so. Such regret, with the attendant sensitivities that make genuine regret possible, will, in turn, make it more difficult for us to proceed with excessively painful animal research in the future. And as we look back on Harlow's research — research that we may now find offensive — the problem may have been not so much with Harlow and his associates as with the larger professional culture in which animal research was conducted. Perhaps, being inadequately sensitive to animal pain and suffering, experiencing no regret and seeing no choices as tragic, an environment was created in which one could feel quite comfortable doing what Harlow did.

59. Rowan, *Of Mice, Models, and Men,* p. 142.

CHAPTER 11

Christianity, the Bible, and Animal Concern

INTRODUCTION

We shall begin this chapter by briefly examining the concern for animal welfare and the respect for animal life that finds expression in a number of the world's religions. The teachings of these religions pose a challenge for those Christians who have an emerging moral concern for animals. After seeing the explicit support for moral concern for animals that can be found in the official teachings of these religions, one may wonder, Is Christianity *alone* among the religions of the world in providing no substantial theological basis for such concern? One wants one's deep moral convictions to be vindicated by one's religious beliefs and certainly not to be at odds with them. I will argue, however, that moral concern for animals is not at odds with the Christian faith and shall explore ways in which a moral concern for animal welfare and respect for animal life can find a biblical home. There are, admittedly, biblical texts that seem to be adverse to the cause of animal advocacy. Those must be honestly confronted. In doing so, I shall argue that Christians who call for a substantial revisioning of our moral attitude toward animals are confronted by a biblical challenge no more imposing (indeed, less so) than the challenge that confronted Christians of a former century who called for the abolition of slavery or the challenge that confronts Christians in our own century who seek to bring an end to the subordination of women. Of course, moral concern for animals is not quite the live issue that women's equality has become or that the abolition of slavery was some 150 years ago. For this reason the biblical and theological challenge of providing adequate support for an ethic of animal concern has not yet been fully taken up. Whereas there are those in the Christian community, like Andrew Linzey, who have addressed these concerns, there is much work yet to be done. It must be recognized that in asking Christians to take up these concerns, we are asking them not only to surmount general cultural insensitivity to animal welfare but to overcome the resistance peculiar to the Christian tradition as well. In part because of the influence of Augustine, moral concern for animals has not been a live issue in the Christian church. In recent years, there has been a resurrection of the pre-Augustinian debate over these issues, though this has occurred mainly among secular thinkers. It is time that the debate be resumed in the Christian community as well. It is true that ecology, concern with species survival, and environmentalism have begun to receive attention, but there has been no comparable effort to embrace or even to explore the concerns of animal advocacy.

WORLD RELIGIONS AND ANIMAL CONCERN

Historically, Christianity has not had a good track record when it comes either to words or deeds directed to the welfare of animals. Theologian John Cobb, reflecting on Judaism, Islam, Hinduism, Jainism, Buddhism, and Confucianism, goes so far as to say that none of these "has a record quite as bad as Christianity."[1] If so, Christians with emerging moral concern for animals can only be embarrassed, and a bit envious of those religious traditions that have perhaps seen things more clearly than those of us within the Christian tradition.

Certainly, when it comes to concern for animals it is the Jains who are the pace setters. Indeed, some may very well judge them to be fanatical in their concern for animal welfare. Adherents of the religion (an offshoot of Hinduism), who comprise only about 1 percent of the population of India, adopt a strict lifestyle committed to not harming any living creature. As Lewis Regenstein, Director of the Interfaith Council for the Protection of Animals and Nature, has observed, "it is clear that of all the world's religions, the Jains, without doubt, go to the greatest lengths to live their faith's commitment of reverence for animals and nature."[2] They go so far

1. John Cobb, Review of *Animal Sacrifices: Religious Perspectives on the Use of Animals in Science,* ed. Tom Regan, in *Environmental Ethics* 10, no. 2 (Summer 1988): 181.

2. Lewis Regenstein, *Replenish the Earth: A History of Organized Religion's Treatment of Animals and Nature* (New York: Crossroad, 1991), p. 232.

as to refrain from tilling the soil because it disturbs insects and worms. They run animal sanctuaries where stray, injured, and abandoned animals are cared for, including cows, camels, water buffalo, pigeons, and parrots. They also canvass the animal markets of India, buying sheep, goats, and other animals destined to be slaughtered, in order to care for them.

One particular Jain, a veterinarian who runs the Charity Birds Hospital in Old Delhi, treating over 6,500 birds each year without charge, explains his mission with these words: "All that breathes is precious. Who is to say that the suffering of a sparrow is less worthy of solace than the pain of a man? The spark of life is no dimmer simply because it is encased in fur or feather."[3] It should be noted that this concern for animals has not diminished the Jains' concern for humans. They have "established schools, universities, and hospitals throughout India to help the poor and to educate the population on a variety of subjects."[4] This, again, demonstrates that a robust moral concern for animals is not incompatible with a deep commitment to human welfare.

Hinduism, the religion of 80 percent of India's population, is, along with Jainism and Buddhism, committed to the doctrine of *ahimsa,* that we humans are not to harm any living creature. The Hindu proverb gives expression to this: "Do not kill any animal for pleasure, see harmony in nature, and lend a helping hand to all living creatures." Or as the Hindu prayer that is used to close public gatherings puts it, "May all (those) that have life be delivered from suffering."[5] Certainly the Hindu doctrine of reincarnation lends support to the moral belief that animals are not to be harmed, animals being receptacles of human souls whose lives have been less than exemplary during their human sojourn on earth. Nevertheless, Hindu concern for animals is not exclusively the product of belief in reincarnation, for unquestionably there is present a genuine concern for the suffering of animals.

And yet, unlike the Jains, the Hindus (more like the rest of us) do not always match conduct with precept. According to Regenstein, "Many Hindus willingly eat meat as long as someone else kills the animal; there is no shortage of slaughterhouses in India. Domestic animals and pets are often neglected, abused, and mistreated."[6] Part of the problem is that sick, suffering, and aged animals, along with unwanted puppies and kittens, in

3. Quoted in Regenstein, *Replenish the Earth,* p. 22.
4. Regenstein, *Replenish the Earth,* p. 233.
5. Regenstein, *Replenish the Earth,* p. 22.
6. Regenstein, *Replenish the Earth,* p. 227.

large numbers are allowed to wander about, in many cases starving to death, rather than being put out of their misery. This, in turn, some feel, breeds an indifference to the suffering of animals on the part of a Hindu population whose religion officially places such a strong emphasis on kindness and charity toward animals. No doubt poverty and overwhelming human suffering contribute to desensitizing people to all suffering — animal and human.

Much the same thing can be said about Buddhism. It, too, gives a central place to compassionate concern for animals. Buddha himself was quite emphatic: "The practice of religion involves, as the first principle, a loving compassionate heart for all creatures." Or, again in the words of Buddha, "Be of compassionate mind to all living beings and extend loving kindness thus: May all living creatures and beings . . . be freed from sorrow! Be freed from suffering! and be happiness full!"[7]

The Islamic religion, which in many ways is more akin to Christianity than Jainism, Hinduism, or Buddhism, also is not silent about concern for animals. In the Qur'an, Muhammad declares:

> There is a meritorious reward for every act of charity and kindness to every living creature.
>
> A good deed done to an animal is as meritorious as a good deed done to a human being, while an act of cruelty to an animal is as bad as an act of cruelty to a human being.
>
> He who takes pity even on a sparrow and spares its life, God will be merciful to him on the Day of Judgment.
>
> There is no man who kills even a sparrow, or anything smaller, without a justifiable cause, but God will question him about it.

In Islam, then, we have concern directed to individual animals, not just stewardly concern with species survival. Helping individual animals is approved by God and will be appropriately rewarded, and the gratuitous killing of animals will require an accounting to God. Despite this, as Regenstein comments, "Alas, as with Christianity, Judaism, and others of the world's major religions, most present-day Moslems largely ignore or are unaware of their great Islamic tradition of reverence for animals and nature."[8]

7. Regenstein, *Replenish the Earth,* p. 233.
8. Regenstein, *Replenish the Earth,* p. 260.

It is nevertheless noteworthy that in all of these religions there is clearly taught a moral concern for animals. What they have to say is impressive even if, as Regenstein sadly observes, there is frequently a failure to practice what is preached (adherents of Jainism aside). The fact remains that there is a strand in all of them (admittedly, more prominent in some than in others) that calls us to a respect for animal life and a concern for animal suffering. Someone who seeks direction and nurture in the Scriptures of the Old and New Testaments, however, may wonder if there is a biblical basis for a serious moral concern for animals. Or is it only in other religious traditions that a substantive moral concern for animals has found expression?

SOME BIBLICAL REFLECTIONS

Here we shall seek to show that those Christians with a growing moral concern for animals are not without biblical resources to support and inspire that concern. Some of these resources have already been referred to in earlier chapters, but some further exposition and commentary is appropriate. Regrettably, one may not be fully sensitive to these biblical resources unless one already has an emerging concern for animals or at least an inkling that there might be something morally important here. If one judges moral concern for animals to be either an eccentric concern or simply unworthy of serious reflection, one will be quite content to let sleeping texts lie.

In the Mosaic law are found restrictions on the use of animals that can reasonably be understood as expressions of concern for the welfare of the animal itself. Thus, animals as well as humans are to rest on the Sabbath: "Six days you shall do your work, but on the seventh day you shall rest; that your ox and your ass may have rest, and the son of your bondmaid, and the alien, may be refreshed" (Exod. 23:12; cf. Exod. 20:10 and Deut. 5:13-14). Also in Exodus 23 it is declared, "If you meet your enemy's ox or his ass going astray, you shall bring it back to him. If you see the ass of one who hates you lying under its burden, you shall refrain from leaving him with it, and you shall help him to lift it up" (vv. 4-5). Thus even though it is your enemy's ox or donkey, nevertheless, it is to be cared for. The donkey is to be set free of its crushing burden despite any reluctance on your part to help because it is the property of an enemy. Friend or foe, the animal's needs are to be addressed. In Deuteronomy 22:10, the Hebrews are forbidden to plow with an ox and donkey together. This may be prompted by concern for the welfare of the animals because pairing animals of different size and strength may cause harm to one or the other.

Further, every seventh year the land is not to be sown or harvested. What grows naturally in the fields is to be food not only for humans but "for your cattle also and for the beasts that are in your land" (Lev. 25:7; cf. Exod. 23:10-11). Thus, the wild animals, of no value to the farmer, are worthy of consideration. In doing this, the farmer becomes an extension of God's gracious care for the animal world. Thus the farmer, like God, "gives to the beasts their food, and to the young ravens which cry" (Ps. 147:9). Indeed, "Thou openest thy hand, thou satisfiest the desire of every living thing" (Ps. 145:16).

This theme of God's gracious provision for all his creatures finds eloquent expression in Psalm 104:

> Thou makest springs gush forth in the valleys;
> they flow between the hills,
> they give drink to every beast of the field;
> the wild asses quench their thirst.
> By them the birds of the air have their habitation;
> they sing among the branches. . . .
> Thou dost cause the grass to grow for the cattle. . . .
> The trees of the LORD are watered abundantly,
> the cedars of Lebanon which he planted.
> In them the birds build their nests;
> the stork has her home in the fir trees.
> The high mountains are for the wild goats;
> the rocks are a refuge for the badgers. . . .
> The young lions roar for their prey,
> seeking their food from God. . . .
> O LORD, how manifold are thy works!
> In wisdom hast thou made them all;
> the earth is full of thy creatures. . . . (Ps. 104:10-24)

On this passage Walter Harrelson has commented, "The creative and powerful anthropocentrism of biblical religion is here beautifully qualified: God has interest in badgers and wild goats and storks for their own sake. He has interest in trees and mountains and rock-cairns that simply serve non-human purposes."[9]

Then there is the story of Jonah, who is angered when Nineveh is

9. Quoted in Robert J. Johnston, "Wisdom Literature and Its Contribution to a Biblical Environmental Ethic," in *Tending the Garden,* ed. Welsey Granberg-Michaelson (Grand Rapids: Eerdmans, 1987), p. 71.

spared divine judgment and who is confronted by God with these words: "And should not I pity Nineveh, that great city, in which there are more than a hundred and twenty thousand persons who do not know their right hand from their left, and also much cattle?" (Jonah 4:11). It seems that along with innocent children, cattle are the objects of divine mercy. Indeed, this provides an example of what the Psalmist affirms when he says, "The LORD is good to all, and his compassion is over all that he has made" (Ps. 145:9).

The New Testament is not, admittedly, quite the resource for moral concern for animals that the Old Testament is. This has prompted some to view Judaism as a better friend to animals than Christianity. Christians need to remind themselves, however, that the Old Testament is sacred Scripture too, and would also be assumed as a repository of sacred truth by the writers of the New Testament. That animal needs are not addressed as often in the New Testament may partly be a product of the urban character of the developing Christian movement. Christians were city dwellers, not rural farmers for whom issues of animal treatment might more naturally arise.

A New Testament text often offered in support of concern for animals is Luke 12:6, "Are not five sparrows sold for two pennies? And not one of them is forgotten before God" (cf. Matt. 10:29-31). It is not merely that God retains information about the fate of sparrows like an uncaring computer, merely tabulating births, deaths, and total populations. It is more than this. The sparrow has value (even if humans are of greater value than many sparrows, Luke 12:7), and the sparrow is not forgotten because it has that value. The sparrow has significance for God. Indeed, Jesus' point is that we who have more value than sparrows can take comfort from the fact that a knowing concern is directed by God even to sparrows.

Also, the Old Testament theme of God's generous and caring provision for animals finds expression in Matthew 6:26: "Look at the birds of the air: they neither sow nor reap nor gather into barns, and yet your heavenly Father feeds them. Are you not of more value than they?" (cf. Luke 12:24).

Then there are those sharp words spoken by Jesus in responses to criticism for healing on the Sabbath a woman who had been a cripple for eighteen years: "You hypocrites! Does not each of you on the sabbath untie his ox or his ass from the manger, and lead it away to water it? And ought not this woman, a daughter of Abraham whom Satan bound for eighteen years, be loosed from this bond on the sabbath day?" (Luke 13:15-16). Of course, it might be suggested that the donkey or oxen could be led to water on the Sabbath (or a sheep lifted out of a pit on the Sabbath, Matt. 12:11) only because the owner is concerned with the animal as a farming tool or a vehicle for transporting goods — because of something, in other words, of instrumental value only. But the logic of the argument suggests otherwise: you would even help an animal in need on the Sabbath (rightly, understandably), so, why do you object to my helping a human being in need on the Sabbath? In short, if the animal is worth helping (and it is), then all the more so is a human. As George Frear comments, "If what is involved in the sabbath rescue of the animal is only prudent husbandry, then the extension to the afflicted human, who of course can wait, does not follow."[10]

THE FALL AND KILLING ANIMALS FOR FOOD

Not only is there a biblical basis for concern with animal welfare, but there is a strategy that one could employ to argue for moral vegetarianism if one chooses. In the book of Genesis, prior to the fall there existed a vegetarian world for both humans and animals: "And God said, 'Behold, I have given you every plant yielding seed which is upon the face of all the earth, and every tree with seed in its fruit; you shall have them for food. And to every beast of the earth, and to every bird of the air, and to everything that creeps on the earth, everything that has the breath of life, I have given every green plant for food.' And it was so" (Gen. 1:29-30). Thus, before the fall, humans ate grain and fruit, and animals ate grass. This is what a world is like without sin, a world not yet marred by human rebellion, a world in which humans are at peace with God, with animals, and with the world of nature. Here there is no killing, no eating of flesh, no infliction of pain and suffering on any of God's creatures. Here were realized God's perfect intentions for humans and animals. As the biblical scholar Claus Westermann has observed, we have here "an awareness that the killing of living beings for food by other living beings is not right, and so is not in accordance with the will of the creator at the beginning. . . ."[11]

But sin intervenes, and the results of this are catalogued in subsequent chapters of Genesis, as decline and decay and corruption occur. Hu-

10. George L. Frear Jr., "Caring for Animals: Biblical Stimulus for Ethical Reflection," in *Good News for Animals?* ed. Charles Pinches and Jay B. McDaniel (Maryknoll, N.Y.: Orbis Books, 1993), p. 7.

11. Claus Westermann, *Genesis 1–11: A Commentary* (Minneapolis: Augsburg, 1984), p. 164.

mans finally become so corrupt that divine judgment falls in the form of a cataclysmic flood, with only the family of Noah and the animals on board the ark surviving. Here the transition from the paradise of the Garden of Eden to the subsequent fallen state is completed. This includes a change in diet. In this regard, God declares to Noah, "The fear of you and the dread of you shall be upon every beast of the earth, and upon every bird of the air, upon everything that creeps on the ground and on all the fish of the sea; into your hand they are delivered. Every moving thing that lives shall be food for you; and as I gave you the green plants, I give you everything" (Gen. 9:2-3). Formerly, only the green plants were available for human consumption; now, animal flesh is also available. This is not how things were originally meant to be. This is not an ideal state of affairs. "Fear and dread" is the response of animals to the human presence on the planet, and animals are "delivered into our hands," which, as John Austin Baker has observed, is the language "normally used of a conqueror slaughtering a routed army or sacking a fallen city. Man has become the enemy of all living things."[12] But this is an acknowledgement of sin and fallenness. It is not the ideal.

One day, however, as the biblical vision has it, the effects of the fall will be reversed and paradise will be restored. And what will that day be like? In Isaiah 11, we have a glimpse of that future messianic age when God's perfect will shall once more be realized and things shall be as they were meant to be:

> The wolf shall dwell with the lamb,
> and the leopard shall lie down with the kid,
> and the calf and the lion and the fatling together,
> and a little child shall lead them.
> The cow and the bear shall feed;
> their young shall lie down together;
> and the lion shall eat straw like the ox.
> The sucking child shall play over the hole of the asp,
> and the weaned child shall put his hand on the adder's den.
> They shall not hurt or destroy
> in all my holy mountain;
> For the earth shall be full of the knowledge of the LORD
> as the waters cover the sea.
>
> (Isa. 11:6-9; see also Ezek. 34:25; Hos. 2:18-20)

12. John Austin Baker, "Biblical Attitudes to Nature," in *Man and Nature,* ed. Hugh Montefiore (London: Collins, 1995), p. 96.

And so, in looking back to a time when God's will was perfectly manifest and looking forward to a time when it will be so again, animals are not slain nor are they eaten for food. Killing creatures that God has made is not seen as something compatible with God's perfect will. So, it could reasonably be suggested, when we pray, in the words of the Lord's Prayer, "Thy will be done on earth as it is in heaven," we are praying for a time when killing animals will cease. If so, how, then, can killing and eating animals be for us a matter of complete indifference? Moreover, is not the church an eschatological community? That is, a community that seeks to embody that future manifestation of God's will when God's kingdom comes in its fullness?[13] Stanley Hauerwas and John Berkman put it this way: "So Christian vegetarianism might be understood as a witness to the world that God's creation is not meant to be at war with itself. Such a witness does not entail romantic conceptions of nature or our fallen creation, but rather is an eschatological act, signifying that our lives are not captured by the old order."[14]

This very interpretive strategy – that participating in God's redemptive work and being God's people involves seeking to reclaim, where possible, what has been lost through the fall, not living at peace with the effects of sin, and seeking to secure in some small measure in the present age that righteousness that one day will be secured in its fullness – has also been used by Christians who seek full equality for women. For it is the fall and the effects of sin, it is argued, that resulted in male domination. Following the fall God says to Eve, "I will greatly multiply your pain in childbearing; in pain you shall bring forth children, yet your desire shall be for your husband, and he shall rule over you" (Gen. 3:16). Both pain in childbirth and the man ruling over the woman are the effects of the fall, expressions of sin and not God's original intent for the world. Both, it might be concluded, are states of affairs that are legitimate objects of redemptive reversal. The parallel with killing animals for food is clear. And if the strategy is acceptable in the one case, then it seems equally acceptable in the other.

Not all biblical interpreters would be happy with our use of the messianic vision found in Isaiah 11. The distinguished New Testament scholar

13. George Frear is, of course, right to observe that the biblical passages dealing with the eschatological era are not completely unified. Some suggest a banquet, possibly carniverous (Isa. 25:6; cf. Matt. 22:1-14; Luke 14:15-24). Rather than taming wild beasts, others envision a banishing of them (Lev. 26:6; Isa. 35:9; Ezek. 34:25). See Frear, "Caring for Animals," p. 8.

14. Stanley Hauerwas and John Berkman, "A Trinitarian Theology of the 'Chief End' of 'All Flesh,'" in *Good News for Animals?* ed. Pinches and McDaniel, p. 72.

C. F. D. Moule (Professor of Divinity at Cambridge University), referring to Isaiah 11:5-9, comments, "No one with a grain of sense believes that the passage . . . is intended literally, as though the digestive system of a carnivore were going to be transformed into that of a herbivore. What blasphemous injury would be done to great poetry and true mythology by laying such solemnly prosaic hands upon it!"[15] But acknowledging the poetic dimension of this passage does not mean that one must deny that there is here being expressed a vision of a peaceable kingdom where there will be no killing and no predation. The writer of these words senses that when all God's creatures live in perfect shalom, there will be no spilling of blood, no agonizing deaths, no painful injuries inflicted by predators upon prey. Whatever it will be like, it will not be like that. One might grant (as I see no reason to do) that this is not even a vision of the future, poetic or otherwise, but something quite different, perhaps only an expression of human yearning for the perfection we associate with God's reign. Nevertheless, to yearn for God's perfection *is* to yearn for a day when there will be no predation.

SOME POSSIBLY NOT-SO-CONGENIAL REFLECTIONS

There are, however, biblical considerations that seem to pose problems for moral vegetarianism and for concern for animals for their own sake. For instance, what kind of example does Jesus set for us? Lewis Regenstein raises the question, "Was Jesus a vegetarian?" He concludes that the correct answer to this "long debated question" is uncertain.[16] But I confess to being unaware of any responsible extended debate over whether or not Jesus was a vegetarian. If Jesus had been a vegetarian with a vegetarian's message, it would be strange that this did not find expression in the New Testament. Moreover, Jesus, being a good Jew, would have eaten the Passover lamb. He also assisted the disciples, perhaps miraculously, in catching fish (Luke 5:1-11), and in his resurrected state, on one occasion, he both directed the disciples' fishing efforts to a successful conclusion and invited them to breakfast on the fish with him (John 21:1-14). Finally, Jesus, who came "eating and drinking," contrasts himself with John the Baptist, who came "neither eating nor drinking." Here "eating and drinking"

15. C. F. D. Moule, *Man and Nature in the New Testament* (Philadelphia: Fortress, 1964), p. 11.

16. Regenstein, *Replenish the Earth,* pp. 180-82.

seems to refer to eating meat and drinking wine. There is, then, no reason to think that Jesus was a vegetarian and in reality good reason to think otherwise. But where does this leave us?

Stephen Clark, a British philosopher, a Christian, and a deeply committed moral vegetarian, has said, referring to the fact that Jesus was not a vegetarian, "I would not commit the absurdity of seeking to justify Him, but the question is inevitable: Shall not the Judge of all the earth do right?"[17] One is right to pause before condemning as wrong anything that Jesus himself did. Yet Christians committed to the moral Lordship of Jesus have, for example, been outspoken abolitionists, though Jesus himself remained silent on the issue of slavery, and others have been temperance crusaders, though Jesus himself drank wine. So, what Jesus did or did not do has not on many issues been taken as decisive or universally generalizable. If a Christian does, however, conclude that painlessly killing animals for food is wrong (or at least is wrong in circumstances where there are known to be healthy and life-sustaining alternative diets), one then does, I believe, confront the apologetical task of accounting for why Jesus himself was not a vegetarian. One could certainly be a conditional vegetarian — that is, boycott meat produced by factory farms, which were nonexistent in Jesus' own day, and have no difficulty with the fact that Jesus was not a vegetarian. One could also recognize a wide range of other very serious moral obligations to animals that concern their humane treatment. But if one judges that killing animals for food is wrong in principle, then one must somehow deal with the fact that the Supreme Moral Exemplar was himself not a vegetarian.

Also, it must be acknowledged that animal sacrifice was a part of Old Testament worship. The Jewish sacrificial system was well developed, and it can be seen in all its meticulous detail in the book of Leviticus. To be sure, prophetic condemnation of animal sacrifices occurred from time to time, but the prophetic objection was not directed against animal sacrifices per se; rather, it was an objection to sacrificial offerings in a context devoid of genuine repentance, devoid of compassion for the needy, devoid of a true commitment to justice. (See Psalm 40; Isaiah 1, 59, 65; Jeremiah 6, 7; Amos 5; Micah 6.) It was any ritual divorced from true spirituality, not only animal sacrifice, that was the object of prophetic condemnation. Accordingly, the prophet exhorts the people:

17. Stephen Clark, *The Moral Status of Animals* (New York: Oxford University Press, 1984), p. 196.

I hate, I despise your feasts,
and I take no delight in your solemn assemblies.
Even though you offer me your burnt offerings and grain offerings,
I will not accept them,
and the peace offerings of your fatted beasts
I will not look upon.
Take away from me the noise of your songs;
to the melody of your harps I will not listen.
But let justice roll down like waters,
and righteousness like an everflowing stream. (Amos 5:21-24)

When justice and righteousness resume their rightful place, however, then ritual is transformed and is acceptable to God. It is, therefore, dead, mechanical religion that the prophets attacked, not the killing of animals. Moreover, although the rejection of animal sacrifice is also found in the New Testament, especially in the book of Hebrews (9:6–10:22), this is not an objection to killing animals. Rather, it is a recognition that Christ has made the one sacrifice that renders all other sacrifices unnecessary.

We should not think, however, that ritual animal sacrifices involve placing a low value on animal life. Quite the reverse. Speaking of animal sacrifice, George Frear comments, "It tends to repel modern people. Yet we must remember that in its way it represents respect for animal life, reverence for animal blood. Animals are seen by sacrificers as a valuable gift to God. Their blood can make a reparation; it can by purification restore the sinner, contribute to the ordination of a priest or the return of the Nazarite from a profane status, help maintain the rhythm of the seasons."[18]

Finally, there are the difficult remarks made by Paul: "For it is written in the law of Moses, 'You shall not muzzle an ox when it is treading out the grain.' Is it for oxen that God is concerned? Does he not speak entirely for our sake? It was written for our sake, because the plowman should plow in hope and the thresher thresh in hope of a share in the crop. If we have sown spiritual good among you, is it too much if we reap your material benefits?" (1 Cor. 9:9-11). In this passage Paul is doing two things that biblical commentators frequently find problematic. First, there seems to be an abandonment of a literal for an allegorical interpretation of Scripture. As C. K. Barrett puts it, according to Paul (and contrary to its literal meaning), "in the Old Testament law God has in mind

18. Frear, "Caring for Animals," p. 7.

not oxen, but Christian preachers and their needs."[19] The second problem is that Paul, in support of his allegorical interpretation, argues that because we could not suppose that God is concerned with oxen, some alternative meaning must be assigned to this passage. This is problematic because, as Hans Conzelmann notes, "The quotation – Deut. 25:4 – is, contrary to Paul's exegesis, essentially a rule for the protection of animals."[20]

For our purposes what is problematic is the question posed by Paul, to which he suggests a negative answer: "Is it for oxen that God is concerned?" And if God is not concerned with oxen, then by implication God is not concerned with any other animal either. This is hardly what the proponent of moral concern for animals wants to hear. Barrett, for one, does not believe that the implication holds. He comments, "This does not mean that Paul would have denied the truth . . . that God is concerned even over the fall of a sparrow; but it was a quite different truth that he found in the O.T. and expressed here."[21] So although God is not concerned with oxen in this particular text, that still leaves open the possibility of other texts teaching just such a concern. Other interpreters make a different move. They do not see Paul denying the literal meaning of Deuteronomy 25:4. They only see him claiming that there is also a deeper meaning to be found in the passage in addition to the literal one. Nor do they see Paul denying God's concern with oxen, but only claiming that God's primary concern is with humans.[22] Yet, F. F. Bruce rejects all such efforts at ameliorating the force of Paul's words. Bruce says that Paul's "argument may clash with modern exegetical method [preference for the literal rather than the allegorical method] and western sentiment [a concern for animals], but he must be allowed to mean what he says."[23]

So as we look to Scripture for vindication of moral concern for animals, we do find texts and considerations supportive of that concern, but we also find some problematic texts. This apparent mix is not peculiar to moral concern for animals, as we shall underscore in the next section.

19. C. K. Barrett, *A Commentary on the First Epistle to the Corinthians* (New York: Harper and Row, 1968), p. 205.

20. Hans Conzelmann, *1 Corinthians* (Philadelphia: Fortress, 1975), p. 154.

21. Barrett, *A Commentary on the First Epistle to the Corinthians,* pp. 205-6.

22. Charles F. Pfeiffer and Everett F. Harrison, *Wycliffe Bible Commentary* (Chicago: Moody, 1962), p. 1243.

23. F. F. Bruce, *New Century Bible: First and Second Corinthians* (London: Oliphants, 1971), pp. 84-85.

THE BIBLE, SLAVES, AND ANIMALS

In some ways, Christians who are beginning to take seriously moral concern for animals are in much the same position vis-à-vis the Bible as those Christians in a previous century who began to see the grievous evil associated with slavery, or Christians in our own century who are beginning to see the evil associated with the subordination of women. In both cases, there is now widespread recognition that these are matters of critical moral importance, yet they were not so for the writers of Scripture.

Consider slavery. For eighteen hundred years the Christian community lived more or less at peace with slavery. Christians could build magnificent cathedrals, be deeply moved by the singing of Gregorian chant, and still find slavery unobjectionable. Christian thinkers could engage in detailed biblical and theological analysis in the course of addressing a wide range of moral and social issues, all the while entertaining no serious moral reservations about the practice of buying and selling human beings. Then, in the eighteenth and nineteenth centuries, a moral awakening occurred, as Christians and others in large numbers began to see the evils of slavery. At this time, finally, there occurs a crucial change in the moral sensibilities of the Christian church and the West in general. As Stephen Clark has commented, "Christ promised his disciples that the Spirit would lead them into all truth (John 16:13), but the leading has indeed been long."[24]

But how, one may wonder, did Christians come to apprehend slavery's morally grievous character in a world where attitudes toward slavery were complacent and accepting? It was not the result, I suggest, of sophisticated exegetical analysis of biblical texts, nor — obviously — is it the product of stumbling across a hitherto overlooked text condemning slavery, for there is no such verse. In fact, Scripture may seem to have been more of an impediment to the Christian community's finally making a decisive break with slavery than it was a help. In the Old Testament, slavery, though regulated and restricted in certain ways, is, nevertheless, fully accepted.[25] Prophetic voices in the course of Old Testament history, with majesterial power, call down divine judgment upon many an evil but slav-

24. Clark, *The Moral Status of Animals,* p. 197.

25. It was required that Hebrew slaves be released after six years (Exod. 21:2-4). Hebrew slavery was, then, a bit more like indentured servitude. A slave could, however, pledge himself or herself, with an awl-pierced ear, to serve forever, or until the next Jubilee (Exod. 21:5-6; Deut. 15:16). On the other hand, non-Hebrews could be held as slaves in perpetuity, willing or not.

ery is not among them. In Jesus' own day there were slaves in Israel. One could walk the streets of Jerusalem and rub shoulders with men and women who were the property of others. But Jesus remained silent on the subject. Indeed, in a number of Jesus' parables, the naturalness of the slave-master relationship is assumed (Matt. 25:14-30; Mark 13:34; Luke 12:42-48; Luke 17:7-10). That is, slavery is used as an accepted backdrop to teach certain spiritual lessons.

The teachings of the epistles pose additional difficulties and could be invoked by defenders of slavery, as indeed they were from pulpits in the antebellum South. Thus, Paul enjoins slaves to be obedient to their masters. "Slaves, be obedient to those who are your earthly masters, with fear and trembling, in singleness of heart, as to Christ; not in the way of eye-service, as men-pleasers, but as servants of Christ, doing the will of God from the heart" (Eph. 6:5-6). And in Philemon we read that the runaway slave Onesimus, apparently newly converted to Christ, is to return to his master to serve him faithfully.

Indeed, faithfulness of slaves to their masters becomes a matter of Christian principle in the New Testament: "Slaves, accept the authority of your masters with all deference, not only those who are kind and gentle but also those who are harsh. For it is a credit to you if, being aware of God, you endure pain while suffering unjustly" (1 Peter 2:18-19 NRSV). This particular Scripture portion goes on to say that the slave who willingly submits to unjust punishment is approved by God and that he or she thereby follows in the footsteps of Christ himself. And this is not an isolated text. It is repeated throughout the epistles (cf. Col. 3:22-25; 1 Tim. 6:1-2; Titus 2:9-10). The need for this repetition arises from the fact that gentile Christian communities contained substantial numbers of slaves. Furthermore, there were Christian masters as well. This is seen from the admonitions directed at masters to treat their slaves justly and fairly (Eph. 6:9; Col. 4:1; 1 Tim. 6:2).

So there seems to be considerable textual ammunition for the southern white preacher in the 1850s to rebut attacks on slavery by Christian abolitionists. But despite such texts, Christians — indeed Christians with a high respect for the moral and theological authority of Scripture — came to judge slavery to be evil and took up the abolitionist's cause, a cause deemed worthy of killing and being killed for.

However it is that Christians finally come to judge slavery to be an evil, once they do, then, as an apologetical activity, they seek to handle those difficult texts that seem to suggest otherwise. They are here playing the role of apologists. They are defending Scripture against the charge that it is on the side of slavery and therefore morally defective. They are not principally seeking to decide whether slavery is right or wrong. That has already been done. What stands in need of argument and defense is the claim that there is a scriptural basis for that judgment. Various interpretive moves may be made and prominent among them has been contextualizing or relativizing biblical passages concerning slavery, so that their application is limited and rendered irrelevant to our present condemnation of the practice. However, what necessitates these interpretive moves (and a range of other observations that could be helpfully made) is the independent conviction that slavery is wrong. Thus, the working with these specific texts is typically an activity that occurs after we have come to see slavery to be an evil, not before.

But in saying this, I do not want to leave the impression that when it comes to slavery Scripture is merely an obstacle to be overcome or a book to be defended by hermeneutical and exegetical gymnastics. Scripture and its teachings are a force for good, and they are so here as elsewhere. They can shape attitudes toward other human beings and engender convictions about appropriate treatment of human beings that may render us increasingly uncomfortable with slavery and even bring us to the point of severely condemning it.

There are several themes in Scripture that might serve to awaken sensitivity to the evil of slavery. For example, all humans are made in the image of God (Gen. 1:26) and are to be respected accordingly; humans are not, because they are divine image bearers, to be killed (Gen. 9:6) or to be cursed (James 3:9). If cursing and killing is a failure to recognize the dignity of those who are in the image of God, might not reducing them to property also be such a failure? Moreover, we are, Jesus tells us, to do to others as we would have them do to us (Luke 6:31). As we reflect on what it would be like to be a slave and to have the status of property, we may ask ourselves, "Would I want this for myself and for those I love?" Further, as Christians we are nurtured by biblical stories and parables and poetry and exhortations that teach love and compassion. So nurtured we may increasingly become the kind of people who will rest uneasy with the practice of slavery, or at least become the kind of people who will be receptive to challenges to slavery when, in the course of historical events, those challenges come. It is in this way that Scripture bears negatively on slavery, not so much with specific anti-slavery texts, but by the creation of people with sensitivities and a moral vision that are, in the final analysis, at odds with it.

It is certainly not the case, then, that all anti-slavery sentiments have their source outside of Scripture. By no means. There are biblical themes – admittedly often very broad and general themes – of a moral and theological nature that can render one deeply uncomfortable with slavery and do so despite the presence of certain problematic texts. Similarly they may render us uncomfortable with the subordination of women and (maybe in time) with the denial of significant moral standing to animals – again, in both cases, despite certain problematic biblical texts.

I would suggest, then, that Christians who are committed to a dramatic revisioning of our attitudes toward and treatment of animals, and who are seeking a biblical basis for this, are no worse off, possibly better off, than those who in an earlier century turned to Scripture in order to condemn slavery. The biblical/exegetical task is no more daunting for, say, the Christian moral vegetarian or the Christian who wishes to argue for moral standing for animals than it was for the Christian abolitionists or for those who seek to articulate a biblical vision of full female equality.

The Christian community's attitude toward animals, as toward many a social and moral issue, is not merely the product of honest and tough-minded exegesis of Scripture, coupled with rigorous theological reflection. Working with Scripture and engaging in moral reflection do not occur in a vacuum. The questions that we put to Scripture and what we want Scripture to do for us change in the course of history, though we do not want to deny that Scripture can also play a role in raising new issues for us. But attitudes and moral outlooks can become so settled that reflective biblical engagement and self-critical moral analysis do not occur. So it has been with our moral attitudes toward animals. Animals have been simply placed outside the pale of moral concern. For most Christians it has not occurred to think about animals in connection with certain biblical texts and theological themes.

AUGUSTINE AND AFTER

As with so many things in the Christian tradition, so also with moral concern for animals, Augustine (354-430) has proved to be a watershed.[26] Augustine's view of animals emphasized their existence for humans. They had, to use contemporary terminology, instrumental but not intrinsic value. It is not that Augustine invented such a view, for it was expressed by both Chris-

26. What I have to say here is heavily indebted to Richard Sorabji, *Animal Minds and Human Morals: The Origins of the Western Debate* (Ithaca, N.Y.: Cornell University Press, 1993).

tian and pagan writers prior to Augustine. The difference was that prior to Augustine there was a debate over this issue, but with Augustine the debate virtually came to a close. Richard Sorabji puts matters this way:

> The Stoic view of animals, with its stress on their irrationality, became embedded in Western, Latin-speaking Christianity above all through Augustine. Western Christianity concentrated on one half, the anti-animal half, of the much more evenly balanced ancient debate. Although there were other strands in Western Christianity, I think this accounts for the relative complacency of our Western Christian tradition about the killing of animals. The ancient philosophers were less complacent. In the eighteenth century the tide began to turn, and in the last fifteen years it has accelerated, with a widespread rethinking of our treatment of animals.[27]

Prior to Augustine, John Chrysostom (c. 347-407), for example, claimed "that animals exist not necessarily for our use, but to proclaim the power of the Creator." Basil of Caesarea (c. 329-379), also known as Basil the Great, insisted "that animals live not for us alone, but for themselves and for God."[28] Indeed, Basil could pray,

> For those, O Lord,
> the humble beasts,
> that bear with us
> the burden and heat of the day,
> and offer their guileless lives
> for the well-being of humankind;
> and for the wild creatures
> whom Thou hast made
> wise, strong, and beautiful
> we supplicate for them
> Thy great tenderness of heart
> for Thou hast promised to save
> both man and beast
> and great is Thy loving kindness,
> O Master,
> Saviour of the world.[29]

27. Sorabji, *Animal Minds and Human Morals,* pp. 2-3.

28. Sorabji, *Animal Minds and Human Morals,* pp. 199-200.

29. *Love and Animals,* ed. Andrew Linzey and Tom Regan (New York: Crossroad, 1989), p. 86.

Basil thus prays for both domesticated and wild animals, commending them, along with their needs, to a compassion that extends to all creatures. Appropriately, those seeking to become like their Creator seek to be characterized by a similarly extensive compassion. Indeed, the prayer itself is an expression of such compassion and a liturgical means of encouraging and confirming it. Furthermore, the logic of prayer is surely such that we be prepared to help with deeds those for whom we have interceded with words.

But the influence of Augustine moved the Christian church in a different direction. Augustine adopted the Stoic view toward animals. The Stoics argued that the possession of reason was a necessary requirement for being a legitimate object of moral concern. In words that could have been written by a Stoic philosopher, Augustine declared, "For we see and appreciate from their cries that animals die with pain. But man disregards this in a beast, with which, as having no rational soul, he is linked by no community of law."[30] That animals feel pain and suffer is recognized by Augustine, but this generated no obligations to the animals who thus suffer. Moreover, he attributed to Christ the same Stoic view. He appealed to the Gospel account of the Gadarene swine, where Jesus, having cast out unclean spirits, sent them into a herd of about two thousand swine that, as a result, ran down a steep bank and into the sea where they drowned (Matt. 8:28-34; Mark 5:1-20; Luke 8:26-39). He appealed also to Jesus' cursing of the fig tree and causing it to wither because of its failure to bear fruit (Matt. 21:18-19; Mark 11:12-13, 20). Augustine commented that Jesus "judged that we had no community of justice with beasts and trees, and sent the devils into a flock of swine, and withered a tree by his curse, when he had found no fruit in it. . . ."[31]

In this attempt to establish that there is nothing wrong with killing animals because we have no obligations of any kind to them, Augustine was not arguing in a vacuum. He was explicitly responding to the "superstitious" vegetarianism of the Manichean movement. Augustine himself had been a Manichean for some nine years. The movement, started by a third-century Persian prophet, Mani, taught, among other curious doctrines, that by eating vegetables one is feeding on the divine light concealed in fruits and plants. This "holy feeding" was supposed to have transforming effects on the individual, something not achievable by eat-

30. From *De Moribus Manichaeorum* (2.17), quoted in Sorabji, *Animal Minds and Human Morals,* p. 196.

31. From *De Moribus Manichaeorum* (2.59), quoted in Sorabji, *Animal Minds and Human Morals,* p. 196.

ing animal flesh. On the contrary, because meat derives from the prince of darkness and consuming it strengthens the body's sensual lusts, it is not to be eaten. Moreover, Manicheans were forbidden from doing anything that could harm plant or animal life.

It was a concern to combat Manichean teaching that prompted Augustine, in the course of commenting on the sixth commandment, "Thou shalt not kill," to observe that the commandment doesn't apply to plants or to "irrational living things, whether flying, swimming, walking, or crawling, because they are not associated in a community with us by reason, since it is not given to them to have reason in common with us. Hence it is by a very just ordinance of the Creator that their life and death is subordinated to our use."[32] Here, then, we have the view that has become standard in the West among both secular and Christian thinkers. (1) The moral community is open only to rational creatures. (2) Only humans are rational creatures. (3) We have no (direct) moral obligations to animals. (4) Animals exist for the purpose of serving human ends.

The threats posed by the Manichean movement were not the only concern that prompted Augustine to address the place of animals within a Christian worldview. Interestingly, the suggestion that God is not concerned with individual animals also posed a serious problem for Augustine. There were farmers, according to Henry Chadwick, the eminent ancient church historian, who were attracted to paganism because they concluded that only the pagan gods would care for their animals. Paul's comments in 1 Corinthians 9:9-10 seemed to indicate that God had no concern with individual animals — in this particular case, no concern with the farmer's oxen.[33] Augustine sought to assure these farmers, despite Paul's words, that God's providential care extends to individual animals, not merely to species. In making his case, Augustine refers them to Jesus' words: "Are not two sparrows sold for a penny? And not one of them will fall to the ground without your Father's will" (Matt. 10:29; cf. Luke 12:6). This, he argued, reflects God's providential care for individual animals.[34] So, curiously, although God's providential care extends to each animal, nevertheless we humans have no moral obligations to individual animals. Divine concern is not to translate into human moral concern.

In arguing that we can kill animals with no moral reservations because we have no obligations at all to animals, we are led to awkward con-

32. Augustine, *City of God* 1.20.

33. Sorabji, *Animal Minds and Human Morals,* p. 195 n. 2.

34. Sorabji, *Animal Minds and Human Morals,* p. 168.

clusions. Not only does this argument grant us moral permission to kill, but it serves equally well to grant us moral permission to torture animals for fun or to do with animals whatever we please. Augustine, however, makes no attempt to address such issues or to provide us with anything approximating a fully thought-out position on our treatment of animals, for his comments on animals are incidental to his pastoral concern with Manicheanism and with farmers attracted to paganism. Nevertheless, despite the somewhat incidental character of these discussions, Augustine's influence has been enormous.

Augustine's use of the biblical account of the Gadarene swine, whatever it may show, does not demonstrate that Jesus endorsed the Stoic view that we have moral obligations only to rational creatures. It is consistent with such a view, of course, but it does not entail it. Jesus could have believed that we have no moral obligations to pigs (and other animals) but have believed this for reasons quite other than the one attributed to him by Augustine. Or it could be that we have moral obligations to animals but that refraining from killing them is not one of those obligations. Or it could be that we have moral obligations to animals, including not killing them unless there is present an overriding reason for doing so, and possibly Jesus had an overriding reason for casting the demons into the swine.[35]

The fact remains that Augustine is a pivotal figure in determining Western and Christian attitudes toward animals. As Sorabji notes, he brought the debate over moral attitudes toward animals to a close. Fortunately, the debate is being reopened in the larger community, and it would be salutary for this debate to reopen in the Christian community as well.

Thomas Aquinas continued Augustine's line of thought. Indeed, he quoted *City of God* 1:20 with approval[36] and thus reaffirmed the Stoic view that Augustine had adopted, that we have no direct moral duties to animals because they are not rational beings. Aquinas also observed, "If any passage in holy scripture seems to forbid us to be cruel to brute animals that is either . . . lest through being cruel to animals one becomes cruel to

35. It may be worth a passing observation that Porphyry, the most able, systematic critic of Christianity in the ancient world, in his *Against the Christians,* used the story of the Gadarene swine to attack Christianity. Porphyry says, in Sorabji's words, "Christ was not much of a Saviour. He cast the devils out of the man possessed by devils. So far, so good. But why should he not banish them from the universe altogether? All he did was transfer them from a party he did care about to the swine whom he didn't" (Sorabji, *Animal Minds and Human Morals,* p. 181).

36. Thomas Aquinas, *Summa Theologica* 2.2., q. 64, a. 1.

human beings or because injury to an animal leads to the temporal hurt of man."[37] This has become standard Roman Catholic thinking.[38] And Protestants, with equal enthusiasm, have supported this view. Thus Calvin, for example, claimed that resting animals on the Sabbath had nothing to do with concern for animals but was to release men from the burden of caring for them on that day.[39]

This apparent turning of Old Testament teaching on its head, something Keith Thomas judges the Apostle Paul to have done in 1 Corinthians 9:9, prompts Thomas to comment, "It can indeed be argued that the Greek and Stoic influence distorted the Jewish legacy so as to make the religion of the New Testament much more man-centered than that of the Old; Christianity, it can be said, teaches, in a way that Judaism has never done, that the whole world is subordinate to man's purposes."[40] I would suggest that while Thomas's claim may be true of Christianity as it has often been interpreted through the centuries, nevertheless, Christians who reclaim their Old Testament heritage and sensitively interpret the New Testament will emerge with a quite different vision. They shall not have an anthropocentric vision, one that sees everything in the universe having meaning and point only so far as it serves human ends. On such a view, so much of creation turns out to be superfluous and seems to have no point at all, since it does not serve any discernible human ends. Rather, in contrast, they shall have a theocentric vision, one that sees God's purposes as multiple, investing creation and the world in which we live with purposes and meaning at many different levels. Indeed, they shall see themselves living in what one philosopher has called "a morally deep world," a world in which we are morally significant and in which "beings on many different levels are morally significant."[41]

37. Thomas Aquinas, *Summa contra Gentiles* iii.113.

38. Cf. Henry Daves, *Moral and Pastoral Theology*, vol. 2, *Commandments of the Church*, fifth ed. (London: Sheed and Ward, 1946), pp. 258-59.

39. Charles William Bingham, ed., *Commentaries on the Four Last Books of Moses* (Edinburgh, 1852-55), iii.56-57. Cited in Keith Thomas, *Man and the Natural World* (New York: Pantheon Books, 1983), p. 358 n. 9.

40. Thomas, *Man and the Natural World*, p. 24.

41. Lawrence E. Johnson, *A Morally Deep World: An Essay on Moral Significance and Environmental Ethics* (Cambridge: Cambridge University Press, 1991), p. 28.

CONCLUSION

This chapter provides some encouragement, I trust, to Christians with a moral concern for animals. It also provides them with a significant challenge. The encouragement is that there is a biblical basis for such concern, that Christianity is not religiously isolated in having sacred texts that are indifferent to animals and their appropriate treatment. The challenge is to come to terms with all of Scripture and to begin the task of articulating a thorough and defensible theological vision of animals and their place in the moral universe. This is a task that requires many hands – in short, a community effort.

In the most general sense, concern for animals is sharing in a concern that we believe to be God's and involves seeing our concern as an extension of God's concern. It is seeking to understand God's concern that is our central task. Moral, biblical, and theological reflection will all be involved in this effort. Nevertheless, one can begin to act on that concern without having all the answers to all the questions that might reasonably be put to one. In this regard moral concern for animals is no different than other legitimate and recognized moral concerns. Theoretical reflection and debate will continue forever, no matter what the moral subject matter. One does not want, however, to have one's active concern for animals paralyzed by the existence of this unfinished theoretical task. The call to moral engagement is a call that is always accompanied by a theoretical agenda that is incomplete. Thus a recognition that there is more to do at the reflective level should not mean that active moral concern, compassion, and respect for animals must wait to find living expression in our lives and in our advocacy.

CHAPTER 12

Animal Suffering and the Problem of Evil

INTRODUCTION

The most serious objection to belief in a good and all-powerful God has always been an objection based on the presence of evil in the world — that vast amount of sin and suffering witnessed and experienced in every generation. How, we wonder, can a good and all-powerful God allow the savagery and horror of disease, starvation, war, and death that afflicts our world? This, of course, is a classic objection to theistic belief, the well-known problem of evil. And the Christian community has provided a range of responses in an effort to show that the presence of evil in the world does not constitute an insuperable obstacle to rational belief in a morally perfect and all-powerful God. But in articulating these responses, both in assessing the extent of evil in the world and in fashioning an explanation for the presence of that evil, often little or no serious consideration is given to the suffering of animals. This constitutes a serious omission, for we live in a world where not only humans suffer, experience pain, and die, but where an even larger number of nonhuman animals suffer, experience pain, and die. Indeed, as Andrew Linzey comments, "In principle, the question of how an almighty, loving God can allow suffering in a mouse is no different to the same question that may be posed about man. Of course there are important differences between men and mice, but there are no morally relevant ones when it comes to pain and suffering."[1]

1. Andrew Linzey, *Christianity and the Rights of Animals* (New York: Crossroad, 1987), p. 60.

We must come to recognize that animal suffering constitutes at least a part – and a neglected part – of the problem of evil. Consider the kind of incident that forcefully raises for us the problem of evil in its *human* dimension: a woman is kidnapped, brutally tortured, and then killed. Possibly we read about this in the newspaper. We are shocked and understandably wonder: how could a loving and powerful God allow such a thing? In asking that question we have, of course, dramatically raised for ourselves the problem of evil. But does not the following incident also raise for us that same problem? "They administered beatings to dogs with perfect indifference, and made fun of those who pitied the creatures as if they felt pain. . . . They nailed poor animals up on boards by their forepaws to vivisect them and see the circulation of the blood which was a great subject of conversation."[2] Do we not wonder here, as with the previous case of the kidnapped and tortured woman, why a loving and powerful God would allow such a thing to happen? We may believe that what happened to the woman was worse than what happened to the dogs, but it does not follow that what happened to the dogs was inconsequential. And would not a perfectly good Being want to stop what happened to the dogs as well as what happened to the woman? Would not compassion intercede for both and is not our God a God of compassion? So in addition to human suffering, we have animal suffering to exacerbate the problem of evil for us.

It is not that animal pain and suffering exacerbates the problem of evil by adding to the pain and suffering in the world. Rather, animal suffering intensifies the problem of evil, as C. S. Lewis noted, "because the Christian explanation of human pain cannot be extended to animal pain. So far as we know beasts are incapable either of sin or virtue: therefore they can neither deserve pain nor be improved by it."[3] Yet animals suffer, innocent of sin and without guilt, who cannot be morally or spiritually benefited by the ravages of pain, who cannot place any meaningful or elevating interpretation upon their suffering, and who will not (according to most) be compensated for their suffering by another life beyond the grave. It would seem that some animals have been brought into existence only to suffer and die, and possibly along the way be put to use by humans: killed for food and clothing, harnessed as beasts of burden, hunted for sport, experimented upon, and in general valued only to the extent that they con-

2. From a 1738 memoir by Nicholas Fontaine quoted in James Rachels, *Created from Animals* (New York: Oxford University Press, 1990), p. 130.

3. C. S. Lewis, *The Problem of Pain* (New York: Macmillan, 1962), p. 129.

tribute one way or another to the satisfaction of human interests. And so the question emerges: how can we understand animal pain and suffering so as to make peace with a vision of a God whose compassion extends to all his creatures?

Lewis, for one, struggled with these difficulties but retained his belief in a loving and powerful God, but this has not been true for all who have confronted the enormity of animal suffering. One of the most famous casualties was Charles Darwin, who in describing the development of his own religious thought — from orthodoxy to agnosticism[4] — points to animal suffering and his inability to make religious sense out of it as a crucial factor in his abandoning Christianity. Darwin wrote:

> That there is much suffering in the world no one disputes. Some have attempted to explain this in reference to man by imagining that it serves for his moral improvement. But the number of men in the world is as nothing compared with that of all other sentient beings, and these often suffer greatly without any moral improvement. A being so powerful and so full of knowledge as a God who could create this universe, is to our finite minds omnipotent and omniscient, and it revolts our understanding to suppose that his benevolence is not unbounded, for what advantage can there be in the suffering of millions of the lower animals throughout almost endless time? This very old argument from the existence of suffering against the existence of an intelligent first cause seems to me a strong one. . . .[5]

But this is not simply the old argument from suffering. It is the old argument from suffering bolstered considerably by appeal to the great amount of animal suffering in the world. And what should we in the Christian community say to Darwin? Indeed, is there anything we can say?

ANIMALS DO NOT FEEL PAIN

One straightforward way to deal with this difficulty is to deny that animals experience pain. If animals do not feel pain, then of course they cannot be said to suffer pain unjustly, and this perplexing aspect of the prob-

4. Charles Darwin, *The Autobiography of Charles Darwin, 1809-1882* (New York: W. W. Norton and Company, 1958), pp. 85-96.

5. Darwin, *The Autobiography of Charles Darwin,* p. 90.

lem of evil need no longer detain us. The denial of animal pain, if credible, would circumvent the need for a protracted theological justification that might in the final analysis fail, and perhaps this is what prompts some within the Christian tradition to choose just such a response. This is exactly how contemporary Roman Catholic philosopher Dom Trethowan responds. In prose that borders on the humorous, he says, "a cat is so arranged that if you pull its tail, a noise comes from the other end."[6] There is, apparently, no pain between the pulling of the tail and the subsequent squealing. Still another Christian apologist asserts,

> It appears to me that an examination of instinctive animal behavior reveals a very interesting and, indeed, very mysterious, psychism, but one that is devoid of consciousness of any kind. . . . If this is indeed the case, the problem of animal "suffering" is an empty one, as "unconscious suffering" is a contradiction in terms. To suffer and not be aware of the fact, to suffer and not to be conscious of suffering, is the same as not suffering at all.[7]

We are further told that those who interpret animal cries as expressions of pain are "victims of a serious illusion." In short, because there is no animal pain and suffering, there is no challenge to God's goodness calling for an apologetical response.

Nicholas Malebranche (1638-1715), the principal disciple of Descartes, and a Roman Catholic priest as well as a philosopher, argued that since it would make no theological sense for animals, who have never sinned and who are completely free of guilt, to experience pain, that therefore we must conclude, for that reason alone, that they simply don't experience any pain. Referring to animals, Malebranche wrote, "Being innocent, if they were capable of feeling, the effect would be that under the government of an infinitely just and all-powerful God an innocent creature would suffer pain, which is a penalty, and the punishment of some sin."[8] Certainly Malebranche senses the problem here: it makes no moral sense for a good God to inflict pain and suffering on any creature unless it deserves that pain and suffering, which would not be true of innocent animals. So confident was Malebranche that a just and powerful God was

6. Dom Trethowan, *An Essay in Christian Philosophy* (London: Longmans, Green and Co., 1954), p. 41.

7. Fernand van Steenberghen, *Hidden God* (St. Louis: B. Herder Book Co., 1966), p. 252.

8. Quoted in John Passmore, "The Treatment of Animals," *Journal of the History of Ideas* 36 (1975): 204.

in control of the universe that he was quite prepared to deny the reality of animal pain. Driven by theological necessity (and supported by Cartesian arguments) he concludes that animals are not sentient: "They eat without pleasure, they cry without sorrow . . . they desire nothing, they fear nothing, they know nothing."[9] Because a good God is in charge of the universe it follows that innocent animals will not be allowed to suffer and feel pain, and therefore they don't, appearances to the contrary.

Peter Harrison is the most recent apologist to seek to solve the problem of animal pain by denying its existence.[10] His is a protracted and in many ways interesting discussion. Harrison argues that whereas humans experience pain, there are good (e.g., evolutionary) reasons to believe that animals do not; he also seeks to refute standard arguments on behalf of the reality of animal pain (e.g., higher animals have a nervous system similar to our own; pain research carried out on animals is applicable to human beings; animals will howl or scream and seek to escape from what we judge to be pain-producing situations; etc.) After presenting his case (which I have only alluded to) he concludes: "The case I have presented is not clearly false, and at best is highly plausible."[11] But, as with all such arguments, which are never indisputable, matters seem to come down to this: Can we bring ourselves to believe and act on the conclusion that animals do not experience pain? If we cannot – and it seems as difficult to believe that animals do not feel pain as it does to believe that plants and rocks do – then consistency at least requires that we seek a response that acknowledges the reality of animal pain. To seek to exonerate God by appealing to the possibility of a state of affairs that I myself cannot help but believe not to be the case, is not to argue with full integrity. I cannot, for example, rigorously support laws that prevent what I judge to be severe cruelty to animals or vigorously condemn (for their cruelty) those who break those laws or be appalled by tales of such cruelty and at the same time declare that God cannot be faulted for animal pain because there is no animal pain. Indeed, if we cannot join those particular followers of Descartes who "kicked about their dogs and dissected their cats without mercy, laughing at any compassion for them and calling their screams the noise of breaking machinery,"[12] then we must part

9. Quoted in Passmore, "The Treatment of Animals," p. 204.

10. Peter Harrison, "Theodicy and Animal Pain," *Philosophy* 64 (1989): 79-92.

11. Harrison, "Theodicy and Animal Pain," p. 92.

12. J. P. Mahaffy, *Descartes* (London, 1901), p. 118, cited in A. Richard Kingston, "Theodicy and Animal Welfare," *Theology* LXX, no. 569 (November 1967): 485.

company with those who would seek to construct an apology based on a denial of animal pain.[13]

ANIMALS FEEL LITTLE PAIN

While the denial that animals experience pain is not found believable by most people, a more persuasive line of thought suggests that animals suffer much less than many of us at first suppose and much less than do human beings. To reach this conclusion it is argued that animal awareness is more or less confined to the present moment, being neither vividly linked to the past by strong memory nor vividly linked to the future by foresight and anticipation.[14] Therefore, one could well suppose that when it comes to mental anguish, at least, this is a distinct advantage – the animal does not carry with it agonizing memories (e.g., the zebra does not continue to sorrow for its young offspring killed by beasts of prey, for such memories soon fade into oblivion) nor is the animal burdened by the anticipation of future ills (e.g., the zebra is not concerned with the fate that may befall it as it grows old).[15] Thus the animal's lot may be just what John Hick claims it to be: "The animal's goods and evils are exclusively those of the present moment, and in general it lives from instant to instant either in healthy and presumably pleasurable activity, or in a pleasant state of torpor. The picture, then, of animal life as a dark ocean of agonizing fear and pain is quite gratuitous and arises from the mistake of projecting our dis-

13. Harrison denies that he advocates beating pets and infants (who also, he argues, do not experience pain) but claims that there are other good reasons for not beating pets and infants. But as with most attempts at taking a common moral belief (e.g., it is wrong to beat pets and infants), removing the commonly accepted basis for that belief (e.g., it causes the pet and the infant to unnecessarily suffer great pain), and providing an alternative basis (e.g., it will offend onlookers or prompt us to mistreat those who do feel pain), we end up with a radically truncated moral belief, one that we hardly recognize. For one thing, the action of beating a dog with a baseball bat is no longer appalling in and of itself; for another, we may legitimately want to work for the day when we can beat the dog without it spilling over to mistreatment of those who do feel pain; finally, whenever we are reasonably convinced that the beating of the pet (or non-pet) will have no negative secondary effects, we can beat without restraint.

14. Cf. George B. Wall, *Is God Really Good?* (Washington, D.C.: University Press of America, 1983), pp. 97-100.

15. Here one thinks of the words of Bobby Burns, who wrote, comparing his condition to that of animals, "Still thou art blest, compar'd wi' me! The present only toucheth thee. But, Och! I backward cast my e'e, On prospects drear! An' forward, tho' I cannot see, I guess an' fear!"

tinctively human quality of experience into creatures of a much lower and simpler order."[16] And even when death comes, though it usually comes violently, it more often than not comes swiftly, possibly being preferable to a lingering death in a cancer ward.[17] Further, the concept of death, in the sense of annihilation, is not a concept that we have reason to suppose is possessed by any animal: for them there can be no fear of passing out of existence, no dread of death's finality. There are no Kierkegaards in the animal kingdom.

This is not to deny that animals suffer, sometimes horribly, often at human hands, nor is it to deny that they can experience painful emotions (such as fear and frustration). Nor should we think that an animal's confinement to the present moment, reducing as it does its mental anguish, has only positive value. Thus, precisely because animals lack vivid links to the future (or to the past) physical pain may actually be worse, since "there are no future-oriented distractions to mitigate these powerful sensations."[18] Further, although being largely restricted to the present means that animals do not suffer the anguish of painful memories or anticipated evils, it also denies animals the pleasure of happy memories and happy anticipations. Whether on balance this is a plus or a minus, or just a draw, is difficult to say.

These qualifying remarks only serve to confirm that animal pain continues to be a problem for us. For in order to generate the problem of evil in its human dimension it was never necessary to establish that human life is a "dark ocean of agonizing fear and pain" (which it is not), so why should it be necessary to establish this to be the case for animals in order to generate the problem of evil in its animal dimension? Thus to argue, even successfully, that animal life is *not* a "dark ocean of agonizing

16. John Hick, *Evil and the God of Love,* rev. ed. (New York: Harper and Row, 1978), p. 314.

17. Predators are not, however, always efficient killers quickly dispatching their prey. One thinks of those animals that are the prey of the spotted hyena, which has no specific, quick method of killing but rather kills its prey simply by eating it. An expert on the spotted hyena describes the process as follows: "It is rare that the victim puts up any significant active defence; usually a group of hyenas has no difficulty in attacking the hind-quarters of an animal, biting its loins and anal region and, if there are many hyenas, also the throat and chest. They tear chunks away of skin, muscles and intestines, and this will bring down the victim and kill it in anything from 1 to 13 minutes" (H. Krunk, *The Spotted Hyena,* quoted in Marian Stamp Dawkins, *Animal Suffering* [New York: Chapman and Hall, 1980], p. 52).

18. Burt Gruzalski, "The Case Against Raising and Killing Animals for Food," in *Ethics and Animals,* ed. Harlan B. Miller and William H. Williams (Clifton, N.J.: Humana, 1983), p. 257.

fear and pain" does not solve our problem. The fact remains (it is reasonable to believe) that animals suffer physical pain and suffer from negative emotions, and at times they suffer considerably. In the wild, animals can die of starvation and thirst (which we have every reason to believe is unpleasant); they usually die violently, being devoured by beasts of prey (which we also have reason to believe is unpleasant whether or not preferable to many human deaths); animals, in large numbers, have been treated painfully by humans (whether justifiably or not), and here we need only reflect on fur trapping, toxicity testing, and various forms of experimentation (and for some of these animals perhaps life does become a "dark ocean of agonizing fear and pain"). And whether animals suffer more or less than humans is not quite to the point. The fact remains that they suffer and in given instances suffer considerably. That itself is sufficient to pose a serious problem for the construction of a satisfactory vision of a loving and powerful Creator providentially in control of all life that he has called into existence.

IT DOESN'T MATTER THAT ANIMALS FEEL PAIN

It may be suggested that although animals do suffer and at times suffer considerably, that fact is of no moral consequence, and therefore it casts no doubt on the goodness of God. It would be argued that because animals lack some essential feature that human beings possess (e.g., a soul, being in the image of God, the attainment of a certain level of rationality) their pain, unlike human pain, is not an evil and does not need to be removed. So, it is not pain per se that is an evil but (for example) pain experienced by one who has a soul or pain experienced by one who is in the image of God or pain experienced by one who has a certain level of rationality. Since animals lack the requisite property, their suffering, though it may be every bit as intense as the suffering of one with a soul or whatever other qualification is being used, is still of no consequence — it simply does not matter that they suffer.

There are two immediate difficulties with such a view. First, there is no reason to believe that such an argument rests on any credible moral principle, as, for example, "Pain is not an evil if the one suffering has no soul, is not in the image of God, or lacks a human-level rationality." Indeed, why should one even be tempted to adopt such a principle? A second difficulty with the proposal that animal pain doesn't matter is one already encountered when dealing with the denial that animals experience pain. That denial, we noted, is not something that most of us can bring ourselves to believe, nor can we bring ourselves, certainly in severe cases, to believe that it simply doesn't matter that animals experience pain. Our laws against cruelty to animals bespeak not only our conviction that animals suffer and can be cruelly treated, but also our conviction that it would be better that they not suffer. In other words, we strongly believe it does matter.

But possibly animal pain, although a source of concern to us, is not of concern to God. The distinguished contemporary philosopher Peter Geach has made the suggestion that God is in fact indifferent to animal suffering and that he cannot be faulted for this indifference because in God's case such indifference is not a failure to have the appropriate virtue, as it would be with human beings should they be similarly indifferent.[19] There are many virtues, Geach argues, that we can ascribe to humans that we cannot ascribe to God (for a range of reasons): chastity, courage, honesty, gratitude. Additionally, according to Geach, we cannot ascribe to God "the virtue of sympathy with physical suffering." Geach says "physical suffering" unqualified by "animal" or "nonhuman," so God must be indifferent not only to physical suffering in animals but also to physical suffering in humans. And why does it make no sense to ascribe to God the virtue of sympathy with physical suffering? Because, Geach argues, God does not share our animal nature. In contrast, because we do share an animal nature, being animals ourselves, it is a virtue in us to sympathize with the physical suffering of animals (to a point, Geach cautions) and a vice not to; but with God, who lacks an animal nature, matters are entirely different. So, although I should sympathize with the intense physical suffering, say, of a dog being cruelly abused, God cannot sympathize and because he cannot sympathize it is not a vice that he does not.

This seems to amount to the position that God is ignorant of the fact that physical suffering is an evil, God being ignorant because he cannot appreciate the character of such suffering as a result of his lack of an animal nature and hence his indifference. On the other hand, unlike God, we humans do understand and appreciate the evil of physical suffering, ought to sympathize with those who suffer, and ought to relieve suffering wherever we can reasonably do so, becoming thereby agents of mercy, but not, apparently, agents of divine mercy. This, however, is theologically problematic. To conclude that there are evils that we, but not God, recog-

19. Peter Geach, *Providence and Evil* (New York: Cambridge University Press, 1977), pp. 76-80.

nize and abhor is to attribute to God an unacceptable moral ignorance. Or to claim that God knows that physical suffering is an evil but that he is still indifferent to it would be to attribute to God a moral fault – indifference to known evil. Further, a divine indifference to physical suffering seems incompatible with an incarnational theology that worships a God who has entered history in human form and has identified with and participated in the full range of suffering that characterizes our historical-biological existence. In the incarnation God knows physical suffering and what God knows incarnationally God knows eternally. This is not to suggest that without an incarnation God could not have known and fully appreciated the character of physical suffering: God is, after all, the Creator who has designed and made all physical organisms in all of their neurological intricacy (in the words of one hymn, "well our feeble frame he knows"). But with the incarnation God identifies with our suffering in its varied dimensions and declares to us that he understands. And so the believer who, prostrate in prayer, intercedes for those who suffer physically is not met with dull incomprehension but with compassion – a compassion that extends, we may well suppose, to *all* his creatures.

ANIMAL PAIN CAN BE COMPENSATED FOR IN AN AFTERLIFE

Perhaps, we may ponder, could not God's compassion prompt him to grant to all his sentient creatures, human and nonhuman, an afterlife? Could we not find in just such an exercise of divine power a partial answer to the perplexing problem of animal pain? Could this not at least alleviate our problem, even if not completely solve it? Indeed, for many, the problem of evil in its human dimension would be insoluble and an insurmountable obstacle to faith were it not for the possibility of an eschatological resolution – an afterlife in which an earthly spiritual journey finds its fulfillment and where the redeemed enter fully into the joy of their salvation. With this possibility, all unjust pain and suffering can be accepted because it is not the last word to the one who suffers. There awaits for her a greater good that renders all the suffering worthwhile. But do not such considerations also apply to animals, as well as to human beings? Should not animals be included in this eschatological resolution? The Christian philosopher Keith Ward thinks so and comments, "if one supposes that every sentient being has an endless existence which offers the prospect of supreme happiness, it is surely true that the sorrows and troubles of this life will seem very small by comparison. Immortality for animals as well as humans is a necessary condition of any acceptable theodicy. . . ."[20] Ward argues that if we reject the idea of animal immortality, then we face the difficult task of making peace with a God who brings into existence creatures "whose sole destiny was to suffer pain"; but that, he contends, is incompatible with the doctrine that God is love.[21]

ANIMAL IMMORTALITY: ITS HISTORY

"At present," it has been observed, "if a member of the Christian clergy begins seriously to wonder if there is salvation for dogs and cats, he or she is quite likely to be either laughed at, sent for psychiatric examination, or excommunicated."[22] This may be so, but these clerics will at least have the consolation of finding themselves in good company, indeed even in illustrious company. For it was in 1767 that Richard Dean's book *Essay on the Future Life of Brutes* was published in Great Britain. In that book Dean sought to establish the immortality of nonhuman animals, or "brutes," as he called them. Even then Dean could observe, as he did in his preface, that the thesis for which he was arguing was "not quite so novel as some folks perhaps have been inclined to imagine." The contemporary Oxford historian Keith Thomas, from whom Dean's words are taken, notes that Dean was "correct" to observe that the central idea of his book was not novel.[23] For what Richard Dean was advocating in 1767, the salvation of cats and dogs, was not original with him, nor was he a lonely advocate.[24] Those of his own era, the eighteenth century, who considered animal immortality at least an open possibility and argued accordingly included Samuel Clark (1675-1729), the English philosopher and defender of orthodox Christianity against deism; Bishop Joseph Butler (1692-1752), bishop of Bristol and Durham, Dean of St. Paul's, author

20. Keith Ward, *Rational Theology and the Creativity of God* (New York: Pilgrim, 1982), pp. 201-2.

21. Keith Ward, *The Concept of God* (Oxford: Basil Blackwell, 1974), p. 223. Ward, no doubt, overstates the case here. For animals, though they suffer pain, also experience pleasure, so they are not simply condemned to pain.

22. Harlan B. Miller, introduction to *Ethics and Animals,* ed. Miller and Williams, p. 3.

23. Keith Thomas, *Man and the Natural World* (New York: Pantheon Books, 1983), p. 140.

24. For the names of those eighteenth- and nineteenth-century figures who advocated or were open to the possibility of animal immortality I am dependent upon Keith Thomas, *Man and the Natural World,* pp. 137-42. I have selected some (but not all) of those that he lists, and I have added my own biographical comments.

of the famous *The Analogy of Religion,* whose work in the field of ethics is still widely anthologized; William Whiston (1667-1752), the English theologian and mathematician who succeeded Newton as Lucasian Professor of Mathematics at Cambridge, and whose translation of the works of Josephus is still read; David Hartley (1705-1757), the philosopher and psychologist, "sincere and fervent Christian," fellow of the Royal Society, and influential ethicist. Those less tentative and even more emphatic in their advocacy of an animal afterlife included Matthew Henry (1662-1714), clergyman and author of what has proved to be the most enduring devotional commentary written on the Bible in the English language, *Matthew Henry's Commentary;* Augustus Toplady (1740-1778), clergyman and proponent of Calvinism within the Church of England who was the author of "Rock of Ages" and other hymns; John Wesley (1703-1791), the founder of Methodism and perhaps the most famous advocate of animal immortality, who, in his sermon "The General Deliverance," declared that opposition to this idea was a "vulgar prejudice" and "contrary to the plain word of God." No – Richard Dean was not a lonely eighteenth-century advocate of animal immortality; indeed, those of greater fame and ability stood with him in his advocacy.

Also in the following century, and throughout the Victorian era, the idea of animal immortality continued to have able defenders. They included the poets Samuel Taylor Coleridge (1772-1834) and Robert Southey (1774-1843); Adam Clarke (1762-1832), a distinguished Wesleyan preacher whose commentary on the whole Bible, theological writings, translations, and wide-ranging intellectual interests brought him considerable scholarly acclaim; William Hamilton Drummond (1778-1865), Presbyterian minister, poet, hymn writer, and member of the Royal Irish Academy; Mary Sommerville (1780-1872), mathematician and scientist, after whom Sommerville College, Oxford, is named; and Anthony Ashley Cooper, Seventh Earl of Shaftesbury (1801-1885), philanthropist and reformer, strong supporter of evangelical causes, and president of the British and Foreign Bible Society.

In our own twentieth century, sympathizers with the notion of an animal afterlife have included C. S. Lewis,[25] the popular and widely read Christian apologist; more recently Roman Catholic theologian Edward Quinn;[26] and Anglicans Keith Ward,[27] Regius Professor of Divinity at Ox-

25. Lewis, *The Problem of Pain,* pp. 125-28.

26. Edward Quinn, "Animals in Heaven," *New Blackfriars* (May 1984), pp. 224-26.

27. Ward, *Rational Theology and the Creativity of God,* pp. 201-2.

ford University, and Andrew Linzey,[28] who holds the first fellowship in theology and animal welfare at Oxford University.

SCRIPTURE AND ANIMAL RESURRECTION

Animal resurrection is not explicitly taught in Scripture, despite John Wesley's conviction that Romans 8:21 "plainly" teaches just such a doctrine.[29] The context of that significant verse is as follows:

> For the anxious longing of the creation waits eagerly for the revealing of the sons of God. For the creation was subjected to futility, not willingly, but because of Him who subjected it, in hope that the creation itself also will be set free from its slavery to corruption into the freedom of the glory of the children of God. For we know that the whole creation groans and suffers the pains of childbirth together until now. (Rom. 8:19-22 NASB)

Here Paul declares that one day nature, along with the children of God, will be completely redeemed and that in that day the natural order will attain the beauty, perfection, harmony, and imperishability that was God's original intent. Although in the twenty-first verse Paul asserts that creation (most likely both animate and inanimate nature) will be set free from corruption, "There is," as Frederick Godet comments, "nothing to show that the apostle has in view the return to life of the individual beings comprising the present system of nature."[30] Nevertheless, that would be quite compatible with Paul's vision of a perfected natural order set free from all corruption. Here we might distinguish between two theories, each consistent with Romans 8:19-22, each projecting a future redeemed natural order populated by animals.

The first theory can be called *creation de novo:* animals will be newly created by God expressly for this perfected cosmic order, being made free from the "corruption" that characterizes those animals that inhabit our present fallen world. It is not, on this view, that formerly existing animals

28. Linzey, *Christianity and the Rights of Animals,* pp. 36-39.

29. Wesley set forth his view on this subject in his sermon "The General Deliverance," which can be found in *The Works of John Wesley,* vol. 2, ed. Albert C. Outler (Nashville: Abingdon, 1985), pp. 437-50.

30. Frederick L. Godet, *Commentary on the Epistle to the Romans* (Grand Rapids: Zondervan, 1969), p. 315.

are to be individually renewed and restored to life but rather they are to be replaced by a new creation, discontinuous with the old. Former species may be preserved (the lion and the lamb will be there to lie down together) but former members of these species will not be preserved (no formerly existing lion will lie down with any formerly existing lamb). Thus Christ's work of cosmic redemption is to be understood differently as it relates to human beings, on the one hand, and to animals, on the other. In the case of human beings, Christ's redemptive power reaches back into time and preserves for eternity all those who are his children – not one will perish but each individual identity will be protected and preserved forever. But the animal kingdom will be redeemed in a different fashion: various species (lions and lambs, etc.) may be preserved and rendered free of corruption but not so for any formerly existing member of those species. They have perished forever. Strictly speaking, the nonhuman inhabitants of the present natural order are not so much redeemed as they are replaced. It is only in an extended sense, then, that animals can be said to be "redeemed."

The second theory is resurrection: animals will be resurrected and transformed after the pattern of the resurrection and transformation of human beings. Just as the resurrection of humans restores to life the formerly existing individual human being, so the resurrection of animals will restore to life formerly existing animals. Individual members of those species that are to be preserved will themselves be preserved. There will be lions and lambs in the redeemed world of nature because lions and lambs that once walked this earth will walk again. It is the individual animal that was at one time part of the present fallen order of nature that will be restored, renewed, and preserved, and thereby redeemed. It is just such a vision that is defended by those advocates of animal immortality who operate within the Christian tradition.

AN OBJECTION TO ANIMAL RESURRECTION CONSIDERED

In discussions over the possibility of an animal afterlife the question is not infrequently raised, "Where does one draw the line? Are all animals to be resurrected?" In asking this question the suggestion often is that somehow all of this is faintly ridiculous, as if one is asked to envision a resurrected order in which all the fleas and flies, lizards and lice, that have ever existed are brought back to life. The implication is that this is absurd. Here two observations are in order. First, a comparable line of questioning can be asked even if one rejects the idea of animal resurrection and advocates instead creation *de novo.* One can still press the question: "Are all species of animals to be created *de novo,* including fleas and flies, lizards and lice?" The one theory no more invites this kind of query than the other. Indeed, John Calvin in his own advocacy of what I have called creation *de novo* confronted this very question when he observed, "Some shrewd but unbalanced commentators ask whether all kinds of animals will be immortal."[31] Indeed, will those animals created especially to populate the heavenly realm and invested with immortality represent *each* species? Will immortal lions lie down with immortal lambs, as well as immortal anteaters with immortal ants? Calvin, however, admonishes his readers: "If we give free rein to these speculations, where will they finally carry us? Let us, therefore be content with this simple doctrine – their constitution will be such, and their order so complete, that no appearance either of deformity or of impermanence will be seen."[32] In essence, Calvin responds: only God knows the answer to such questions, and better we simply leave it to him; we are to accept the doctrine in its broad outline and leave the details for eternity. So whether animals are to be resurrected (as some have claimed) or newly created (as others have claimed), the same question can be raised. "Will all species be present in this new cosmic order or only some selected species?" Whatever embarrassment – if any – attaches to the one theory attaches to the other as well. And to this supposedly awkward question, it seems, Calvin has already given the most satisfactory response.

A second observation should also be made, namely, that whether we are concerned with the resurrection of animals or the resurrection of humans, the issue of drawing lines will confront us. For who, among what is broadly construed as human, will be resurrected? Will all those who die in infancy, for example? Some have thought so, but others have demurred. Austin Farrer ponders, "We shall still have to ask why the fact of being born should be allowed a decisive importance; we shall wonder what of children dying in the womb or suffering abortion; and we shall be at a loss where to draw the line."[33] Indeed, will a newly fertilized ova (a human zygote) that perishes (and millions upon millions of them do annually whether by spontaneous abortion or artificially induced means) share in the general resurrection from the dead? And what about the massively re-

31. John Calvin, *The Epistles of Paul the Apostle to the Romans and to the Thessalonians* (Grand Rapids: Eerdmans, 1961), p. 74.

32. Calvin, *The Epistles of Paul the Apostle to the Romans and to the Thessalonians,* p. 74.

33. Austin Farrer, *Love Almighty and Ills Unlimited* (Garden City, N.Y.: Doubleday, 1961), p. 166.

tarded who function at a level much below that of a normal chimpanzee, what of their fate? And what about the anencephalic infant, born without a cerebral cortex? Indeed, where do we draw the line? No doubt this matter needs to be left just where Austin Farrer left it when he wrote, "We may be sure that he (God) loves and saves whatever is there to be saved or loved; if his love or power does not act, it is because there is nothing to act upon. . . . But there is no certain light on this painful matter; nor is there any honesty in dogmatizing where we have nothing to go upon."[34] Thus it is that, even when dealing with human resurrection, issues of line-drawing emerge, and Farrer's judicious response applies, I suggest, to both animal and human resurrection – "We may be sure that God loves and saves whatever is there to be saved or loved."

ANOTHER OBJECTION TO ANIMAL RESURRECTION CONSIDERED

In part the rationale for invoking an animal resurrection is to provide a means whereby compensation for animal suffering can occur. For this to occur, however, it must be the case that the animal who suffers in this life and the animal who is resurrected in the next life are the same animal. It is not sufficient that the resurrected animal merely be of the same species or that it be a very good copy (even an exact copy) of the previously existing animal. It must be the numerically identical animal. But there may be problems here. Indeed, it has been seriously questioned whether even talk of a *human* resurrection is sensible or coherent, let alone an animal resurrection. Here one is quickly immersed in complicated questions of personal identity. What makes a person the same person over time? By virtue of what feature or features can we sensibly say that the resurrected Jones is really Jones rather than a copy of Jones? And so forth. But a careful analysis of the intelligibility of postmortem survival for human beings, which the Christian tradition assumes and which Christian apologists defend, would require a protracted discussion. Here I only wish to suggest that the resurrection of Fido is logically no more problematic than the resurrection of Jones.

As far as the resurrection of *bodies* is concerned, there are no differences between animals and humans that would warrant the claim that reconstituting or re-creating the body of Fido would be any more difficult than reconstituting or re-creating the body of Jones. As far as the *psychic*

34. Farrer, *Love Almighty and Ills Unlimited,* pp. 167-68.

life of animals is concerned, it is reasonable to affirm that animals (at a certain level of development) possess a mental life, an awareness and consciousness, an inner subjective existence, that is real, though less complex than that enjoyed by human beings. Further, if we believe that mental life is a radically different form of reality than physical existence, as body-mind dualists believe, then there is no reason to deny that animals have a nonphysical mind or what is also called a "soul." Indeed, if we are of the conviction that human consciousness is not a physical but an immaterial state, then we should be of the same conviction when it comes to animal consciousness. Therefore, if we believe that there is a nonphysical dimension of human beings that can be preserved by God beyond the grave, it is not difficult to believe that many animals possess a nonphysical or immaterial dimension that can also be preserved by God beyond the grave.[35]

But do animals also have self-awareness and therefore a self or a continuing ego that can (somehow) be preserved by God in a future resurrected order? If some kind of psychic continuity makes it possible for an animal who suffered in this life to be identical with the animal who is resurrected in the next life, this seems to require a continuing ego or self. It is plausible to affirm, however, that some animals are, in fact, self-conscious, and therefore that they possess a self or ego. Interestingly, the issues of animal self-consciousness may be an issue from which the Christian apologist can only emerge a winner. For where there is no self-consciousness and hence no ego or self, it may be the case that there can be no experience of pain and thus no need for a resurrection to secure compensation for undeserved pain. C. S. Lewis[36] and more recently Peter Harrison[37] have argued that with no self-consciousness there can be no painful experiences because, as Harrison argues, there can be no experiences that I own, that belong to me, and hence are painful to me.[38] Thus

35. Of course, it has been argued that the existence of a nonmaterial mind or soul is not necessary for postmortem existence and that human beings, even if they were only physical beings, could be preserved in conscious existence by God beyond the grave. Cf. Bruce Reichenbach, "Monism and the Possibility of Life After Death," *Religious Studies* 14, no. 1 (March 1978): 27-34; Clifford Williams, "The Irrelevance of Non-Material Minds," *Christian Scholars Review* 12, no. 4 (1983): 310-23. This is not a debate directly relevant to our present concerns. If a nonmaterial mind is not necessary for postmortem survival, then so be it. If such a dimension is required, then it is reasonable to believe that many animals have such a dimension.

36. Lewis, *The Problem of Pain,* p. 119.

37. Harrison, "Theodicy and Animal Pain," pp. 90ff.

38. David Bakan comments, "unless there is a psyche, unless there is an awake and conscious organism, there is nothing to which one can sensibly refer as pain. Pain exists

whereas the lack of an ego may preclude the possibility of resurrecting a formerly existing animal, it may also preclude the necessity for any such resurrection. So either way, the apologist can only benefit from the outcome of this debate. It may very well be, however, that higher animal forms have an ego, do experience pain, and can be resurrected, but that lower animal forms lack an ego, experience no pain, and cannot have what they do not need, namely, a resurrection.

BUT DOES AN ANIMAL RESURRECTION HELP?

In the context of the problem of evil, interest in an animal afterlife is prompted by a desire to find a means by which animals can be compensated for the pain and suffering they have endured in this life. If, in a resurrected state, the animal's quality of life is endlessly happy, then, it is suggested, that will offset the suffering and deprivation it may have undergone in this life. But, even granting the possibility and coherence of a doctrine of an afterlife for animals, it may not be clear how an afterlife would actually help. In this vein John Hick comments, "it is extremely doubtful whether even a zoological paradise, filled with pleasure and devoid of pain, could have any compensating value in relation to the momentary pangs of creatures who cannot carry their past experience with them in conscious memory."[39] Because animals are largely (though one need not say "exclusively") restricted in their consciousness to the present moment, with few or no vivid memories to link them to the past, it is difficult, it is argued, to see how a future life for animals can be compensation for past suffering. The difficulty is not how a future life of bliss can compensate for a past life of suffering but how this can be so for those who lack strong memories. And why are memories crucial? One might suppose (though Hick doesn't tell us) that memories are crucial because they are essential to recognizing and appreciating one's new circumstances, and only if one recognizes and appreciates one's new circumstances as an improvement over the past can those circumstances compensate for past suffering and deprivations.

But one can contest this claim. For "to compensate" only involves extending a sufficiently generous benefit to one who has suffered harm or

---

only in a conscious ego. . ." (*Disease, Pain and Sacrifice: Toward a Psychology of Suffering* [Chicago: University of Chicago Press, 1968], p. 70).

39. Hick, *Evil and the God of Love,* p. 316.

loss so as to offset that harm or loss. Thus, would not a painful operation performed on my dog, say, be justified were its condition after the operation significantly better than it was before the operation? The improved condition compensates for the pain endured as a result of the operation, and that is so, it would seem, whether or not the animal can vividly recollect its situation prior to the operation and compare it with its new and improved state. As with operations, so with resurrections. It is reasonable to suppose that to restore by resurrection a sentient animal to a life that is filled with pleasures, satisfactions, and fulfillments (proper to its own kind) is to benefit generously that animal and could be a means of compensating for past suffering, whether or not the animal has a conscious awareness of its improved state.

Further, if God has brought into existence animals and has allowed them to suffer considerably but then drops them out of existence, that seems more problematic than God resurrecting them to a new life filled with satisfactions. This is so for the simple reason that the animal is better off being resurrected than not being resurrected, and it is easier (all else being equal) to justify circumstances where animals are better off than where they are worse off. So we may at least hope that Wesley is right when he declares of animals, "As a recompense for what they once suffered, while under the 'bondage of corruption,' when God has 'renewed the face of the earth,' and their corruptible body has put on incorruption, they shall enjoy happiness suited to their state, without alloy, without interruption, and without end."[40]

THE ORIGINS OF ANIMAL PAIN: AN ANGELIC FALL?

To look to a future resurrection of animals to help resolve the problem of animal pain is paralleled by another attempt to resolve this difficult issue — one that looks to the past, indeed to the remote past, to Adamic and angelic falls. Thus, within the Christian tradition, it is often argued that all the physical evil in the world, including animal pain, is the consequence of human sin and rebellion. Because of this rebellion, the natural order has been grossly distorted, resulting in a wide range of imperfections such as earthquakes, hurricanes, disease, death, and physical pain. The result is that not only are humans fallen but nature is also fallen, neither one exemplifying the perfection that was God's original intent. Significantly,

40. Wesley, "The General Deliverance," in *The Works of John Wesley,* vol. 2, p. 447.

there is a crucial connection between sin and nature's distortion, God having linked the fate and destiny of nature to that of his human creation. Thus with the entry of sin, there are disastrous consequences that corrupt not only human nature (predisposing us to sin) but also corrupt the natural order; hence the presence in the world of animal pain and other distortions.

The problem with such an account is that animals were experiencing pain, were dying, were being devoured by other animals millions of years prior to the appearance of human beings. And the same could be said for the occurrence of earthquakes, hurricanes, and other so-called natural disasters (though these are not evils, we may well suppose, until they cause suffering to some sentient creature), since they too pre-date the appearance of human beings. This makes it impossible, observed C. S. Lewis, to any longer trace animal suffering back to Adam's fall. But, not wanting to trace such evils and imperfections back to the creative hand of God, Lewis makes the following suggestion:

> Now it is impossible at this point not to remember a certain sacred story which, though never included in the creeds, has been widely believed in the Church and seems to be implied in several Dominical, Pauline, and Johannine utterances – I mean the story that man was not the first creature to rebel against the Creator, but that some older and mightier being long since became apostate and is now the emperor of the darkness and (significantly) the Lord of this world.[41]

Here Lewis is talking about what is commonly referred to as Satan, and he goes on to observe, "It seems to me, therefore, a reasonable supposition, that some mighty created power had already been at work for ill on the material universe . . . before ever man came on the scene; and that when man fell, someone had, indeed, tempted him."[42] Why physical evil then? Not because of a human fall but because of an angelic fall, because a rebellious fallen angel with his minions has attacked and distorted God's creation.

Now it must be admitted that talk of Satan and other demonic spirits does not "at present enjoy either the extensive popularity or the high esteem of, say, quantum mechanics," as Alvin Plantinga puts it.[43] Peter

41. Lewis, *The Problem of Pain,* pp. 133-34.

42. Lewis, *The Problem of Pain,* p. 135.

43. Alvin Plantinga, *God and Other Minds* (Ithaca, N.Y.: Cornell University Press, 1967), p. 150.

Geach calls Lewis's suggestion of a Satanic origin of physical evil "grotesque"[44] and finds it more reasonable to argue, as we have seen, that God is indifferent to the physical suffering of animals. Peter Harrison rejects Lewis's proposal as "ad hoc" and "lacking a certain credibility" with its appeal to "mythological beings."[45] Indeed, Harrison finds Lewis's proposal sufficiently lacking in credibility to the point where he judges it more reasonable to defend the claim that animals feel no pain at all.

John Hick finds the appeal to an angelic fall seriously problematic because (among other considerations) it involves the "paradox of finitely perfect creatures, dwelling happily and untempted in the presence of God, turning to sin."[46] Whether this is a proper characterization of the angelic hosts – "finitely perfect" and "untempted in the presence of God" – is unclear. Scripture is, after all, virtually silent on the circumstances and conditions under which any angelic fall may have occurred and extra-biblical fantasizing about this event does not constitute firm data on which theological reflection is to be based. Some interpreters have found allusions to the fall of Satan in Isaiah 14 and Ezekiel 28 but the focus in those passages is on earthly rulers. Second Peter 2:4 says that angels who "sinned" were cast into hell and Jude 6 says that angels who "left their proper dwelling" have been kept in eternal bonds awaiting judgment. Even assuming that these are references to a prehistoric angelic fall, it still tells us little or nothing of its character or circumstances. What we must assume, however, is that angels are moral agents, possessed of free will, who at one time were confronted with a choice between good and evil. That God had arranged the circumstances that called for this choice does not make God the author of sin. The choice, we assume, was freely made. Nor are the angels created sinful or fallen by virtue of having desires. These desires, legitimate in themselves, can nevertheless in particular circumstances conflict with their moral and spiritual obligations, requiring of them a choice in which one of the alternatives involves a defection from the divine will. None of this seems so paradoxical that reason requires its rejection as Hick suggests.

Lewis's proposal has had and continues to have able advocates. E. L.

44. Geach, *Providence and Evil,* p. 69.

45. Harrison, "Theodicy and Animal Pain," p. 80.

46. Hick, *Evil and the God of Love,* p. 62. Obviously the argument advanced by Hick to establish the incoherence of an angelic fall applies to humans, so that if his argument is sound it invalidates the possibility of any fall, human or angelic. Hick does in fact apply it to humans and concludes that human beings must have been created "fallen" because morally and spiritually good creatures could not fall. Cf. pp. 280ff.

Mascall (who as Professor of Historical Theology at the University of London wrote extensively on issues of theology and science) attributes the distortion of the "evolutionary plan" (apparently with its excessive pain and ferocity) to fallen angels.[47] Oxford philosopher Richard Swinburne observes that the hypothesis of demonic activity may be "indispensable" if we are to reconcile belief in a good, all-powerful God with the existence of "animal pain."[48] And there is no reason to balk at such a suggestion simply because the climate of opinion is not conducive to its acceptance. As Keith Ward comments, "It is a perfectly coherent supposition that there are spiritual beings of great power who have chosen evil and who involve this world in the anarchy and distortion of their struggle to accept or reject the powers of love."[49] Certainly, to place our own spiritual struggle in the larger context of a cosmic struggle between forces of good and evil is very much a New Testament theme. That those forces were at work prior to the appearance of human beings and that the world into which we were born has been negatively interfered with by destructive spiritual powers should not be a doctrine beyond our capacity to accept as religious believers. Once one believes in God, one has opened the door to a supernatural realm, and to assert that this realm can be characterized only by good and never by evil powers is an arbitrary and gratuitous stipulation.

SORTING OUT OUR OPTIONS

To trace the existence of physical evil back to the destructive operations of rebellious angelic forces is not, however, to provide anything approaching a justification of physical evil. It is only to provide a causal account, not an apologetical one. "Satan did it," we are told, but the question a theodicy must answer is "Why did God allow Satan to do it?" Indeed, granting that there was an angelic fall, why did God not immediately nullify the consequences of that fall or restrain the activity of these rebellious forces so that there would be no physical evil and no animal pain? It is that question that needs to be asked and then answered in order to have a genuine theodicy.

Whether or not we can successfully answer this question, it remains

47. E. L. Mascall, *Christian Theology and Natural Science* (London: Longmans, Green and Co., 1956), pp. 299-304.

48. Richard Swinburne, "The Problem of Evil," in *Contemporary Philosophy of Religion*, ed. Steven M. Cohen and David Shatz (New York: Oxford University Press, 1982), p. 12.

49. Ward, *Rational Theology and the Creativity of God*, pp. 205-6.

the case that the theory of an angelic fall does at least serve to place God one step removed from the physical evil in the world. God permits Satan to distort the natural order but God himself does not create a distorted natural order featuring animal pain and suffering. Importantly, then, it may be felt, the supposition of an angelic rebellion enables us to preserve the principle that God never directly wills or creates evil. God uses evil that others have created, brings good out of evil, but does not call into existence the evil he employs for his own good ends.

Here, perhaps, we begin to see more clearly some of the options before us. *First,* we can deny that animal pain is an evil, thereby dispensing with the need to posit an angelic rebellion to account for it, and we can do this by arguing either that there is no animal pain or that animal pain, though real, is not an evil — alternatives we have already examined and rejected. *Second,* we can grant that animal pain is real, is evil, and did exist prior to the appearance of human beings, but invoke, as Lewis suggests, an angelic rebellion to account for its presence in the world, while asserting that God has his reasons for allowing Satanic forces their extensive power to corrupt the natural order. A *third* option also acknowledges that animal pain is real, is evil, and was in the world prior to the appearance of human beings, but dispenses with the notion of an angelic (or Adamic) rebellion as its cause and forthrightly affirms that God himself is the direct cause of animal pain — this is how he made the world and it is not the result of any rebellious angel's activity. Again, it would be claimed, God has his justifying reason for creating in this manner rather than creating a suffering-free environment.[50]

A crucial difference between the second and third suggestions is that in the one instance God permits animal pain and in the other God directly wills animal pain. Here we can put to work the distinction between the permissive will of God and the intentional will of God. Using that distinction we can say, referring to Lewis's theory, that the Satanic rebellion, with the subsequent destructive attacks on the natural order, is embraced within the permissive will of God but it is not directly or intentionally willed by God. The introduction of this distinction was never meant to constitute a theodicy or anything approaching a solution to the mystery of sin and evil in the world. It was simply an attempt to ensure that we not attribute to God authorship of evil. It is not a justification for anything

50. John Hick argues that both human beings and nature are created fallen; he, therefore, would be an example of someone who argues in this third way. Cf. *Evil and the God of Love,* pp. 243-364.

(no theological writer thought that it was), but it was an attempt to make clear what it was that needed justification, or if a justification was not forthcoming what it was that remained a mystery. And what needs a justification or remains a mystery, as the case may be, is God's permitting evil – in this case, God's permitting an angelic fall and the subsequent Satanic onslaught on the natural order. So then, to the extent that we wish to keep God "one step removed" from the production of animal suffering by its being permissively willed, to that extent we will find attractive the theory of an angelic fall. This does mean that we will have to embrace a theological belief that is, as Alvin Plantinga says, "repugnant to 'modern' habits of thought," though as he also says, "that is scarcely evidence against it."[51] On the other hand, the price we have to pay for a neater, simpler (and perhaps, for many, easier to believe) theology, one with no angelic cause of animal suffering, is that we make God the direct cause of such suffering. That is, animal suffering is the product of the intentional will of God.

But we should note that on neither of these latter two views is the creative process free from the presence of evil. If we assume that God creates human beings by an evolutionary process that involves the death, pain, and suffering of animals, then the divine creating itself involves death, pain, and suffering. God directly wills to create by such a process. If, on the one hand, we adopt the theory of an angelic fall, then we are saying that the disruptive attack by the angelic rebels does not come after a good creation has been completed but during the very process of creating. In both cases, to the extent that we view the suffering of animals as an evil, to that extent we must conclude that evil is part of the creative process, though in the one instance it is intentionally willed and in the other permissively willed.

ADAM'S FALL REVISITED

An angelic fall was invoked in order to account for the existence of animal pain and other imperfections in the world because it was judged that a human fall could no longer satisfactorily serve that purpose, since we now know that these imperfections were present prior to the appearance of any human beings in the world. Humans cannot be the cause of animal suffering if there were no humans in the world at the time animals began

51. Plantinga, *God and Other Minds*, p. 155.

to suffer and experience pain. It is thus assumed that a human fall can be a plausible explanation of physical evil only if the fall occurs before (or perhaps contemporaneously with) the emergence of physical evil. This crucial assumption has been challenged, and it has been argued that the doctrine of a human fall can continue to serve its traditional function of explaining physical evil despite the fact of pre-human evil. Indeed, at the turn of this past century when evolutionary thought was beginning to make deep inroads in the intellectual world, some conservative theologians sought to accommodate the acknowledged fact of pre-human physical evil (forcefully impressed upon them by evolutionary theory) with this ancient judicial account of physical evil. One such individual was the well-known Baptist theologian A. H. Strong, who argued for what he called "anticipative consequences" (a term that Strong says he borrowed from Horace Bushnell). Strong put forth his understanding of matters in the following way:

> This is not a perfect world. It was not perfect even when originally constituted. Its imperfection is due to sin. God made it with reference to the Fall, — the stage was arranged for the great drama of sin and redemption which was to be enacted therein. . . . If sin had not been an incident, foreseen and provided for, the world might have been a paradise. . . . God made the world what it is in view of the events that were to take place in it.[52]

So God, foreknowing that Adam would sin, prepared the world with its physical evils so that when God's protective hand was removed from those first humans (Eden was "reserved to show what a sinless world would be") and they were sent forth into the world, it was a world already prepared by natural disaster, pain and death, as a fitting home for a sinful and rebellious humanity.

Whatever one may think of a judicial or penal understanding of physical evil and whatever one may think of the notion of "anticipative consequences" (and Strong himself acknowledged that in his own day "much sport has been made of this doctrine"), it still remains unclear how animals, who do not sin and do not incur guilt, can legitimately bear the penalty of human sin. Of course, if they *do* share in the curse of Adam's sin, with its pain and death, one might not be too bold to suggest that it would be fitting that they also share in the cancellation of that curse in

52. A. H. Strong, *Systematic Theology* (Old Tappan, N.J.: Fleming H. Revell, 1954), p. 403. The 1954 edition is a reprint of the 1907 version of this work.

Christ, participating in the resurrection and sharing, in their own way, in the glory that is to come.

JUSTIFYING ANIMAL PAIN: SOME POSSIBILITIES

One reason why God might have allowed animal pain has been suggested by Alvin Plantinga,[53] who invokes an angelic fall (as a logical possibility) and applies the free will defense to angels, as traditionally it has been applied to human beings; thus angels, like human beings, have been given free will and allowed to make choices for good and evil. Some angels, however, have misused their freedom, rebelled against God, and attacked God's created order, with the result that there is, among other undesirable things in the world, animal pain. Why does God permit this to happen? For the same reason that God permits human beings to misuse their freedom, rebel against God, and cause suffering. And why does God permit this? Plantinga argues that it is possible that the possession and exercise of free will, by both humans and angels, and its use to do more good than evil (something that God foreknows will be the case), is a good of such value that it outweighs all the evil in the world (including animal pain).

In order to present another complementary reason why God might permit (or decree) animals to be a part of a vast system of nature that involves pain, suffering, and death, we need to briefly sketch a response to the problem of evil and then place animal pain in the context of that response. First, it could be asserted, God's purpose in creating human beings is to bring into existence spiritual-moral agents capable of freely coming to know and love God, and capable of being transformed into the image of Christ. This is to suggest a decision-making and soul-making theodicy: life for human beings is the divinely appointed occasion to seek God (see Acts 17:26-27), and in general to determine ultimate loyalties and to live them out — to participate, in other words, in a process that has as its outcome one's destiny as a moral and spiritual being. Indeed, as Karl Barth maintained, life is "the one great opportunity of meeting God and rejoicing in his praise."[54] Second, this world with the possibility of moral evil (sin) and with the presence of natural evil (natural suffering) is the

53. Plantinga, *God and Other Minds,* pp. 149-51.

54. Karl Barth, *The Doctrine of Creation,* vol. 3 of *Church Dogmatics* (Edinburgh: T&T Clark, 1961), p. 336.

best kind of world for this decision-making and soul-making to occur. Animal pain is part of the natural order and part of a context that makes the divine purpose for human beings possible. Third, the outcome of this process of decision-making and soul-making is a good of sufficient magnitude that it justifies God in both allowing sin and placing us in a world where there is physical suffering, including animal suffering. This, in broad outline, is one theodicy that has received a certain prominence in recent years.[55]

But how does animal pain and suffering contribute to the creation of an environment in which human decision-making and soul-making can best occur? In general, it would be observed, this environment must be one in which human beings can freely move toward or away from God. This is to say, it must be an environment in which God is not overwhelmingly and dominatingly present, intimidating with his power, perfection, and glory, as he would be should he wish to ensure that the natural order not merely reflect his majesty but reflect his majesty *perfectly* (and without equivocation). That is, all natural imperfections that cause pain and suffering would be eliminated and sentient creatures would be miraculously protected against all such threats by a constant interposing of divine power. In such a world, there would not be adequate "space" or "distance" between the Creator and his human creation to allow for fully free commitments to a range of alternative loyalties. On the opposite extreme, a world with no pointers to God, devoid of beauty, pleasure, goodness, harmony, and order, a world only of pain and suffering, chaos, and disorder, yet where human beings somehow managed to cling to existence, would make commitment to a God of love and justice, if not an impossibility, certainly difficult beyond measure. Therefore, the best kind of world for the making and working-out of a free commitment to God would be a world that is somewhere between these two extremes, a mix as it were. It would be neither a world characterized only by light and perfection, demanding one and only one kind of commitment, to God and his righteousness, nor a world of utter darkness and chaos, demanding rejection of God. This middle way would be a world very much like ours, an ambiguous world, with pointers to God, yet with features, such as physical evil including animal pain, that give one pause, that make one wonder, features that seem to point away from God — all in all an environment that

55. This particular theodicy is usually referred to as a soul-making theodicy and its most prominent contemporary exponent is John Hick. Cf. *Evil and the God of Love.*

does not dictate or coerce what one believes, an environment that makes room for an appropriate human freedom.

Further, such an environment also proves to be a test of what one wants to be true, of what one hopes to be true, and the supreme test of the heart is always what one desires to be true, not simply what one believes to be true. (Contrast the woman who only believes that her husband exists with one who *wants* him to exist.) An ambiguous environment, one in which there is good and evil, light and darkness, is one in which one's hopes and desires must play a role in one's ultimate commitment. And so one moves toward the light and goodness, in part, because one *wants* it to be the truth about the universe. One wants there to be a God of love and justice who will ultimately triumph over all forces of evil, death, and destruction. And one's faith is partly expressive of that hope. Or if one has other desires one can, of course, move in a different direction, focusing on the evil in the world and providing oneself with another interpretation of the universe, one that eliminates God or seriously truncates God's character. It is a commitment to God made in this context that has deep value and significance, a context in which desires and wants, in addition to arguments and reasons, are important features. It is the very ambiguity of the human situation, created in part by the perplexity of physical evil, *including animal pain,* that makes possible the play of desires and hopes in framing and making one's ultimate commitments. It is in this context that we can give God our heart with its hopes and desires, and not merely offer to God a mental assent with the appropriate epistemic status.

WHY SOMETHING MORE IS NEEDED

The free will defense and its soul-making variant, however attractive we may find them, cannot be the whole story. Marilyn McCord Adams in the course of her critique of the free will defense has helpfully distinguished between two aspects of God's goodness in relation to creation: (1) God as a producer of global goods and (2) God as a lover of individual persons.[56] To argue that the possession and exercise of free will by angels and humans will secure goods of such great value that they outweigh all the evils associated with the misuse of this freedom, including those evils neces-

56. Marilyn McCord Adams, "Horrendous Evils and the Goodness of God," in *Philosophy of Religion: The Big Questions,* ed. Eleanore Stump and Michael J. Mussary (Oxford: Blackwell Publishers, 1999), p. 252.

sary to preserve it, is to argue in support of God's goodness and effectiveness as a producer of global goods. It does not serve to defend God's goodness as a lover of individuals, certainly not in a world of horrendous evils where, for example, a woman witnesses the extermination of her whole family in a Nazi concentration camp, finally going to the gas chamber herself. Here we must do more than argue that God will maximize *overall* good, the woman's suffering being the price that has to be paid for some global advantage. Rather, we must be able to affirm and argue for the maximizing of good in the context of her individual life, if we are to continue to believe in God's goodness as a powerful lover of each of his creatures. It is not just overall good but her good that God wants and to which God's power is devoted. As with humans so with animals, I would argue, God's compassion and concern is directed to the welfare of each individual animal, certainly each animal that has an inner life that can go better or worse for it, that is capable of experiencing pain and pleasure and possibly a range of other positive and negative feelings and emotions. In face of the considerable pain and suffering that befalls individual animals, to invoke the value of free will in producing goods that are exclusively associated with human advantage (of whatever kind, global or individual, material or spiritual) does little to defend the goodness of One whose compassion embraces *all* his creatures.

A second distinction introduced by Adams that will be helpful in our present discussion is between *engulfing* evil and *defeating* evil.[57] Individual persons who undergo horrendous evil might have that evil engulfed by their subsequent life (here or in the hereafter), which would be filled with good things and positive experiences so that they would declare that on the whole life was a great good for them. *Defeating* evil, on the other hand, cannot be achieved by adding more positive value to a life, as in the case of engulfing evil; rather, it involves integrating the horrendous evil suffered into one's relationship with God. To use an analogy, a mediocre collection of paintings, which include some rather inferior pieces, might be turned into a great collection by adding a large number of excellent paintings. In this case the mediocre collection of paintings has been engulfed. In contrast to this, there might be a particular painting in the collection that includes a small ugly patch, but because of the organic unity that obtains among the parts, the painting as a whole is aesthetically excellent and is so in part because of that ugly patch. The ugly patch has been defeated, so to speak. In the case of the sufferer of horrendous evils,

57. Adams, "Horrendous Evils and the Goodness of God," p. 251.

Adams has in mind (only partially and inadequately hinted at here) one's suffering serving as a vision into the inner life of God, ultimately deepening one's beatific intimacy with God.[58] Because of the suffering, horrendous though it is, one's life is actually enriched and better for it, and God ensures that eventually it will be so.

So when an animal has suffered horribly, God might engulf that evil with subsequent good, ensuring that life on the whole is good for it. Otherwise God would be bringing into existence creatures whose life was a curse for them, such that in essence it would have been better for them not to have existed. In some cases this process might seem to require a postmortem existence, a possibility discussed earlier. Although evil might be engulfed by a benign and pleasant afterlife, it is difficult, in the case of animals with their limited rational powers, to imagine how it might be defeated. The defeat of evil in a life seems to be reserved for those individuals with the kind of spiritual comprehension associated with humans, since only humans can, in the first place, suffer in ways that cry out for the kind of defeat that Adams has in mind. To be a candidate for the defeat of evil in one's life, one must possess interpretative capacities whereby one can take the evil suffered as a challenge to the very meaning of one's own life. This capacity would appear to be something animals lack.

Here a crucial question arises for us: would the fact that God guarantees that a creature's life, despite its considerable pain and suffering, is good on the whole thereby render unproblematic a good and compassionate God's permitting that pain and suffering *solely* for ends that do not benefit the one who suffers? In the case of *defeating* evil in the life of a human, the pain and suffering are used by God to benefit the very one who suffers, deepening one's relationship with God, even though it may be used to serve additional good ends extrinsic to the sufferer. But where pain and suffering are *not* defeated, as with (apparently) animals, there we have pain and suffering that bring no advantage to the sufferer but only make the life of the sufferer worse, despite God's ensuring that this life will be good on the whole. This pain and suffering, then, would be permitted by God for the sake of various goods associated with human advantage (à la the free will defense) but *not* for the sake of the sufferer, in this case the individual animal. Would a compassionate and all-powerful God, we may wonder, use sentient creatures in this way?

One can at least begin to imagine, in the context of postmortem

58. Marilyn McCord Adams, *Horrendous Evils and the Goodness of God* (Ithaca, N.Y.: Cornell University Press, 1999), pp. 155ff.

possibilities, how God might render good on the whole of the life of a zebra eaten alive by spotted hyenas on the plains of the Serengeti. It is even possible that the zebra's life was good on the whole without any postmortem existence and despite its painful demise, and hence there was no need for any subsequent engulfing. Nevertheless, this painful death brings no advantage to the zebra; its suffering, if not completely gratuitous, would at best serve human ends, possibly contributing to an ambiguous environment protective of human freedom as previously suggested. What one would desire, however, is that this pain and suffering might be defeated, perhaps in some extended sense, the zebra actually being better off because of that very death. It is difficult to see how this might be so, but one hopes this is a failure of imagination on our part.

A CAUTIONARY ETHICAL NOTE

Here we need to introduce a word of caution. Although we have introduced the possibility that God permits animal pain and suffering for human advantage, that is, as part of the context for human soul-making and decision-making, and although we have not been able to see how some terrible suffering can be made to benefit the individual animal who suffers it (yet remaining hopeful in our ignorance), *nevertheless* leaving matters there does not give us license to use animals for our advantage in just any way we see fit. Some, however, such as the philosopher Frederick Ferré, have argued to the contrary. Those who seek to understand animal pain "in terms of divine ends applicable only to human persons" are in essence, Ferré contends, denying the intrinsic value of animals, morally turning their back on animals, considering animal suffering a trivial matter and judging as acceptable treatment of animals that would be found seriously objectionable to sensitive theists with environmental or animal welfare concerns (e.g., blood sports like bull fighting and cock fighting, unrestricted vivisection).[59]

I believe that Ferré is mistaken in this, for he appears to be reasoning that because God uses animals for human ends, that is, for ends that *God* has for humans, that humans are thereby licensed to use animals for any end they may choose. This does not follow. First, as Oliver O'Donovan comments (in another context but applicable to the present one), "God

59. Frederick Ferré, "Theodicy and the Status of Animals," *American Philosophical Quarterly* 12, no. 1 (January 1986): 25-26.

has evils at his own disposal which he does not put at ours. Though he works good through war, death, disease, famine, and cruelty, it is not given to us to deploy these mysterious alchemies in the hope that we may bring good from them."[60] Because God uses animal suffering for his own ends, it does not follow that humans can inflict suffering on animals for God's ends, let alone for their own ends. Second, and more specifically, the end for which animal suffering is a divinely chosen means is the creation of a context in which the very purpose for human existence can occur – decision-making and soul-making. That such an exalted end as this justifies animal suffering does not entail the conclusion that any lesser end (e.g., being entertained by bull fights) also justifies animal suffering. Third, to be sure, the ends that God pursues in soul-making and decision-making are ends that God has for humans, but ultimately *God himself* is the End, the One who is to be loved, worshiped, and glorified. For this End humans have been called into existence and put in this mysterious place we call earth, along with other wonderful creatures who also experience pain, suffer, and die. These creatures have their own value and significance, but their pain and suffering may be permitted (in part) as a means to create lovers, worshipers, and glorifiers of God, and – who knows – caretakers of these very animals in some glorified state. This is to say that the permitted pain and suffering is for *divine* advantage. Nothing follows from this about the legitimacy of using animals exclusively for human advantage.

CONCLUSION

In the course of our discussion we have contemplated a range of speculative possibilities, offered in an effort to come to some understanding of the presence of animal pain in a world created by a good, all-powerful God. It is important to acknowledge that many of these are *speculative* possibilities, and therefore should not be given the assured status of central tenets of the Christian faith. It is important, nevertheless, that we recognize that these are *possibilities,* both logically and theologically, providing faith with options that it can at least tentatively embrace as it struggles with the problem of animal suffering. Indeed, theological speculation can keep alive wonder and faith's continued openness to possibilities and realities still unthought of.

60. Oliver O'Donovan, *Begotten or Made?* (New York: Oxford University Press, 1984), p. 83.

Also, we should be aware that God's working in the world may be multi-purposed and therefore layered with different goals that may overlap and interpenetrate in ways we are unable to fully discern. It could be, for example, that animal pain is causally linked to the activity of fallen angels, who, given free will for much the same reason it was given to human beings, have rebelled and attacked God's creation with malevolent intent. And it could be that the results, including animal suffering, are used by God in the construction of an arena in which human decision-making and soul-making may occur. Animal pain is, then, intended for the construction of a world appropriate to a fallen humanity, appropriate for children of Adam, one that is characterized by suffering and death, but one that finds its denouement in a general resurrection that embraces the animal as well as the human world. What God might ensure by this is that the pain and suffering of animals will be, as needed, engulfed by good, securing for each animal a life that is good on the whole for it. No sentient creature, then, will be painfully used and then simply discarded. Nevertheless, we might still hope for something more, something that presently escapes our capacity to see clearly, God's using extreme pain and suffering for the benefit of the very animal who suffers it.

In seeing animal pain as a significant part of the larger problem of evil and wrestling with it as we have done, we are paying homage to the moral significance of animals. To enlarge the problem of evil in this way is simply a consequence of the Christian acknowledging that animals count morally and that animal welfare is to be a human as it is a divine concern.

BIBLIOGRAPHY

BOOKS

Adams, Carol J. *The Sexual Politics of Meat: A Feminist-Vegetarian Critical Theory.* New York: Crossroad, 1990.

Adams, Marilyn McCord. *Horrendous Evils and the Goodness of God.* Ithaca, N.Y.: Cornell University Press, 1999.

Adler, Mortimer J. *The Difference of Man and the Difference It Makes.* New York: Holt, Rinehart and Winston, 1967.

Aldo, Leopold. *A Sand County Almanac.* New York: Oxford University Press, 1949.

Ammon, William H. *The Christian Hunter's Survival Guide.* Old Tappan, N.J.: Fleming H. Revell, 1989.

Amory, Cleveland. *Man-Kind? Our Incredible War on Wildlife.* New York: Harper and Row, 1974.

Aquinas, Thomas. *Summa Theologica.* New York: Benziger Brothers, 1947.

Attfield, Robin. *The Ethics of Environmental Concern.* Oxford: Blackwell, 1983.

Augustine. *City of God.* New York: Random House, 1950.

Bakan, David. *Disease, Pain and Sacrifice: Toward a Psychology of Suffering.* Chicago: University of Chicago Press, 1968.

Barrett, C. K. *A Commentary on the First Epistle to the Corinthians.* New York: Harper and Row, 1968.

Barth, Karl. *The Doctrine of Creation.* Volume 3 of *Church Dogmatics.* Edinburgh: T&T Clark, 1961.

Bickerton, Derek. *Language and Species.* Chicago: University of Chicago Press, 1990.

Blum, Lawrence. *Friendship, Altruism, and Morality.* London: Routledge and Kegan Paul, 1980.

Bostock, Stephen. *Zoos and Animal Rights.* New York: Routledge, 1993.

Brambell, F. W. R (Chairman). *Report of the Technical Committee to Enquire into the Welfare of Animals Kept Under Intensive Livestock Husbandry Systems.* London: HMSO, 1965.

Brown, Les. *Cruelty to Animals: The Moral Debt.* New York: Macmillan, 1988.

Bruce, F. F. *New Century Bible: First and Second Corinthians.* London: Oliphants, 1971.

Budiansky, Stephen. *The Covenant of the Wild: Why Animals Chose Domestication.* New York: William Morrow, 1992.

Callard, Andree. *Rape of the Wild.* Bloomington: Indiana University Press, 1989.

Callicott, J. Baird, ed. *A Companion to a Sand Country Almanac.* Madison: University of Wisconsin Press, 1987.

Calvin, John. *The Epistles of Paul the Apostle to the Romans and to the Thessalonians.* Grand Rapids: Eerdmans, 1961.

Carruthers, Peter. *The Animal Issue.* New York: Cambridge University Press, 1992.

Carson, Gerald. *Men, Beasts, and Gods: A History of Cruelty and Kindness to Animals.* New York: Charles Scribner's Sons, 1972.

Chomsky, Noam. *Cartesian Linguistics.* New York: Harper and Row, 1966.

Clark, Henry. *The Ethical Mysticism of Albert Schweitzer: A Study of the Sources and Significance of Schweitzer's Philosophy of Civilization.* Boston: Beacon, 1962.

Clark, Stephen. *The Moral Status of Animals.* New York: Oxford University Press, 1984.

Coetzee, J. M. *The Lives of Animals.* Princeton, N.J.: Princeton University Press, 1999.

Comroe, Julius H., Jr. *Retrospectoscope: Insights Into Medical Discovery.* Menlo Park, Calif.: Von Gehr Press, 1977.

Conzelmann, Hans. *1 Corinthians.* Philadelphia: Fortress, 1975.

Darwin, Charles. *The Autobiography of Charles Darwin, 1809-1882.* New York: W. W. Norton and Company, 1958.

———. *The Expression of the Emotions in Man and Animals.* Chicago: University of Chicago Press, 1965.

Daves, Henry. *Moral and Pastoral Theology,* vol. 2, *Commandments of the Church.* Fifth ed. London: Sheed and Ward, 1946.

Davis, David Brion. *Slavery and Human Progress.* New York: Oxford University Press, 1986.

Dawkins, Marian Stamp. *Animal Suffering.* New York: Chapman and Hall, 1980.

Descartes. "Discourse on Method." In *The Philosophical Works of Descartes,* trans. E. S. Haldane and G. R. T. Ross. Vol. 1. New York: Dover Publications, 1955.

Devine, Philip. *The Ethics of Homicide.* Ithaca, N.Y.: Cornell University Press, 1978.

Diner, Jeff. *Physical and Mental Suffering of Experimental Animals.* Washington, D.C.: Animal Welfare Institute, 1979.

Farrer, Austin. *Love Almighty and Ills Unlimited.* Garden City, N.Y.: Doubleday, 1961.

Fox, Michael Allan. *The Case for Animal Experimentation: An Evolutionary and Ethical Perspective.* Berkeley and Los Angeles: University of California Press, 1986.

Frey, R. G. *Interests and Rights: The Case Against Animals.* Oxford: Clarendon, 1980.

———. *Rights, Killing, and Suffering: Moral Vegetarianism and Applied Ethics.* Oxford: Blackwell, 1983.

Geach, Peter. *Providence and Evil.* New York: Cambridge University Press, 1977.

Gilligan, Carol. *In a Different Voice.* Cambridge, Mass.: Harvard University Press, 1982.

Godet, Frederick L. *Commentary on the Epistle to the Romans.* Grand Rapids: Zondervan, 1969.

Godlovitch, Stanley, Roslind Godlovitch, and John Harris, eds. *Animals, Men and Morals: An Inquiry into the Maltreatment of the Non-Human.* London: Gollancz, 1972.

Gold, Mark. *Assault and Battery.* London: Pluto, 1983.

Gould, James. *Ethology: The Mechanism and Evolution of Behavior.* New York: W. W. Norton and Company, 1982.

Graham, George. *Philosophy of Mind: An Introduction.* Oxford: Blackwell, 1993.

Granberg-Michaelson, Wesley, ed. *Tending the Garden: Essays on the Gospel and the Earth.* Grand Rapids: Eerdmans, 1987.

Griffin, Donald. *Animal Thinking.* Cambridge, Mass.: Harvard University Press, 1984.

———. *Animal Minds.* Chicago: University of Chicago Press, 1992.

Griffiths, Richard. *The Human Use of Animals.* New York: Grove Books, 1982.

Grimshaw, Jean. *Philosophy and Feminist Thinking.* Minneapolis: University of Minnesota Press, 1986.

Hall, Douglas John. *The Steward: A Biblical Symbol Come to Age.* New York: Friendship, 1982.

Hargrove, Eugene C., ed. *The Animal Rights/Environmental Ethics Debate.* Albany: State University of New York Press, 1992.

Harrison, Ruth. *Animal Machines.* London: Vincent Stuart, 1964.

Held, Virginia. *Feminist Morality.* Chicago: University of Chicago Press, 1993.

Hick, John. *Evil and the God of Love.* Rev. ed. New York: Harper and Row, 1978.

———. *Philosophy of Religion.* Second ed. Englewood Cliffs, N.J.: Prentice Hall, 1973.

Hinman, Lawrence. *Ethics: A Pluralistic Approach to Moral Theory.* Fort Worth, Tex.: Harcourt Brace Jovanovich, 1994.

Hume, C. W. *The Status of Animals in the Christian Religion.* Second ed. N.p.: Universities Federation for Animal Welfare, 1957.

Hume, David. *A Treatise of Human Nature.* Ed. L. A. Selby-Bigge. New York: Oxford University Press, 1960.

Humm, Maggie. *The Dictionary of Feminist Theory.* Columbus: Ohio State University Press, 1990.

Hursthouse, Rosalind. *Beginning Lives.* New York: Basil Blackwell, 1989.

Jasper, James M., and Dorothy Nelkin. *The Animal Rights Crusade.* New York: Free Press, 1992.

Joachim, Jeremias. *The Eucharistic Words of Jesus.* London: SCM Press, 1966.

Johnson, Andrew. *Factory Farming.* Oxford: Basil Blackwell, 1991.

Johnson, Lawrence E. *A Morally Deep World: An Essay on Moral Significance and Environmental Ethics.* Cambridge: Cambridge University Press, 1991.

Kant, Immanuel. *Lectures on Ethics: Duties Toward Animals and Other Spirits.* Trans. Louis Infield. New York: Harper and Row, 1963.

Kellert, Stephen, and Joyce Berry. *Knowledge, Affection and Basic Attitudes toward Animals in American Society.* Phase III. Washington, D.C.: U.S. Government Printing Office, 1980.

Kleinig, John. *Valuing Life.* Princeton, N.J.: Princeton University Press, 1991.

Kohlberg, Lawrence. *The Philosophy of Moral Development.* New York: Harper and Row, 1981.

La Mettrie. *Man a Machine.* Chicago: Open Court, 1927.

Laidler, Keith. *The Talking Ape.* Glasgow: Collins, 1980.

Langacker, Ronald W. *Language and Its Structure.* Second ed. New York: Harcourt Brace Jovanovich, 1973.

Langley, Gill, ed. *Animal Experimentation: The Consensus Changes.* New York: Chapman and Hall, 1989.

Lembeck, Fred. *Scientific Alternatives to Animal Experiments.* Chichester, Eng.: Ellis Horwood Limited, 1989.

Lemos, Noah M. *Intrinsic Value: Concept and Warrant.* Cambridge: Cambridge University Press, 1994.

Leopold, Aldo. *A Sand County Almanac.* New York: Oxford University Press, 1949.

Lewis, C. S. *Mere Christianity.* New York: Macmillan, 1960.

———. *The Problem of Pain.* New York: Macmillan, 1962.

Linden, Eugene. *Apes, Men and Language.* Harmondsworth: Penguin, 1976.

Linzey, Andrew. *Animal Rights: A Christian Assessment.* London: SCM Press, 1976.

———. *Animal Theology.* Urbana: University of Illinois Press, 1995.

———. *Christianity and the Rights of Animals.* New York: Crossroad, 1987.

Linzey, Andrew, and Tom Regan, eds., *Animals and Christianity.* New York: Crossroad, 1988.

———, eds. *Love the Animals.* New York: Crossroad, 1989.

Lovelock, James. *Gaia: A New Look at Life on Earth.* London: Oxford University Press, 1974.

Magel, Charles R. *Keyguide to Information Sources in Animal Rights.* London: Mansell, 1989.

Mascall, E. L. *Christian Theology and Natural Science.* London: Longmans, Green and Co., 1956.

Mason, Jim, and Peter Singer. *Animal Factories.* New York: Harmony, 1990.

McDaniel, Jay B. *Of God and Pelicans: A Theology of Reverence for Life.* Louisville: Westminster/John Knox Press, 1990.

McKeon, Thomas. *The Role of Medicine: Dream, Mirage or Nemesis?* Princeton, N.J.: Princeton University Press, 1979.

Meilaender, Gilbert. *The Theory and Practice of Virtue.* Notre Dame, Ind.: University of Notre Dame Press, 1984.

Midgley, Mary. *Animals and Why They Matter.* Athens, Ga.: University of Georgia Press, 1983.

———. *Beast and Man.* Rev. ed. London: Routledge, 1995.

Migliore, Daniel. *Faith Seeking Understanding: An Introduction to Christian Theology.* Grand Rapids: Eerdmans, 1991.

Miller, Harlan B., and William H. Williams, eds. *Ethics and Animals.* Clifton, N.J.: Humana, 1983.

Moule, C. F. D. *Man and Nature in the New Testament.* Philadelphia: Fortress, 1964.

Murdoch, Iris. *The Sovereignty of Good.* London: Routledge and Kegan Paul, 1970.

Nash, Roderick. *The Rights of Nature: A History of Environmental Ethics.* Madison: University of Wisconsin Press, 1989.

Noddings, Nel. *Caring: A Feminine Approach to Ethics and Moral Education.* Berkeley and Los Angeles: University of California Press, 1984.

Norton, Bryan. *Why Preserve Natural Variety?* Princeton, N.J.: Princeton University Press, 1987.

O'Donovan, Oliver. *Begotten or Made?* New York: Oxford University Press, 1984.

Paget, S. F., ed. *Methods in Toxicology.* Cambridge, Mass.: Blackwell Scientific Publications, 1970.

Passmore, John. *Man's Responsibility for Nature.* New York: Charles Scribner's Sons, 1974.

Paton, William. *Man and Mouse: Animals in Medical Research.* Oxford: Oxford University Press, 1984.

Patterson, F., and E. Linden. *The Education of Koko.* New York: Holt, Rinehart and Winston, 1981.

Pfeiffer, Charles F., and Everett F. Harrison. *Wycliffe Bible Commentary.* Chicago: Moody Press, 1962.

Piaget, Jean. *The Moral Judgment of the Child.* New York: Free Press, 1965.

Pinches, Charles, and Jay B. McDaniel, eds. *Good News for Animals? Christian Approaches to Animal Well-Being.* Maryknoll: Orbis, 1993.

Plantinga, Alvin. *God and Other Minds.* Ithaca, N.Y.: Cornell University Press, 1967.

Pluhar, Evelyn B. *The Moral Significance of Human and Nonhuman Animals.* Durham, N.C.: Duke University Press, 1995.

Pratt, Dallas. *Painful Experiments on Animals.* New York: Argus Archives, 1976.

Premack, D. *Intelligence in Ape and Man.* Hillsdale, N.J.: Erlbaum, 1976.

Premack, D., and A. J. Premack. *The Mind of an Ape.* New York: Norton, 1983.

Rachels, James. *Created from Animals: The Moral Implications of Darwinism.* New York: Oxford University Press, 1990.

Radner, Daisie, and Michael Radner. *Animal Consciousness.* Buffalo: Prometheus Books, 1989.

Regan, Tom, ed. *Animal Sacrifices: Religious Perspectives on the Use of Animals in Science.* Philadelphia: Temple University Press, 1985.

Regan, Tom. *The Case for Animal Rights.* Berkeley and Los Angeles: University of California Press, 1983.

Regan, Tom, and Peter Singer, eds. *Animal Rights and Human Obligations.* Second ed. Englewood Cliffs, N.J.: Prentice-Hall, 1989.

Regenstein, Lewis. *Replenish the Earth: A History of Organized Religion's Treatment of Animals and Nature.* New York: Crossroad, 1991.

Richardson, Alan. *Genesis I–XI.* London: SCM Press, 1953.

Rodd, Rosemary. *Biology, Ethics, and Animals.* New York: Oxford University Press, 1990.

Rollin, Bernard. *Animal Rights and Human Morality.* Buffalo: Prometheus Books, 1981.

———. *The Unheeded Cry.* New York: Oxford University Press, 1989.

Rosen, Steven. *Food for the Spirit: Vegetarianism and the World Religions.* New York: Bala, 1987.

Rowan, Andrew N. *Of Mice, Models, and Men: A Critical Evaluation of Animal Research.* Albany: State University of New York Press, 1984.

Ruesch, Hans. *Slaughter of the Innocent.* Armonk, N.Y.: Futura, 1979.

Rumbaugh, D. M. *Language Learning by a Chimpanzee: The Lana Project.* New York: Academic Press, 1977.

Ryder, Richard. *Animal Revolution: Changing Attitudes towards Speciesism.* New York: Basil Blackwell, 1989.

———. *Victims of Science: The Use of Animals in Research.* Second ed. London: National Anti-vivisection Society, 1983.

Santmire, Paul H. *The Travail of Nature: The Ambiguous Ecological Promise of Christian Theology.* Philadelphia: Fortress, 1985.

Sapontzis, Steve. *Morals, Reason, and Animals.* Philadelphia: Temple University Press, 1987.

Schriver, A. M., and F. Stollnitz, eds. *Behavior of Nonhuman Primates: Modern Research Trends.* Vol. 4. New York: Academic Press, 1971.

Schweitzer, Albert. *The Philosophy of Civilization.* Third ed. Trans. C. T. Campion. London: A & C Black; New York: Macmillan, 1949.

———. *The Teaching of Reverence for Life.* New York: Holt, Rinehart and Winston, 1965.

Scruton, Roger. *Animal Rights and Wrongs.* Third ed. London: Metro Books, 2000.

Sebeok, T. A. *Perspectives in Zoosemiotics.* The Hague: Moulton, 1972.

Sequoia, Anna. *67 Ways to Save the Animals.* New York: Harper Collins, 1990.

Serpell, James. *In the Company of Animals.* Oxford: Basil Blackwell, 1986.

Sharp, Robert. *The Cruel Deception: The Use of Animals in Medical Research.* San Francisco: Thorsons, 1988.

Singer, Peter. *Animal Liberation.* Berkeley and Los Angeles: University of California Press, 1978.

———. *Practical Ethics.* Cambridge: Cambridge University Press, 1979.

———, ed. *In Defense of Animals.* New York: Basil Blackwell, 1985.

Skinner, B. F. *Reflections on Behaviorism and Society.* Englewood Cliffs, N.J.: Prentice Hall, 1978.

Smith, A. Delafield. *The Right to Life.* Durham: University of North Carolina Press, 1965.

Smyth, D. H. *Alternative to Animal Experiments.* London: Scholar Press, 1978.

Sorabji, Richard. *Animal Minds and Human Morals: The Origins of the Western Debate.* Ithaca, N.Y.: Cornell University Press, 1993.

Sorrell, Roger D. *St. Francis of Assisi and Nature: Tradition and Innovation in Western Christian Attitudes toward the Environment.* New York: Oxford University Press, 1988.

Sperling, Susan. *Animal Liberation.* Berkeley and Los Angeles: University of California Press, 1988.

Spiegel, Marjorie. *The Dreaded Comparison: Human and Animal Slavery.* New York: Mirror Books, 1988.

Strong, A. H. *Systematic Theology.* Old Tappan, N.J.: Fleming H. Revell, 1954.

Swanson, Wayne, and George Shultz. *Prime Rip.* Englewood Cliffs, N.J.: Prentice-Hall, 1982.

Taylor, Argus. *Magpies, Monkeys and Morals.* Orchard Park, N.Y.: Broadview, 1999.

Taylor, Paul W. *Respect for Nature: A Theory of Environmental Ethics.* Princeton, N.J.: Princeton University Press, 1986.

Terrace, H. S. *Nim.* New York: Knopf, 1979.

Tester, Keith. *Animals and Society: The Humanity of Animal Rights.* New York: Routledge, 1991.

Thomas, Keith. *Man and the Natural World.* New York: Pantheon Books, 1983.

Thorpe, W. H. *Animal Nature and Human Nature.* Garden City, N.Y.: Doubleday, 1974.

Trethowan, Dom. *An Essay in Christian Philosophy.* London: Longmans, Green and Co., 1954.

Turner, E. S. *All Heaven in a Rage.* New York: St. Martin's, 1964.

Turner, James. *Reckoning with the Beast.* Baltimore: Johns Hopkins University Press, 1980.

U.S. Air Force School of Aerospace Medicine, Report No. USAFSAM-TR-82-24, August 1982.

U.S. Air Force School of Aerospace Medicine, Report No. USAFSAM-TR-87-19, October 1987.

U.S. Congress Office of Technology Assessment. *Alternatives to Animal Use in Research, Testing, and Education.* Washington, D.C.: Government Printing Office, 1986.

Van de Veer, Donald, and Christine Pierce Van de Veer, eds. *People, Penguins and Plastic Trees: Basic Issues in Environmental Ethics.* Belmont, Calif.: Wadsworth, 1986.

Van Steenberghen, Fernand. *Hidden God.* St. Louis: B. Herder Book Co., 1966.

Wainwright, Geoffrey. *Doxology.* New York: Oxford University, 1980.

Walker, Stephen. *Animal Thought.* London: Routledge and Kegan Paul, 1983.

Wall, George B. *Is God Really Good?* Washington, D.C.: University Press of America, 1983.

Ward, Keith. *The Battle for the Soul: The End of Morality in a Secular Society.* London: Hodder and Stoughton, 1985.

———. *The Concept of God.* Oxford: Basil Blackwell, 1974.

———. *Rational Theology and the Creativity of God.* New York: Pilgrim, 1982.

Warnock, Mary. *The Uses of Philosophy.* Oxford: Blackwell, 1992.

Webb, Stephen H. *On God and Dogs.* New York: Oxford University Press, 1998.

Westermann, Claus. *Creation.* London: SPCK, 1974.

———. *Genesis 1–11: A Commentary.* Minneapolis: Augsburg, 1984.

Wolfe, Alan. *The Human Difference.* Berkeley and Los Angeles: University of California Press, 1993.

Wolterstorff, Nicholas. *Until Justice and Peace Embrace.* Grand Rapids: Eerdmans, 1983.

Zink, Sidney. *The Concept of Ethics.* London: Macmillan, 1962.

ARTICLES

Adams, Marilyn McCord. "Horrendous Evils and the Goodness of God." In *Philosophy of Religion: The Big Questions,* ed. Eleanore Stump and Michael J. Mussary. Oxford: Blackwell, 1999.

Baker, John Austin. "Biblical Attitudes to Nature." In *Man and Nature,* ed. Hugh Montefiore. London: Collins, 1995.

Baldwin, Elizabeth. "The Case for Animal Research." *Journal of Social Issues* 49, no. 1 (1993): 125-26.

Bateson, Patrick. "When to Experiment on Animals." *New Scientist* 20 (February 1986).

Callicott, J. Baird. "Animal Liberation: A Triangular Affair." *Environmental Ethics* 2 (Winter 1980).

———. "Elements of an Environmental Ethics: Moral Considerability and the Biotic Community." *Environmental Ethics* 1 (1979).

Chomsky, Noam. "Language: Chomsky's Theory." In *The Oxford Companion to the Mind,* ed. Richard L. Gregory. New York: Oxford University Press, 1987.

Crocker, Joe. "Respect Your Feathered Friends." *New Scientist* (October 10, 1985).

Davis, Michael. "The Moral Status of Dogs, Forests and Other Persons." *Social Theory and Practice* 12 (Spring 1986).

Donavan, Josephine. "Animal Rights and Feminist Theory." *Signs* 15 (1990).

Doyle, James F. "Schweitzer's Extension of Ethics to All Life." *Journal of Value Inquiry* 11 (Spring 1977).

Ferré, Frederick. "Theodicy and the Status of Animals." *American Philosophical Quarterly* 12, no. 1 (January 1986).

Fouts, R. S. "Language: Origins, Definitions, and Chimpanzees." *Journal of Human Evolution* 3 (1974).

Fox, Michael Allan. "Animal Experimentation: A Philosopher's Changing Views." *Between the Species* 3 (1987).

———. *The Scientist* (December 15, 1988).

Franz, Carol G. "Effects of Mixed Newton-Gamma Total-Body Irradiation in Physical Activity Performance of Rhesus Monkeys." *Radiation Research* 101 (1985).

Freud, Sigmund. "Some Physical Consequences of the Anatomical Distinction between the Sexes." In vol. 7 of *On Sexuality,* ed. A. Richards. Harmondsworth: Penguin, 1977.

Friedman, Marilyn. "Beyond Caring." In *An Ethic of Care,* ed. Mary Jeanne Larrabee. New York: Routledge, 1993.

Gallup, G. G. Jr., and S. D. Suarez. "On the Use of Animals in Psychological Research." *Journal of Psychological Research* 30 (1980).

Gardner, R. A., and B. T. Gardner. "Teaching Sign Language to a Chimpanzee." *Science* 165 (1969).

Geddes, Leonard. "On the Intrinsic Wrongness of Killing People." *Analysis* 33 (January 1973).

Goodpaster, Kenneth E. "On Being Morally Considerable." *Journal of Philosophy* 75 (1978).

Gunn, Alastair S. "Traditional Ethics and the Moral Status of Animals." *Environmental Ethics* 5 (1983).

Halpin, Zuleyma Tang. "Scientific Objectivity and the Concept of 'the Other.'" *Women's Studies International Forum* 12, no. 3 (1989).

Harrison, Peter. "Theodicy and Animal Pain." *Philosophy* 64 (1989).

Heffernan, James D. "The Land Ethic: A Critical Appraisal." *Environmental Ethics* 4 (1982).

Heil, John. "Speechless Brutes." *Philosophy and Phenomenological Research* XLII, no. 3 (March 1982).

Holland, Alan J. "On Behalf of Moderate Speciesism." *Journal of Applied Philosophy* 1 (October 1984).

Horenstein, D. "The Dynamics and Treatment of Child Abuse: Can Primate Research Provide the Answers?" *Journal of Clinical Psychology* 33 (1977).

Hunt, W. Murray. "Are Mere Things Morally Considerable?" *Environmental Ethics* 2 (Spring 1980).

Johnson, Lawrence E. "Can Animals Be Moral Agents?" *Ethics and Animals* 4 (1983).

———. "Do Animals Have an Interest in Life?" *Australasian Journal of Philosophy* 62 (1983).

———. "Humanity, Holism, and Environmental Ethics." *Environmental Ethics* 5 (1983).

Jones, David Albert. "Do Whales Have Souls?" *New Blackfriars* 73, no. 866 (December 1992).

Kellert, Stephen R., and Joyce K. Berry. "Attitudes, Knowledge, and Behavior toward Wild Life as Affected by Gender." *Wild Life Society Bulletin* 11.5 (1987).

Kevler, Daniel J. "Some Like It Hot." *The New York Review of Books* (March 26, 1992).

Kingston, A. Richard. "Theodicy and Animal Welfare." *Theology* LXX, no. 569 (November 1967).

Kohlberg, Lawrence, and R. Kramer. "Continuities and Discontinuities in Child and Adult Moral Development." *Human Development* 12 (1969).

Lawler, Justus George. "On the Rights of Animals." *Anglican Theological Review* (April 1965).

Lember, J. "Language in Child and Chimp?" *American Psychology* 32 (1977).

Lennberg, E. H. "Of Language, Knowledge, Apes and Brains." *Journal of Psychological Research* 1 (1971).

Lockwood, Michael. "Singer on Killing and the Preference for Life." *Inquiry* 22 (Summer 1979).

Lombardi, Louis G. "Inherent Worth, Respect, and Rights." *Environmental Ethics* 5 (Fall 1983).

Lovelock, James E. "Gaia: The World as Living Organism." *New Scientist* 118 (1986).

Marshall, Paul. "Does Creation Have Rights?" *Studies in Christian Ethics* 6, no. 2 (Autumn 1993).

Masserman, Jules H., Stanley Weckin, and William Terris. "'Altruistic Behavior in Rhesus Monkeys." *American Journal of Psychiatry* 121 (1964).

McKinlay, John B., Sonja M. McKinlay, and Robert Beagehole. "Trends in Death and Disease and the Contribution of Medical Measures." In *Handbook of Medical Sociology,* fourth ed., ed. Howard E. Freeman and Sol Levine. Englewood Cliffs, N.J.: Prentice Hall, 1989.

Mill, John Stuart. "Three Essays on Religion." In *John Stuart Mill: Essays on Ethics, Religion and Society,* ed. J. M. Robson. London: Routledge and Kegan Paul, 1969.

Miller, N. E. "The Value of Behavioral Research on Animals." *American Psychologist* 40 (1985).

Mounin, G. "Language, Communication, Chimpanzees." *Current Anthropology* 17 (1976).

Naess, Arne. "The Shallow and the Deep, Long-Range Ecology Movement." *Inquiry* 16 (1973).

Nagel, Thomas. "What Is It Like to Be a Bat?" Reprinted in *Mortal Questions.* Cambridge: Cambridge University Press, 1979.

Narveson, Jan. "Animal Rights." *Canadian Journal of Philosophy* 7 (March 1977).

Nowell-Smith, P. H. "Morality: Religious and Secular." In *Christian Ethics and Contemporary Philosophy,* ed. Ian Ramsey. New York: Macmillan, 1966.

Nozick, Robert. "About Mammals and People." *New York Times Book Review* (November 27, 1983).

Paske, Gerald H. "Why Animals Have No Right to Life: A Response to Regan." *Australasian Journal of Philosophy* 66 (December 1988).

Passmore, John. "The Treatment of Animals." *Journal of the History of Ideas* 36 (1975).

Patterson, Francine. "Ape Language." *Science* 211 (1981).

———. "Conversations with a Gorilla." *National Geographic* 154 (1978).

Paton, William. "Animal Experiment and Medical Research: A Study in Evolution." *Conquest* 169 (1979).

Preus, Anthony. "Respect for the Dead and Dying." *Journal of Medicine and Philosophy* 9 (November 1984).

Quinn, Edward. "Animals in Heaven." *New Blackfriars* 65, no. 767 (May 1984).

Raz, Joseph. "The Nature of Rights." *Mind* 93 (1984).

Regan, Tom. "An Examination and Defense of One Argument Concerning Animal Rights." *Inquiry* 22, nos. 1-2 (Summer 1979).

———. "The Moral Basis of Vegetarianism." *Canadian Journal of Philosophy* 5 (October 1975).

Reichenbach, Bruce. "Monism and the Possibility of Life After Death." *Religious Studies* 14, no. 1 (March 1978).

Robinson, John A. T. "Need Jesus Have Been Perfect?" In *Christ, Faith and History: Cambridge Studies in Christology,* ed. S. W. Sykes and J. P. Clayton. London: Cambridge University Press, 1972.

Rosenthal, David M. "Two Concepts of Consciousness." *Philosophical Studies* 49 (1986).

Rowley, H. H. "Sacrifice and Morality: A Rejoinder." *The Expository Times* 17 (March 1959).

Rumbaugh, D. M., and T. V. Gill. "Language and the Acquisition of Language-Type Skills by a Chimpanzee (Pan)." *Annals of the New York Academy of Sciences* 270 (1976).

———. "Mastery of Language-type Skills by the Chimpanzee (Pan)." *Annals of the New York Academy of Sciences* 280 (1976).

Rumbaugh, D. M., T. V. Gill, and E. C. von Glaserfeld. "Reading and Sentence Completion by a Chimpanzee (Pan)." *Science* 182 (1973).

Sapontzis, Steve F. "Must We Value Life to Have a Right to It?" *Ethics and Animals* 3 (March 1982).

Schönfeld, Martin. "Who or What Has Moral Standing?" *American Philosophical Quarterly* 29 (October 1992).

Shepard, P. S. "Reverence for Life at Lambarene." *Landscape* 8 (1959).

Sommers, Christina Hoff. "Tooley's Immodest Proposal: Abortion and Infanticide" (Book Review). *Hastings Center Report* 15 (June 1985).

Stevenson, Lloyd. "Religious Elements in the Background of the British Anti-Vivisection Movement." *Yale Journal of Biology and Medicine* 29 (November 1956).

Swinburne, Richard. "The Problem of Evil." In *Contemporary Philosophy of Religion,* ed. Steven M. Cohen and David Shatz. New York: Oxford University Press, 1982.

Taylor, Paul. "The Ethics of Respect for Nature." *Environmental Ethics* 3 (Fall 1981).

———. "Are Humans Superior to Animals and Plants?" *Environmental Ethics* 6 (Summer 1984).

Terrace, H. S. "Animal Cognition: Thinking Without Language." In *Animal Intelligence,* ed. Laurence Weiskuentz. Oxford: Clarendon, 1985.

Terrace, H. S., L. A. Petitto, R. J. Sanders, and T. G. Beves. "Can an Ape Create a Sentence?" *Science* 206 (November 23, 1979).

Thompson, J. "A Refutation of Environmental Ethics." *Environmental Ethics* 12, no. 2 (1990).

Tuck, W. P. "Schweitzer's Reverence for Life." *Theology Today* 30 (January 1974).

Walker, Lawrence J. "Sex Differences in the Development of Moral Reasoning." *Child Development* 57 (1986).

Weisenkrantz, L. "Varieties of Residual Experience." *Quarterly Journal of Experimental Psychology* 32 (1980).

Wesley, John. "The General Deliverance." In *The Works of John Wesley,* vol. 2, ed. Albert C. Outler. Nashville: Abingdon, 1985.

West, D. "On Goodrich's 'The Morality of Killing.'" *Philosophy* 45 (1970).

Williams, Clifford. "The Irrelevance of Non-Material Minds." *Christian Scholars Review* 12, no. 4 (1983).

Winterscheid, L. C. "Animal Experimentation Leading to the Development of Advanced Surgical Techniques." *American Journal of Public Health* 5 (1967).

Zbinden, G., and M. Flury-Roversi. "Significance of the LD50 Test for the Toxicological Evaluation of Chemical Substances." *Archives of Toxicology* 47 (1981).

INDEX